P9-AFE-441

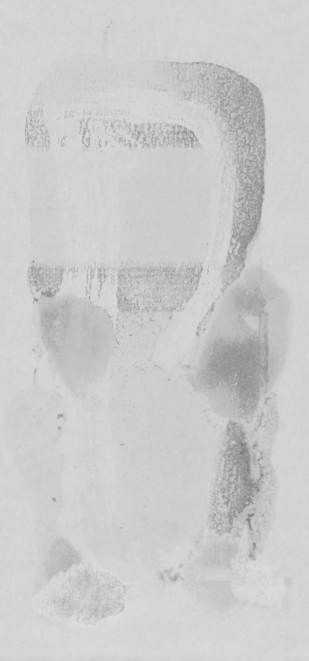

The Catholic Tradition

REV. CHARLES J. DOLLEN
DR. JAMES K. McGOWAN
DR. JAMES J. MEGIVERN
EDITORS

The Catholic Tradition

Sacred Scripture

Volume 1

A Consortium Book

Library of Congress Card Catalog Number: 79-1977
ISBN: 0-8434-0734-4
ISBN: 0-8434-0725-5 series

The publisher gratefully acknowledges permission to quote from the
following copyrighted sources. In cases where those properties contain
scholarly apparatus such as footnotes, such footnotes have been omitted
in the interest of the general reader.

BRUCE PUBLISHING COMPANY
  Selections from *The Two-Edged Sword, An Interpretation of the Old
  Testament* by John L. McKenzie, S.J., © 1956. Reprinted by permis-
  sion of Bruce Publishing Company.

THE CATHOLIC UNIVERSITY OF AMERICA PRESS, INC.
  "The Trinity" from *The Fathers of the Church*, Volume 67, *Novatian*,
  translated by Russell J. DeSimone, O.S.A., copyright © 1974; *The
  Homilies of St. Jerome*, Volume I from *The Fathers of the Church*,
  Volume 48, translated by Sister Marie Ligouri Ewald, I.H.M., copyright
  © 1964; *The Homilies of St. Jerome*, Volume II from *The Fathers of the
  Church*, Volume 57, translated by Sister Marie Ligouri Ewald, I.H.M.,
  copyright ©1966.

FABER & FABER, LTD.
  "Commentary on the Gospel According to St. John" from *Meister
  Eckhart: Selected Treatises and Sermons* by James Midgley Clark and
  John Vass Skinner. © 1958 by James Midgley Clark and John Vass
  Skinner. Reprinted by permission of Faber and Faber, Ltd.

JOHN J. GAVIGAN, O.S.A.
  "Christian Instruction" from *The Fathers of the Church*, Volume 2, *Writ-
  ings of St. Augustine*, Volume 4, translated by John J. Gavigan, O.S.A.,
  John Courtney Murray, S.J., Robert P. Russell, O.S.A., Bernard M.
  Peebles. Copyright 1947, The Catholic University of America Press, Inc.
  Copyright renewed 1975 by John J. Gavigan, O.S.A., John Courtney
  Murray, S.J., Robert P. Russell, O.S.A. "Christian Instruction" reprinted
  by permission of John J. Gavigan, O.S.A.

WORLD PUBLISHING COMPANY
Selections from *On the Inspiration of Scripture* by John Henry Newman,
edited by J. Derek Holmes and Robert Murray, S.J., ©1967.

Table of Contents

VOLUME 1

Introduction   *ix*

ORIGEN   1
  On First Principles   3

NOVATIAN   27
  The Trinity   29

ST. JEROME   63
  The Homilies   65

ST. AUGUSTINE   121
  Christian Instruction   123

ALCUIN OF YORK   147
  Commentary on the Epistle to Titus   149

RUPERT OF DEUTZ   165
  The Victory of God's Work   167

ST. THOMAS AQUINAS   179
  Commentary on St. Paul's Epistles to the Galatians
    and to the Ephesians   181

THE CATHOLIC TRADITION: Sacred Scripture

MEISTER ECKHART   207
    Commentary on the Gospel According to John   209

JACQUES BENIGNE BOSSUET   233
    Panegyrics of the Saints   235

JOHN HENRY NEWMAN   249
    On the Inspiration of Scripture   251

MARIE JOSEPH LAGRANGE   271
    The Gospel of Jesus Christ   273

POPE PIUS XII   299
    Divino Afflante Spiritu   301

RONALD ARBUTHNOTT KNOX   327
    The Trials of a Translator   329

LUCIEN CERFAUX   343
    Christ in the Theology of St. Paul   345

PIERRE MAURICE BENOIT   365
    Jesus and the Gospel   367

JOHN LAWRENCE McKENZIE   387
    The Two-Edged Sword   389

Introduction

The Catholic Tradition is a 14 volume anthology of excerpts from the great Catholic writers from antiquity to the present day. *The Catholic Tradition* is intended for the armchair reader who has not studied theology or church history and has not time to struggle unassisted through 198 books. The publisher's intention is to provide such a reader with a compact home library that will permit him to familiarize himself with the great Catholic writers and their works. The works included in *The Catholic Tradition* are all religious in subject. The publisher did not include fiction or nonfiction books on secular subjects written by Catholic authors.

The Catholic Tradition arranges the writings according to religious subjects. There are seven religious subjects, each of which is covered in two volumes: The Church; Mass and the Sacraments; Sacred Scripture; The Saviour; Personal Ethics; Social Thought; and Spirituality. Within each subject, the writings are arranged in chronological order, which permits the reader to follow the development of Catholic thought across 2000 years.

Each excerpt in *The Catholic Tradition* is preceded by a brief biographical and explanatory introduction to help the reader understand the world in which the writer lived and wrote, and the problems with which he was dealing.

THE CATHOLIC TRADITION: Sacred Scripture

The selection of the excerpts and the writing of the introductions has been a long and difficult process. The task of making the final selections was particularly arduous (as such choices always are); the most modern authors, about whose writing there is yet no final judgment provoking the most debate. The selection of authors was made originally in the publisher's offices and then submitted to the three editors of the series who refined the selection. The editors submitted their selection to an unofficial board of scholars who very kindly made constructive comments.

The process of assembling the many hundreds of books from which to make the final selection was in itself a vast task. Many of the books under consideration were very scarce and not available in bookstores or libraries. The work of collecting the books and then making selections among them stretched over a three year period, and many books were selected for inclusion and later rejected after careful scrutiny and reflection.

The editing of *The Catholic Tradition* was a long and difficult job because the literature of Roman Catholicism is a vast and complex body. Of all the Christian denominations, the Roman Catholic Church is by far the oldest and largest. Its ranks include a tremendous number of saints and scholars, writers and thinkers, mystics and preachers: many of whom felt so strongly about their faith that they were willing to die for it. They have left an incomparably rich legacy of art and writing. Selecting from it is not simple.

The selections that we made are representative of the best of mainstream Catholic writing. Generally, they should be intelligible to a thoughtful layman. Some however, may prove more technical than others, and some of the very recent writers may seem controversial. The reader should bear in mind that some theological questions simply do not admit of facile answers, and that some of the earlier writers were considered controversial in their own days. It is also well to remember that the writings gathered here, brilliant and revered as their authors may be, are not necessarily official statements of Church policy. But they are, all of them, solidly part of the Catholic tradition.

The writers are all Catholics, many of them clergymen, some of them converts to Catholicism. They all wrote as loyal

Introduction

servants of the Church and from a Catholic point of view. When they wrote on personal ethics they proceeded from the assumption that man's goal was to imitate Christ, not simply to follow a secular set of ethical rules. When they wrote on social problems they expressed the need to solve social problems because they loved their neighbors, not for the material enrichment of society. Their writings on Christ reflect an intense struggle to bend human language to divine definition. Taken together, their writings form a literary tradition that is Roman Catholic at heart. That tradition has certain ingredients that are not present in the literary traditions of the other Christian denominations. Particularly, the heritage of liturgical ceremony and mystical contemplation have left an incomparable treasure of literature that is here presented in the volumes entitled *Mass and the Sacraments,* and *Spirituality.*

The whole corpus of Catholic thinking and writing, distilled here in *The Catholic Tradition,* is generally considered by scholars to have three important periods: the ancient, or patristic, period; the high middle-ages, which is the era of St. Thomas Aquinas and sometimes called the scholastic period; finally the time in which we live today, the last 100 years. These three epochs are golden ages of Catholic writing. They are separated from each other by the generally unproductive eras of the dark ages and the Reformation.

Through all these epochs the great Catholic writers have preserved and developed the Christian message: love God; love your fellow man. Each writer wrote conscious of the tradition behind him, conscious that he was building on the work of men before him, adapting their work to changed conditions or continuing their work on the outer edges of human speculation.

The present day writers, those of the third great era of Catholic writing, are the most important part of *The Catholic Tradition.* Here for the first time their thinking is presented along with the work of their predecessors; here can be seen the stunning achievement of today's Catholic writing, and how it follows logically from the writing of the patristic and scholastic thinkers.

The present day writers presented in *The Catholic Tradition* number 114, over half of the total number of writers chosen.

Their writing will probably prove more intelligible to the average reader because they write in today's idiom and they address contemporary problems.

Oddly enough, many if not most of the modern writers are not familiar to the average Catholic. St. Augustine, and St. Thomas Aquinas are household names, but only serious Catholic readers today are familiar with the masterful writings of Karl Rahner, Edward Schillebeeckx, Raymond Brown, and Gustavo Gutiérrez. None the less, these men are representative of a great historical flowering of Catholic writing today and their names may well echo down the ages.

THE PUBLISHER

Origen
185-253

Origen was "the outstanding teacher and scholar of the early Church, a man of spotless character, encyclopaedic learning, and one of the most original thinkers the world has ever seen" (J. Quasten). From 202 to 230 (interrupted by the persecution of Caracalla, 215-217) he was the pride of the Church in Alexandria, teaching and writing at a prolific pace. Then from 230 until his death he continued his phenomenal work in Caesarea.

Among his many claims to fame, Origen is usually considered to be the founder of biblical science. His four books On First Principles are often looked upon as his greatest achievement. In them he brings Greek philosophy to bear on Christian faith, developing an unparalleled speculative system for his time. It is in the fourth book On First Principles that he formulates the first theoretical approach to discovering the meaning of the Scriptures, and it would be difficult to overestimate the impact of this work on all subsequent Christian history.

In granting him his due, however, contemporary scholars are also very much aware of some basic problems introduced by Origen's very brilliance. G. W. Butterworth has expressed it well: "It is obvious that, however sincerely Origen started from the simple Christian faith, he ended in speculations which were only remotely connected with it. The real source of these specu-

*lations is to be found in the intellectual atmosphere of the time
. . . But Origen claimed to find it all in the Scriptures."*

*The basic problem alluded to is the allegorical method
which he inherited from Philo and applied unremittingly. The
selection that follows consists of all three of his chapters dealing with this method of interpretation. As Butterworth further
elaborates, "It would be an exaggeration to say that the method
is wholly arbitrary, for it has its rules. But it despises the history,
ignores the poetry, and turns all that is warm and human into
frigid intellectual reasonings. Its greatest value was that, in the
hands of Origen at any rate, it kept the idea of God on a high
moral and spiritual level and free from the distortions that are
bound to creep in when the Old Testament is accepted in its
literal sense as a perfect revelation."*

*The influence of the Alexandrian school on all subsequent
Christian biblical interpretation in the patristic age was over-
whelming. Origen's allegorism introduces so totally subjective
an approach that any common meaning of biblical passages can
seldom be agreed upon. History is unimportant; one must
search for the supra-historical truth behind (or above, or below)
the text. The method lends itself readily to absurdity so that
things never mean what they seem to mean. This was especially
true of the Old Testament, since its only meaning was supposedly
derived from the New.*

*So, while one of the greatest problems in biblical interpre-
tation lies squarely on Origen's doorstep, this should not obscure
the power and beauty, the insight and ingenuity demonstrated
in his commentaries. His incredible industry and capacity for
work are indicated by the fact that a century and a half later
Jerome knew of at least 290 books and over 600 homilies, all
centered on the Bible and attributed to Origen. Then, of course,
there was also his famous Hexapla ("sixfold" Old Testament),
most of which has been lost, as so many of his works. Seldom,
if ever, have the church or the Bible received such indefatigable
service.*

2

ON FIRST PRINCIPLES

BOOK IV

CHAPTER I

THE INSPIRATION OF DIVINE SCRIPTURE

N ow in our investigation of these important matters we do not rest satisfied with common opinions and the evidence of things that are seen, but we use in addition, for the manifest proof of our statements, testimonies drawn from the scriptures which we believe to be divine, both from what is called the Old Testament and also from the New, endeavouring to confirm our faith by reason. We have not yet, however, discussed the divine character of the scriptures. Well then, let us deal in a brief manner with a few points concerning them, bringing forward in this connexion the reasons that influence us to regard them as divine writings. And first of all, before we make use of statements from the writings themselves and from the events disclosed in them, let us speak of Moses, the Hebrew lawgiver, and of Jesus Christ, the introducer of the saving doctrines of Christianity.

For although there have been very many lawgivers among both Greeks and barbarians, and teachers who proclaimed doctrines which professed to be the truth, we have no record of a lawgiver who has succeeded in implanting an enthusiasm for the acceptance of his teachings among nations other than his own. A great apparatus of supposed logical proof has been introduced by men who profess that their philosophy is concerned with truth, and yet none of them has succeeded in implanting what he regarded as the truth among different nations or even among any number of persons worth mentioning in a single nation.

Yet it would have been the wish of the lawgivers to put in force the laws which appeared to them to be good among the whole race of mankind, had that been possible; while the teachers would have wished that what they imagined was the truth should be spread everywhere throughout the world. But knowing that they could not summon men of other languages and of many nations to the observance of their laws and the acceptance of their laws and the acceptance of their teachings they wholly refrained even from attempting to do this, considering not unwisely how impossible it was that such a result should happen to them. Yet all over Greece and in the barbarian part of our world there are thousands of enthusiasts who have abandoned their ancestral laws and their recognised gods for observance of the laws of Moses and of the teaching contained in the words of Jesus Christ, in spite of the fact that those who submit to the law of Moses are hated by the worshippers of images and that those who accept the word of Jesus Christ are not only hated but in danger of death.

Now if we consider how in a very few years, although those who profess Christianity are persecuted and some are put to death on account of it while others suffer the loss of their possessions, yet the word has been able, in spite of the fewness of its teachers, to be 'preached everywhere in the world', so that Greeks and barbarians, wise and foolish have adopted the religion of Jesus, we shall not hesitate to say that this achievement is more than human, remembering that Jesus taught with all authority and convincing power that his word should prevail.

Consequently we may reasonably regard as oracles those utterances of his such as, 'Ye shall be brought before kings and governors for my sake, for a testimony to them and to the gentiles'; and. . . . 'Many shall say to me in that day, Lord, Lord, did we not eat in thy name and drink in thy name and in thy name cast out daemons? And I shall say unto them. Depart from me, ye workers of iniquity; I never knew you'. Now there was once a possibility that in uttering these words he was talking idly, because they were not true; but when words spoken with such authority have come to pass it shows that God has really become man and delivered to men the doctrines of salvation.

And what need is there to say also that it was predicted that those who are called 'ruler' 'shall fail from Judah and the leaders from his thighs, when he shall come for whom it'—

that is, clearly, the kingdom—'is reserved', and when 'the expectation of the gentiles shall dwell here'. For it is abundantly clear from history and from what we see at the present day that after the times of Jesus there were no longer any who were called kings of the Jews, and that all those Jewish customs on which they prided themselves, I mean those connected with the temple and the altar and the performance of worship and the garments of the high priest, have been destroyed. For the prophecy has been fulfilled which says, 'The children of Israel shall sit for many days without king or ruler, without sacrifice or altar or priesthood or oracles'.

Now we use these sayings as an answer to the difficulty arising from the words in Genesis spoken by Jacob to Judah, say that the Ethnarch, who comes from the tribe of Judah, is the ruler of the people, and that men of his seed will not fail until the advent of the Christ as they picture him. For if 'the children of Israel shall sit for many days without king or ruler, without sacrifice or altar or priesthood or oracles,' and if from the time the temple was rased to the ground there has been 'neither sacrifice nor altar nor priesthood', it is clear that a ruler has 'failed from Judah and a leader from his thighs'. And when the prophecy says, 'A ruler shall not fail from Judah nor a leader from his thighs until there shall come what is reserved for him', it is clear that he has come for whom are the things reserved, that is, he who is the expectation of the gentiles. This is evident from the number of gentiles who through Christ have believed in God.

And in the song in Deuteronomy it is prophetically revealed that there shall be an election of foolish nations on account of the sins of God's former people; which has come to pass through no other than Jesus. For it says: 'They moved me to jealousy with that which is not God; they have provoked me to anger with their idols; and I will move them to jealousy with that which is not a nation, and with a foolish nation I will provoke them to anger'. Now it can be very clearly perceived in what manner the Hebrews, who are said to have moved God to jealousy with that which is not God and to have provoked him to anger with their idols, have themselves been provoked to anger and jealousy with that which is not a nation, and with

5

a 'foolish nation', which God chose through the advent of Christ Jesus and his disciples.

We see, then, our calling, that 'not many wise after the flesh, not many mighty, not many noble are called; but God chose the foolish things of the world, that he might put to shame them that are wise; and the base things and the things that are despised did God choose, yea, and the things that are not, that he might bring to nought those things that were before them'. So let not 'Israel after the flesh', which is called by the apostle 'flesh', 'glory before God'.

And what need is there to speak of the prophecies relating to Christ in the Psalms, in which a certain ode is headed 'For the beloved', whose tongue is said to be the 'pen of a ready writer' who is 'fairer than the children of men' because 'grace was poured on his lips'? Now a proof that 'grace was poured on his lips' is the fact that although the time he spent in teaching was short—for he taught only about a year and a few months—the world has been filled with this teaching and with the religion that came through him. For there has arisen 'in his days' 'righteousness and an abundance of peace' lasting until the consummation, which is here called the 'taking away of the moon'; and he continues to 'have dominion from sea to sea and from the rivers to the ends of the earth'. And a 'sign' has been given to the house of David, for 'the virgin' did 'conceive and bear a son', and his name is 'Emmanuel', which means 'God with us'.

There has also been fulfilled that which the same prophet says, 'God is with us. Know it, ye nations, and be overcome; ye that are strong, be overcome'. For we who have been captured from among the nations have been overcome and conquered by the grace of his word. Moreover the place of his birth is foretold in Micah. 'And thou, Bethlehem,' it says, 'land of Judah, art in no way least among the rulers of Judah; for out of thee shall come a governor, who shall shepherd my people Israel'. And the 'seventy weeks' until the coming of Christ the governor were fulfilled in accordance with Daniel's prophecy. He, too, has come who according to Job has 'subdued the great fish' and who has given to his true disciples authority to 'tread on serpents and scorpions and over every power of the enemy', without being in any way harmed by them.

6

Let anyone also consider how the apostles who were sent by Jesus to preach the gospel sojourned everywhere, and he will see that their daring venture was not merely human and that the command was from God. And if we examine how, when people heard the new teachings and strange words, they welcomed these men, the desire to plot against them being frustrated by some divine power that watched over them, we shall not refuse to believe that they even worked miracles, 'God bearing witness with their words, and through signs and wonders and manifold powers'.

Now when we thus briefly demonstrate the divine nature of Jesus and use the words spoken in prophecy about him, we demonstrate at the same time that the writings which prophesy about him are divinely inspired and that the words which announce his sojourning here and his teaching were spoken with all power and authority and that this is the reason why they have prevailed over the elect people taken from among the nations. And we must add that it was after the advent of Jesus that the inspiration of the prophetic words and the spiritual nature of Moses' law came to light. For before the advent of Christ it was not at all possible to bring forward clear proofs of the divine inspiration of the old scriptures. But the advent of Jesus led those who might have suspected that the law and the prophets were not divine to the clear conviction that they were composed by the aid of heavenly grace.

And he who approaches the prophetic words with care and attention will feel from his very reading a trace of their divine inspiration and will be convinced by his own feelings that the words which are believed by us to be from God are not the compositions of men. Now the light which was contained within the law of Moses, but was hidden away under a veil, shone forth at the advent of Jesus, when the veil was taken away and there came at once to men's knowledge those 'good things' of which the letter of the law held a 'shadow'.

It would be a long business if we were to record at this point the ancient prophecies relating to every future event, in order that the doubter might be struck by their divine origin and, putting away all hesitation and indecision, might devote himself with his whole soul to the words of God. But if in every

7

passage of the scriptures the superhuman element of the thought does not appear obvious to the uninstructed, that is no wonder. For in regard to the works of that providence which controls the whole world, while some show themselves most plainly to be works of providence, others are so obscure as to appear to afford grounds for disbelief in the God who with unspeakable skill and power superintends the universe. The skilful plan of the providential ruler is not so clear in things on earth as it is in regard to the sun and moon and stars, and not so plain in the events that happen to men as it is in regard to the souls and bodies of animals, where the purpose and reason of the impulses, the mental images and the natures they possess and the structures of their bodies are accurately discovered by those who investigate these matters.

But just as providence is not abolished because of our ignorance, at least not for those who have once rightly believed in it, so neither is the divine character of scripture, which extends through all of it, abolished because our weakness cannot discern in every sentence the hidden splendour of its teachings, concealed under a poor and humble style. For 'we have a treasure in earthen vessels, that the exceeding greatness of the power of God may shine forth' and may not be reckoned as coming from us who are but men. For if it had been the hackneyed methods of demonstration used among men and preserved in books that had convinced mankind, our faith might reasonably have been supposed to rest in the wisdom of men and not in the power of God. But now it is clear that 'the word and the preaching' have prevailed among the multitude 'not in persuasive words of wisdom, but in demonstration of the Spirit and of power.'

Since therefore it is a celestial or even super-celestial power that impels us to worship only him who created us, let us endeavour to 'leave behind the doctrine of the first principles of Christ', that is, of the elements, and 'press on to perfection', that the wisdom which is spoken to the perfect may be spoken also to us. For he who had acquired this wisdom promises that he speaks it to the perfect, and that it is a wisdom different from the 'wisdom of this world, and the wisdom of the rulers of this world, which is coming to nought'. And this wisdom will be distinctly stamped upon us 'according to the revelation of the mystery which hath been kept in silence through times eternal, but now is manifested both through the scriptures and through the appearing of our Lord and Saviour Jesus Christ'; to whom be glory for ever and ever. Amen.

CHAPTER II

HOW DIVINE SCRIPTURE SHOULD BE READ AND INTERPRETED

Now that we have spoken cursorily about the inspiration of the divine scriptures it is necessary to discuss the manner in which they are to be read and understood, since many mistakes have been made in consequence of the method by which the holy documents ought to be interpreted not having been discovered by the multitude. For the hard-hearted and ignorant members of the circumcision have refused to believe in our Saviour because they think that they are keeping closely to the language of the prophecies that relate to him, and they see that he did not literally 'proclaim release to captives' or build what they consider to be a real 'city of God' or 'cut off the chariots from Ephraim and the horse from Jerusalem' or 'eat butter and honey, and choose the good before he knew or preferred the evil.'

Further, they think that it is the wolf, the four-footed animal, which is said in prophecy to be going to 'feed with the lamb, and the leopard to lie down with the kid, and the calf and bull and lion to feed together, led by a little child, and the ox and the bear to pasture together, their young ones growing up with each other, and the lion to eat straw like the ox'; and having seen none of these events literally happening during the advent of him whom we believe to be Christ they did not accept our Lord Jesus, but crucified him on the ground that he had wrongly called himself Christ.

And the members of the heretical sects, reading the passage, 'A fire has been kindled in mine anger'; and 'I am a jealous God, visiting the sins of the fathers upon the children to the third and fourth generation'; and 'It repenteth me that I have anointed Saul to be king'; and 'I, God, make peace and create evil'; and elsewhere, 'There is no evil in a city, which the

Lord did not do'; and further, 'Evils came down from the Lord upon the gates of Jerusalem'; and 'An evil spirit from the Lord troubled Saul'; and ten thousand other passages like these, have not dared to disbelieve that they are the writings of God, but believe them to belong to the Creator, whom the Jews worship. Consequently they think that since the Creator is imperfect and not good, the Saviour came here to proclaim a more perfect God who they say is not the Creator, and about whom they entertain diverse opinions. Then having once fallen away from the Creator, who is the sole unbegotten God, they have given themselves up to fictions, fashioning mythical hypotheses according to which they suppose that there are some things that are seen and others that are not seen, all of which are the fancies of their own minds.

Moreover, even the simpler of those who claim to belong to the Church, while believing indeed that there is none greater than the Creator, in which they are right, yet believe such things about him as would not be believed of the most savage and unjust of men.

Now the reason why all those we have mentioned hold false opinions and make impious or ignorant assertions about God appears to be nothing else but this, that scripture is not understood in its spiritual sense, but is interpreted according to the bare letter. On this account we must explain to those who believe that the sacred books are not the works of men, but that they were composed and have come down to us as a result of the inspiration of the Holy Spirit by the will of the Father of the universe through Jesus Christ, what are the methods of interpretation that appear right to us, who keep to the rule of the heavenly Church of Jesus Christ through the succession from the Apostles.

That there are certain mystical revelations made known through the divine scriptures is believed by all, even by the simplest of those who are adherents of the word; but what these revelations are, fair-minded and humble men confess that they do not know. If, for instance, an inquirer were to be in a difficulty, about the intercourse of Lot with his daughters, or the two wives of Abraham, or the two sisters married to Jacob, or the two hand-maids who bore children by him, they can say nothing except that these things are mysteries not understood by us.

But when the passage about the equipment of the tabernacle is read, believing that the things described therein are types, they seek for ideas which they can attach to each detail that is mentioned in connexion with the tabernacle. Now so far as concerns their belief that the tabernacle is a type of something they are not wrong; but in rightly attaching the word of scripture to the particular idea of which the tabernacle is a type, here they sometimes fall into error. And they declare that all narratives that are supposed to speak about marriage or the begetting of children or wars or any other stories whatever that may be accepted among the multitude are types; but when we ask, of what, then sometimes owing to the lack of thorough training, sometimes owing to rashness, and occasionally, even when one is well trained and of sound judgment, owing to man's exceedingly great difficulty in discovering these things, the interpretation of every detail is not altogether clear.

And what must we say about the prophecies, which we all know are filled with riddles and dark sayings? Or if we come to the gospels, the accurate interpretation even of these, since it is an interpretation of the mind of Christ, demands that grace that was given to him who said, 'We have the mind of Christ, that we may know the things that were freely given to us by God. Which things also we speak, not in words which man's wisdom teacheth, but which the Spirit teacheth.' And who, on reading the revelations made to John, could fail to be amazed at the deep obscurity of the unspeakable mysteries contained therein, which are evident even to him who does not understand what is written? And as for the apostolic epistles, what man who is skilled in literary interpretation would think them to be plain and easily understood, when even in them there are thousands of passages that provide, as if through a window, a narrow opening leading to multitudes of the deepest thoughts?

Seeing, therefore that these things are so, and that thousands of men make mistakes, it is dangerous for us when we read to declare lightly that we understand things for which the 'key of knowledge' is necessary, which the Saviour says is with 'the lawyers'. And as for those who are unwilling to admit that these men held the truth before the coming of Christ, let them explain to us how it is that our Lord Jesus Christ says that the 'key of knowledge' was with them, that is, with men who as these objectors say, had no books containing the secrets of knowledge and the all-perfect mysteries. For the passage runs as follows: 'Woe unto you lawyers, for ye have taken away the key of knowledge. Ye entered not in yourselves, and them that were entering in ye hindered.'

The right way, therefore, as it appears to us, of approaching the scriptures and gathering their meaning, is the following, which is extracted from the writings themselves. We find some such rule as this laid down by Solomon in the Proverbs concerning the divine doctrines written therein: 'Do thou pourtray them threefold in counsel and knowledge, that thou mayest answer words of truth to those who question thee'.

One must therefore pourtray the meaning of the sacred writings in a threefold way upon one's own soul, so that the simple man may be edified by what we may call the flesh of the scripture, this name being given to the obvious interpretation; while the man who has made some progress may be edified by its soul, as it were; and the man who is perfect and like those mentioned by the apostle: 'We speak wisdom among the perfect; yet a wisdom not of this world, nor of the rulers of this world, which are coming to nought; but we speak God's wisdom in a mystery, even the wisdom that hath been hidden, which God foreordained before the worlds unto our glory'— this man may be edified by the spiritual law, which has 'a shadow of the good things to come'. For just as man consists of body, soul and spirit, so in the same way does the scripture, which has been prepared by God to be given for man's salvation.

We therefore read in this light the passage in The Shepherd, a book which is despised by some, where Hermas is bidden to 'write two books', and after this to 'announce to the presbyters of the Church' what he has learned from the Spirit. This is the wording: 'Thou shalt write two books, and shalt give one to Clement and one to Grapte. And Grapte shall admonish the widows and the orphans. But Clement shall send to the cities without, and thou shalt announce to the presbyters of the Church.'

Origen

Now Grapte, who admonishes the widows and orphans, is the bare letter, which admonishes those child souls that are not yet able to enrol God as their Father and are on this account called orphans, and which also admonishes those who while no longer associating with the unlawful bridegroom are in widowhood because they have not yet become worthy of the true one. But Clement, who has already gone beyond the letter, is said to send the sayings 'to the cities without', as if to say, to the souls that are outside all bodily and lower thoughts; while the disciple of the Spirit is bidden to announce the message in person, no longer through letters but through living words, to the presbyters or elders of the whole Church of God, to men who have grown grey through wisdom.

But since there are certain passages of scripture which, as we shall show in what follows, have no bodily sense at all, there are occasions when we must seek only for the soul and the spirit, as it were, of the passage. And possibly this is the reason why the waterpots which, as we read in the gospel according to John, are said to be set there 'for the purifying of the Jews', contain two or three firkins apiece. The language alludes to those who are said by the apostle to be Jews 'inwardly', and it means that these are purified through the word of the scriptures, which contain in some cases 'two firkins', that is, so to speak, the soul meaning and the spiritual meaning, and in other cases three, since some passages possess, in addition to those before-mentioned, a bodily sense as well, which is capable of edifying the hearers. And six waterpots may reasonably allude to those who are being purified in the world, which was made in six days, a perfect number.

That it is possible to derive benefit from the first, and to this extent helpful meaning, is witnessed by the multitudes of sincere and simple believers. But of the kind of explanation which penetrates as it were to the soul an illustration is found in Paul's first epistle to the Corinthians. 'For,' he says, 'it is wirtten; thou shalt not muzzle the ox that treadeth out the corn'. Then in explanation of this law he adds, 'Is it for the oxen that God careth? Or saith he it altogether for our sake? Yea, for our sake it was written, because he that ploweth ought to plow in hope, and he that thresheth, to thresh in hope of partaking.' And most of the interpretations adapted to the multitude which are in circulation and which edify those who cannot understand the higher meanings have something of the same character.

But it is a spiritual explanation when one is able to show of what kind of 'heavenly things' the Jews 'after the flesh' served a copy and a shadow, and of what 'good things to come' the law has a 'shadow'. And, speaking generally, we have, in accordance with the apostolic promise, to seek after 'the wisdom in a mystery, even the wisdom that hath been hidden, which God foreordained before the worlds unto the glory' of the righteous, 'which none of the rulers of this world knew'. The same apostle also says somewhere, after mentioning certain narratives from Exodus and Numbers, that 'these things happened unto them figuratively, and they were written for our sake, upon whom the ends of the ages are come.' He also gives hints to show what these things were figures of, when he says: 'For they drank of that spiritual rock that followed them, and that rock was Christ.'

In another epistle, when outlining the arrangements of the tabernacle he quotes the words: 'Thou shalt make all things according to the figure that was shown thee in the mount.' Further, in the epistle to the Galatians, speaking in terms of reproach to those who believe that they are reading the law and yet do not understand it, and laying it down that they who do not believe that there are allegories in the writings do not understand the law, he says: 'Tell me, ye that desire to be under the law, do ye not hear the law? For it is written, that Abraham had two sons, one by the handmaid and one by the free woman. Howbeit the son by the handmaid is born after the flesh; but the son by the free woman is born through promise. Which things contain an allegory; for these women are two covenants', and what follows. Now we must carefully mark each of the words spoken by him. He says, 'Ye that desire to be under the law' (not, 'ye that are under the law') 'do ye not hear the law?' hearing being taken to mean understanding and knowing.

And in the epistle to the Colossians, briefly epitomising the meaning of the entire system of the law, he says: 'Let no man therefore judge you in meat or in drink or in respect of a feast day or a new moon or a sabbath, which are a shadow of the things to come.' Further, in the epistle to the Hebrews, when discoursing about those who are of the circumcision, he writes: 'They who serve that which is a copy and shadow of the heavenly things.' Now it is probable that those who have once admitted that the apostle is a divinely inspired man will feel no difficulty in regard to the five books ascribed to Moses; but in regard to the rest of the history they desire to learn whether those events also 'happened figuratively'. We must note the quotation in the epistle to the Romans: 'I have left for myself seven thousand men, who have not bowed the knee to Baal, found in the third book of the Kings. Here Paul has taken it to stand for those who are Israelites 'according to election', for not only are the gentiles benefited by the coming of Christ, but also some who belong to the divine race.

This being so, we must outline what seems to us to be the marks of a true understanding of the scriptures. And in the first place we must point out that the aim of the Spirit who, by the providence of God through the Word who was 'in the beginning with God', enlightened the servants of the truth, that is, the prophets and apostles, was pre-eminently concerned with the unspeakable mysteries connected with the affairs of men—and by men I mean at the present moment souls that make use of bodies—his purpose being that the man who is capable of being taught might by 'searching out' and devoting himself to the 'deep things' revealed in the spiritual meaning of the words become partaker of all the doctrines of the Spirit's counsel.

And when we speak of the needs of the souls, who cannot otherwise reach perfection except through the rich and wise truth about God, we attach of necessity pre-eminent importance to the doctrines concerning God and His only-begotten Son; of what nature the Son is, and in what manner he can be the Son of God, and what are the causes of his descending to the level of human flesh and completely assuming humanity; and what, also, is the nature of his activity, and towards whom and at what times it is exercised. It was necessary, too, that the doctrines concerning beings akin to man and the rest of the rational creatures, both those that are nearer the divine and those that have fallen from blessedness, and the causes of the fall of these

15

latter, should be included in the accounts of the divine teaching; and the question of the differences between souls and how these differences arose, and what the word is and why it exists, and further, how it comes about that evil is so widespread and so terrible on earth, and whether it is not only to be found on earth but also in other places—all this it was necessary that we should learn.

Now while these and similar subjects were in the mind of the Spirit who enlightened the souls of the holy servants of the truth, there was a second aim, pursued for the sake of those who were unable to endure the burden of investigating matters of such importance. This was to conceal the doctrine relating to the before-mentioned subjects in words forming a narrative that contained a record dealing with the visible creation, the formation of man and the successive descendants of the first human beings until the time when they became many; and also in other stories that recorded the acts of righteous men and the sins that these same men occasionally committed, seeing they were but human, and the deeds of wickedness, licentiousness and greed done by lawless and impious men.

But the most wonderful thing is, that by means of stories of wars and the conquerors and the conquered certain secret truths are revealed to those who are capable of examining these narratives; and, even more marvellous, through a written system of law the laws of truth are prophetically indicated, all these having been recorded in a series with a power which is truly appropriate to the wisdom of God. For the intention was to make even the outer covering of the spiritual truths, I mean the bodily part of the scriptures, in many respects not unprofitable but capable of improving the multitude in so far as they receive it.

But if the usefulness of the law and the sequence and ease of the narrative were at first sight clearly discernible throughout, we should be unaware that there was anything beyond the obvious meaning for us to understand in the scriptures. Consequently the Word of God has arranged for certain stumbling-blocks, as it were, and hindrances and impossibilities to be inserted in the midst of the law and the history, in order that we may not be completely drawn away by the sheer attractiveness of the language, and so either reject the true doctrines absolutely, on the ground that we learn from the scriptures nothing worthy of God, or else by never moving away from the letter fail to learn anything of the more divine element.

And we must also know this, that because the principal aim was to announce the connexion that exists among spiritual events, those that have already happened and those that are yet to come to pass, whenever the Word found that things which had happened in history could be harmonised with these mystical events he used them, concealing from the multitude their deeper meaning. But wherever in the narrative the accomplishment of some particular deeds, which had been previously recorded for the sake of their more mystical meanings, did not correspond with the sequence of the intellectual truths, the scripture wove into the story something which did not happen, occasionally something which could not happen, and occasionally something which might have happened but in fact did not. Sometimes a few words are inserted which in the bodily sense are not true, and at other times a greater number.

A similar method can be discerned also in the law, where it is often possible to find a precept that is useful for its own sake, and suitable to the time when the law was given. Sometimes, however, the precept does not appear to be useful. At other times even impossibilities are recorded in the law for the sake of the more skilful and inquiring readers, in order that these, by giving themselves to the toil of examining what is written, may gain a sound conviction of the necessity of seeking in such instances a meaning worthy of God.

And not only did the Spirit supervise the writings which were previous to the coming of Christ, but because he is the same Spirit and proceeds from the one God he has dealt in like manner with the gospels and the writings of the apostles. For the history even of these is not everywhere pure, events being woven together in the bodily sense without having actually happened; nor do the law and the commandments contained therein entirely declare what is reasonable.

CHAPTER III

THE PRINCIPLE UNDERLYING THE OBSCURITIES IN DIVINE SCRIPTURE AND ITS IMPOSSIBLE OR UNREASONABLE CHARACTER IN PLACES, IF TAKEN LITERALLY.

Now what man of intelligence will believe that the first and the second and the third day, and the evening and the morning existed without the sun and moon and stars? And that the first day, if we may so call it, was even without a heaven? And who is so silly as to believe that God, after the manner of a farmer, 'planted a paradise eastward in Eden', and set in it a visible and palpable 'tree of life', of such a sort that anyone who tasted its fruit with his bodily teeth would gain life; and again that one could partake of 'good and evil' by masticating the fruit taken from the tree of that name? And when God is said to 'walk in the paradise in the cool of the day and Adam to hide himself behind a tree, I do not think anyone will doubt that these are figurative expressions which indicate certain mysteries through a semblance of history and not through actual events.

Further, when Cain 'goes out from the face of God' it seems clear to thoughtful men that this statement impels the reader to inquire what the 'face of God' is and how anyone can 'go out' from it. And what more need I say, when those who are not altogether blind can collect thousands of such instances, recorded as actual events, but which did not happen literally?

Even the gospels are full of passages of this kind, as when the devil takes Jesus up into a 'high mountain' in order to show him from thence 'the kingdoms of the whole world and the glory of them'. For what man who does not read such passages carelessly would fail to condemn those who believe that with the eye of the flesh, which requires a great height to enable us to perceive what is below and at our feet, the kingdoms of the Persians, Scythians, Indians and Parthians were seen, and the manner in which their rulers are glorified by men? And the careful reader will detect thousands of other passages like this in the gospels, which will convince him that events which did not take place at all are woven into the records of what literally did happen.

Origen

And to come to the Mosaic legislation, many of the laws,
so far as their literal observance is concerned, are clearly irrational, while others are impossible. An example of irrationality
is the prohibition to eat vultures, seeing that nobody even in the
worst famine was ever driven by want to the extremity of eating
these creatures. And in regard to the command that children of
eight days old who are uncircumcised 'shall be destroyed from
among their people', if the law relating to these children were
really meant to be carried out according to the letter, the
proper course would be to order the death of their fathers or
those by whom they were being brought up. But as it is the
Scripture says: 'Every male that is uncircumcised, who shall not
be circumcised on the eighth day, shall be destroyed from
among his people'.

And if you would like to see some impossibilities that are
enacted in the law, let us observe that the goat-stag, which
Moses commands us to offer in sacrifice as a clean animal, is a
creature that cannot possibly exist; while as to the griffin,
which the lawgiver forbids to be eaten, there is no record that
it has ever fallen into the hands of man. Moreover in regard to
the celebrated sabbath, a careful reader will see that the command, 'Ye shall sit each one in your dwellings; let none of you
go out from his place on the sabbath day,' is an impossible one
to observe literally, for no living creature could sit for a whole
day and not move from his seat.

Consequently the members of the circumcision and all
those who maintain that nothing more than the actual wording
is signified make no inquiry whatever into some matters, such
as the goat-stag, the griffin and the vulture, while on others
they babble copiously, bringing forward lifeless traditions, as
for instance when they say, in reference to the sabbath, that
each man's 'place' is two thousand cubits. Others, however,
among whom is Dositheus the Samaritan, condemn such an
interpretation, and believe that in whatever position a man is
found on the Sabbath day he should remain there until evening.

Further, the command 'not to carry a burden on the sabbath day' is impossible; and on this account the teachers of the
Jews have indulged in endless chatter, asserting that one kind
of shoe is a burden, but another is not, and that a sandal with

19

nails is a burden, but one without nails is not, and that what is carried on one shoulder is a burden, but not what is carried on both.

If now we approach the gospel in search of similar instances, what can be more irrational than the command: 'Salute no man by the way', which simple people believe that the Saviour enjoined upon the apostles? Again, to speak of the right cheek being struck is most incredible, for every striker, unless he suffers from some unnatural defect, strikes the left cheek with his right hand. And it is impossible to accept the precept from the gospel about the 'right eye that offends'; for granting the possibility of a person being 'offended' through his sense of sight, how can the blame be attributed to the right eye, when there are two eyes that see? And what man, even supposing he accuses himself of 'looking on a woman to lust after her' and attributes the blame to his right eye alone, would act rationally if he were to cast his eye away?

Further, the apostle lays down this precept: 'Was any called being circumcised? Let him not become uncircumcised'. Now in the first place anyone who wishes can see that these words have no relation to the subject in hand; and how can we help thinking that they have been inserted at random, when we remember that the apostle is here laying down precepts about marriage and purity? In the second place who will maintain that it is wrong for a man to put himself into a condition of uncircumcision, if that were possible, in view of the disgrace which is felt by most people to attach to circumcision?

We have mentioned all these instances with the object of showing that the aim of the divine power which bestowed on us the holy scriptures is not that we should accept only what is found in the letter; for occasionally the records taken in a literal sense are not true, but actually absurd and impossible, and even with the history that actually happened and the legislation that is in its literal sense useful there are other matters interwoven.

But someone may suppose that the former statement refers to all the scriptures, and may suspect us of saying that because some of the history did not happen, therefore none of it happened; and because a certain law is irrational or impossible when taken literally, therefore no laws ought to be kept to the letter; or that the records of the Saviour's life are not true in a physical sense; or that no law or commandment of his ought to be obeyed. We must assert, therefore, that in regard to some things we are clearly aware that the historical fact is true; as that Abraham was buried in the double cave at Hebron, together with Isaac and Jacob and one wife of each of them; and that Shechem was given as a portion to Joseph; and that Jerusalem is the chief city of Judaea, in which a temple of God was built by Solomon; and thousands of other facts. For the passages which are historically true are far more numerous than those which are composed with purely spiritual meanings.

And again, who would deny that the command which says: 'Honour thy father and thy mother, that it may be well with thee', is useful quite apart from any spiritual interpretation, and that it ought certainly to be observed, especially when we remember that the apostle Paul has quoted it in the self-same words? And what are we to say of the following: 'Thou shalt not kill; thou shalt not commit adultery; thou shalt not steal; thou shalt not bear false witness'?

Once again, in the gospel there are commandments written which need no inquiry whether they are to be kept literally or not, as that which says, 'I say unto you, whosoever is angry with his brother', and what follows; and, 'I say unto you, swear not at all'. Here, too, is an injunction of the apostle of which the literal meaning must be retained: 'Admonish the disorderly, encourage the faint-hearted, support the weak, be longsuffering toward all;' though in the case of the more earnest readers it is possible to preserve each of the meanings, that is, while not setting aside the commandment in its literal sense, to preserve the 'depths of the wisdom of God.'

Nevertheless the exact reader will hesitate in regard to some passages, finding himself unable to decide without considerable investigation whether a particular incident, believed to be history, actually happened or not, and whether the literal meaning of a particular law is to be observed or not. Accordingly he who reads in an exact manner must, in obedience to the Saviour's precept which says, 'Search the scriptures', carefully investigate how far the literal meaning is true and how far it is impossible, and to the utmost of his power must trace out

from the use of similar expressions the meaning scattered everywhere through the scriptures of that which when taken literally
is impossible.

When, therefore, as will be clear to those who read, the
passage as a connected whole is literally impossible, whereas the
outstanding part of it is not impossible but even true, the reader
must endeavour to grasp the entire meaning, connecting by an
intellectual process the account of what is literally impossible
with the parts that are not impossible but are historically true,
these being interpreted allegorically in common with the parts
which, so far as the letter goes, did not happen at all. For our
contention with regard to the whole of divine scripture is, that
it all has a spiritual meaning, but not all a bodily meaning; for
the bodily meaning is often proved to be an impossibility.
Consequently the man who reads the divine books reverently,
believing them to be divine writings, must exercise great care.
And the method of understanding them appears to us to be as
follows.

The accounts tell us that God chose out a certain nation
on the earth, and they call this nation by many names. For the
nation as a whole is called Israel, and it is also spoken of as
Jacob. But when it was divided in the days of Jeroboam the son
of Nebat, the ten tribes said to have been subject to him were
named Israel, and the other two together with the tribe of Levi,
which were ruled over by men of the seed of David, were called
Judah. The entire country which was inhabited by men of this
race and which had been given them by God, is called Judaea,
the metropolis of which is Jerusalem, this being the mother city
of a number of others whose names lie scattered about in many
different places of scripture but are gathered together into one
list in the book of Joshua the son of Nun.

This being so, the apostle, raising our spiritual appre-
hension to a high level, says somewhere: 'Behold Israel after
the flesh', inferring that there is an Israel after the spirit. He
says also in another place: 'For it is not the children of the flesh
that are children of God', nor are 'all they Israel, who are of
Israel'.

And again: 'Neither is he a Jew, who is one outwardly, nor
is that circumcision, which is outward in the flesh; but he is a

Jew, who is one inwardly, and circumcision is of the heart, in the spirit, not in the letter'. For if we take the phrase 'a Jew inwardly' as a test, we shall realise that as there is a race of bodily Jews, so, too, there is a race of those who are 'Jews inwardly', the soul having acquired this nobility of race in virtue of certain unspeakable words. Moreover there are many prophecies spoken of Israel and Judah, which relate what is going to happen to them. And when we think of the extraordinary promises recorded about these people, promises that so far as literary style goes are poor and distinguished by no elevation or character that is worthy of a promise of God, is it not clear that they demand a mystical interpretation? Well, then, if the promises are of a spiritual kind though announced through material imagery, the people to whom the promises belong are not the bodily Israelites.

But we must not spend time discussing who is a 'Jew inwardly' and who an Israelite 'in the inner man', since the above remarks are sufficient for all who are not dull-witted. We will return to the subject before us and say that Jacob was the father of the twelve patriarchs, and they of the rulers of the people, and they in their turn of the Israelites who came after. Is it not the case, then, that the bodily Israelites carry back their descent to the rulers of the people, the rulers of the people to the patriarchs, and the patriarchs to Jacob and those still more ancient; whereas are not the spiritual Israelites, of whom the bodily ones were a type, descended from the clans, and the clans from the tribes, and the tribes from one whose birth was not bodily, like that of the others, but of a higher kind; and was not he born of Isaac, and Isaac descended from Abraham, while all go back to Adam, who the apostle says is Christ? For the origin of all families that are in touch with the God of the whole world began lower down with Christ, who comes next after the God and Father of the whole world and is thus the father of every soul, as Adam is the father of all men. And if Eve is interpreted by Paul as referring to the Church, it is not surprising (seeing that Cain was born of Eve and all that come after him carry back their descent to Eve) that these two should be figures of the Church; for in the higher sense all men take their beginning from the Church.

THE CATHOLIC TRADITION: Sacred Scripture

Now if what we have stated about Israel, its tribes and its clans, is convincing, then when the Saviour says, 'I was not sent but unto the lost sheep of the house of Israel', we do not take these words in the same sense as the poor-minded Ebionites do (men whose very name comes from the poverty of their mind, for in Hebrew *ebion* is the word for poor), so as to suppose that Christ came especially to the Israelites after the flesh. For 'it is not the children of the flesh that are children of God'.

Again, the apostle gives us the following instances of teaching about Jerusalem: 'The Jerusalem which is above is free, which is our mother'; and in another epistle: 'But ye are come to Mount Sion and to the city of the living God, the heavenly Jerusalem, and to an innumerable company of angels, to the general assembly and church of the firstborn who are written in heaven'.

If therefore Israel consists of a race of souls, and Jerusalem is a city in heaven, it follows that the cities of Israel have for their mother city the Jerusalem in the heavens; and so consequently does Judaea as a whole. * * * * * * * * * * * *
(*A sentence appears to be missing from the Greek at this point.*)

In all prophecies concerning Jerusalem, therefore, and in all statements made about it, we must understand, if we listen to Paul's words as the words of God and the utterances of wisdom, that the scriptures are telling us about the heavenly city and the whole region which contains the cities of the holy land. Perhaps it is to these cities that the Saviour lifts our attention when he gives to those who have deserved praise for the good use of their talents authority over ten or over five cities.

If therefore the prophecies relating to Judaea, to Jerusalem, and to Israel, Judah and Jacob suggest to us, because we do not interpret them in a fleshly sense, mysteries such as these, it will follow also that the prophecies which relate to Egypt and the Egyptians, to Babylon and the Babylonians, to Tyre and the Tyrians, to Sidon and the Sidonians, or to any of the other nations, are not spoken solely of the bodily Egyptians, Babylonians, Tyrians and Sidonians. If the Israelites are spiritual, it follows that the Egyptians and Babylonians are also spiritual.

For the statements made in Ezekiel about Pharaoh king of Egypt entirely fail to apply to any particular man who was or will be ruler of Egypt, as will be clear to those who study the passage carefully.

Similarly the statements concerning the ruler of Tyre cannot be understood of any particular man who is to rule over Tyre. And as for the numerous statements made about Nebuchadnezzar, especially in Isaiah, how it is possible to interpret them of that particular man? For the man Nebuchadnezzar neither 'fell from heaven', nor was he the 'morning star', nor did he 'rise in the morning' over the earth.

Nor indeed will any man of intelligence interpret the statements made in Ezekiel concerning Egypt, that it shall be 'laid waste forty years' so that 'no foot of man' shall be found there, and that it shall one day be so overwhelmed with war, that throughout the whole land there shall be blood up to the knees, as referring to the Egypt which lies next to the Ethiopians whose bodies are blackened by the sun.

And perhaps, just as people on earth, when they die the common death of all, are in consequence of the deeds done here so distributed as to obtain different positions according to the proportion of their sins, if they are judged to be worthy of the place called Hades; so the people there, when they die, if I may so speak, descend into this Hades, and are judged worthy of different habitations, better or worse, in the whole of this region of earth * * * * * * * * * * * * * * * *

and of being born of such or such parents, so that an Israelite will occasionally fall among Scythians and an Egyptian descend into Judaea. Nevertheless the Saviour came to gather together the 'lost sheep of the house of Israel', and since many from Israel have not submitted to his teaching, those from the Gentiles are also called. * * * * * * * * * * * * * *

But these truths, as we think, have been concealed in the narratives. For 'the kingdom of heaven is like unto a treasure hid in a field, which when a man findeth he hideth it, and for joy thereof goeth and selleth all that he hath, and buyeth that field.' Now let us consider whether the outward aspect of scripture and its obvious and surface meaning does not correspond to the field as a whole, full of all kinds of plants, whereas the truths that are stored away in it and not seen by all, but lie as if buried beneath the visible plants, are the hidden 'treasures of wisdom and knowledge', which the Spirit speaking through Isaiah calls 'dark and unseen and concealed'.

These treasures require for their discovery the help of God, who alone is able to 'break in pieces the gates of brass' that conceal them and to burst the iron bars that are upon the gates, and so to make known all the truths taught in Genesis concerning the various legitimate races and as it were seeds of souls, whether closely akin to Israel or far apart from him, and the descent of the 'seventy souls' into Egypt, in order that they may there become 'as the stars of the heaven in multitude'. But since not all who are sprung from these are a 'light of the world', for 'they are not all Israel, who are of Israel' there come from the seventy a people 'even as the sand which is by the sea shore innumerable.'

But if we continue our inquiries as far as the passion, to seek for this in the heavenly places will seem a bold thing to do. Yet if there are 'spiritual hosts of wickedness' in the heavenly places, consider whether, just as we are not ashamed to confess that he was crucified here in order to destroy those whom he destroyed through his suffering, so we should not fear to allow that a similar event also happens there and will happen in the ages to come until the end of the whole world * * * * * * *

Novatian
200-258

Novatian was a distinguished member of the Roman clergy
up to 251. In that year, he refused to acknowledge the newly-
elected Cornelius as bishop of Rome, and allowed himself to be
chosen rival bishop by a minority group. The cause of the split
was a disagreement over policy in readmitting to the Church
those who had fallen away during persecution. Novatian was a
rigorist who held they should never be allowed to return. His
followers, known as Cathari (puritans) lasted until at least the
sixth century, but we have no information about Novatian after
this schism, neither how long he lived nor how he died, but in
1932 a richly decorated tomb was discovered in Rome designat-
ing someone named Novatian as "a most blessed martyr."

Whatever the circumstances of his later life, there is no
escaping the fact of his earlier importance. "He was the first
theologian of Rome to publish in Latin and he is thus one of the
founders of Roman theology . . . (His work on the Trinity) is the
first great Latin contribution to theology to appear in Rome . . .
Composed in poetical prose, outstanding in form and content, it
is the most valuable and most extensive of Novatian's productions
and the cause of his high reputation as a divine" (J. Quasten).

The Trinity was probably written between 240 and 250. It
consists of 31 chapters, using the baptismal confession of faith
as its framework, so that the bulk of the book is about Christ.

Amidst the numerous heresies that had arisen, Novatian would show what the true Christian positions were, appealing to scripture and tradition. He brings his training in Stoic philosophy to bear on the topic and utilizes all the resources of ancient rhetoric.

Our purpose in including it here, however, is because of the way in which the Bible is appealed to. The following selection contains chapters 10 through 22, the real heart of the book, in which the appeal to Biblical proof is relentless. In clear, calm, and careful Latin he takes up point after point and in dialectical fashion insists that Christ is God, that Christ is man, that the Old Testament foretells this, that the New Testament declares it. To appreciate Novatian one must keep in mind that he was writing nearly a century before Arius, before any of the Councils, before a very reliable Latin translation of the Bible was on hand.

Novatian's tenacity in arguing reminds one of a bulldog. At one point in the middle of the following selection he applies the hammer by repeating at least 25 times in a row: "If Christ is only man, how is it that . . ?," "If Christ is only man, why is it that . . ?" As the rhetorical questions multiply, the heart of his concern becomes more and more apparent, and objectionable positions are left in disarray.

A powerful model of theological argumentation is thus presented for posterity: reason used for probing the depths and implications of the text of the Bible. Novatian does not show the fascination that Origen does for the allegorical method, although he can also engage in it. But the precedent is firmly and strikingly established that there is no such thing as Christian theology that is not totally and radically biblical theology.

THE TRINITY

CHAPTER 10

I must warn you that no other Christ should have been sought for in the Gospel than this one who was promised before by the Creator in the writings of the Old Testament, especially because the things that were predicted about Him have been fulfilled, and all that has been fulfilled was predicted beforehand. To that counterfeit and spurious Christ, devised somehow from old wives' tales by heretics who reject the authority of the Old Testament, I can, with reason, truly and boldly say: Who are you? From what place did you come? By whom were you sent? Why did you wish to come now? Why are you what you are? By what way did you manage to come? Why did you not go to your own people, if not to prove, by coming among strangers that you have no people of your own? What have you to do with the Creator's world, or with man, the Creator's handiwork, or with the semblance of a body to which you deny the hope of resurrection? Why do you come to another man's servant, and why do you desire to disturb another man's son? Why are you trying to take me away from the Lord? Why do you drive me to blaspheme against the Father and make me impious? Or what will I obtain from you in the resurrection, if, when I lose my body, I do not get myself back? If you wish to save, you should have made man to whom you could give salvation. If you desire to deliver me from sin, you should have granted me the grace beforehand not to fall into sin. What approval of the Law do you carry about with you? What testimony for your stand have you in the voice of the prophets? Or what genuine good can I promise myself from you, when I see that you have come as a phantom and not in reality? And if you hate the body, what are you doing with the semblance of a body? In fact, you are proved false in your claim to hate carrying about with you the substance of a body when you did not hesitate to assume the very semblance of one.

For you ought to have hated even the imitation of a body, if you hated its reality. If you are another, you should have come in a different manner, so that you would not be called the Creator's son by your possession of even the appearance of flesh and body. Surely, if birth was odious to you because you hated the Creator's ordinance of marriage, you should have refused to assume even the very resemblance of a man born according to the Creator's ordinance of marriage.

Nor, in fact, do we acknowledge the Christ of the heretics, who existed (as they say) in appearance and not in reality. If he were a phantom and not reality, then he did not really perform any of these actions that he is said to have performed. Nor do we acknowledge him to be Christ who in no way took upon himself our human body, inasmuch as he took nothing from Mary and consequently never came to us because he was not seen in our own bodily substance when he appeared. Finally, we do not acknowledge him to be a Christ who put on ethereal or sidereal flesh, as other heretics would have it, lest we should see any salvation of ours in him, if we did not also recognize the real substance of our own body. And we utterly reject anyone else who bears a body of any other kind whatever of heretical figment. Not only Our Lord's Nativity but even His death refutes all these heretics. "And the Word," says John, "was made flesh and dwelt among us"; consequently, He must have had our human body because the Word truly took our flesh. Blood flowed from His hands and feet and even from His very side, that He might prove Himself to be a sharer of our human body by dying according to the laws of our human dissolution. The wounds of His very body proved that He was raised again from the dead in the same corporeal substance in which He died. Thus He showed us the conditions of our resurrection in His own flesh, by restoring in His Resurrection the same body which He had from us. Hence a law of resurrection is laid down because Christ is raised up in the substance of His body as a model for others. Because it is written: "Flesh and blood shall not obtain the kingdom of God," it is not meant that the substance of our flesh, which was fashioned by the hands of God so as not to perish, was condemned. On the contrary, only the guilt of the flesh is censured, the guilt which was caused by man's deliberate and rash rebellion against the claims of divine law. After this guilt has been taken away in baptism and in the dissolution brought about by death, then the flesh is restored to salvation, because the flesh is recalled to a state of innocence, after the mortal condition of sin has been put aside.

CHAPTER 11

Lest we seem—by our assertion that Our Lord Jesus Christ, the Son of God the Creator, manifested Himself in the substance of a real body—to have joined forces with or given material for controversy to other heretics, who in this connection maintain that He was solely and simply a man and who therefore are very eager to prove that He was a mere man and nothing more, we do not express ourselves in such a manner concerning the substance of His body and claim that He was simply and solely a man. On the contrary we maintain that, by the fact that the divinity of the Word was permixed in that very matter, He was also God according to the Scriptures. It is very dangerous to say of Christ—the Saviour of the human race, the Lord and Prince of the whole world, to whom "all things have been" entrusted and "granted by His Father," by whom all things were made, all things created, all things set in order, the King of all ages and of all times, the Ruler of all the angels, before whom there was nothing besides the Father—to say that He is only man and to deny His divine authority in these things. This insult from the heretics will also extend to God the Father, if God the Father could not beget God the Son. No blindness on the part of the heretics shall lay down the law for the truth. Because they maintain one thing about Christ and do not maintain the other, and because they see one side of Him and not the other, never shall the heretics take away from us the truth which they do not see for the sake of what they do see. For they consider in Him the frailties of man, but they do not regard the powers of a God. They reflect on the infirmities of His flesh, but they exclude from their minds the power of His divinity. If this proof drawn from the infirmities of Christ has such efficacy as to prove that He is man precisely because of those infirmities, then the proof of His divinity, drawn from His miracles, will have enough efficacy to show on account of

His mighty works that He is also God. If His sufferings manifest human frailty in Him, why should not His works confirm the divine power in Him? If the miracles do not suffice to prove Him God, then neither will the sufferings alone suffice to prove Him man. Whatever principle is posited in either case will be found to be suspect in the other. If it cannot be proved that He is God because of His miracles, there will also be the danger of not being able to show that He is man because of His sufferings. One must not lean to one side and incline away from the other, for whoever rejects a portion of the truth will never hold the complete truth. Just as Scripture proclaims that Christ is also God, so, too, does it proclaim that God is very Man. It describes Jesus Christ as Man, just as it describes Christ the Lord as God. Scripture proclaims Him to be not only the Son of God but also the Son of Man; it not only calls Him the Son of Man but has also been accustomed to refer to Him as the Son of God, so that He is both because He is of both. Otherwise—if He were only the one—He could not be the other. Nature itself demands that we believe that he is a man who is of man. Likewise it demands that we believe that he is God who is of God; otherwise, if He were not also God, when He is of God, then He would not be man, though He is of man. Both natures alike would be endangered by the denial of one or the other, inasmuch as one proves to have been discredited by the overthrow of the other. Therefore, let those who read in Scripture that the Man Christ Jesus is the Son of Man, also read there that this same Jesus is called both God and Son of God. In the same manner that He, as Man, is of Abraham, even so, as God, is He also before Abraham himself. In the same manner that He, as Man, is the Son of David, so is He also, as God, called the Lord of David. And in the same manner that He, as Man, is made under the Law, so is He also, as God, declared to be the Lord of the Sabbath. In the same manner that He, as Man, endured the sentence of death, we find that, as God, He has all judgment over the living and the dead. In the same manner that He, as Man, is born after the world existed, so, as God, is He shown to have existed before the world. In the same manner that He, as Man, was born "of the seed of David," so in like manner is it said that through Him, as God, the world was made. In the same manner that He, as Man, was after many, He was, as God, before all men. In the same manner that He, as Man, was lower in rank than the others, as God He was greater than all. In the same manner, that He, as Man, ascended into heaven, as God, He first descended from heaven. In the same manner that he, as Man, goes to the Father, so as a Son obedient to His Father shall he descend from the Father. Therefore, if limitations give evidence of human frailty in Him, His majesty affirms His divine power. However, when you read about both these truths, there is danger that you will believe not both of them but only one. Since we read of both attributes in Christ, we should believe both of them so that our faith may be true only if it is also complete. If one of these two truths ceases to have a part in our faith, while the other truth (and precisely that truth which is of lesser importance) is accepted as a matter of faith, then the Rule of Truth has been shaken. Such temerity will not give salvation; in its stead it will, through the rejection of faith, bring about a serious danger of death.

CHAPTER 12

Why, then, should we hesitate to say what Scripture does not hesitate to express? Why should the truth of Faith waver where the authority of Scripture has never faltered? For behold, the prophet Hosea says in the person of the Father: "I will not save them by bow, nor by horses; but I will save them by the Lord their God." If God says that He will save them by God and if God does not save except by Christ, then why should man hesitate to call Christ God when he realizes that the Father declares, through the Scriptures, that He is God. In fact, if God the Father can not save, except by God, no one can be saved by God the Father, unless he has aknowledged that Christ is God, in whom and through whom the Father promises to grant salvation. Consequently, whoever acknowledges that He is God, finds salvation in Christ who is God; whoever does not acknowledge that He is God, has lost salvation, which he cannot find elsewhere but in Christ who is God.

For just as Isaiah says: "Behold a virgin shall conceive and bear a son, and you shall call His name Emmanuel," "which is interpreted 'God with us,' " so too, does Christ Himself say:

"Behold I am with you, even to the consummation of the world." God, then, is with us, and what is more, He is even in us. Christ is with us; therefore it is He whose name is "God with us," because He is also with us. Or is it possible that He is not with us? Then, how can He say that He is with us? He is, therefore, with us, and because He is with us, He is called Emmanuel, "God with us." God, then, because He is with us, was called "God with us." The same prophet says: "Be strong, you feeble hands and weak knees; be comforted, you that are faint-hearted, be strong, fear not. Behold, our God will render judgment: He will come and save us: then shall the eyes of the blind be opened, and the ears of the deaf shall hear; then shall the lame man leap as the hart, and the tongue of the dumb shall be eloquent." If the prophet says that these signs—which have already been wrought—will be the future signs of God's advent, then let the heretics either acknowledge that Christ is the Son of God, at whose coming and by whom these miracles of healing were wrought, or—defeated by the truth of Christ's divinity and falling into the other heresy, inasmuch as they refuse to confess that Christ is the Son of God and God—let them confess that He is the Father. Since they have been restrained by the words of the prophets, they can no longer deny that Christ is God. What, then, can they reply, when the miracles which were prophesied as taking place at the coming of God, were actually wrought at the advent of Christ? In what way do they think Christ is God? For they can no longer deny that He is God. Do they think He is the Father or the Son? If they accept Him as the Son, why do they deny that the Son of God is God? If they accept Him as the Father, why are they not following those who are seen to hold such blasphemies? At any rate, in this debate with them about the truth, it suffices for our present purpose that, no matter how they are refuted, they confess that Christ, whose divinity they wished to deny, is also God.

He says through Habakkuk the prophet: "God shall come from the south, and the holy one from the dark and dense mountain." Whom would they have come from the South? If they say that God the Father almighty came, then God the Father came from a place; consequently, He is also enclosed by space and contained within the limits of some abode. Thus the sacrilegious heresy of Sabellius, as we said, takes concrete form because of these men who believe that Christ is not the Son but the Father. It is strange how these heretics, while insisting that Christ is a mere man, make an about-face and acknowledge that Christ is the Father, God almighty. If Christ, who is also called God by the Scriptures, was born in Bethlehem, which geographically faces towards the South, then this God is rightly described as coming from the South, because it was foreseen that He would come from Bethlehem. Therefore let them decide just who this Person from the South is, the Father or the Son? For Scripture says that God will come from the South. If He is the Son, why do they hesitate to say that Christ is also God, for Scripture says that God will come? If He is the Father, why do they hesitate to associate themselves with the rashness of Sabellius, who says that Christ is the Father? The truth of the matter is that, whether they call Him the Father or the Son, they are compelled, though against their will, to abandon their own heresy since they are accustomed to say that Christ is only a man. The very facts constrain them to declare that He is God, whether they choose to call Him the Father or the Son.

CHAPTER 13

In like manner, John, in his description of Christ's Nativity, says: "The Word was made flesh and dwelt among us. And we saw His glory—the glory as of the only-begotten of the Father—full of grace and of truth." For "His name is called the Word of God" also, and not without reason. "My heart," he says, "has uttered a good word," the word which he subsequently calls by the name of king, when he says: "I speak my works to the king." For "through Him all things were made, and without Him nothing was made." "For whether they be Thrones," says the Apostle, "or Dominations, or Virtues, or Powers, all things, visible and invisible, exist through Him." This is the Word who "came into His own and His own received Him not." For "the world was made through Him, and the world knew Him not." However, this "Word was in the beginning with God, and the Word was God." When John states in the latter part of his prologue that "the Word was made flesh and dwelt among us," who can doubt that Christ, whose birth it is, and because He was made flesh, is Man? And because He is the Word of God, who can hesitate for a moment to declare that He is God, especially when one realizes that the Gospel account has associated both these natures in the unique union of Christ's Nativity?

He it is who "comes forth as a bridegroom from His bridal chamber and rejoiced as a giant to run His course; His going forth is from the highest heaven and His return even to the height thereof." For He [returns] even to the height; "since no one has ascended into heaven except Him who has descended from heaven, the Son of Man who is in heaven." He repeats this very same fact when He says: "Father, glorify Me with the glory that I had with You before the world existed." If this Word descended from heaven as a bridegroom to take on our flesh, so that in taking flesh He might ascend again as Son of Man to that place whence, as Son of God, the Word had descended, then assuredly, because of a mutual bond, the flesh bears the Word of God, and the Son of God assumes the weakness of the flesh. He ascends with His spouse, the flesh, to the same place from which He had descended without the flesh and receives now that glory which He is shown to have had before the creation of the world. This proves, without the least doubt, that He is God. Nevertheless, since the world itself is said to have been created after Him, it is evident that it was created through Him. This fact itself gives proof of the glory and the authority of the divinity that is in Him, through whom the world was made.

Now if Christ sees the secrets of the heart, Christ is certainly God, since God alone knows the secrets of the heart. If the same Christ forgives sins, Christ is certainly God because no one can forgive sins but God alone. If Christ came down from heaven in coming into the world, Christ is certainly God, because no mere man can come from heaven. If the statement: "I and the Father are one," can be said by no man and if Christ in the consciousness of His divinity makes this statement, Christ is certainly God. If the apostle Thomas, finally convinced by all the proofs and the facts of Christ's divinity, says in reply to Christ: "My lord and My God," Christ is certainly God. If the apostle Paul also writes in his epistles: "Of whom are the fathers, and of whom is Christ according to the flesh, who is over all things, God blessed forever," Christ is certainly God. If the same apostle declares that he is "an apostle sent not from men by man, but by Jesus Christ," and asserts that "he learned the Gospel not from men or through man, but received it from Jesus Christ," Christ is certainly God.

At this point, therefore, one of two alternatives must be true. Since it is evident that all things were made through Christ, either He is before all things, because "all things are through Him," and consequently He is God, or else, because He is man, He is after all things, and consequently nothing was made through Him. But we cannot say that nothing was made through Him, since we know that it is written: "All things were made through Him." He is not after all things; that is, He is not a mere man who is after all things; for He is also God because God is before all things. He is before all things because "all things are through Him"; otherwise, were He only a man, nothing would be through Him. On the other hand, if all things were made through Him, He would not be a mere man. Were He merely a man, all things would not be made through Him; in fact, nothing would be made through Him. What, then, do the heretics reply: that nothing is through Him, hence He is a mere man? Then, how are all things through Him? Therefore He is not only Man but also God because all things are through Him. Consequently, we must understand not only that Christ is not a mere man who is after all things but that He is also God because all things were made through Him. Or how can you say that He is only man, when you behold Him also in the flesh? Certainly if both these truths are carefully considered, one must necessarily believe both truths.

CHAPTER 14

Yet the heretic still hesitates to say that Christ is God, even though he notes that it has been proved in so many words and by so many facts that He is God. If Christ is only man, how did He "come unto His own" when He came into this world, since man could not have made a world? If Christ is only man, how is "the world" said to have been "made through Him," when it is stated, not that the world was created through man but that man was created after the world? If Christ is only man, how is it that Christ is not only of the seed of David but "the Word was made flesh, and dwelt among us"? Though the first man was not born of human seed, still he was not compounded from the union of the Word and flesh, simply because he is not "the Word made flesh, [who] dwelt among us." If Christ is only man, how does "He who comes down from heaven bear witness to that which He has seen and heard," when it is evident that man cannot come from heaven because he cannot be born there? If Christ is only man, how are "things visible and invisible, Thrones, Virtues and Dominations" said to have been "created through Him and in Him," when the heavenly powers could not have been created through man, since they must have existed before man? If Christ is only man, how is He present wherever He is invoked—since it is not man's nature but God's to be able to be present everywhere? If Christ is only man, why is a man called upon in prayer as a mediator, when calling upon a man to grant salvation is considered useless? If Christ is only man, why is hope put in Him, when hope in man is declared to be accursed? If Christ is only man, why cannot He be denied without ruin to one's soul, when it is declared that an offense against man can be forgiven? If Christ is only man, how does John the Baptist bear witness of Him when he says: "He who comes after me was made before me, for He was before me"? If Christ were only man, then, being born after John, He could not be before John, unless he preceded him as God. If Christ is only man, how is it that "what the Father does, the Son also does in like manner," when man cannot do works like the heavenly works of God? If Christ is only man, how is it that "as the Father has life in Himself, so has He given to the Son to have life in Himself," when man cannot have life in himself after the manner of God the Father, because he is not glorious in eternity, but is made with the perishable matter of mortality? If Christ is only man, how could He say: "I am the bread of eternal life that came down from heaven," when man who is himself mortal neither can be the bread of life, nor has descended from heaven, since no matter of frailty can be found in heaven? If Christ is only man, how does He assert: "For no man has ever seen God the Father; but He who is from God, He has seen"

God? For if Christ is only man, He could not have seen God because "no man has seen God." If He has seen God because He is of God, then he wished Himself to be considered more than man since He has seen God. If Christ is only man, why does He say: "What if you shall see the Son of Man ascending to that place where He was before?" But He did ascend into heaven; therefore He was there before, in that He returned to the same place where He was before. Now if He was sent from heaven by the Father, He certainly is not a mere man; for as we said, man could not come from heaven. Therefore He was not there before as man; He ascended to that place where as man He had not been. However the Word of God, who was there, descended—the Word, I say, of God who is also God, through whom "all things were made, and without whom nothing was made." Thus it was not man that came thence from heaven but the Word of God, that is, God, descended from that place.

CHAPTER 15

If Christ is only man, how is it that He says: "Even if I bear witness to Myself, my witness is true, because I know where I came from and where I go. You judge according to the flesh"? Note that He also says in this passage that He will return to the place from which He testified that He previously came—sent, namely, from heaven. Therefore He descended from the place from which He came, just as He goes to the place from which He descended. Consequently, if Christ were only man, He would not have come from that place and—since He had not come from that place—He could not return there. By coming, however, from that place from which man cannot come, He showed that He came as God. But the Jews, ignorant and unacquainted, as they were, with this descent of His, made these heretics their heirs, addressing them with the very same words: You do not know from what place I come, nor where I go. You judge according to the flesh." So these heretics, as well as the Jews, maintaining that the carnal birth of Christ was His only birth, believed that Christ was nothing else but a man. They do not reflect that since man could not come down from heaven, so as to be able accordingly to return to heaven,

He who descended from heaven, whence man could not have come, is God.

If Christ is only man, how does He say: "You are from below, I am from above; you are of this world; I am not of this world"? Does it follow that Christ is a mere man simply because every man is of this world, and Christ, as one of them, is in this world? Not at all! Rather, consider what He says: "I am not of this world." Does He lie then? If He is only man, He is of this world. On the other hand, if He is not lying, He is not of this world. Therefore, He is not a mere man since He is not of this world. In order that His identity might not remain unknown, He made it quite clear whence He was: "I", said He, "am from above"; that is, from heaven, whence man cannot come, for man was not made in heaven. He who is from above is God; therefore He is not of this world. In a certain sense, He is of this world; consequently, Christ is not only God, but also Man. Accordingly, just as He is not of this world according to the divinity of the Word, so is He of this world according to the frailty of the body which He assumed. Man is joined to God, and God is coupled to Man. However, in this passage Christ emphasized only one side, His divinity. Since the Jews in their blindness considered only the human side of Christ, in this passage He passed over in silence the fragility of the body, which is of this world, and spoke only of His divinity, which is not of this world. To the same extent that the Jews were inclined to believe that He was only man did Christ, on His part, draw them to consider His divinity so that they would believe He was God. He wished to overcome their incredulity regarding His divinity by omitting, for the time being, any mention of His human heritage and by simply placing before them His divinity alone.

If Christ is only man, how does He say: "From God I came forth and have come," when it is a well-known fact that man was made by God and did not come forth from God? Man, then, did not come forth from God in the same manner that the Word of God came forth, concerning whom it is said: "My heart has brought forth a good Word." Since this Word is from God, therefore, it is "with God"; and because it was not uttered without effect, it rightly does all things: "All things were made through Him and without Him, nothing was made." Now this Word, through whom all things were made, [is God]. "And the Word," John says, "was God." Therefore God proceeded from God, since the Word who proceeded is God who proceeded from God. If Christ is only man, how does He say: "If any man keep my word, he will never see death"? What is never seeing death but immortality? Immortality, however, is the companion of divinity because divinity is immortal, and immortality is the fruit of divinity. Now every man is mortal; so immortality cannot come from what is mortal. Therefore immortality cannot derive its origin from Christ as mortal man. However, He says: "Whoever keeps my word will never see death." Hence the word of Christ bestows immortality and through immortality bestows divinity. If man, since he is himself mortal, cannot claim to make someone else immortal and if Christ's word not only claims but actually bestows immortality, then you can be certain that He who grants this immortality is not just a mere man. He could not bestow it, were He only a man. But He proves that He is God by bestowing divinity through immortality and by offering divinity which He could not bestow unless He were God.

If Christ is only man, how does He say: "I am before Abraham"? No man can be before him from whom he himself takes his origin; nor is it possible that a thing existed before that from which it itself took its origin. Yet, Christ, even though He descends from Abraham, says that He is before Abraham. Either He is lying, therefore, and deceiving us (if He, who actually descended from Abraham, was not before Abraham), or He is not deceiving us (if He is also God because He was before Abraham). For if He had not been God, it is evident that He could not have been before Abraham because He had really descended from Abraham. If Christ is only man, how does He say: "And I shall know them, and my own follow Me; and I give them everlasting life, and they shall never perish." Now, every man is bound by the laws of mortality and therefore cannot even keep himself alive forever; much less can he keep another man alive forever. Christ, nevertheless, promises to give salvation forever. And if He does not give it, He is a liar; if He does give it, He is God. But He does not deceive, for

41

He gives what He promises. Therefore He is God, who offers eternal salvation, which man, who cannot even save himself, cannot grant to another.

If Christ is only man, what does He mean when He says: "I and the Father are one"? How can "I and the Father be one," if He is not both God and Son, who therefore can be said to be one thing [with the Father] because He is of Him and because He is His Son and because He is born of Him inasmuch as He is found to have proceeded from Him? This proves that He is also God. The Jews considered this odious and believed that it was blasphemy, since Christ has shown by these words that He was God. Therefore they ran to get stones and passionately set about to cast them at Him. He vigorously refuted His adversaries with the precedent and testimony of the Scriptures. "If [the Law] called them gods," He says, "to whom the words of God were addressed—and the Scripture cannot be broken— do you say to Me whom the Father has made holy and sent into this world. 'You blaspheme,' because I said, 'I am the Son of God'?" With these words He did not deny that He was God; on the contrary he affirmed that He was God. If, beyond any question of a doubt, they are said to be gods to whom the words of God were addressed, much more is He God who is found to be better than all of them. And yet He refuted their slanderous blasphemy in a fitting manner by a proper ordering [of relations]; for He wants Himself to be considered God and considered precisely as the Son of God, not the Father Himself. In fact, He said that He was sent, and pointed out to them: "Many works have I shown you from My Father." Therefore, He wanted Himself to be considered not the Father but the Son. Also, in the last part of His defense He made mention of the Son, not the Father: "You say, 'You blaspheme,' because I said, 'I am the Son of God.' " So, with regard to the charge of blasphemy, He answered that He was the Son, not the Father, whereas, in regard to His own divinity, He proved that He was the Son and God when He said: "I and the Father are one." Therefore, He is God, but God in such a manner that He is the Son, not the Father.

CHAPTER 16

If Christ is only man, how is it that He himself says: "And whoever sees and believes in Me, shall never die"? Whereas he who trusts in a mere man is said to be accursed, he who believes in Christ is not accursed; on the contrary, it is stated that he will never die. Consequently, if He is only man, as the heretics would have it, how is it that whoever believes in Him shall never die, since he who trusts in man is considered accursed? Or if he is not accursed, but rather, as one reads, destined for the attainment of eternal life, Christ is not man only but God; and whoever believes in Him not only avoids the danger of such a curse but also attains to the fruit of justice.

If Christ is only man, how does He say that the Paraclete will receive of what is His and will declare these things? For the Paraclete does not receive anything from man, but rather gives knowledge to man. Nor does the Paraclete learn future things from man; He instructs him about things to come. Therefore, either the Paraclete did not receive from Christ, as Man, what He should make known, simply because man will never be able to give anything to the Paraclete, from whom he himself must receive (and in that case, Christ not only errs but also deceives in the present passage when He says that the Paraclete will receive from Him, as Man, the things which He will make known), or He does not deceive us—just as He does not deceive—and the Paraclete receives from Christ the things which He will make known. If He received from Christ the things which He will make known, then surely Christ is greater than the Paraclete, since the Paraclete would not receive from Christ unless He were less than Christ. Now, the fact that the Paraclete is less than Christ proves that Christ is also God, from whom He received what He makes known. This, then, is a great testimony to Christ's divinity, inasmuch as the Paraclete, having been found to be less than Christ, takes from Him what He gives to others. If Christ were only man, Christ would receive from the Paraclete what He should say; the Paraclete would not receive from Christ what He should make known.

If Christ is only man, why did He lay down for us a rule to be believed when He said: "Now this is everlasting life, that they may know Thee, the one and true God, and Jesus Christ, whom Thou hast sent"? If He did not wish Himself to be considered also God, why did He add: "and Jesus Christ, whom Thou hast sent," unless He wished to be acknowledged also as God. If He did not wish Himself to be considered God, He would have added: "and the man Jesus Christ, whom Thou hast sent." As a matter of fact, He did not add anything; nor did Christ teach us in this present passage that He was only man; He associated Himself with God. He wanted us to understand that He was, on account of this association, also God—as He truly is. Therefore we must believe, according to the prescribed Rule, in the Lord, the one true God. Similarly we must believe in Him whom He has sent, Jesus Christ, who would never have associated Himself with the Father, as we have said, unless He had wished to be acknowledged also as God. He would have separated Himself from Him if He had not wished to be understood to be God. He would have ranked Himself only with men, if He had known that He was only man; and He would not have associated Himself with God, if He had not known that He was also God. Now He does not even mention His humanity, because no one doubts that He is man. He associates Himself with God, and rightly so, in order to lay down a formal statement of His divinity for those who were to believe in Him.

If Christ is only man, how does He say: "And now glorify Me with the glory which I had with Thee before the world was"? If He had glory with God before the world was and retained His glory with the Father, certainly He existed before the world. For He could not have had this glory unless He had existed before the world, so as to keep the glory. No one who possesses anything can have anything unless He exists before it. But Christ has glory before the creation of the world; therefore, He existed before the creation of the world. Unless He had existed before the creation of the world, He could not have had glory before the creation of the world, because He Himself would not have existed. In fact, man, who existed after the world, could not have glory before the creation of the world. Christ had it; therefore, He existed before the world. Consequently, He who existed before the world was not man only but God, for He existed before the world and possessed glory before the world existed.

Nor can anyone say that it is a question here of predestination, since Scripture contains nothing to that effect. Let those who think this add it [to the written word]. However, woe is as much pronounced upon those who add to, as upon those who take away from, what is written. Therefore what cannot be added to the written word cannot be asserted. Accordingly, after we have eliminated the possibility of predestination because it is not contained in the written word, we conclude that Christ existed in substance before the creation of the world. In fact, He is "the Word" through whom "all things were made, and without whom nothing was made." Even if someone does say that He was glorious in predestination and that this predestination took place before the creation of the world, due order must be observed. And there will be a considerable number of men before Christ destined to glory. In such a determination to glory, Christ will be considered less than other men, because He is ranked after them in time. In fact, if this glory was in predestination, then Christ was the last to receive this predestination to glory; for we see that Adam was predestined before Him, as were also Abel, Enoch, Noah, Abraham, and the rest. Since the order of all persons and things is at the disposal of God's arrangement, many will be said to have been predestined to glory before the predestination of Christ. Accordingly, Christ is found to be less than other men, He who is really better and greater and more ancient even than the angels themselves. Either all these arguments are to be discarded, so that divinity may not be asserted of Christ, or if these arguments cannot be refuted, let the heretics give back to Christ His own divinity.

CHAPTER 17

What would you reply if I should say that Moses follows this same Rule of Truth and has given us enough in the beginning of his writing to teach us that all things are created and founded through the Son of God, that is, through the Word of God? He states what John and the rest affirm. In fact, John and the others are known to have received from Him what they assert. For John says, "All things were made through Him and nothing was made without Him," and the Prophet says, "I speak of my works to the king," and Moses represents God as commanding first that there be light, then that the heavens be firmly established, the waters be gathered together, the dry land appear, fruit come forth according to its seed, animals be produced, the luminaries and stars be set in the heavens. He thus makes it clear that no one else was then present with God, on whom could be enjoined the task of executing these works, save Him through whom "all things were made, and without whom nothing was made." And as He is the Word of God ("My heart has uttered a good word"), he shows that the Word was in the beginning, that this Word was with the Father, and that the Word was God, all things were made through Him. Furthermore, this "Word was made flesh and dwelt among us," namely, Christ, the Son of God. We acknowledge Him to be later Man according to the flesh, just as we know that He was the Word of God and God before the creation of the world. Consequently, we believe and hold, according to the teaching of the Old and the New Testaments, that Christ Jesus is both God and Man.

Again, what would you reply, if I should say that Moses introduces God as saying; "Let us make man to our image and likeness"; and further on, "and God made man, to the image of God He made him, male and female He made them"? If, as we have already shown, it is the Son of God through whom all things were made, then assuredly, it is the Son of God through whom man—for whose sake all things were made—was also created. When God commands that man be made, He who makes man is said to be God; however, it is the Son of God, namely, the Word of God, "through whom all things were made and without whom nothing was made, who makes man. Furthermore, this "Word was made Flesh and dwelt among us"; therefore Christ is God. Accordingly, man was made through Christ, through the Son of God. If God made man to the image of God, then He who made man to the image of God must be God. Therefore Christ is God. Consequently, the authority of the Old Testament regarding the Person of Christ remains unshaken because it is supported by the testimony of the New

Testament. Nor is the force of the New Testament undermined, since its truth has under it the roots of this same Old Testament. They who take it for granted that Christ, the Son of God and the Son of Man, is only man and not also God are really acting contrary to both the Old and the New Testament, inasmuch as they are destroying the authority and the truth of both the Old and the New Testaments.

Finally, what would you reply if I should say that the same Moses everywhere represents God the Father as boundless, without end? He cannot be confined by space, for He includes all space. He is not in one place, but rather all place is in Him. He contains all things and embraces all things; therefore He cannot descend or ascend inasmuch as He contains all things and fills all things. Yet Moses represents God as descending to the tower which the sons of men were building, seeking to inspect it and saying: "Come, let us go down quickly, and there confuse their language, so that they may not understand one another's speech." Who do the heretics think was the God that descended to the tower in this passage, and then sought to visit these men? Was He God the Father? In that case, God is enclosed in a place; how then does He embrace all things? Or is it possible that he speaks of an angel descending with other angels and saying: "Come, and let us go down quickly, and confuse their language"? On the contrary, we note in Deuteronomy that it was God who recounted these things and God who spoke, where it is written: "When He scattered abroad the sons of Adam, He set up the boundaries of the people according to the number of the angels of God." Therefore the Father did not descend, nor did an angel command these things, as the facts clearly indicate. Accordingly, the only remaining conclusion is that He descended of whom the apostle Paul says: "He who descended, He it is who ascended also above all the heavens, that He might fill all things," that is, the Son of God, the Word of God. But "the Word was made flesh and dwelt among us." This must be Christ. Therefore we must affirm that Christ is God.

CHAPTER 18

Please note that the same Moses says in another passage that God appeared to Abraham. Yet the same Moses hears from

God that no man can see God and live. If God cannot be seen, how did God appear? If He appeared, how is it that He cannot be seen? For John says in like manner: "No one has ever seen God." And the apostle Paul says: "Whom no man has seen or can see." But certainly, Scripture does not lie; therefore, God was really seen. Accordingly, this can only mean that it was not the Father, who never has been seen, that was seen, but the Son, who is wont both to descend and to be seen, for the simple reason that He has descended. In fact, He is "the image of the invisible God," that our limited human nature and frailty might in time grow accustomed to see God the Father in Him who is the Image of God, that is, in the Son of God. Gradually and by degrees human frailty had to be strengthened by means of the Image for the glory of being able one day to see God the Father. Great things are dangerous if they happen suddenly. Even the light of the sun, striking suddenly with excessive brilliance upon eyes accustomed to the darkness, will not manifest the light of day but rather will cause blindness. There-fore, so that our human eyes may not suffer much injury, the darkness is gradually dispersed and driven away, and that luminary stealthily shows itself by rising little by little. Thus men's eyes are slowly accustomed, by the gradual intensification of its rays, to bear its full orb. In like manner Christ, the image of God and the very Son of God, was presented to the eyes of men only insofar as He was able to be seen. Thus the frailty and weakness of man's present condition is sustained, assisted, and fostered by Him, so that in time, by being accustomed to behold the Son, it may be able to see God the Father Himself as He is. Otherwise, human frailty would succumb to the sudden and unbearable brightness of God's majesty, and would be so overwhelmed that it could not possibly see God the Father, whom it has always desired to see. Therefore, it is the Son who is seen here. But the Son of God is the Word of God: "The Word" of God "was made flesh and dwelt among us"; and He is Christ. What in the world is the reason we hesitate to call Him God, when we have so many proofs that He is God?

When Hagar, Sarah's maidservant, had been banished, from her home and put to flight, she was met at a spring of water on the road to Shur by an angel, who questioned her and learned the reason for her flight. She was advised to humble herself, with the hope that she would later bear the title of mother. Furthermore, the angel vowed and promised that the progeny of her womb would be numerous. Not only was Ishmael to be born of her but the angel also made known to her, among other things, the place of Ishmael's abode and described his manner of life. Now Scripture portrays this angel as both Lord and God, for He would not have promised the blessing of progeny if He had not been both angel and God. Let the heretics try to explain away this passage. Was it the Father who was seen by Hagar, or not? For it was stated that He was God. Far be it from us to call God the Father an angel, lest He be subject to another, whose angel He would be. But they will say that He was an angel. If He was an angel, how could He possibly be God since this name has never been given to angels? However, if we examine both sides of the question, truth itself drives us to this conclusion: we must acknowledge that He was the Son of God. Because He is of God, He is rightly called God, since He is the Son of God; and because He is subject to the Father and herald of the Father's will, he is proclaimed "Angel of Great Counsel." Therefore, if this passage is not appropriate to the person of the Father, lest He be called an angel, nor to the person of an angel, lest He be called God, it does, however, suit the person of Christ, since He is not only God, inasmuch as He is the Son of God, but also an angel, inasmuch as He is the herald of the Father's dispensation. Heretics must realize that they are acting contrary to the Scriptures when they say they believe that Christ was also an angel, but do not want to admit that He is also the God who they read came frequently to visit the human race in the Old Testament.

Moses also added that God appeared to Abraham "at the oak of Mamre, as he was sitting at the entrance of his tent at midday," and though he saw three men, he addressed only one of them as Lord. When he had washed their feet and offered them bread baked on ashes with butter and an abundance of milk, he pleaded with them to remain as his guests and dine. Later, he hears from them that he will be a father and learns that Sarah, his wife, will bear him a son. He is informed of the destruction of the Sodomites and what they deserved to suffer. Finally, he learns that God has come down because of the ill repute of the Sodomites. If in this passage the heretics are of the opinion that it was the Father who was hospitably received at that time with the two angels, then the heretics believe that the Father is visible. If they say that it was an angel, then why is an angel addressed with the unusual title of God, since one of the three angels was called Lord? The only possible explanation that will render to God the Father His proper invisibility and to an angel His proper inferior position is to believe that no one but the Son of God, who is also God, was seen and hospitably received by Abraham. As Abraham's guest, He was prefiguring in a mystery what He would one day be, when He would find Himself among the sons of Abraham. For He washed their feet to prove that it was really He; thus, He repaid Abraham's sons their claim to hospitality which their father had previously extended to Him. And that there might not remain any doubt that He had been the guest of Abraham, it is written regarding the destruction of the Sodomites: "When the Lord poured down on Sodom and Gomorrah fire and sulphur from the Lord out of heaven." In fact, the prophet also says in the person of God: "I destroyed you, as the Lord destroyed Sodom and Gomorrah." The Lord, therefore, destroyed Sodom; that is, God destroyed Sodom. In the destruction of the Sodomites, however, it was the Lord who rained fire from the Lord. This Lord was the God seen by Abraham. This God is Abraham's guest and was undoubtedly seen because He was touched. Now, since the Father, inasmuch as He is invisible, was assuredly not seen at that time, He who was seen and who was hospitably received and taken in was He who was wont to be seen and touched. This one then is the Son of God, "the Lord, who rained upon Sodom and Gomorrah fire and sulphur from the Lord." But He is the Word of God: and the "Word" of God "was made flesh, and dwelt among us." This one then is Christ. Therefore, it was not the Father who was the guest of Abraham but Christ. Nor was it the Father who was seen, but the Son; therefore, it was Christ who was seen. Consequently, Christ is both Lord and God, who could be seen by Abraham only because He was God, the Word, begotten of God the Father before Abraham even existed.

Furthermore, Moses relates that this same angel, who is also God, visited and consoled Hagar when she fled from Abraham's home with her son. For when she had abandoned the child in the desert because there was no more water in the bottle and when the boy cried out, she mourned and wept aloud. "And God," says Scripture, "heard the voice of the boy from the place where he was." When Scripture had recounted that it was God who had heard the child's voice, Scripture added: "And the angel of the Lord called to Hagar from heaven." Scripture calls Him an angel whom it has just called God and declares that He is Lord whom it had just represented as an angel. And He, being angel and God, promises Hagar even greater consolations, saying: "Do not fear, for I have heard the voice of the boy from the place where he was. Arise, take up the boy and hold him, for I will make him a great nation." Why does this angel, if he be only an angel, claim for himself the right to say: "For I will make him a great nation," since this kind of power undoubtedly belongs to God and cannot belong to an angel? Consequently, it proves that He who can do this is also God. To prove this very point, Scripture immediately adds: "And God opened her eyes, and she saw a well of spring water, and she went and filled the bottle with water and gave the boy a drink, and God was with the child." Therefore He, who was with the child and opened the eyes of Hagar so that she might see the well of spring water and draw water to satisfy the child's urgent need of a drink, was God. On the other hand, if He who called to her from Heaven was God, then we must realize that He who was called an angel is really not only an angel but God as well—even though earlier in the narrative, when He heard the cry of the boy, He was simply called God. Now, although all this cannot be appropriately and suitably applied to the Father, who is only God, it can, however, be appropriately applied to Christ who has been proclaimed not only God but an angel also. It is quite evident, then, that it was not the Father who spoke to Hagar in the present passage but rather Christ, because He is God. The title of angel is also appropriate to Christ because He was made "the Angel of Great Counsel." He is an angel because

He lays bare the heart of the Father, as John declares. For if John says that this Word, who lays bare the bosom of the Father, was also made flesh, so that He could lay bare the heart of the Father, it follows that Christ is not only man but also an angel. And the Scriptures show not only that He is an angel but also that He is God. This is what we too believe. For, if we will not admit that it was Christ who then spoke to Hagar, we must either make an angel God or reckon God the Almighty Father among the angels.

CHAPTER 19

What will you reply if in another passage we read also that God was described as an angel? In fact, when Jacob was complaining to his wives, Leah and Rachel, of the injustice of their father and when he told them that now he desired to go and return to his native land, he pleaded on the authority of a dream of his and related that an angel of God had said to him in a dream: " 'Jacob, Jacob.' And I," he continues, "said, 'What is it?' And he said, 'Lift up your eyes, and take note: the he-goats and rams are mating with the she-goats and the sheep, and are streaked with white, of divers colors, grizzled and speckled. For I have seen all that Laban has done to you. I am the God who appeared to you in the place of God, where you anointed the memorial pillar in my behalf and made a vow to me. Now therefore arise, depart from this land, and go to the land of your birth and I shall be with you' " If the angel of God speaks these things to Jacob and the angel himself goes on to say: "I am the God who appeared to you in the place of God," we immediately perceive that He is declared to be not only an angel but also God, since He says that Jacob's vow was made to Him "in the place of God," and does not say, "in my place." It is therefore the place of God, and He who speaks is also God. Furthermore, it is simply written: "in the place of God," not "in the place of the angel and of God," but only "of God." Now He who promises these things is said to be God and angel. Consequently, there must be a distinction between Him who is called simply God and Him who is declared to be not simply God, but an angel as well. Accordingly, if there is no other angel, whose authority can here be judged so great that he can claim to be God and attest that a vow had been made to him, except Christ alone—to whom a vow can be made not as to a mere angel but as to God—then it is quite evident that He cannot be regarded as the Father, but the Son who is both God and angel. If He is Christ—as indeed He is—that man is in great danger who says that Christ is only a man or only an angel and denies Him the power due His Holy Name, a power He has frequently received according to the authority of the heavenly Scriptures, which repeatedly call Him both God and angel.

To all these considerations, we can add that, just as divine Scripture repeatedly asserts that Christ is God and angel, so too does the same divine Scripture assert that He is both God and Man, when it explains what He was to be and represents in a figure, even at that early period, what nature He was to have in very substance. Scripture recounts "Jacob remained alone; and a man wrestled with him until the break of day. And he saw that he could not prevail against him, and he touched the broad part of Jacob's thigh while he struggled against him, and he with him, and he said to him, 'Let me go, for the morning star is rising.' And he said, 'I will not let you go, unless you bless me.' And he said, 'What is your name?' And he said, 'Jacob.' And he said to him, 'Your name shall not be called Jacob any longer, but Israel shall be your name; for you have prevailed with God, and with men you are powerful.' " Furthermore, Scripture adds: "And Jacob called the name of that place Vision of God; for 'I have seen God face to face, and my life has been spared.' And the sun rose upon him and soon he passed the Vision of God; but he limped because of his thigh." A man, Scripture says, wrestled with Jacob. If he is a mere man, who is he? Where did he come from? Why does he struggle and wrestle with Jacob? What had come between them? What had happened? What was the cause of so great a conflict and struggle as that? Moreover, why is it that Jacob proves to be the stronger even to the holding of the man with whom he was struggling? And why still, because the morning star was rising, is it he who, on that account, asks a blessing from him whom he held? It can only mean that this struggle was prefiguring that future contention between Christ and the sons of Jacob, which is said to have had its completion in the Gospel. For Jacob's people struggled against this man and proved to be more powerful in the conflict, because they obtained the triumph of their own unrighteousness over Christ. Then, on account of the crime they had perpetrated, they began to limp very badly in the gait of their own faith and salvation, stumbling and slipping in their course. Tough Jacob's people proved superior by their condemnation of Christ, they still need His mercy and still need His blessing. Now, this man who wrestled with Jacob says to him. "Your name shall no longer be called Jacob, but Israel shall be your name." And if Israel is a man who 'sees God,' then the Lord was showing in an elegant manner that he who wrestled with Jacob was not only man, but also God. Undoubtedly, Jacob saw God with whom he wrestled, though it was a man whom he held in his grip. That there might not remain any doubt, he himself gave the interpretation when he said: "For you have prevailed with God, and with men you are powerful." That is why this same Jacob, understanding now the meaning of the prefiguration and realizing the authority of him with whom he had wrestled, called the name of the place where he had wrestled "Vision of God." Furthermore, he added his reasons for giving his interpretation of God: "I have seen God face to face, and my soul has been saved." For he saw God with whom he wrestled, as though he were wrestling with a man; but while as if victor he held the man, as an inferior he asked a blessing of him, as one would of God. Thus he wrestled with God and with man. Now if this struggle was then prefigured and has been actually fulfilled in the Gospel between Christ and Jacob's people—a struggle in which the people proved superior, yet were found to be inferior because of their guilt—who will hesitate to acknowledge that Christ in whom this figure of a struggle was fulfilled was not only Man but also God, when that very figure of a struggle seems to have proved that He is both God and Man?

And yet, even after all these arguments, Scripture rightly does not cease to call an angel God, and God an angel. When this same Jacob was about to bless Manasseh and Ephraim, the sons of Joseph, he placed his hands crosswise upon the heads of the boys and said: "May God who has nourished me from my youth even to this day, the angel who has delivered me from all evils, bless the boys." So conclusively does he affirm that the same one whom he had called God is an angel that he does not hesitate towards the end of his sentence to place the person of whom he was speaking in the singular number, saying: "May He bless these boys." For if he had meant the angel to be taken as a separate person, he would have joined two persons together in the plural number; instead he used the singular number for one person in the blessing. Consequently, he wished the same person to be considered God and angel. Although God the Father cannot be considered to be an angel, Christ can readily be taken to be both God and angel. By laying his hands crosswise on the heads of the boys, Jacob designated Christ as the author of this blessing, implying that Christ was their father. Accordingly, by the way in which he placed his hands, he was manifesting a figure and a future symbol of the Passion. Just as no one hesitates to call Christ an angel, so too let no one hesitate to call Him also God, especially when he sees that He was invoked as both God and angel in the blessing of the boys through the mystery of His Passion, shown forth in the figure of the crossed hands.

CHAPTER 20

If any heretic obstinately resisting the truth would want to imply or even insist that an angel in the proper sense of the word must be understood in all these instances, he must also be defeated in this stand of his by the forces of truth. Now if all things, celestial, terrestrial, and infernal, which have been subjected to Christ, even the very angels, with all possible creatures subject to Christ, are called gods; then rightly Christ also is God. And yet any angel subject to Christ can be called god; furthermore, if this is said, it can even be said without blasphemy. Hence, it is indeed much more fitting that Christ, the very Son of God, should be proclaimed God. For if an angel, who is subject to Christ, is declared to be a god, much more and more fittingly will Christ, to whom all angels are subject, be said to be God. In fact, it is not in accord with natural propriety to deny to the greater what has been granted to the lesser. So if an angel who is less than Christ, is, nevertheless, called a god, it follows quite readily that Christ, who is both greater and better than not just one angel but all of them, is to be called God. Now if "God stood in the assembly of the gods and in their midst God judges the gods," and Christ stood several times in the assembly, then Christ stood in the assembly as God judging the gods, to whom He says: "How long do you respect the persons of men?" He thereby accused the men of the assembly of judging unjustly. Furthermore, if they who are reproved and blamed seem for some reason or other to acquire this name without blasphemy, so that they can be called gods, much more, assuredly, shall He be regarded as God who is said not only to have stood as the God of gods, but to have been revealed to us by the authority of the same passage, as judging and passing sentence on gods. Now if they who "fall like one of the princes" are, nevertheless, called gods, much more shall He be called God who not only does not fall as one of the princes, but even overcomes the very author and prince of wickedness. Why in the world, after reading that this name was also given to Moses, when it is stated: "I have made you as God to Pharaoh," should they deny this title to Christ who we find has been constituted not a god to Pharaoh, but rather the Lord and God of all creation? And in the former case the name is given with a qualification in the latter unreservedly; in the former case, by measure, in the latter, beyond all measure whatever ("for the Father," says Scripture, "does not give by measure to the Son, for the Father loves the Son"); in the former case, for a time; in the latter, without reference to time. In fact, Christ received the power of the Divine Name, not only over all things but for all time. Now if he who received power over one man, notwithstanding the limited power given him, is without hesitation granted the name of God, how much more shall we believe that He who has power even over Moses has received the authority of the name given to Him?

CHAPTER 21

I could have very well sifted through the statements of all the Heavenly Scriptures and, if I may use the expression, produced a veritable forest of texts on this question of Christ's divinity. However, I did not intend to speak against this particular heresy, but rather to explain briefly the Rule of Truth regarding the person of Christ. Although I must hasten on to other matters, I do not think that I ought to omit what the Lord expressed in the Gospel as a mysterious indication of His majesty, when He said: "Destroy this temple, and in three days I will raise it up" or when He stated in another place, and in a different context: "I have power to lay down My life and take it up again, for I have received this command from the Father." Now, who is this who says that He has power to lay down His life or that He can restore His life again, because He has received this command from the Father? Or who says that He can raise up again and rebuild the ruined temple of His body? He can be no other than the Word who is of the Father, who is with the Father, through whom "all things were made, and without whom nothing was made." He is the imitator of the Father's works and mighty deeds, the "image of the invisible God," who "came down from heaven," who "bore witness to that which He has seen and heard," who did not come to do His own Will but rather to do the Will of the Father, by whom He had been sent for this very purpose. He was constituted the "Angel of Great Counsel" that He might reveal to us the laws of heavenly mysteries. He, the Word made flesh, dwelt among us. He, therefore, is this Christ who, as one of us, has been clearly demonstrated to be not only Man inasmuch as He is the Son of Man, but also God because He is the Son of God.

Now, if Christ is called by the Apostle "the firstborn of all creatures," how could He be the firstborn of all creatures unless—in virtue of His divinity—He came forth, as the Word from the Father before every creature? But if the heretics do not interpret the above passage in this manner, they will be compelled to prove that Christ, as man, is the firstborn of all creatures, something they have not been able to do. Therefore, either He is before every creature, so as to be the firstborn of all creatures (then He is not merely a man because man is after every created thing) or else He is merely a man and consequently after every created thing. And how is He the firstborn of all creatures, if not by virtue of His being that divine Word that is before every creature? Therefore, the firstborn of all creatures is made flesh and dwells among us—that is, He assumes this humanity which is after all creation—and thus, with it and in it, dwells among us, so that neither is humanity taken away from Christ nor is divinity denied Him. For if He is merely before every creature, humanity is taken away from Him. On the other hand, if He is only man, His divinity, which is before every creature, is done away with. Both then are united in Christ, both are conjoined, both are linked together. This is rightly so, since there is something in Him that surpasses every creature, inasmuch as the union of the divinity and the humanity seems to be secured in Him. For this reason, He who is declared to have been made "the Mediator between God and man" is found to have associated in Himself both God and Man.

And when the same Apostle says of Christ: "He, having put off the flesh, dishonored the Powers, openly triumphing over them in Himself," certainly he did not intend that the phrase, "having put off the flesh," should have no meaning at all. On the contrary, he intended it to mean that He put on the flesh again in His Resurrection. Let the heretics, then, find out for themselves who it is that puts off and again puts on the flesh. For we know that it was the Word of God who put on the substance of flesh and that this selfsame Word divested Himself of the very same material of His body, which he took again in His Resurrection, and put on anew, as though it were a garment. If Christ had been only a man, He could neither have divested Himself of nor clothed Himself with humanity since no one is ever divested of or clothed with himself. Whatever is taken way from or put on by someone must of necessity be something other than the person himself. Consequently, it was assuredly the Word of God who put off the flesh and in His Resurrection put it on again. He discarded it because He had put it on in His Nativity. So in Christ it is God who is clothed, and it must also be God who was divested because He who is clothed must likewise be divested. He, then, puts on and puts off humanity, as though His body were a woven tunic. Therefore it was the Word of God, as we have already stated, who is found to have at one time put on and at another time to have put off the flesh. He even foretold this in the blessing: "He shall wash His garment in wine, and His clothing in the blood of the grape." If in Christ the garment is His flesh and the clothing His body, then one may ask, who it is whose body is His clothing and His flesh His garment. It is quite evident to us that the flesh was the garment and the body was the clothing of the Word who washed the substance of His body and the matter of His flesh in the blood, that is, in wine, cleansing by His Passion that humanity He had taken upon Himself. Therefore, inasmuch as He is washed, He is man, because the garment that is washed is flesh; but He who washes it is the Word of God, who, in order to wash the garment, was made the wearer of the garment. Accordingly, He is declared to be Man by that substance which was assumed that it might be washed, just as He who washed it is shown to be God, by the authority of the Word.

CHAPTER 22

Although we find ourselves hurrying on to another part of the discussion, we cannot omit that well-known passage of the Apostle: "Who though He was in the form of God, thought it not robbery to be equal to God, but emptied Himself, taking the form of a slave, being made in the likeness of men, and in habit found as a man. He humbled Himself, becoming obedient even to death, the death of the Cross. Therefore God also has exalted Him exceedingly, and has bestowed upon Him the name that is above every name; so that at the name of Jesus every knee should bend of those in heaven, on earth and under the earth, and every tongue should confess that the Lord Jesus is in the glory of God the Father." The Apostle says: "Who though He was in the form of God." If Christ, then, were only man, He would have been referred to as in the image of God, not as in the form of God. For we know that man was made to the image, not according to the form of God. Who, then, is this, who was made, as we have said, in the form of God? An angel? But nowhere in Scripture do we read about angels in the form of God, simply because He alone is the first and of noble birth before all others: the Son of God, the Word of God, the Imitator of all His Father's works. Inasmuch as He also works as His Father does, He is, as we have said, in the form of God the Father. Rightly, then, has He been declared to be in the form of God, because He is above all things, holds divine authority over every creature, and is God after the likeness of His Father. However, He received this from His own Father, that He might be both God and Lord of all and God according to the form of God the Father, begotten and brought forth from Him. Therefore, though "He was in the form of God, He did not think it robbery to be equal to God." For though He was ever mindful that He was God the Father, He never compared or ranked Himself with God the Father, knowing that He is of His Father; and this very thing (that He is) He had, because the Father had given it to Him. Hence, not only before He took upon Himself the flesh but even after He had taken a body, and again, after His Resurrection, He rendered and still renders perfect obedience to His Father in all things. Consequently, this proves that He never regarded His divinity as a means of unlawfully arrogating to Himself equality with God the Father. On the contrary, obedient and subject to His Father's every command and will, He was even content to take upon Himself the form of a slave—that is, to become man. He took upon Himself by His birth the substance of flesh and of the body which fell to His lot from the bondage incurred by the transgressions of His forefathers and according to His human nature.

At that time, He also emptied Himself, for He did not refuse to take upon Himself the human frailty of human existence. Had he been born a mere man, He would never, because of that, have been emptied. Man, by being born, is not emptied but rather acquires something. When he begins to be, he acquires what he could not have had when He did not exist; as a result, he is not emptied, as we have said, but rather acquires and is enriched. And if Christ is emptied, since He is born, taking the form of a slave, how, then, is He merely a man? Of Christ it would have been more correct to say that He was enriched when He was born, not emptied, for the simple reason that the majesty of the Divine Word, condescending for the moment to take upon itself humanity and not exercising itself in its powers, lowers and abases itself for a time, while bearing the humanity that it has taken upon itself. He empties Himself when He condescends to affronts and insults, when He hears blasphemies and suffers unbecoming things.

His abasement, however, bears excellent fruit, since He received a "name which is above every name," which name indeed we know can only be the name of God. In fact, since God alone is above all things, it follows that that name is above all things, which belongs to Him who is above all things, namely God. It is therefore, that name which is above every name, which name consequently must assuredly belong to Him who, though he had been in the form of God, thought it not robbery to be equal to God. For if Christ were not also God, every knee of those in heaven, on earth, and under the earth would not bend at His name. Neither things visible nor those invisible, nor creation itself would be subject and subservient to a man, since they would be mindful of the fact that they existed before man. Christ, then, is said to be in the form of God. He is shown to have emptied Himself in His Nativity according to the flesh. He is said to have received from His Father a name that is above every name. It is clear to all that every knee of those in heaven, on earth, and under the earth bends and bows at His name; furthermore, it is stated that this redounds to the glory of God the Father. Consequently, the fact that He "became obedient" to the Father "unto death, even to the death of the cross" does not mean that He is only man. On the contrary, if we consider the foregoing proofs which loudly proclaim Christ's divinity, we find that the Lord Christ Jesus proves to be also God. The heretics do not accept this truth.

St. Jerome
348-420

St. Jerome was The Scripture Scholar of the early Church. He was born in Stridon, Dalmatia, and went to Rome for literary studies at a young age. He was baptized there by Pope Liberius around 365. Thereupon he went to Trier, where he studied theology and resolved to become a monk. He spent six or seven years in Aquileia. In 374 he went to the East where he practiced rigorous austerities for a time in the Syrian desert. He also devoted himself to learning Hebrew and Greek, and at the end of this period he was ordained a priest in Antioch.

379 was an important year for Jerome, for it was then that he went to Constantinople and heard Gregory Nazianzen preach and teach. He became acquainted with the works of Origen and got very interested in Biblical translation and interpretation. In 382 he returned to Rome and became secretary to Pope Damasus. When the latter died in 385, Jerome left Rome to live in Palestine. The following year he settled in Bethlehem and immersed himself in Biblical studies. There in the final three and a half decades of his life he produced an incredible output, translating the entire Bible into Latin, writing commentaries, giving homilies, and engaging in historical and theological work of immense proportions.

As an interpreter of the Bible, Jerome belongs to the Alexandrian school. The influence of Origen was inescapable.

Jerome says at one point that he tried to steer his course "between history and allegory," but the pull toward the latter invariably won out. But ordinarily he does try to base the "spiritual sense" on a well-founded literal sense.

The amount and variety of scriptural studies produced by Jerome make it difficult to decide on what to select as representative. What follows, however, are seven of his homilies to his fellow monks in Bethlehem. They reveal how his scholarship was never pursued in isolation. Its purpose was pastoral; the goal of aiding others to come to a deeper knowledge and love of God was always there as its motive force. The first three homilies are on Psalms (84, 86, 91), and reveal how deeply Jerome loved the Psalter as the "prayerbook of the Church." The latter four are on different Gospel passages, the last one being on the prologue of the Fourth Gospel.

It would be difficult to evaluate the full impact of Jerome on subsequent Western Christianity. Before long his translation, the Latin Vulgate, became the Bible of the Western World, and remained so for a thousand years. His work on Famous Men *was the first real history of Christian literature. His translations of Origen assured the latter of a central role in Western theology. His commentaries on the Bible set the tone for ages to come, and his homilies stood as models for biblical preaching that influenced all later monasticism. A capable exegete, a skillful philologist, a trained critic, a master translator, a superb stylist, Jerome was the right man in the right place at the right time, as far as the Latin Church was concerned. He had his faults, as every genius does, but they were far outweighed by the magnitude of his achievements and the relevance of his contributions. In more ways than one, it was Jerome who opened the Bible to the Western world.*

THE HOMILIES

U nto the end. A psalm of the son of Core' is the title of the eighty-fourth psalm. As I have said frequently before, you will always find joy and never sadness in a psalm that has 'for the sons of Core' in its title. This is so because the sons' joy is to console the father's sorrow. Reread the psalms with that in mind and you will discover that wherever you come upon the title, 'of the sons of Core,' you will find no sadness. I have remarked likewise many times that the name Core signifies the place of Calvary [or the skull] and must, therefore, connote joy.

Now, then, who is this Core? He is the man who was making his way up from Jericho to Bethel. Bethel means the 'House of God.' Note this carefully: anyone in Jericho who wants to go to the House of God has to climb upward along the road; hence, our Core, that is, Eliseus, is making his way upward from Jericho to Bethel, the House of God. As he approaches the city, forty-two young boys come out from Bethel—from the House of God, from the synagogue where first had been the House of God—and mock Eliseus, our Core, crying out: 'Go up, thou bald head; go up, thou bald head.' He is on his way to his own house and he is made sport of by urchins from Bethel. Eliseus, truly that most patient of men who had come to Bethel in order to save the city, at length turned and looked back; looked back and commanded two bears to come forth from the forest, and the bears came and they tore the forty-two boys to pieces. Even so our Lord, that is, our Core, when He had come into Bethel ready for His Ascension and was mocked by young boys, commanded two bears, Vespasian and Titus, to come forth, and they destroyed the forty-two boys. Who are these forty-two boys? From the Ascension of Christ to the destruction of

Jerusalem, there are forty-two years. Ponder this diligently and you will find that it is so. Thus, for forty-two years after His Resurrection and Ascension to Bethel, the Lord gave His people the opportunity to repent, but because they cried out in derision: 'Go up, thou bald head; go up, thou bald head,' two bears came out and killed them.

'You have favored, O Lord, your land.' This refers to the coming of the Savior and is properly historical; later, after we have considered its history, we shall discuss its tropological significance. 'You have favored, O Lord, your land.' We have said that this verse speaks of the coming of the Redeemer. The land which had offended You and had been defiled by idolatrous worship has been redeemed at Your advent. 'You have favored, O Lord, your land.' Let this be the prayer of the sinner, in view of the fact that he has obtained pardon: Lord, You have blessed this clay of Yours. Even though it has brought forth thistles and thorns, it is, nevertheless, Your creature and for that reason has been restored. 'You have restored the well-being of Jacob,' of those who have believed in Christ. 'You have restored the well-being of Jacob': every sinner is held captive. 'You have forgiven the guilt of your people'; not on account of their works, but because of Your mercy, You have delivered Your people; 'you have covered all their sins.' Down to the very last word, this psalm, as I have indicated, tells of the coming of the Savior.

'Kindness and truth shall meet. Near indeed is his salvation to those who fear him, glory dwelling in our land.' Veritably has the glory of God dwelt in our land, and furthermore: 'Justice has looked down from heaven; the Lord himself will give his benefits.' What benefits? 'Our land shall yield its increase': Mary, our clay, our flesh, has yielded her fruit. 'Justice shall walk before him': the virgin earth has brought forth the fruit of justice.

Thus far, we have given the historical character of the psalm; now let us turn to the tropological method of interpretation. 'You have forgiven the guilt of your people.' Remission presupposes a debt. 'You have covered all their sins': You have covered them with virtues, so their sins do not appear; You have, for example, covered injustice with justice, impurity with purity, blackness with whiteness. 'You have withdrawn all your wrath; you have revoked your burning anger.' 'Restore us, O God of our salvations.' Note the meaning: Because it was Your will to do so, You have mercifully revoked Your burning anger. 'Restore us, O God': You have turned away from wrath; You have turned us away from sin.

'Restore us, O God of our salvations.' Why did not the psalmist say 'our salvation' instead of 'our salvations'? If we were sinning just once, we would need but one salvation; but we have sinned many times, hence, are in need of many salvations. 'Will you not instead, O God, give us life? Until the Lord restores us to life, we are dead. 'Show us, O Lord, your kindness, and grant us your salvation.' The Savior's descent is the work of God's mercy. He would not have come as a Physician if most men were not sick. Because so many were sick, He came as Physician; because we were in need of compassion, He came as Savior.

'I will hear what the Lord God proclaims within me.' Many there are who think that when Moses and Isaia, and the others, say: 'Thus saith the Lord'; and that when the Scripture says: 'The word of the Lord came to Isaia'—or to Ezechiel—'the prophet,' that the communication comes from God externally and that the prophet hears actually with his ears the word of the Lord. This is not so. What does our Lord Himself say to the Pharisees and the Jews? 'He who has ears to hear, let him hear.' And Isaia says: 'The Lord has given me an ear.' Comprehend what he means: 'The Lord has given me an ear.' Because I did not possess that ear which is of the heart, He gave me one that I might hear God's message. Whatever the prophet hears, therefore, he hears in his heart, for just as we cry in our hearts, 'Abba, Father,' and the cry is a silent one and the silence is heard by the Lord, in that same way the Lord speaks to our heart that cries, 'Abba, Father.' So it is that the prophet now says: 'I will hear what the Lord God proclaims within me.' Such is the meaning also of the prophet Habacuc in: 'I will stand at my guard post, and keep watch to see what answer the Lord will give me and what answer I will give Him,' and I will hear what the Lord God proclaims within me. The words: 'I will hear what the Lord God proclaims within me,' refer, therefore, to what the Lord speaks in the heart—in the understanding.

Would you like to know what this cry of the heart is? Would you like to know that the cry that rises to God is not that of the voice but that of tears? Listen to the Lamentations of Jeremia: 'Let there be no repose for your eyes.' 'For he proclaims peace to his people.' This is appropriate for the Jews who were to believe in Christ, for it speaks of the Advent of Christ and of the faith of the Jews, that is, the faith of the apostles and all those who believed them. 'For he proclaims peace to his people.' Peace implies that there is war.

'And to his faithful ones, and to those who put in him their hope': this points to those who first obeyed the flesh, but afterwards came back to Him with all their heart. That you may be sure that this versicle is about the Jews—those of them who believed in the Savior—think over the examples we have considered. Suppose with me that a Jew is reading Leviticus, about all the rites described there: under what conditions the leper enters the synagogue, how a hen is bled by having its neck wrenched, what it says about the sprinkling of blood, and about water and hyssop; how the leper's garments are torn away from him, and how, then, he enters the synagogue. If we were to take all of this literally, what benefits would we derive from such reading? If, however, our conversion has been genuinely wholehearted, if we have a spiritual hold on what we have read, we shall discern that it is not possible for the leper to go before the people of God without first having his garments rent, without first revealing what had been concealed.

In the second place, perceive that this leper does not gain entrance to the synagogue except through blood and water and hyssop; hence, you, too, who up to this very day have been a leper, were not conscious of your leprosy until you had come to the priest. But since you came to the priest, he tore open your garments, and what seemed to be sound while it was covered up, proved to be leprous when exposed. The priest made you see your sins and your leprosy, and led you back into God's assembly through blood and water: through blood, the Passion of Christ; through water, by baptism. After you have contracted the leprosy of corruption, you cannot be healed save through the Blood of Christ and through baptism. When you have been healed, then the following words are in order: 'Cleanse me of sin with hyssop, that I may be purified; wash me, and I shall be whiter than snow.'

You are still in Egypt to this day; as long as you do not come to blood and water, you cannot be saved. Do you want to be spared the destroying angel of Egypt? Take some hyssop, dip it in blood, sprinkle your door posts, and when the destroyer sees the blood on your forehead, he will leave you untouched. Why have I dwelled so long on all this? Because it is written: 'And to those who put in Him their hope.' God cannot speak peace to His people except to those who hope in Him with all their heart.

'Near indeed is his salvation to those who fear him': I have shown you the way of salvation; I am merciful to you. Although your conversion is not yet complete, nevertheless, I am waiting; I am giving you time for repentance. And all this, indeed, 'that glory may dwell in our land.' He calls you to repentance in order that you, who were a leper, may have Christ for your Guest.

'Kindness and truth shall meet; justice and peace shall kiss.' O what wonderful friendship! 'Kindness and truth shall meet.' Are you a sinner? Heed that it says 'Kindness.' Are you a faithful servant? Hear that it says, 'and truth.' If you are a sinner, do not despair; if you are just, do not yield to complacency.

Let us state this in a different way. There are two peoples that believe: the Gentiles and the Jews. To the Jews was given the promise that the Savior would come, but the promise was not made to us who were outside the law of God. Kindness, therefore, is symbolic of the Gentiles; truth, of the Jews, for the promise has been fulfilled; the promise made to the fathers is fulfilled in the sons. 'Justice and peace shall kiss'; mark: 'Justice and peace shall kiss.' This is equivalent to what was said above: kindness and truth shall meet, kindness equates to peace, truth to justice. Whatever pertains to peace belongs, likewise, to kindness; whatever refers to truth applies also to justice. Realize to the full what the psalm says: 'Justice and peace shall kiss,' kindness and truth have embraced in friendship. In other words, the Gentiles and the Jews are under one Shepherd, Christ.

'Truth shall spring out of the earth.' 'I am the way, and the truth, and the life.' He who said: 'I am the truth,' has sprung out of the earth. What is this truth that has risen up out of the earth? 'But a shoot shall sprout from the stump of Jesse, and from his roots a bud shall blossom'; and in another place: 'O God, you doer of saving deeds on earth.' What have you to say, Manichaeus, who deny that the Savior assumed a body? Behold Truth, the Savior, is born of earth, that is, of Mary. 'And justice shall look down from heaven,' for it was just that the Savior have mercy on His people. Think what this means:—O, the just judgments of God, and how unsearchable his ways!—'Truth shall spring out of the earth': that means the Savior. Again, 'justice shall look down from heaven': justice is the Savior. How has He sprung out of the earth? How has He looked down from heaven? He grew up out of the earth since He was born as man; He has looked down from heaven since God is always in heaven. Assuredly, He is born of earth, but He who was born of earth is always in heaven, for God is everywhere. His appearance on earth was such that He never left heaven. He looked down; as long as we were given to sinning, He turned His eyes away from us.

Now listen to what that means. It is right for the Potter to feel pity for His works, for the Shepherd to be compassionate of His flock. We are His people, we are His creatures. He sprang out of the earth and looked down from heaven to fulfill His justice and take pity on the work that He wrought. That you may know, moreover, that justice bespeaks not cruelty, but mercy, the psalmist says: 'The Lord himself will give his benefits.' To be compassionately kind to all His works, He looked down from heaven. 'Our land shall yield its increase.' Truth has sprung out of the earth, indeed; that refers to the past. Now the psalmist turns to the future: our land shall yield its harvest. Do not give up hope because He was born once of Mary; every day He is born in us. 'Our land shall yield its increase.' We, too, have the power to bring forth Christ if we so desire. 'Our land shall yield its increase.' These words refer to Him who became the Bread of Heaven, to Him who says: 'I am the bread that has come down from heaven.'

St. Jerome

We have stressed the mercy of the Lord because His whole purpose in coming was to redeem mankind. We ought, nevertheless, to know that He Himself is going to sit in judgment over the living and the dead; that He Himself will come to judge us. 'Justice shall walk before him.' Do not be heedless: justice will lead Him. 'And salvation, along the way of his steps.' Note the exact words: 'his steps'—where there are no rocks, where there are no thorns nor thistles, where the path is even, where He may walk, where He cannot stumble. Let us, therefore, make way for the Lord in our heart, that way for which John was giving his life's effort, and for which he was crying in the desert that we should make ready the way of the Lord. That is why the psalmist says now: 'And salvation, along the way of his steps'; where He finds the way, there He will walk. Although formerly we had obstacles of thorns and thistles, although we had stones, He declares to us in Isaia: 'clear the highway of stones.' He proclaims this, furthermore, lest He stumble upon them when He is ready to walk in the way of our heart. Now the stones that He bids us throw out from our way are our sins. Christ does not walk in our heart if there is any sin there. He stumbles at once against these stones. 'And salvation, along the way of his steps.' Let us make ready the way, and Jesus will set His steps in it.

HOMILY 18

ON PSALM 86 (87)

A psalm of the sons of Core. A song.' I have called your attention frequently to the difference between the psalm and the song. The psalm is named from the psalter, but a song comes forth from the voice. The psalm, a work of art, relates to the practical; the song, to meditation and is speculative.

'His foundation upon the holy mountains.' The psalmist did not predicate whose foundation, but merely stated: 'His foundation, upon the holy mountains.' These are the utternaces of a prophet; the sons are Core's sons. The meaning of the name Core, as I have indicated before, is 'Calvary'; hence, his sons are 'sons of the Resurrection.'

'His foundation': either God's, or surely, the Church's. What, in truth, is the foundation, if not the Father and the Son and the Holy Spirit? This foundation is not, therefore, in valleys, but upon mountains; and not upon any mountains, but upon holy mountains. Paul declares: 'As a wise builder, I laid the foundation,' namely, faith in the Trinity. Then, in another place he says: 'For he was looking for the city that has foundations, of which city the architect and builder is God.' 'His foundation upon the holy mountains.' The psalmist specified holy mountains simply because there are other mountains that are not holy. Besides, Isaia says: 'Upon the dark mountains set up a signal.' In another passage of Holy Writ we find: 'What are you, O perverse mountain?' and Jeremia says: 'Give glory to the Lord, your God, before it grows dark. Before your feet stumble on darkening mountains.' You see, then, there are dark mountains, and Jeremia warns us that we should give glory to God before our feet begin to stumble on them, for if our feet should be bruised in stumbling upon these mountainways, we cannot give glory to the Lord. 'His foundation upon the holy mountains.' Whom can we name as foundations? The apostles. Upon them the foundations were laid; where the faith of the Church was first established, there, too, the foundations were laid.

Because everyone builds upon a foundation, one gold, another silver, another precious stones, 'The Lord loves the gates of Sion, more than any dwelling of Jacob.' Does He love the gates that we see fallen in ruins? Does He love these gates, and this Sion that has become a plowed field? But just consider what it says: the gates of Sion are dearer to the Lord than any dwelling of Jacob. Mark: more than all the cities of Jacob—of Judea—so much does He love this city! How does it happen, then, that we see other cities preserved in part, but this one completely in ruins? Let us read the Apocalypse of John; let us read Isaia, too, where the city of Jerusalem is being built and its twelve gates are said to be wrought of precious stones, and the city itself is coming down from heaven with its walls of gold and its broad streets covered with jasper and each gate made from a single precious stone. These are altogether the riches of the Lord, and how does the Lord love them and mankind also? Does He restrain us from avarice and He Himself build a city

because of avarice? But the Lord loves the gates of Sion, those
twelve gates of Sion. Obviously, then, the psalmist wrote of the
apostles. 'More than any dwelling of Jacob,' more than all the
saints of old.

Thus far in our interpretation, we have confined ourselves
to one figurative meaning. Let us now consider another trope.
'The Lord loves the gates of Sion.' It seems to me that the gates
of Sion are the virtues. Just as vice and sin are the gates of death,
I think the gates of Sion are the virtues. Furthermore, there is
another passage in the psalms that says: 'You have raised me up
from the gates of death.' If the gates of death are sins, surely
the gates of Jerusalem are virtues. 'More than any dwelling of
Jacob.' Note that the people of old—Jacob—do not have a
foundation nor a house built upon foundations, but instead
they dwell in tents that they readily carry from place to place.

'Glorious things are said of you, O city of God!' As we have
suggested, we may refer the verse: 'His foundation upon the
holy mountains,' to God Himself. Moreover, we may also refer
to God the words: 'Glorious things are said of you, O city of
God!' What city is this? Where shall we find these glorious
sayings? All the prophets speak of this city. Isaia says: 'Awake,
awake! put on your strength, O Jerusalem,' and again: 'I am a
strong city, the city that is being brought down.' David says in
one psalm: 'There is a stream whose runlets gladden the city of
God'; in another: 'O Lord, in your city you will set at nought
their phantoms.' Also the Savior Himself has spoken gloriously
of this city: 'A city set on a mountain cannot be hidden.'

'I will be mindful of Rahab and Babylon among those that
know me.' Since the psalmist said: 'Glorious things are said of
you, O city of God,' and we understand this city to be the
Church gathered together from the nations, the psalm now
speaks of the calling of the Gentiles: 'I will be mindful of Rahab
and Babylon among those that know me.' Let the sinner be at
peace; the Lord was mindful of Rahab. I mean, at peace, if the
sinner returns to the Lord; otherwise, there is no healing peace
in a tearless security. 'I will be mindful of Rahab,' of Rahab,
that harlot who lodged Jesus' secret agents, who lived in Jericho
whither Jesus had come and had dispatched the two spies.
Jericho, that collapsed in seven days, is a type of this world, and

73

as such is determined to kill the secret agents. Because, therefore, Jericho is bent upon killing the spies, Rahab, the harlot,
alone received them, lodged them not on the ground floor, but
in the upper story of the roof—or, in other words, in the sublimity of her faith. She hid them under her stalks of flax.

We have been following so far the historical interpretation
and you perceive how from the history itself we are ascending
upward gradually to a mystical understanding. Jesus, the leader,
who had led the people out of Egypt; Jesus, whose name means
Savior, after the death and burial of Moses in the land of Moab
in the land of Arabia—that is, after the law was dead—Jesus
desires to lead His people into the Gospel and sends out two
men on secret mission to Jericho. Two messengers He sends:
one to the circumcised; the other to the Gentiles, Peter and
Paul. Jericho seeks to kill them; the harlot takes them in, meaning, of course, the Church gathered together of the Gentiles.
She believes in Jesus; and those whom Jericho is determined to
destroy, she protects in safety on her own roof. She harbors
them on the roof—in the loftiness of her faith—and hides them
under the stems of flax. Even though she is a harlot, she covers
them with flax.

Flax with much labor and care becomes of dazzling whiteness. You yourselves know that flax grows from the soil and
that when it has come forth from the ground, it is black; it has
no beauty; it has no use. First, it is pulled up from the ground,
broken, then twisted, afterwards washed. Next, it is pounded;
finally, combed, and after so much care and hard work, it
finally becomes white. Here, then, is the meaning: this harlot
took the messengers in and covered them with her flax so that
these agents might turn her flax into dazzling whiteness. And
then what? She counsels them and says: 'Wait here for three
days.' Not one day does she specify, nor two days, but definitely
three days. Notice what she says: 'Wait three days.' She does
not designate three nights, but three days, for hers was an
enlightened heart. Then she says, and after three days—but
what does she say? 'Do not go through the open plains,' she
warns, 'but go up the mountain way.' The faith of the Church is
not laid in the valleys, but is established on the mountains.
Later, indeed, Jericho is overthrown, but this harlot alone is

preserved untouched; hence, the Lord says: 'I will be mindful of Rahab'; that is, on the day of judgment, I will be mindful of her who welcomes My messengers.

'I will be mindful of Rahab.' Rahab; what is the force of her name? We have been following the historical sense; let us now reflect upon the anagogic significance of the name. Rahab thus admits of two interpretations: the name may imply either a 'broad space' or, better, 'pride.' Consider, therefore, its impact. She who formerly walked the broad, spacious road to death, she whose pride was driving her to destruction, was later converted unto humility. 'I will be mindful of Rahab and Babylon.' The meaning of Babylon is 'confusion.' See what the Lord says: Not only of Rahab will I be mindful, but even of Babylon, and of any soul that is troubled over its faults and sins. 'And of Babylon among those that know me.' Realize what this actually means. Even though anyone has been a Rahab, even though anyone has been a Babylon, nevertheless, I will be mindful of him who knows Me. So if we have been Rahabs and Babylons, even we ought to be at peace and say: The Lord said, I will be mindful of Rahab and Babylon. But now see what follows: 'among those that know me.' They have been Rahab and they have been Babylon, but later they turned to Me in hope. 'I will be mindful of Rahab and Babylon among those that know me.' She who was at one time on the broad road to perdition, afterwards mounted upward into the memory of God.

So far, the psalmist has been speaking almost enigmatically, but now he speaks more plainly of the calling of the Gentiles, for notice what he says: 'Of Philistia, Tyre, Ethiopia: "These were born there."' He designates Philistines to distinguish them from the Jews, for we are the Philistines. 'Tyre.' Tyre connotes tribulation, or SOR. 'Ethiopia': black and cloaked in the filth of sin. 'Ethiopia.' We find the same typology in the versicle: 'Let Ethiopia extend its hands to God.' 'Of Philistia, Tyre, Ethiopia.' Now for the meaning: they who before were strangers, they who previously were in tribulation, who had dwelt in the midst of the sea (for it is said of Tyre: 'Tyre that is situated in the heart of the sea'), they, therefore, who at first were in the sea and beaten about by waves, are found later in the Church. 'Ethiopia.' At one time we were Ethiopians in our vices and sins. How so? Because our sins had blackened us. But afterwards we heard the words: 'Wash yourselves clean!' And we said: 'Wash me, and I shall be whiter than snow.' We are Ethiopians, therefore, who have been transformed from blackness into whiteness. 'Of Philistia, Tyre, Ethiopia: "These were born there." ' Where were they born? 'Glorious things are said of you, O city of God!' 'These were born there': in the city of God.

'Shall not Sion say a man, a man is born in her?' The rendition of the translators of the Septuagint is: 'Shall not Sion say a man?' Many, therefore, have surmised, but have not understood, the meaning of μήτι Σιών and have added the letter 'r' to make the reading μήτηρ Σιών ἐρεῖ ἄνθρωπος. They base their emendation on the words that immediately follow: 'and a man is born in her.' It is, likewise, their supposition that this verse should read: 'Mother Sion shall say a man.' Since there is the implication that a son has been born, they go astray on a word for 'mother.' Let us consider this interpretation first (for we cannot afford to overlook it) and also translate: Mother Sion shall say a man, and a man is born in her. These, then, are they who had been begotten in the Church: Philistia, Tyre, and Ethiopia; these are they who are born in the Church. They believe in the Church and begin life in the Church, for unless they have been baptized, they are not sons of the Church. They, indeed, who have been baptized in the Church call the Church 'Mother.'

Now let us turn to the Hebrew truth. 'Shall not Sion say a man, and a man is born in her?' The true sense of the Hebrew is this: Who will be able to announce to Sion, who of men will be able to announce to her, that a man shall be born in her and shall be her Savior? In other words, no mere man has the power to announce to Sion that she will be saved in the man who will be born in her. 'And a man is born in her.' Who is this man? 'And he who has established her is the Most High Lord.' Let the Arians answer, for they say that the Father alone is the Highest. Behold, here it speaks of the Son and says: 'And he who has established her is the Most High Lord.' The psalmist did not say, the Son of God who was in the beginning with the Father, but what did he say? 'A man is born in her, and he who has established her is the Most High Lord.' If, moreover, He is said to be the Most High Lord, how much the more is He the Word of God?

'In his record of the peoples and princes the Lord shall tell of these who have been born in her.' Now the psalm did not say, those who are born in her, but who have been born in her. 'The Lord shall tell.' How shall He tell? Not by word of mouth, but in His writings. In His writings of whom? Of the peoples. That is not enough, for it also speaks of the princes. And which princes? Those who are born in her? No, it did not say that; but, those who have been born in her. Just see how full of mystical meaning Sacred Scripture is! We have read the Apostle Paul; we have read Peter; and we have read Paul's words: 'Do you seek a proof of the Christ who speaks in me?' What Paul speaks, Christ speaks, for: 'He who receives you, receives me.' Our Lord and Savior, therefore, speaks to us in the writings of His princes.

'In his record of the peoples the Lord shall tell': in the sacred writings, in His Scripture that is read to all peoples in order that all may know. Thus the apostles have written; thus the Lord Himself has spoken, not merely for a few, but that all might know and understand. Plato wrote books, but he did not write for all people but only for a few, for there are not many more than two or three men who know him. But the princes of the Church and the princes of Christ did not write only for the few, but for everyone without exception. 'And princes': the apostles and the evangelists. 'Of those who have been born in her.' Note: 'who have been' and not 'who are.' That is to make sure that, with the exception of the apostles, whatever else is said afterwards should be removed and not, later on, hold the force of authority. No matter how holy anyone may be after the time of the apostles, no matter how eloquent, he does not have authority, for 'in his record of the peoples and princes the Lord shall tell of those who have been born in her.'

'The home as it were of all rejoicing is within you.' The prophet is speaking to the Church and tells her that all who dwell in her are, as it were, full of joy and gladness. Why did he not say, 'the home of all rejoicing is within you,' rather than 'as it were of all rejoicing'? Another psalm says: 'When the Lord brought back the captives of Sion, we were like men dreaming,' not 'we were men dreaming'; hence, this verse: 'The home as it were of all rejoicing is within you.' Why have I made such a point of all this; For the reason that in the present world no matter how faithful one may be, no matter to what degree he renounces the world, his is not a perfect victory. In fact, the Gospel says: 'Blessed are they who mourn, for they shall be comforted.' If, moreover, it has been said: 'Blessed are you who weep now, for you shall laugh,' it is evident that in the present world there is no lasting joy; our joy is only ephemeral. 'The home is within you.' Grasp what that means: no one may ever withdraw from the Church.

We ought to know that what we have interpreted in reference to the Church can be understood also as applying to our soul. If Sion is taken to mean a watchtower, our soul ascends to a contemplation ever more sublime. The true Church, the true temple of Christ, is no other than the human soul. The Church of Christ is nothing other than the souls of those who believe in Christ. 'Do you not know that you are the temple of God and that the spirit of God dwells in you?' 'His foundation upon the holy mountains': there are no foundations of God except upon the holy mountains, upon the doctrine in the soul of the one who believes in Christ. 'The lord loves the gates of Sion.' Our Sion has any number of gates, and if we open them wide to our Spouse, He will enter and will rest with us. Indeed, He Himself says: 'Behold, I stand at the door and knock. If anyone listens to my voice and opens the door to me, I will come into him and will sup with him.'

'Glorious things are said of you, O city of God!' A city is not just one building, but many. Even so the Church, and also our Sion, unless it has many virtues, will not be the city of God. 'I will be mindful of Rahab and Babylon among those that know me.' She who of old walked the broad road of sinners climbed up afterwards into the remembrance of God. 'Shall not Sion say a man, and a man is born in her?' Shall I tell you something marvelous but true? Our Sion, in which at times there are Philistines, and Tyre, and Ethiopia; that watchtower, that meretrix, that harlot, that Rahab, that Babylon, that one who, according to Ezechiel, has prostituted herself to everyone on the crossroads; that meretrix, if she wills it, suddenly becomes a

virgin. A virgin she becomes, conceives the Son of God, and
brings Him forth. 'From your fear, O Lord, we conceived, and
suffered the pangs of childbirth, bringing forth the spirit of
your salvation upon the earth.' Understand, therefore, that she
who was a prostitute conceives of God and is in labor and brings
forth the Savior. We have brought forth upon earth the spirit
of Your salvation. Thus, our soul, that Rahab, that meretrix,
has the power to conceive and bring forth the Savior.

'And a man is born in her.' If it is our desire, every day
Christ is born; through each virtue Christ is born. If 'Christ is
the power [virtue] of God, and the wisdom of God,' whoever
performs virtuous acts, engenders virtue. 'And he who has
established her is the Most High Lord.' The very one who is
born in you has Himself established your Sion. 'In his record of
the peoples the Lord shall tell.' It is clear that what the Lord
speaks in Scripture, He speaks to no one as he speaks to Sion.
Yet, although all these things are so, although Christ has been
born in her, nevertheless, victory is not complete nor secure, for
we are always in peril. 'The home as it were of all rejoicing is
within you.' He who is joyful is fearless from joy itself; but he
who is fearless is soon deceived. The man, however, who is wary
of snares through fear can readily escape them, with the help of
the Lord to whom be glory forever and ever. Amen.

HOMILY 21

ON PSALM 91 (92)

The ninety-first psalm is inscribed with the title: 'A psalm;
a song for the Sabbath day.' There could be no sabbath day
without six preceding days. We work for six days, on the seventh
day we rest. We cannot sing to the Lord, therefore, save on the
day of the sabbath. As long as we are engaged in the works of
the world, that is, for the six days, we cannot sing to the Lord.
Leviticus says: 'On the sabbath day you shall do no servile
work.' No one, therefore, on the day of the sabbath and on the
day of the Lord's rest may do servile work—work pertaining to
this world; but he ought to do the work that belongs to the
sabbath. Would you know that on the sabbath the priests work
in the temple of the Lord? It is not permitted anyone to cut

wood on the sabbath; in fact, the man who was discovered gathering wood in the wilderness was stoned to death. Neither may one even kindle a fire nor do any kind of work.

You will observe, however, that all the things that the lay-man is not allowed to do on the sabbath, the priests alone are permitted to do, for they cut wood, enkindle a fire, and perform other services, and immolate victims. Why am I making such a point of this? To show you that it is written in the law that we must withdraw from all worldly pursuits on the sabbath and perform only those works that pertain to God. A psalm, there-fore, is a song on the sabbath day when we do not work for the world, but for God. Let us see now what we must sing on the sabbath when we are abstaining from the works of the world.

'It is good to confess to the Lord, to sing praise to your name, Most High.' The psalmist did not say that it is good to sing and after that confess; but note the order; it is good to confess, and it is good to sing. First repent and wash away sins with your tears; then sing to the Lord. 'It is good to confess to the Lord': not to men, but to God; confess your sins to Him who is able to heal you. 'And to sing praise to your name, Most High.'

'To proclaim your kindness at dawn, and your truth throughout the night.' Attend closely: To proclaim Your kind-ness at dawn and Your truth throughout the night. Each of these versicles refers in turn to a different versicle. 'It is good to confess to the Lord, to proclaim your kindness at dawn.' If you confess to the Lord, you are proclaiming His kindness at dawn. 'And to sing praise to your name, Most High.' This versicle is related to the following one: 'and truth throughout the night.' When we confess to the Lord, we are trusting in His mercy; when we sing, we are performing a good work.

'To proclaim your kindness at dawn.' Where are they who take the Scriptures literally? Are we not able to proclaim the kindness of God at noon? Certainly, too, it is the duty of Christians, and monks especially, to confess their sins at night. What, then, does 'to proclaim your kindness at dawn' mean? It means this. It is not possible for us to confess to the Lord and obtain His mercy unless a clear light has begun to en-lighten our heart. Unless the shades of night have withdrawn and dawn has arrived, we cannot attain the compassionate mercy of God. Then, in truth, do you proclaim at dawn the kindness of God, when the sun of justice has risen in your heart.

'And your truth throughout the night.' The truth of the Lord does not shine forth in its brilliance save at night. In the daytime it cannot be proclaimed because the weak are not able to sustain its sublimity nor endure its dazzling splendor. For this reason another psalm says of God: 'And he made darkness the cloak about him.' In other words, the Lord shrouds Himself in darkness. That is how the truth of the Lord if proclaimed at night; it is shrouded, so to speak, in an obscurity of words. In parables, moreover, and enigmatically, the Lord says: 'Seeing they may not see, and hearing they may not understand.'

We read in Osee that the prophet is bid: 'Go take a harlot wife.' The Jews hear this and the heathens, too, and they laugh. Why do they laugh? Because truth is set forth in the darkness of night, not in the light of day. Do you want proof that the truth of God is in the night, and, as it were, cloaked in darkness and enclosed in parables? Moses went up into Mount Sinai; and he went up in a cloud and in a mist and in darkness, and there he spoke with the Lord. The Israelites, however, could not see the mysteries of God because they had not entered the cloud that covered God.

'With ten-stringed instrument and lyre, with melody upon the harp.' I shall paraphrase this in simple language: Whenever we lift up pure hands in prayer, without deliberate distractions and contention, we are playing to the Lord with a ten-stringed instrument. 'With ten-stringed instrument and lyre, with melody upon the harp.' Our body and soul and spirit—our harp—are all in harmony, all their strings in tune.

'For you make me glad, O Lord, by your deeds; at the works of your hands I rejoice.' No matter what the Christian looks upon, it becomes for him a source of edification. Nothing injures the monk save sin. Whatever you gaze upon holds a lesson for you. You look up at the sky; you see the sun; you behold the stars, the moon; these are all grist for your meditation. You ought to reflect upon them and say: 'If the sun, and moon, and heaven, and the stars serve God, why do I not serve

Him?' You look down at the ground; you see the tiny animals and everything that is there. Apply this to your soul, learn from it, and say to your soul: 'Everything proceeds at its appointed time, for example, spring and summer, autumn and winter; why do they not change the order of their course? Because all creatures serve God as He ordains. Heaven obeys, and earth obeys, and I, unhappy man, do not obey.'

Let us focus our attention now on tiny beings. I am dismissing elephants, lions, all the various kinds of animals; I come down to little insects. Consider the bee or the ant; see its body and search into its wisdom—a wisdom far greater than the magnitude of its body! Bees and ants plan ahead for the winter that is to come, but the monk and the Christian give no thought to the judgment that is on its way. The bee and the ant know that they can be imperiled by hunger if they do not labor in the summertime for their winter supply of food; we do not reflect that without good works we shall be tormented in hell. Why have I said all this? Because the psalm says: 'For You make me glad, O Lord, by your deeds.' Whatever I look upon fills me with gladness, for I recognize the Creator and I bless God.

'At the works of your hands I rejoice.' I look at a tree and I reflect upon the bark that clothes it like a garment; I notice how the tree is ready to burst into flower just like a bud. Then, I muse how like a flower it is, how the blossom fades, and the flower itself becomes a fruit. I meditate on how gradually, day by day, in every season, nature works for me and becomes my food. I ponder over how God in all His creatures labors for me that I may lack nothing; and then I rejoice in You, O Lord.

'How great are your works, O Lord!' This is the verse in which Marcion and Manichaeus make their noisy entrance. What, pray, are they saying? If God has made all things, and has made them all for the needs of man, why did He have to make bugs and fleas? I shall make my answer to you brief and to the point: in order to expose your frailty, O man. You, who set your thoughts in heaven, look down; you are being bitten by a bug and you are trembling. Why do you hold your head on high and even transcend heaven with your thought? Look, you are being bitten by a bug! 'How great are your works, O Lord!'

Tiny bodies, indeed, but mighty planning. They all have their own proper usefulness.

Just as I marvel at the Lord in the elephant, I wonder at the Lord in the ant. As I proclaim Him in the camel, even so I proclaim Him in the gnat. Look at the gnat, how it is practically a mere dot with its tiny body. Yet in that tiny speck of a body all the parts, every member is distinct from the other. It has six feet, it has two eyes, it has a mouth and a paunch, it has also a trumpet for its voice, and it has wings. If you concentrate on each member by itself, you cannot find the rest of the body and you marvel at the work of God, for where there seems to be no body at all, not a single member is missing!

'How very deep are your thoughts!' However much I probe, I cannot fathom them. 'Your judgments, like the mighty deep.' 'Oh, the depth of the riches of the wisdom and of the knowledge of God!' With Ecclesiastes I, too, shall say: 'I said, "I will acquire wisdom"; but it was beyond me, much farther than before; it is deep, very deep: who can find it out?' What Ecclesiastes is saying is this: Before I turned my thoughts to ponder over God's work, I was not aware of God's magnificence. I said, I must have wisdom; that is, I must inquire into the nature of every cause; and wisdom withdrew farther away from me than it ever was before. By that I mean, formerly I was not in quest of wisdom because I was unaware of it, and afterwards, when I began to seek it, I could not find it. 'A senseless man knows not, nor does a fool understand this.' Anyone who is not a Christian and does not recognize the Creator in His creatures is a fool.

'Though the wicked flourish like grass.' You have seen generals, you have seen governors, you have observed armies, you have witnessed victories and triumphs. Yesterday they were and today they are no more. 'And all evildoers thrive, they are destined for eternal destruction.' Yesterday, a flower was barely in blossom; today, the flower is not to be seen. Yesterday, a plant was fresh and green; today, it is dried up and withered. What has become of all that beauty?

Nothing is good save the eternal; nothing is good except the everlasting. Anything that is finite is not to be counted among the good. What good does it do me if yesterday I feasted and today I am dying with hunger? What good to me if in the days gone by I was king and today I am dying in prison? Whatever is passing and has an end is nothing. Each one of us has come from the world to embrace this state of life. One has left his mother; another, his children; one, his wife; another, his parents. Let us recall our childhood, our youth; let us recall the time when we had wealth and each one through his own efforts possessed whatever he could. Behold, we have crossed over to this life. Where are all those possessions of ours? Reminiscence brings more pain than pleasure. Nothing is good except that which lasts forever.

'While you, O Lord, are the Most High forever. For behold, your enemies, O Lord, for behold, your enemies shall perish; all evildoers shall be scattered.' If they shall perish, how shall they be scattered? He who has once perished cannot be scattered. It ought to say: Behold they shall be scattered, and shall vanish, for, what it means is: Your enemies, O Lord, shall perish; since every creature is subject to You, everyone who has been Your enemy is afterwards made a friend; that means, of course, that not man shall perish, but the enemy shall vanish. The one-time enemy will become a friend, so the enemy will perish. 'For behold your enemies shall perish; all the evildoers shall be scattered.' Just as when holy men live together, it is a great grace and blessing; so, likewise, that congregation is the worst kind when sinners live together. The more sinners there are at one time, the worse they are. Indeed, when the tower was being built up against God, those who were building it were disbanded for their own welfare. The conspiracy was evil; the dispersion was of true benefit even to those who were dispersed.

'You have exalted my horn like the wild bull's.' A horn is always set up in a kingdom. 'Our foes through you we struck down with the horn.' As a matter of fact, no animal is immolated to the Lord in the temple unless it is horned. In the temple there are three animals sacrificed to the Lord: the bull, the ram, and the buck. Three are sacrificed and all three are horned. Unless one has a horn with which to rout his enemies, he is not worthy to be offered to God. That is why, too, the Lord is described as a horn to those who believe in Him; and it was with the horns of the cross that He routed His enemies. On the cross

He confounded the devil and his entire army. To be sure, Christ was crucified in His body, but on the cross, it was He who was crucifying there the devils. It was not a cross; it was a symbol of triumph, a banner of victory. His whole purpose in mounting the cross was to lift us up from earth. I think the cross of the Savior was the ladder that Jacob saw. On that ladder, angels were descending and ascending; on that ladder, that is, the cross, the Jews were descending and the Gentiles ascending. 'You have exalted my horn like the wild bull's.' Others may have many horns; I have only one. 'But as for me, God forbid that I shall glory save in the cross of the Lord, through whom the world is crucified to me, and I to the world.'

'And my old age with the rich oil of mercy.' Our old age needs the oil of God. Just as our bodies, when they are wearied from toil (I am speaking very simply for the sake of our guileless brethren who are unable to grasp a more subtle analogy), just as our bodies, when they are tired from manual labor, are refreshed by rubbing them with oil; just as the light in a lamp burns out unless you feed it oil; so, likewise, the light of my old age required the oil of God's mercy to keep it burning brightly. Then, too, the apostles ascended Mount Olivet in order that they might be illuminated with the oil of the Lord because they were weary and their lamps were in need of His oil. In line with this thought, the just man says: 'But I, like a green olive tree in the house of God.' And in another place Holy Writ says: 'Your children like olive plants around your table.'

Was there no other mountain, moreover, except Mount Olivet from which the Lord might ascend into the kingdom of heaven? Was there not a higher mountain in Galilee, Thabor? Why was it necessary for the Lord to ascend into the kingdom of heaven from Mount Olivet? But just realize what Scripture is teaching you. Unless you oil yourselves and your lamps, you shall not be able to ascend into the kingdom of heaven. You have to be on Mount Olivet; not in the Valley of the Olives, but on the Mount. Someone may ask: What is this Valley of Olives? The devil, too, has his own olives; he has the philosophers; he has the heretics; they also have oil; they also promise the light of knowledge. But those olive groves lead down into the valley: 'Let not the festive oil of sinners anoint my head.' Let us pray, then, to the Lord, that our old age and all our labor and all our darkness be illuminated with oil of the Lord.

I am reviewing carefully the places in Scripture where I might find old age mentioned for the first time. Adam lived for 930 years, yet he is not called an old man. Mathusala's life was 969 years, and he is not called old man. I am coming down all the way to the Flood, and after the Flood for almost three thousand years, and I find no one who has been called old. Abraham is the first one, and certainly he was much younger than Mathusala, but he is called an old man because his old age had been anointed with rich oil. In fine, it is written there in the Scripture: 'Abraham died at a good old age; full of days.' His was a good old age because it was full of days, for the whole of his life was day and not night. This same attribute is given also to Isaac and to Jacob. They who had served the Lord in the same age, rightly should be called old men of the Lord at the same time.

'Like a cedar of Lebanon shall he grow,' a truly fragrant wood, the wood from which the roof of the temple had been constructed. 'Like a cedar of Lebanon shall he grow,' a wood that never decays.

'They that are planted in the house of the Lord shall flourish in the courts of our God.' In one place we are planted; in another place we flourish; here we are planted; in the kingdom of God we shall flourish. 'I have planted,' says the Apostle, 'Apollos watered, but God has given the growth.' I have been planted in the house of the Lord, I mean in the Church; not in the walls, but in its doctrines: 'For the kingdom of God,' the Lord says, 'is within you.' Everyone who has been planted in the house of the Lord, who has grown roots here, brings forth flowers there.

'They that are planted in the house of the Lord shall flourish in the courts of our God.' These are the eternal dwelling places. What are these courts? Different mansions in heaven. At the same time, note that: 'They that are planted in the house of the Lord shall flourish in the courts of our God.' Here is the house; there is the court. According to proper order, it should have said court first and then house. But just see what it means. Even though we seem to be in a house here, nevertheless, when we shall have migrated to the kingdom of heaven, in comparison with the angels and the other powers, we shall not be in the house at all but only in the court. We are at the beginning, not at the end of perfection. We shall not be angels, but like angels. Do not let that seem a slight thing to you, O man, if you shall be like an angel.

'They shall bear fruit even in old age.' Happy the man who grows more vigorous from day to day; he who grows feeble in age grows feeble likewise in virtue.

We have been talking about the psalter, we have said a few words about the Gospel; we have also mentioned the Apostle. Let us beg the Lord that everything that we have said—both that which we have said and that which you have heard—we may fulfill in good works; that we may translate words into works; that we, who have been planted here in the house of the Lord, may flourish there in the court of Christ. To Him be glory forever and ever. Amen.

HOMILY 76 (II)

ON MARK 1.13-31

The passage from the gospel that we considered previously, closed with the words: 'He was with the wild beasts, and the angels ministered to him.' Since there was not enough time last Sunday to go as far as this text, we ought to begin with it today, for all of Holy Writ is animated and held together by one Spirit. It is not unlike a necklace held together by the union of its links, so that whichever link you pick up, another suspends from it. 'He was with wild beasts, and angels ministered to him.' Jesus was with beasts, and on that account angels ministered to Him. 'Give not to the beasts,' Scripture says, 'the soul of thy confessor.' These are the beasts that the Lord trampled down with the foot of the Gospel—the lion and the dragon. 'Angels ministered to him.' Not that it should seem grand and wonderful if angels ministered to God, for there is nothing remarkable about servants paying homage to their master; but this is all expressed in the language of the Incarnation. He was lodging with beasts. God cannot lodge with beasts, but the body that He assumed could, that flesh subject to human temptations;

that body, that flesh that thirsted, hungered, is tempted, conquers, and in which we are triumphant.

'After John had been delivered up, Jesus came into Galilee.' The historical sense is clear enough to those who are listening without any explanation on our part. Let us ask Him: 'who has the key of David, he who opens and no one shuts, and who shuts and no one opens,' to open for us the inner chambers of the Gospel that we, too, may say with David: 'Open my eyes that I may consider the wonders of your law.' To the multitudes, the Lord spoke in parables; He spoke to them from the outside, not interiorly or in the spirit, but externally in the letter. So we beg the Lord to introduce us to His mysteries, to bring us into His chamber, to permit us to say with the spouse in the Canticle of Canticles: 'The king brought me to his chambers.' The apostle says that a veil was placed over the eyes of Moses, but I say, not only is there a veil over the Law, but also over the Gospel for the one who does not understand. The Jew hears, but does not comprehend; for him a veil has been placed over the Gospel; the Gentiles hear, heretics hear, but for them also there is the veil. Let us leave the letter, therefore, with the Jews, and follow the spirit with Jesus; not that we scorn the letter of the Gospel—for everything has come to pass that is written—but that, by mounting certain steps, we may climb to higher places.

'After John had been delivered up, Jesus came into Galilee.' When we were commenting upon the Gospel last Sunday, we distinguished John in the Law and Jesus in the Gospel, for John says: 'One mightier than I is coming after me, the strap of whose sandals I am not worthy to stoop down and loose.' And in another place, he says: 'He must increase, but I must decrease.' He is drawing a comparison, therefore, between the Law and the Gospel. Farther, he says: 'I have baptized you with water,' that is, the Law; 'but he will baptize you with the Holy Spirit,' that is, the Gospel. Jesus came, therefore, because John had been imprisoned; hence, it is the Old Law that is closed up, and gone is its freedom; from the Law, we have crossed over into the Gospel. Notice that: 'After John had been delivered up, Jesus came into Galilee'; by no means into Judea nor Jerusalem, but into Galilee of the Gentiles. 'Jesus came into Galilee.'

St. Jerome

Galilee in our language means 'katakuliste' [rolling down]. There was nothing sublime nor lofty there before the coming of the Savior; everything base was tolerated: luxury, filth, impurities, the wallowing place for the muck of swine.

'Preaching the gospel of the kingdom of God.' As far as I am able to recall reading the Law, perusing the prophets, reciting the psalter, I have never heard of the kingdom of heaven except in the Gospel. Only after He came, by whom it was said: 'the kingdom of God is within you,' the kingdom of God was opened. 'Preaching the gospel of the kingdom of God.' 'From the days of John the Baptist the kingdom of heaven has been enduring the violent assault, and the violent have been seizing it by force.' Before the advent of the Savior and the glory of the Gospel, until Christ with the robber opened the door of Paradise, all the souls of the faithful were consigned to the nether world. As a matter of fact, even Jacob says: 'I will go down mourning to the nether world.' If Abraham descended to the land of the dead, who did not? In the Law, Abraham is in hell; in the Gospel, the robber is in heaven. We are not depreciating Abraham in whose bosom we all long to find rest, but we prefer Christ to Abraham, the Gospel to the Law. We have read that, after the Resurrection of Christ, many of the saints appeared in the holy city. Our Lord and Savior preached on earth and also among the dead, for that is why He died and why he descended into hell: to release the souls that had been confined there.

'Preaching the gospel of the kingdom of God, and saying, "The time [of the Law] is fulfilled," ' the Gospel has begun ' "and the kingdom of God is at hand." ' He did not say, the kingdom of God has already arrived, but the kingdom is at hand. Until I suffer and shed My blood, the kingdom of God is closed; it is near at hand, therefore, because not yet have I suffered the Passion. 'Repent and believe in the gospel': by no means in the Law, but in the Gospel; nay, rather through the Law into the Gospel, as it is written: 'From faith unto faith.' The faith of the Law has confirmed the faith of the Gospel.

'Passing along the sea of Galilee, he saw Simon and his brother Andrew, casting their nets into the sea (for they were fishermen).' Simon, not yet Peter—for not yet had he followed

89

the Rock that he should be called Peter—Simon and his brother, Andrew, were at sea and were casting their nets. Scripture does not say that they cast their nets and caught fish. He saw Simon, it says, and his brother, Andrew, casting their nets into the sea, for they were fishermen. The Gospel reports, to be sure, that they were casting nets; still it does not say that they caught anything; hence, it is clear that before the Passion, they cast nets, but it is not recorded that they caught anything. After the Passion, however, they let down their net and drew up a catch, so great that it broke the nets. 'Casting their nets into the sea, for they were fishermen.'

'Jesus said to them, "Come, follow me, and I will make you fishers of men." ' Happy exchange of fishing! Jesus fishes for them that they may become fishers of other fishermen. First, they become fish that they may be caught by Christ; afterwards, they will fish for others. Jesus says: 'Come, follow me and I will make you fishers of men.' 'And at once they left the nets, and followed him.' 'At once.' True faith does not hesitate; it responds at once, believes at once, it follows at once, becomes a fisherman at once. 'At once they left the nets.' I think that in the nets, they left behind the vices of the world. It was impossible, indeed, for them to keep their nets and follow Jesus.

'Going on a little farther, he saw James the son of Zebedee, and his brother John; they also were in their boat mending the nets.' The fact that it says 'mending' shows that the nets were torn. They were casting their nets into the sea, but, because they were torn, they could not catch any fish. They were mending their nets in the sea; sitting in a little boat in the sea, with their father, Zebedee, they were mending the nets of the Old Law. That, by the way, is the spiritual interpretation. 'They also were in their boat mending the nets,' 'they also who were in the boat.' They were in the boat, not on the shore where it was steady and firm, but in a boat washed back and forth by the waves.

'Immediately he called them. And they left their father Zebedee in the boat with the hired men, and followed him.' Someone may remark: Faith is rash. What sign had they seen, what majesty had they beheld, that they should follow Him immediately upon being called? Certainly, there is evidence here that Jesus' eyes and countenance radiated a certain divinity that readily attracted those whom He met. Even without Jesus ever saying, 'Follow Me,' they would have followed Him, for if they had followed Him without cause, it would not have been faith as much as temerity. If I were seated and anyone passing by should say to me, 'Come, follow me,' and I should follow him, is that faith? Why do I make such a point of all this? Because the very speech of the Lord was efficacious. Whatever He spoke accomplished His purpose, for if: 'he spoke and they were made, he commanded and they were created,' assuredly, He is the same and the very One who called; therefore, they followed.

'Immediately he called them. And they left their father Zebedee.' 'Hear, O daughter, and see; turn your ear, forget your people and your father's house. So shall the king desire your beauty.' 'They left their father Zebedee in the boat.' Take heed, O monk, and imitate the apostles; listen to the voice of the Savior and pay no attention to your temporal father. Recognize your true Father of the soul and of the spirit, and leave your natural father. The apostles leave their father; they leave the boat; in a moment, they leave all their wealth. They leave the world and innumerable possessions. They surrendered all that they had. God does not consider the extent of property, but the disposition of the soul that renounces it; they who have given up little would have given up much just as promptly.

They left their father Zebedee in a boat with the hired men, and followed Him. This goes back to what we said a little earlier in allegory about the apostles, that they were mending the nets of the Law. By now the nets had been torn and could not hold a catch, by now they had been eaten away by the brine of the sea and could no longer have been repaired if the blood of Jesus had not come and renewed them. They leave, then, their father Zebedee; they forsake the Law that in truth had begotten them; they abandon the Law in the boat, in the midst of the billows of the sea. Note, also, that they leave their father—that is the Law—with the hired men. Everything the Jews do, they do for the sake of the present life; hence, they are hired men. 'The man who carries out the Law will find life through it.' Scripture did not say, he will find life through it, in the sense that through the Law he will live in heaven, but he will find life through it to the extent that what he merits, he reaps in the present world. It is written for a fact in Ezechiel: 'I gave them statutes that were not good and regulations not the best, which they shall observe and thereby find life.' The Jews find life in them, for they look for nothing else than to have children, to possess health and wealth. They seek the things of earth; they give no thought to those of heaven; they are hired men. Would you be convinced that the Jews are hired men? That son who had squandered all his fortune, and who, by interpretation, prefigures the Gentiles, exclaims: 'How many hired men there are in my father's house!' 'They left their father Zebedee in the boat with the hired men, and followed him.' They left their father—the Law—with the hired men in the boat. To this very day, the Jews are navigators, navigating in the Law and in the sea, but they cannot reach the harbor. They have not believed in the harbor; hence, for them there is no arriving in haven.

'They entered Capharnaum.' O happy and grand and glorious exchange! They quit the sea; they abandon the ship; they renounce the bonds of the nets and enter Capharnaum. The first change is to give up the sea, to surrender the boat, to desert their father, to reject their earlier errors. In the nets, I say, and in the attraction of the nets, all vices are left behind. Just realize the exchange! They renounce them and, because they have renounced them, what do they find? They enter Holy Writ, says Capharnaum, the field of consolation. Now CAPHAR means field; NAVM, consolation. If, however, we mean Naum—in Hebrew there are multiple meanings, and the sense differs according to the difference in pronunciation—it can be taken as either consolation or beautiful. Capharnaum, therefore, may be translated as field of consolation or most beautiful land. In Scripture, where we read: 'Behold, how good it is, and how pleasant,' where we say 'terpnón [pleasing], and Aquila translates, 'eùprepés [fitting], the Hebrew has NAVM, which means beautiful.

'They entered Capharnaum. And immediately on the Sabbath he went into the synagogue and began to teach them,' in order that they might forsake the leisure of the Sabbath and take up the work of the Gospel. 'He was teaching them as one having authority, and not as the Scribes.' He was not saying, for instance, 'This the Lord says,' and He who sent me says that; He was speaking Himself in person who previously had spoken by the prophets. It is one thing to say, 'it is written,' and another to say, 'the Lord says this,' and still another to say, 'amen I say to you.' In another passage: 'It is written in the Law: thou shalt not kill, thou shalt not dismiss thy wife.' 'It is written.' By whom is it written? By Moses at God's command. If it is written with the finger of God, how dare you say: 'Amen I say to you,' unless you are He who first gave the Law? No one ventures to change the law except the king himself. But did the Father give the Law, or the Son? Answer, heretic. Whichever you say, I gladly support; for me, it is one as well as the other. If the Father gave the Law and changes it, the Son who changes it with Him who gave it, is equal to him. Whether, moreover, He is the one who gave or the one who changes, it takes equal authority to have given and to have changed—a thing which no one is able to do except the king.

'They were astonished at his teaching.' Now I ask what new doctrine had He taught, what had He said that was new? He was saying the same things that He had spoken by the prophets, but that is exactly why they were astonished; He was teaching as one who had authority, and not as the Scribes. He was not speaking as a teacher, but as the Lord; He was not speaking in reference to a greater authority, but He was teaching that which was His very own. In fine, He was speaking in this manner because He who had spoken by the prophets was talking now in person. 'It is I who have foretold it: Here I am!'

The unclean spirit that before had been in the synagogue and had led them into idolatry, of whom it is written: 'the spirit of harlotry has led them astray'; the spirit that had gone out of a man and was roaming in the dry places in search of a resting place and could find none, and that took with him seven other demons and returned into his former dwelling place; all these spirits were in the synagogue and could not bear the presence of the Savior. Indeed: 'What harmony is there between Christ and Belial?' Christ and Belial could not abide in the same assembly.

'Now in their synagogue there was a man with an unclean spirit, and he cried out, saying, "What have we to do with thee?" ' Who is asking: 'What have we to do with you?' He is only one, but he cries out the recognition of many. He is aware that, in his own defeat, his devils have been vanquished with him.

'He cried out,' like one undergoing torture, gripped in pain, unable to endure scourging. 'He cried out, saying, "What have we to do with thee, Jesus of Nazareth? Hast thou come to destroy us? I know who thou art, the Holy One of God." ' He was in extreme torture and, by his cry, betrayed the excess of his torments, but there is no end to his guile. He is driven to utter the truth; the torments compel him, but malice forbids: 'What have we to do with thee, Jesus of Nazareth?' Why do you not admit that it is the Son of God? Is it a Nazarene who torments you and not the Son of God? Do you feel the punishments, but refuse to confess the name? 'Jesus of Nazareth, have you come to destroy us?' What you are saying is true: 'You have come to destroy us. I know who You are.' Let us examine the title you give Him: the Holy One of God. Was not Moses the holy one of God? Was not Isaia? Was not Jeremia? 'Before I formed you in the womb, I sanctified you.' That is said to Jeremia, and he yet was not the holy one of God? If not they, then, who were holy men? But why do you not say to them, 'I know who you are, the Holy One of God'? O perversity of heart! He is held in the midst of scourgings and torments and knows what is true but will not admit it. 'I know who you are, the Holy One of God.' Do not say: 'Holy One of God'; but, 'Holy God.' You pretend to know, but you do not know, for either you know and are guilefully silent, or actually you are ignorant. Indeed, He is not the Holy One of God, but Holy God. Why do I stress all this? That we may not give assent to the testimony of demons.

The devil never tells the truth, since he is a liar, the father of lies. 'Your father is a liar, and from the beginning he is a liar just as the father of lies.' The father, Holy Writ says, is a liar and does not speak truth, the father of lies, the father of the Jews. The devil is certainly a liar from the beginning. Who is the devil's father? 'For his father is a liar and from the beginning spoke lies, just as the father of lies.' This means that the devil is a liar and utters lies, and, therefore, is the father of lies. Not that the devil has another father, but the devil is the father of untruth. Scripture says, therefore: He is a liar and, from the beginning of the world, does not tell the truth; what he speaks is a lie and he is its father; he is the father of lying itself. We have digressed on this point, because we must not give credence to the testimony of demons. The Lord and Savior teaches: 'This kind can only be cast out by much prayer and fasting.' But look here, I see many dissipated in drunkenness who belch up wine and, in the midst of feasting, get rid of demons and the demons cry out: we also believe that Christ has lied, for He said: This kind can only be cast out by much prayer and fasting. My purpose in saying all this is to warn you against too readily believing in the testimonies of demons.

What does the Savior say next? 'Jesus rebuked him, saying, "Hold thy peace, and go out of the man." ' Truth has no need for the witness of falsehood; I have not come to give proof to your testimony, but to cast you out of My creature. 'Unseemly is praise on a sinner's lips.' I do not need the witness of one whose torture I have commanded. Silence! Let your silence be My praise. I do not want your voice to praise Me, but your torments; your punishment is My praise. Not because of your praise do I rejoice, but because you are departing. Hold your peace and go out of the man. It is as if He were saying: Go out from My dwelling place; what are you doing in My guest chamber? I wish to enter it; be silent and go out from the man, from the rational animal. Go out from the man; leave the guest chamber that has been prepared for Me. The Lord desires His own dwelling place; depart from the man, from a rational animal. 'Go out of the man.' In another place in Holy Writ, He commanded a legion to come out of a man and go into swine. Realize how precious is the soul of man! This contradicts those who think that we and brute animals have one and the same soul and receive one and the same spirit. He is driven out of one man and is sent into two thousand swine; the precious is saved, and the mean is destroyed. Go out of the man, go into the swine; go into brute creatures; go into whatever else you wish; go into the bottomless pits. Relinquish man, My own proper possession of him; it is a wrong to Me for you to dwell in him since he is My dwelling place. I have assumed a human body, I dwell in man; the body that you are holding in possession shares in My body; depart from the man.

'The unclean spirit, convulsing him.' By this sign, he reveals his anguish; he threw the man into a convulsion. He could not wound the soul; the body he afflicted, yes, because in no other way could it be perceived that the demon was coming out of him; by such bodily contortions, he reveals that he is departing. 'The unclean spirit, convulsing him.' Because the clean spirit was holding its own steadfastly, the unclean spirit fled. 'Crying out with a loud voice, went out of him.' He protested his departure with a loud cry and the convulsion of the body. 'They were all amazed, so that they inquired among themselves.' Let us read the Acts of the Apostles and the miracles that the ancient prophets performed. Moses works wondrous signs, and what do Pharo's magicians say? 'This is the finger of God.' Moses performs, and they acknowledge the power of another. The apostles, too, worked miracles: 'In the name of Jesus, arise and walk'; 'In the Spirit of Jesus, go out'; always in the name of Jesus. But here, what does He say? 'Go out of the man.' Not in the name of another, but by His own power, He compels them to depart. 'They were all amazed, so that they inquired among themselves, saying, "What is this? What new doctrine is this?"' It was nothing new that a demon had departed; it was unusual for the Hebrew exorcists to expel evil spirits. What new doctrine is this, then? What is new? 'With authority he commands even the unclean spirits.' He does not command in the name of another, but He gives the command Himself; not in the name of another does He speak, but in His own.

'Rumor concerning him went forth immediately into all the region round about Galilee.' Not into Judea nor Jerusalem did the Jewish rabbis, in envy of Jesus' fame, suffer the rumor to enter. Besides, Pilate and the others had known that the Pharisees had delivered Jesus up out of envy. Fame finds entrance only into ears that are not closed up by envy. Why do I say all this? Because rumor concerning Him went forth into all regions of Galilee. It reached all Galilee. It reached all Galilee, but did not enter into one little village of Judea. Again, why do I say this? Because once the soul has been possessed by envy, it is very difficult for it to receive virtue; it is almost impossible to restore the soul that envy has mastered. It was, in fact, envy that caused the first fratricide. There were two men in the world, Abel and Cain; the Lord accepted the gift of Abel, but not Cain's. He who should have made virtue his model did not, but immediately killed him whose gift had been acceptable to the Lord.

'As soon as they came out of the synagogue, they, with James and John, came into the house of Simon and Andrew.' The Lord had drawn up His team of four and was carried above the Cherubim—and entered in the house of Peter, whose soul was worthy to receive so great a guest. They 'came into the house of Simon and Andrew.' 'Now Simon's mother-in-law was keeping her bed sick with a fever.' O, may He come to our house and enter in and by His command cure the fever of our sins! Each one of us is sick with a fever. Whenever I give way to anger, I have a fever; there are as many fevers as there are faults and vices. Let us beg the apostles to intercede for us with Jesus, that He may come to us and touch our hand, for if He but does so, at once our fever is gone. Excellent physician and truly the chief physician! Moses is a physician; Isaia, a physician; all the saints are physicians, but He is the archphysician. He knew how carefully to touch veins and thoroughly search out the hidden secrets of diseases. He does not touch the ear or any other part of the body; He touches only the hand. The cause of sickness and fever is the lack of good works. So, first of all, deeds are made right; afterwards, the fever is lifted. The fever cannot be dissipated unless works are amended. When our hands are guilty of evil deeds, we are sick in bed; we cannot rise or walk; we are sick all over.

'Drawing near' to her who was sick . . . she could not rise, for she was lying sick upon a couch, unable to go to meet Him, but this compassionate physician went Himself to her couch; He who had carried the sick lamb upon His shoulders went Himself to the sick bed. 'Drawing near.' Of His own will He approaches, so that of His own will He may heal. 'Drawing near.' It is as if He says: Certainly, you ought to have come to meet Me. You ought to have come to the door and received Me so that your cure might be the result, not only of My kindness, but also of your desire. Because, however, you are lying prostrate from the violence of the fever and cannot get up, I come to you Myself. 'Drawing near, he raised her up.' Because she could not rise of herself, the Lord raises her up. 'He took her by the hand and raised her up.' He took her hand. Peter, too, when he was in danger in the sea and was drowning, is raised up by the touch of His hand. He raised her up by touching her hand. He takes her hand in His. O happy friendship! O beautiful kiss! He raised her up by taking her hand! He healed her hand with His hand. He took her by the hand as if He were a physician; He touched her veins; He recognized the intensity of the fever; He is both doctor and cure. At Jesus' touch, the fever is put to flight.

May He also touch our hand, that our works may be cleansed. May He enter our house. Let us now, at last, rise up from the couch; let us not lie prostrate. Jesus stands before our couch, and do we lie down? Let us rise up and stand. It is disgraceful for us to be indolent in the presence of Jesus. Someone may ask: Where is Jesus? He is here in our midst. 'In the midst of you there has stood one whom you do not know.' 'The kingdom of God is within you.' Let us have faith, and we shall see Jesus in our midst. If we cannot touch His hand, let us fall at His feet. If we are unable to reach His head, let us, at least, wash His feet with our tears. Our penitence is perfume to the Savior. Just see how great is the compassionate kindness of the Savior! Our sins are malodorous, putrid; still, if we do penance for our wrongdoings, if we weep over them, our foul offenses become the fragrant perfume of the Lord. Let us, therefore, beg the Lord to take us by the hand.

'The fever left her at once.' As soon as He took her by the hand, the fever fled. Mark what follows. 'The fever left her at once.' Be hopeful, sinner, if only you rise up from the couch! Even holy David who had fallen, who lay on the couch with Bethsabee, the wife of Urias the Hethite, and was feverishly sick of adultery, the Lord cured as soon as he said: 'Have mercy on me, O God, in your goodness,' 'for I acknowledge my offense, and my sin is before me always'; 'free me from blood guilt, O God, my saving God. . . .' David had shed the blood of Urias because he had commanded his death. 'Free me,' he said, 'From blood guilt, O God, my saving God, and a steadfast spirit renew within me.' Notice that he said, 'renew.' When I committed adultery, when I perpetrated homicide, the Holy Spirit in me had grown old. 'Wash me, and I shall be whiter than snow.' Because you have washed me with tears, my tears and my repentance were for me as baptism. See, then, what is wrought of repentance? He repented and wept; therefore, he was cleansed. What follows directly? 'I will teach transgressors your ways, and sinners shall return to you.' He is made the teacher of repentance.

Why now have I said all this? Because it is written here in our text: 'The fever left her at once, and she began to wait on them.' It is not enough that her fever leave her, but she is elevated to the service of Christ. 'She began to wait on them.' She served Him with her feet and with her hand; hither and thither she ran; she worshiped Him by whom she had been cured. Let us also wait on Jesus. Gladly does He accept our service even though we have soiled hands; because He has healed us, He deigns to look upon what He has healed. To Him be glory forever and ever. Amen.

HOMILY 84(X)

ON MARK 13.32, 33 AND 14.3-6

The Gospel reading demands considerable exposition. Before we get to the sacraments, we must remove a stumbling-block lest any obstacle lodge in the minds of those who are going to receive them. They who are going to be baptized must believe in the Father, the Son, and the Holy Spirit; yet right here Holy Writ says, in reference to the Son: 'Of that day or hour no one knows, neither the angels in heaven, nor the Son, but the Father only.' If we receive baptism equally in the Father, Son, and Holy Spirit, and must believe that it is in the one name of the Father, the Son, and the Holy Spirit, which is God, and if God is one, how in one Godhead are there different degrees of knowledge? Which is greater, to be God or to know everything? If to be God is, how can He be unknowing? Scripture says, in fact, of the Lord Savior: 'All things were made through him, and without him nothing was made.' If all things were made through Him, then, the day of judgment that is to come was also made through Him. Is it possible that He does not know what He made? Can the workman be unknowing of his work? We read of Christ in St. Paul: 'In whom are hidden all treasures of wisdom and knowledge.' Note: 'all treasures of wisdom and knowledge.' Not that some are and some are not in Him, but all treasures of wisdom and knowledge are in Him, but they are hidden. That which is in Him, therefore, is not lacking to Him, even though it be hidden to us. If, moreover, the treasures of wisdom and knowledge are hidden in Christ, we must find out why they are hidden. If we men were to know the day of judgment, that, for example, it would not be for two thousand years, and if we knew it so long ahead of time, we would be more careless on that account. We would say, for instance, What is it to me if the day of judgment will not be here for two thousand years? Scripture says, therefore, for our benefit, that 'the Son does not know the day of judgment,' because we do not know when the day of judgment will be upon us; and further: 'Take heed, watch and pray, for you do not know when the time is.' Not, we do not know, but you do not know.

So far, we seem to be forcing Holy Writ and not really explaining it. After the Resurrection, the apostles ask the Lord Savior: 'Lord, when wilt thou restore the kingdom to Israel?' O apostles, you heard before the Resurrection: I know not that day, nor the hour; do you, again, ask what I do not know? But the apostles do not believe the Savior, do not believe that He does not know. See now, there is a mystery. He who does not know before the Passion, does know after the Resurrection. What is His answer to the apostles when, after the Resurrection, they question Him about the time: When will you restore the kingdom to Israel? 'It is not for you to know the time,' He replies, 'which the Father has fixed by his own authority.' Here, He is not saying: I do not know, but, It is not yours to know, it does not profit you to know the day of judgment. Watch, therefore, for you know not when the master of the house will come. There is much more that could be said, but we have drawn your attention to this point in the Gospel to prevent anyone from being scandalized that there might be something unknown to Him in whom he was about to put his trust.

St. Jerome

This same lesson from the Gospel says: 'When he was at Bethany, in the house of Simon the leper, and was reclining at the table, there came a woman with an alabaster jar of ointment, genuine nard of great value.' This woman has a very special message for you who are about to be baptized. She broke her alabaster jar that Christ may make you 'christs,' His anointed. Hear what it says in the Canticle of Canticles: 'Your name spoken is a spreading perfume, therefore the maidens love you. We will follow you eagerly in the fragrance of your perfume!' As long as the perfume was sealed up, as long as Christ was known only in Judea, in Israel alone His name was great, the maidens were not following Jesus. When His perfume spread throughout the world, then, maiden souls of believers followed the Savior.

'When he was at Bethany, in the house of Simon the leper.' Bethany means house of obedience. How, then, is the house of Simon the leper in Bethany, the house of obedience? What is the Lord doing in the house of one who is leprous? That is exactly why He went into the house of a leper, in order to cleanse him. Leper implies, not one who is a leper, but who has been leprous; he was a leper before he received the Lord, but after he received Him, and the jar of perfume was broken in his house, the leprosy vanished. He retains his former identity, however, in order to manifest the power of the Savior. Similar is the case of the apostles who keep their former names to proclaim the power of the One who called them and made of them what they are. In the same way, Matthew, the publican, becomes an apostle and, after his entrance into the apostolate, continues to be called a publican, not because he is one, but because from being one, he became an apostle. He retains his previous title, moreover, that the power of the Savior may be evident. Similarly, Simon the leper is called by his old name to show forth that he has been cured by the Lord.

'There came a woman with an alabaster jar of ointment.' The Pharisees, the Scribes, and the priests are in the temple and they have no ointment. This woman is outside the temple and carries with her a jar of ointment containing nard, genuine nard, from which she has prepared the ointment; hence, you are called genuine [nard], or the faithful. The Church, gathered

101

together from the Gentiles, is offering the Savior her gifts, the faith of believers. She has broken the alabaster jar that all may receive its perfume; she has broken the alabaster jar that was kept sealed in Judea. 'She broke the alabaster jar.' Just as the grain of wheat, unless it falls into the ground and dies, does not bring forth any fruit, so, also, unless the alabaster jar be broken, we cannot spread its fragrance.

'She poured it on his head.' This woman, who broke the alabaster jar and poured the perfume on His head, is not the same woman of whom it says in another Gospel that she washed the Lord's feet. That woman, like a prostitute and sinner, clings to His feet; this one, like a saint, holds His head. The one, like a prostitute, washes the feet of the Savior with her tears and dries them with her hair. She seems, indeed, to be washing the Savior's feet with her tears, but actually she is washing away her own sins. The priests and Pharisees do not give the Savior a kiss; she kisses His feet. You, likewise, who are going to receive baptism, since we are all sinful, and 'there is no one without sin even if he lived but a single day,' 'and with his angels he can find fault,' first, hold fast to the feet of the Savior, wash them with your tears, dry them with your hair. When you have done that, then, you will reach His head. When you descend into the life-giving font with the Savior, then, you must learn how the ointment comes upon the head of the Savior. If the head of every man is Christ, your head must be anointed, and after baptism you are anointed.

'There were some who were indignant among themselves,' not all, but some. To this day, the Jews are indignant when we anoint Jesus' head. Then, too, in another place, it says that Judas the betrayer was indignant; in him, the Jews are represented. Right down to this day, Judas is indignant because the Church anoints Jesus' head. What does he say? 'To what purpose has this waste of ointment been made?' To him, it seems to be wasting the ointment because the jar is broken, but, for us, it was a great good because the perfume spread throughout the world. Why are you indignant, Judas, because the alabaster jar is broken? God, who made you and all the nations, is bedewed with that precious perfume. You wanted to keep the perfume sealed up so that it would not reach others. With truth is it said of you in another text: 'You have the key of knowledge, you have not entered yourselves, and those who were entering you have hindered.' You have the alabaster jar; rather, you had it in the temple and kept it sealed. A woman came along and took it into Bethany; in the house of a leper, she anoints Jesus' head. What do they who are indignant say? 'It might have been sold for three hundred denarii,' for He who was anointed with this perfume was crucified. We read in Genesis that the ark that Noe built was three hundred cubits long, fifty cubits wide, and thirty cubits high. Notice the mystical significance of the numbers. In the number fifty, penance is symbolized because the fiftieth psalm of King David is the prayer of his repentance. Three hundred contains the symbol of the crucifixion. The letter T is the sign for three hundred, whence Ezechiel says: 'Mark THAV on the foreheads of those who moan; and do not kill any marked with THAV.' No one marked with the sign of the cross on his forehead can be struck by the devil; he is not able to efface this sign, only sin can.

We have spoken of the ark, of the number fifty, of the number three hundred. Let us comment on the number thirty because the ark was thirty cubits high and finished above in one cubit. First, we repent in the number fifty; then, through penance, we arrive at the mystery of the cross; we reach the mystery of the cross through the perfect Word that is Christ. As a matter of fact, when Jesus was baptized, according to Luke: 'He was thirty years of age.' These same thirty cubits were finished off one cubit above. Fifty, and three hundred, and thirty were finished above into one cubit, that is, into one faith of God. Why have we said all this? Because it says here in the Gospel: 'It might have been sold for three hundred denarii.' Afterwards, the Lord Savior was sold for thirty pieces of silver. It is not surprising that a jar of nard might have been sold for three hundred denarii, for He was sold for thirty! It is written in Leviticus and in Exodus that the priests did not begin their duties until they were thirty years old. Before they were thirty, it was not permitted them to enter the temple of God, as the perfect age for beasts of burden and brute animals is the third year. It says in Genesis, when Abraham performed the 'dichoto-memata' [division into two], that he used a heifer, a she-goat, and a lamb, of three years each, in order to show that that was the perfect age for brute animals; in like manner, among men the perfect age is thirty. Could not our Lord have received baptism at twenty-five? At twenty-six? At twenty-eight? Yes, but He waited for the perfect age of man in order to give us an example. It is written, also, in the beginning of the Book of Ezechiel: 'In the thirtieth year, while I was among the exiles.' We have mentioned all this in order to unfold the mystical meanings of the numbers that contain thirty. The Jews are indignant, aliens to faith are indignant, because that jar of ointment was broken, but our Lord, on the contrary, says: 'Let her be. Why do you trouble her? She has done me a good turn.'

Because of that woman's good work, we have made these few comments on the Gospel, and, most opportunely, has the fourteenth psalm been read. It is now time to discuss it.

HOMILY 86

ON THE GOSPEL OF LUKE 16. 19-31

The Rich Man and Lazarus

There was a certain rich man.' When the Lord had declared: 'No servant can serve two masters; you cannot serve God and mammon,' and the greedy Pharisees had rebuked Him, He set before them an example, or rather, a truth, in the form of an example and parable. Strictly speaking, it is not really a parable when the names of the characters are given. A parable poses an example, but suppresses identification. Where Abraham is mentioned by name, and Lazarus, the prophets, and Moses, there Lazarus is genuine; if Abraham is a true person, so also is Lazarus. We have read who Abraham was; we have not read of Lazarus, but He who made Lazarus, also made Abraham. If he speaks of Abraham as a real person, then we understand Lazarus, also, as a living reality, for fiction is not congruous with the actual.

'There was a certain rich man.' Just think of the kindness of the Lord! Lazarus, the beggar, is called by his name because he was a saint, but the man who is rich and proud is not deemed worthy of a name. 'There was a certain rich man.' I say, 'certain,'

104

because he has passed like a shadow. 'There was a certain rich man who used to clothe himself in purple and fine linen.' Ashes, dust, and earth, he covered up with purple and silk. 'Who used to clothe himself in purple and fine linen, and who feasted every day in splendid fashion.' As his garments, so his food; and with us, likewise; as our food, so our garments.

'There was a certain poor man, named Lazarus.' The meaning of Lazarus' name is 'boethoúmenos,' one who has been helped; he is not a helper, but one who has been helped. He was a poor man and, in his poverty, the Lord came to his assistance. 'Who lay at his gate, covered with sores.' The rich man, in purple splendor, is not accused of being avaricious, nor of carrying off the property of another, nor of committing adultery, nor, in fact, of any wrongdoing; the evil alone of which he is guilty is pride. Most wretched of men, you see a member of your own body lying there outside at your gate, and have you no compassion? If the precepts of God mean nothing to you, at least take pity on your own plight, and be in fear lest you become such as he. Why do you save what is superfluous to your pleasures? Give in alms to your own member what you waste. I am not telling you to throw away your wealth. What you throw out, the crumbs from your table, offer as alms.

'Who lay at his gate.' He was lying at the gate in order to draw attention to the cruelty paid to his body and to prevent the rich man from saying, I did not notice him; he was in a corner; I could not see him; no one announced him to me. He lay at the gate; you saw him every time you went out and every time you came in. When your throngs of servants and clients were attending you, he lay there full of ulcers. If your eyes disdained to look upon putrid flesh, did not your ears, at least, hear his plea? 'Who lay at his gate, covered with sores.' He did not have just one sore, his whole body was sores, so that the magnitude of his suffering might arouse your utmost compassion. 'Who lay at his gate, covered with sores, and longing to be filled with the crumbs that fell from the rich man's table.' There is some relief to sickness if one has resources, but if you add poverty to extreme weakness the infirmity is doubled. Sickness is always fastidious and cannot take anything indelicate; it is nauseated by it. How much real suffering that causes!

In the midst of so many wounds, he does not, however, think of the pain of his afflictions, but of the pangs of hunger. 'Longing to be filled with the crumbs that fell from the rich man's table.' In a certain way, he is saying to the rich man: The crumbs from your table are enough for me; what you brush off the table, give in alms; draw profit from your losses. 'Even the dogs would come and lick his sores.' What no man deigned to bathe and touch, gentle beasts lick.

'It came to pass that the poor man died and was borne away by the angels into Abraham's bosom; but the rich man also died and was buried; and in hell lifting up his eyes. . . .' We have heard what each has suffered on earth; let us consider how they fare in the nether world. The temporal has passed and is over; what follows is for all eternity. Both are dead; the one is met by angels, the other with torments; the one is borne away on the shoulders of angels, the other goes to his punishment; the one, Abraham receives into his bosom of happiness; the other, hell devours. Lazarus 'was borne away by the angels.' Great sufferings are suddenly exchanged for delights. He is carried by angels and borne away without even the effort of walking. He is carried after his great trials because he was exhausted. 'Was borne away by the angels.' One angel was not enough to carry the pauper, but many came to form a chorus of jubilation. 'Was borne away by angels.' Every angel rejoices to touch so precious a burden. With pleasure, they bear such burdens in order to conduct men into the kingdom of heaven. He was escorted and carried into the bosom of Abraham, not to the side of Abraham, but into the bosom of Abraham, that Abraham might caress him, revivify him; that he might hold him in his bosom and, like a tender and compassionate father, warm him back to life again.

'The rich man also died and was buried,' earth has returned to its earth. 'In hell lifting up his eys.' Note the import and appropriateness of each word. 'In hell lifting up his eyes.' Lazarus was above; he was below; he lifted up his eyes to behold Lazarus, not to despise him. 'Lifting up his eyes, being in torments.' His whole being was in anguish; his eyes alone were free, free to gaze upon the happiness of the other man. He was allowed the liberty of his eyes to be tortured the more because he does not enjoy what the other has. The riches of others are torments to those who are in poverty. 'Lifting up his eyes, being in torments.' The one many angels carry away; the other is held fixed in never-ending torments. Being in torments: the Gospel did not say in torment, but in torments, for such are the rewards of covetous wealth. He saw Abraham afar off; he looked up at him only to increase his torture. 'Lazarus in his bosom.' Abraham's bosom was the poor man's paradise. 'Abraham afar off and Lazarus in his bosom.' Someone may say to me: Is Paradise in the nether world? I say this, that Abraham's bosom is true Paradise, but I also grant that the bosom of a holy man is Paradise.

'He cried out and said,' (excruciating pain increases the volume of the voice) ' "Father Abraham have pity on me." ' 'Father Abraham.' Even though I am in the grip of torments, nevertheless, I call upon my father. Just as that son who squandered all his possessions calls his father, even so I call you father, even though I have lost you as father through sin. Have pity on me. 'In the nether world who gives you thanks?' Vain is your repentance in a place where there is no room for repentance. Torments, not the disposition of your soul, force you to repent. 'Have pity on me.' A saint, indeed, is Abraham, holy and blessed, and all of us are in haste to enter his bosom, but I am not so sure that it is possible for anyone in hell or in heaven to feel pity. The Creator pities His creature; one Physician came to restore the dead, for the others could not.

'Send Lazarus to dip the tip of his finger in water.' 'Send Lazarus.' You are mistaken, miserable man; Abraham cannot send, but he can receive. 'To dip the tip of his finger in water.' Recall your lifetime, rich man; you did not condescend to see Lazarus and now you are longing for the tip of his finger. 'Send Lazarus.' You should have done that for him while he lived. 'To dip the tip of his finger in water.' See the conscience of the sinner; he does not dare ask for the whole finger. 'Cool my tongue, for I am tormented in this flame.' Cool my tongue, for it has uttered many a proud word. Where there is sin, there is also the penalty for sin. 'To cool my tongue, for I am tormented in this flame.' How evil the tongue can be, James has told us in his Letter: 'The tongue also is a little member, but it boasts

107

mightily.' The more it has sinned, the more it is tortured. You long for water, who formerly were so fastidious at the mere sight of smeary and spattered dishes.

'Abraham said to him, "Son, remember that thou in thy lifetime hast received good things." ' Be sure you know what he means: good things to you; but they are not good. You have received what you thought were good, but you cannot have been a lord upon earth and reign here too. It is not possible to have wealth both on earth and in hell. 'Lazarus in like manner evil things.' If ever we are sick, if we are beggars, if we are wasting away in sickness, if we are perishing from the cold, if there is no hospitality for us, let us be glad and rejoice; let us receive evil things in our lifetime. When the crushing weight of informity and sickness bears down upon us, let us think of Lazarus. 'Besides all that, between us and you a great gulf is fixed.' It cannot be bridged, removed, or levelled. We can see it, but cannot cross it. We see what we have escaped; you see what you have lost; our joy and happiness multiply your torments; your torments augment our happiness.

'He said, "Then, father, I beseech thee." ' The miserable creature does not cease to call him father. 'Then, father, I beseech thee.' You should have called him father in former times, for he was your true father. Did you acknowledge your father, you who despised your brother? 'To send him to my father's house.' Notice the perversity; not even in pain does he speak truth. You see what he says: 'Then, father, I beseech thee.' Your father, then, is Abraham; how can you say, therefore, send him to my father's house? You have not forgotten your father; you have not forgotten that he who was your father has destroyed you. Because he was your father, you have five brothers. You have five brothers: sight, smell, taste, hearing, touch. These are the brothers to whom formerly you were enslaved; they were your brothers. Since they were the brothers you loved, you could not love your brother, Lazarus. Naturally, you could not love him as brother, because you loved them. Those brothers have no love for poverty. Your sight, your sense of smell, your taste, your sense of touch, was your brother. These brothers of yours loved wealth; they had no eye for poverty. 'I have five brothers, that he may testify to them.'

They are the brothers who sent you into these torments; they cannot be saved unless they die. 'Lest they too come into this place of torments.' Why do you want to save those brothers who have no love for poverty? It must needs be that brothers dwell with their brother.

'Abraham said to him, "They have Moses and the Prophets, let them hearken to them." ' Why do you ask that Lazarus go? 'They have Moses and the Prophets.' Besides, Moses and the prophets went about in goatskins, wandering in their caves and in holes in the ground; they were poor men just like Lazarus, and they suffered calamities and endured hunger. Why do you ask me to send Lazarus? They have Lazarus in Moses and the prophets. Moses was Lazarus; he was a poor man; he was naked. He esteemed the poverty of Christ greater riches than the treasures of Pharao. They also have the prophets. They have Jeremia who is thrown into a cistern of mud and who fed upon the bread of tribulation. They have all the prophets; let them hearken to them. Every day Moses and the prophets are preaching against your five brothers; let them teach them; let them instruct them. Let them summon the eye; and what do they say to it? Do not look upon the carnal, but discern the spiritual. 'What we have seen with our eyes,' says the apostle, 'what we have heard, what our hands have handled: of the Word of God.' He instructs the ear, too, the sense of smell, of taste. All the prophets and all the saints teach these brothers.

'He answered, "No, father Abraham, but if someone from the dead goes to them, they will repent." ' Here, a dogma is being revealed without our realizing it. One thing is said, another is foreshadowed. He knows that these brothers of his cannot be saved unless someone rises from the dead. The Jews, indeed, hearken only to Moses and the prophets; and no one has come back to them from the dead, therefore, our Savior has such brothers. 'If someone from the dead goes to them, they will repent.' 'If someone from the dead goes.' I do not know who will go, for I who am fixed in punishment do not deserve to know Him who will rise from the dead. This I do know, however. Whoever rises from the dead and teaches can save these brothers. He has saved ears, for He says: 'He who has ears to hear, let him hear'; and eyes, for He says: 'The lamp of the body is your eye.' In His name, the apostle says: 'We are the fragrance of Christ'; and the psalmist: 'Taste and see how good the Lord is.' He saves, also, the sense of touch, for, in a way, John is speaking of all these brothers when he says: 'What we have seen, what we have heard, what our hands have handled.' To these brothers, the Resurrection of the Lord brought salvation.

These brothers were in us, also, before our Lord rose from the dead. My eyes used to look upon evil; they led me in pursuit of a prostitute. I simply could not look at a beautiful woman without her beauty setting me aflame. Formerly, my ear was a snare, for I used to delight in popular songs and to listen gladly to shameful tales. Perfumes were my pleasure, not, indeed, good fragrance, but evil, for they were destroying my soul. Neither land nor sea was able to satisfy my palate. With every kind of delicacy, my slaves catered to me as an epicure. My sense of touch held me captive; I was seduced in the embrace of women. Do you see how these brothers, before the Resurrection of Christ, were leading me into death? He died and I lived; He died and these brothers rose from the dead; rather, they died in order that they might live; they died in the flesh that they might live in the Spirit. Now, my eye looks upon Christ; my ear hears only Him; my taste relishes Him alone; my sense of smell detects Him; my touch embraces Him.

'He said to him, "If they do not hearken to Moses and the Prophets." ' Mark how our Lord instructs the soul by His own word and by recalling Scripture. When we had said, moreover, that these brothers could not be saved unless someone rose from the dead, we had, by no means, given place to Marcion and to Mani, who tear down the Old Testament. They maintain that the soul cannot be saved except through, and only through, the Gospel; they do away completely with the Old Testament. Abraham, on the other hand, does not do away with Him who is going to rise from the dead, for he does not say, let them hearken to Moses and the prophets; why do you wait for Him who is going to rise from the dead? If he had said that, he would have destroyed the Gospel. What does he say? 'If they do not hearken to Moses and the Prophets, they will not believe even if someone rises from the dead.' 'If you believed Moses you would believe me also, for he wrote of me.' See now what Abraham means? You do well, indeed, to wait for Him who will rise from the dead, but Moses and the prophets proclaim that He is the One who is going to rise from the dead. It is Christ, in fact, who speaks in them; if you hearken to them, you will hearken, also, to Him.

There is so much more to be said. The psalm that has been read, the one-hundred-third, is mystical, especially so where it says: 'With Leviathan, which you formed to make sport of it'; and: 'The highest of them is the home of the stork.' The whole psalm is replete with mystical meaning, and but a day, not an hour, is scarcely long enough to do it justice. Since, however, it is already Lent, we shall, if the Lord grants an opportunity, attempt at another time to unveil the mysteries hidden in it. For the present, let it suffice to hear about Lazarus, or rather, to hear that he was the rich man. May the torments of the rich man be a restraint upon us and the example of the poor man an incentive to us. The Christian soul, the soul of the monk, the soul of him who naked follows the naked Christ, when it looks with envy upon a rich man, or when it itself revels in wealth and display, may it call to mind Dives; may it ponder well his voice as he cries out and begs for the touch of Lazarus' finger.

While we are still thinking about Lazarus, let us consider something we had all but forgotten to mention, for someone may, by this question, introduce a false doctrine: Is this scene presented to us as taking place before the last judgment or after? One answer might be, after the judgment because the one is suffering punishment and the other is enjoying consolation. What, then, is the meaning of: 'They have Moses and the Prophets'? On the other hand, if Christ Himself is the one speaking and He is teaching before the Resurrection which, according to our interpretation, is an expectation, then, the scene is taking place before the Resurrection, and, reasonably, is before the last judgment. I shall give an example to bring out the truth. Imagine that a man has been caught in the act of robbery and is sent to a very dark prison; he has been put into prison and is in torments while actually waiting for sentence. He, surely, is subject to some kind of punishment, and comes to realize what he is going to suffer in the future. Even though he has not yet received final condemnation, and the day of the trial, or judgment, has not yet come; nevertheless, from the imprisonment, from the darkness, filth, hunger, creaking of chains, groaning of the fettered, weeping of those who are with him, he understands fully what kind of penalty will be his. If the prelude to punishment is so painful, what will the punishment itself be like? If he has not yet come to trial, and his penalty is not yet meted out, yet he longs for cool water, what will he suffer after judgment!

It must also be taken into account that Abraham was in the nether world. Christ had not yet risen from the dead to lead him into Paradise, for, before Christ died, no one had ascended into heaven, not even the thief. That flaming, flashing sword was keeping Paradise safe; no one could open the gates which Christ had closed. The thief was the first to enter with Christ; his great faith merited the greatest of rewards. His faith in the kingdom was not attendant upon seeing Christ; he did not see Him in His radiant glory nor behold Him looking down from heaven; he did not see the angels administering to Him. Certainly, to put it plainly, he did not see Christ walking about in freedom, but on a gibbet, drinking vinegar, crowned with thorns; he saw Him fixed to the cross and heard Him beseeching help: 'My God, my God, why have you forsaken me?' Under such circumstances, he believed, O fickle, fallen state of man! The apostles had followed Him, and they had run away; this criminal on the cross acknowledged the Lord. O Peter, O John, you who had boldly asserted: 'Even if I should have to die with thee, I will not desert thee!' You make a promise and you do not keep it; behold another who is condemned for homicide fulfills the promise that he had not made! You have been excluded from your place; a thief has shut you out and is the first to enter Paradise with Christ.

We have digressed on the thief, but we have not forgotten the theme of our discussion, for when speaking of Paradise, we had said that no one would go there before the coming of Christ. Let us return, therefore, to that proposition. The thief's crown must not lead us astray; let it rather incite us to win the crown. Abraham was not yet in Paradise because Christ had not yet entered with the thief. Christ came, and He suffered, and

112

many bodies of the saints arose from their graves and were seen in the holy city. The cross of Christ is the key to Paradise, the cross of Christ opened it. Has He not said to you: 'The kingdom of heaven has been enduring violent assault, and the violent have been seizing it by force'? Does not the One on the cross cause the violence? There is nothing between; the cross and, at once, Paradise. The greatest of pains produces the greatest of rewards.

So much for what we have been saying. Let us pray the Lord that we may imitate the thief and this Lazarus, the beggar; if there is persecution, the thief; if peace, Lazarus. If we become martyrs, straightway we are in Paradise; if we endure the pains of poverty, instantly we are in Abraham's bosom. Blood has its own abode and so has peace. Poverty, too, has its martyrdom; need well borne is martyrdom—but need suffered for the sake of Christ and not from necessity. How many beggars there are who long to be rich men and, therefore, commit crime! Poverty of itself does not render one blessed, but poverty for the sake of Christ. Faith does not fear hunger. The lover of Christ has no fear of hunger; he who has Christ, with Him possesses all riches. A certain merchant, a very wise man, sold all his material possessions, all his pearls, and purchased for himself a single pearl, the most precious of all. He, certainly, had pearls, and they were very beautiful and precious pearls. He had Moses, Isaia, Jeremia, the holy prophets, but, in comparison to Christ he deemed these pearls as dung, wherefore the apostle says: 'But the things that were gain to me, I count them as dung that I may gain Christ,' that I may buy the one pearl. Similarly, one of the prophets says: 'Stand beside the roads, ask the pathway.' It is as if he were saying, sell the pearls and, with the pearls, purchase the one pearl. The prophet did not say, abandon the ways, but stand on the ways, and ask and seek the Way, Christ. To whom be glory forever and ever. Amen.

HOMILY 87

ON THE GOSPEL OF JOHN 1.1-14

The gospel says of John: 'There has been a man, one sent from God.' Consider the vast difference between God and man, for of God it says: 'In the beginning was the Word, and the Word was with God; and the Word was God.' Notice how an unlettered fisherman made use of a new word in its proper signification of God: 'In the beginning was the Word'—as we have already quoted; we have no time to repeat the entire passage. He says of man: 'There has been a man sent from God.' Mark the 'has been.' Of the Son of God, he says 'was,' of man, 'has been.' In referring to God, John says: 'In the beginning was the Word'; in referring to the Son of God he says, 'the Word'; of man, 'There has been a man.' Because he is a man, he has been sent from God. 'Whose name was John.' In his name, one senses grace, for the name 'John' means the grace of the Lord. IO means the Lord, ANNA means grace. Whose name was *Ioannes.* Truly, he merits the name he bears (pheronúmos). Why 'pheronúmos'? Because he is true to his name; he has received a very great grace; hence, in the desert, he searches into the reason and nature of things and keeps himself for the coming of Christ. Because he was to announce Christ, from day to day, he is fed in the desert; there, from day to day, he grows. He has no desire to converse with men; in the wilderness, he communes with the angels. John had always known that Christ would come. Not only had he known Him from infancy, but when he was in the womb of his mother, he had recognized Christ and had already greeted Him. It is written, in fact: 'The babe in the womb leapt for joy.' Just think, as he was being formed in his mother's womb, he perceived the advent of the Lord!

Realize your nobility, monks! John is the first one of our calling. He is a monk. Right after his birth, he lives in the wilderness; he is reared in the wilderness; there, he waits for Christ. Meditate on the difference. When John was born and lived in the wilderness, how much wealth was stored away in the Temple that we now see in ruins, how much gold, silver; what crowds worshiped in it. Do you want to know how vast was the throng of worshipers? Josephus, the Jewish historian, gives an account of the number at the time when Jerusalem was captured by Vespasian and Titus. He says that eight-hundred-one-thousand were captured in a single day. Grasp what that means. When that many have been captured, how many inhabitants must there have been altogether; how many died; how many did hunger kill; how many the sword? He also records the quantity of gold there was, the silver, precious gems, silk; the numerous priests, scribes, and various other officials. On the other hand, see how Christ esteems humility. Christ, the Son of God, is not recognized in the Temple, but He is proclaimed in the desert. The humble Christ loves the humble. Why do I lay such stress on this? To teach you that John the Baptist set the example for our way of life. Blessed are they who imitate John, than whom there has not been a greater among those born of women! He was waiting for Christ; he knew that He was to come; he did not deem it fitting for his eyes to look upon anyone else.

'All things were made through him, and without him was made nothing that has been made.' Many read this inaccurately because they add without any punctuation, 'that which has been made in him was life.' The correct statement: 'All things were made through him, and without him was made nothing that has been made,' meaning that that which has been made without Him has not been made. The Holy Spirit has not been made; hence, the Holy Spirit is not through Him. Admittedly, the Holy Spirit, who has made all things, has not been made by the Lord. 'By the word of the Lord the heavens were made; by the Spirit of his mouth all their host.' You perceive that there are two who create. I dismiss the Father, for there is no doubt about Him, although three persons are plainly indicated in this versicle. When Scripture says: 'By the word of the Lord the heavens were made,' it speaks of the 'Lógos,' i.e., it speaks of the Word, and the Lord, Father and Son; two persons are mentioned. 'By the Word of the Lord the heavens were made,' in other words, by the Son of the Father, the heavens were made, 'and by the Spirit of his mouth all their host.' There is clear demonstration in this versicle that the Father, the Son, and the Holy Spirit are the creators of all things. 'All things were made through him.' Now, if all things were made through Him, is the Father, on that account, excluded from creation, or Holy Spirit, and has the Son alone worked? Because the evangelist had said: 'All things were made through him,' lest he take away creation from the Holy Spirit and the Father, he added: 'And without him was made nothing that has been made.'

When he says: 'without him was made nothing,' he reveals that another has made, but has made nothing without Him. In fine, what does wisdom say in Proverbs? 'When he established the heavens I was there.'

'The life was the light of men. And the light shines in the darkness; and the darkness grasped it not.' In general, of course, it is said of God the Creator that He is ever in the midst of His creatures; nevertheless, the creature does not recognize its Creator. In particular, however, this text refers to the Lord Savior, and says that the Word who was God, and was in God, was also in the world to shine in the darkness of the Jews; and the Jews, who are the darkness, did not grasp the Light.

'There has been a man, one sent from God.' We shall comment briefly on each word. 'There has been a man sent from God.' Notice the precision of idiom. What does it say about God? Of the Son of God? 'In the beginning was the Word.' Was. He who was has no beginning; He who was has ever been. Of John, however, although he is a saint and the precursor, it does not say, he was, for he did not exist before he was conceived; he was not before he became the forerunner nor before he was conceived in the womb. Let heresy listen to this. He is not sent who was, but he who was not is sent and becomes the precursor. What is the meaning of: 'There has been a man sent from God'? Notice the propriety of the words. 'In the beginning was the Word, and the Word was with God; and the Word was God. He was in the beginning with God.' We have read secular literature, we have studied Plato and the other philosophers. Our fisherman has found what the philosopher failed to detect. If he had said, In the beginning was God the Son, he would seem to have excluded the Father, or even to be making two gods; and it would have been no gain for us from the Gentiles if we had abandoned many gods to believe in two gods. See, then, how prudently, how gradually, the evangelist moves along? He does not say, in the beginning was God, lest it seem that god and god created, that two gods had been associated, but he calls the Son, the Word. While he is saying that the Word Itself is in the Father, he is also saying that the Son is God, so that there is no misunderstanding that God is one. By the same process of reasoning through which we affirm the Son to be

God and affirm, moreover, one God in the Father and in the Son, so in the Father and in the Son and in the Holy Spirit, there is indeed, a trinity, but one divine nature.

'There has been a man, one sent from God.' John has been, who before was not; he has been made, who before was not; a man has been, not the Word. A man, therefore, has been because he was a man. The Word has not been, but always was. 'There has been a man sent from God.' 'In the beginning was the Word'; the Word is not sent. 'A man has been sent from God.' Whatever, therefore, the man says, it is the One who sent him who is heard. 'He who receives you, receives me,' the honor of the sender is recognized and acknowledged in him who is sent. 'There has been a man sent from God.' Where we say 'sent,' the Hebrews say, one sent forth; in Greek, 'apóstolos'; in Hebrew SILOAS. You see, therefore, that this John, the prophet, is not only a prophet, but also an apostle. Isaia is sent; he was an apostle. 'Here I am, send me!' 'Sent from God.' Well said, 'sent,' for the Lord says in the Gospel: 'All who have come before me are thieves and robbers.' He did not say, all who have been sent are thieves and robbers, but those who have come on their own. Whom does He mean by all those who have come before Me? 'Those who say, "Thus says the Lord!" whereas the Lord has not sent them'; they who have come on their own authority and have not been sent are the thieves and robbers. But this man has been sent from God. 'Whose name was John,' and whose name corresponds to his calling. The name, '*Ioannes*,' is interpreted as the grace of the Lord, for IO means Lord, and ANNA, grace; hence, John is called the grace of the Lord. His mission as messenger, he receives from the Lord. 'This man came as a witness, to bear witness concerning the light.' There is much to be said, but time prevents.

'The Word was made flesh, and dwelt among us.' The Word was made flesh, but how He was made flesh, we do not know. The doctrine I have from God; the science of it, I do not have. I know that the Word was made flesh; how it was done, I do not know. Are you surprised that I do not know? No creature knows. It is a mystery which has been hidden for ages and generations, but now is clearly shown in our time. Someone may object: If it has been revealed, who do you say that you do not know? That it has been brought to pass has been revealed, but how it was brought to pass is hidden. Isaia even says: 'Who can describe his generation?' What had Isaia meant, then, by saying: 'The virgin shall be with child and bear a son'? He is telling us what has happened; but when he says: 'Who can describe his generation,' he is revealing to us the fact that He has been born, but how He has been born, we do not know. Holy Mary, blessed Mary, mother and virgin, virgin before giving birth, virgin after giving birth! I, for my part, marvel how a virgin is born of a virgin, and how, after the birth of a virgin, the mother is a virgin.

Would you like to know how He is born of a virgin and, after His nativity, the mother is still a virgin? 'The doors were closed and Jesus entered.' There is no question about that. He who entered through the closed doors was not a ghost nor a spirit; He was a real man with a real body. Furthermore, what does He say? 'Feel me and see; for a spirit does not have flesh and bones, as you see I have.' He had flesh and bones, and the doors were closed. How do flesh and bones enter through closed doors? The doors are closed and He enters, whom we do not see entering. Whence has He entered? Everything is closed up; there is no place through which He may enter. Nevertheless, He who has entered is within and how He entered is not evident. You do not know how His entrance was accomplished, and you attribute it to the power of God. Attribute to the power of God, then, that He was born of a virgin, and the virgin herself after bringing forth was a virgin still.

We read in Ezechiel in regard to the building of the Temple: 'The east gate facing the east is to remain closed; it is not to be opened for anyone to enter by it except only the chief priest.' The gate is closed and no one enters by it but the chief priest alone. The Savior's tomb had been hewn out in the hardest kind of rock, and it is written that in it no one had ever yet been laid, for it was a new tomb. What has taken place historically is very clear; the sepulchre was hewn out of rock (we must give the literal interpretation first), very hard rock; He was laid in a new tomb, and a great stone was rolled to the entrance; and a military guard was stationed there to prevent any possibility of stealing Him away. Now all this precaution took place that the power of God would be all the more manifest when He arose from the dead. If the tomb had been in the ground, they could say, 'They have dug a tunnel and have stolen Him away.' If a stone of ordinary size had been placed as a seal, they could say, 'It was a small stone and they carried Him away while we were sleeping.' As a matter of fact, what is written in the Gospel? 'The next day the scribes, the Pharisees, and the chief priests went in a body to Pilate, saying, "Sir, that deceiver used to say that he would rise again. Lest, therefore, his disciples may come and steal him away and say, 'He has risen from the dead'; and the last imposture be worse than the first, give us guards to guard his sepulchre lest they take him away by stealth." Pilate said to them, "You have a guard; go, guard it as well as you know how." The extreme caution of the scribes and the enemy has rendered service to our faith. Look out, Pharisees; watch out; God cannot be shut in; God cannot be confined in a sepulchre. He who made heaven and earth, in the palm of whose hand rest heaven and earth, who poises the universe on three of His fingers—the Hebrew expression for this is translated by the Greek 'en trisomati'—He who, as I was saying, balances the universe, cannot be contained in a single sepulchre.

Then, too, when the women, Mary Magdalene and Mary the mother of James and Joseph [sic.], pious and well-meaning women, to be sure, but mistaken, were looking for God in the tomb, He accepted, indeed, their good desire, but the angel who rolled back the stone made known to them their error. He was sitting upon the stone, and what was it he made them understand? This stone upon which I am sitting, I, who am servant of Him who really is, is not able to confine my Lord since He would then be restrained by His own slave. That stone could not shut in Jesus. The angel says to the women who had come to seek Him: 'Are you seeking Jesus? He is not here.' Where is He, in heaven? He is beyond the heavens. On earth? He is beyond earth. Wherever He wills, there He is; wherever He is, He is there whole and entire. Wherever He is and wherever you are, you who are seeking Him are in Him whom you seek.

Listen to what the angel says to the women: 'Why do you seek the living one among the dead?' Why do you seek the Lord in a tomb? You seek Jesus; you seek the Lord; why do you keep looking for Him? Certainly, if you knew that He is living, you would heed the words: 'In the midst of you there has stood one whom you do not know'; and: 'The kingdom of God is within you.' What does the angel say to these women? Do you seek Jesus in the tomb? Believe that He has risen, and ponder well that He whom you seek is within you.

When Mary Magdalene had seen the Lord and thought that He was the gardener . . . she thought that He was the gardener; she was mistaken, indeed, in her vision, but the very error had its prototype. Truly, indeed, was Jesus the gardener of His Paradise, of His trees of Paradise. 'She thought that he was the gardener,' and wanted to fall at His feet. What does the Lord say to her? 'Do not touch me, for I have not yet ascended to my Father.' Do not touch Me; you do not deserve to touch Me whom you looked for in a grave. Do not touch Me whom you only suppose, but do not believe, has arisen. Do not touch Me, for to you I have not yet ascended to My Father. When you believe that I have ascended to My Father, then, it will be your privilege to touch Me; with the help of Christ our Lord, who liveth and reigneth forever. Amen.

St. Augustine
354-430

Augustine was the foremost teacher of the Western Church. The Bible played a central role in his life in several ways. From 383 when he first heard Ambrose preach until 387 when he was baptized by Ambrose, its message had gradually been working on him. Once he became bishop of Hippo in 396 he preached almost daily, always dealing in one way or another with Biblical texts. In 397, the year that he wrote his famous Confessions, he also wrote most of another book, on Christian Instruction. Thirty years later he realized he had not finished it, so went back to it and added what he had left undone.

In his Retractations (427) he explains what the work was meant to be. "The first three (books) help to an understanding of the Scriptures, while the fourth instructs us how to present the facts which we have comprehended." Thus the first three books are about "hermeneutics," while book four is about "homiletics." In the following selection we have chosen the first fifteen chapters of book one, plus chapter 7 and 20 of book four, simply to give a taste of Augustine's twofold approach: how to go about understanding the Bible, and how to go about communicating its message to others.

Christian Instruction has long been regarded as Augustine's most important work concerning the use of the Bible. It is in some ways his counterpart to book four of Origen's On First

Principles. *It received great attention in subsequent centuries, and was one of the first of Augustine's works to be printed in the 15th century.*

Augustine's contribution to Western understanding of the Bible extended far beyond this one book. He wrote four different works on Genesis alone, he has 124 treatises on the Fourth Gospel; of his 363 recorded sermons the vast majority are directly Biblical in content. His work on the Psalms is probably his best effort at exegesis; his study on The Harmony of the Gospels *gave needed attention to a central issue, and his treatments of Paul's letters to the Romans and to the Galatians have been highly valued.*

From his background and the fact that he was thrown into such all-absorbing controversies over Donatism and Pelagianism, Augustine was never able to equip himself for scientific Biblical study as well as Jerome. He was aware of this and several times referred technical questions to Jerome. On the crucial question of the senses of Scripture he had no consistently worked out solution (but neither did anyone else). In preaching he indulged invariably in allegorical and mystical interpretations, while in his theological writings he stayed much closer to literal exegesis. In fact, he was the first to propose the idea that a passage might have more than one literal sense, a position that bristles with serious problems and which he frequently abandoned.

The charm of Augustine, however, is not that he has all the answers but that he was never afraid of the questions. God-given intelligence was not to be set aside; it was to be put to use in humble service to the Word. This was his real legacy to the Western world. He stood at the opposite end of the spectrum from mindless fundamentalism. There is no question about it: were he alive today, he would be leading the vanguard of the Catholic Biblical revival.

CHRISTIAN INSTRUCTION

BOOK ONE
CHAPTER 1

The entire treatment of the Scriptures is based upon two factors: the method of discovering what we are to understand and the method of teaching what has been understood. I shall discuss first the method of discovery and then the method of teaching. This is a worthy and laborious task, and, though it should prove hard to accomplish, I fear that I am rash enough to undertake it. Indeed, I should be, if I were relying solely upon myself. However, since all my confidence of finishing this work depends upon Him from whom I have already received much inspiration through meditation, I need not fear that He will cease to grant me further inspiration when I shall have begun to employ that which He has already granted. Everything which is not exhausted by being given away is not yet owned as it ought to be, so long as we hold on to it and do not give it away. 'For,' He has said: 'He that hath to him shall be given.' Therefore, He will give to those who already have; this is, He will increase and heap up what He has given, when they dispense with generosity what they have received. There were five loaves of bread and, on another occasion, seven loaves, before they were distributed to the hungry multitude. Afterwards, although the hunger of so many thousands was satisfied, they filled baskets and baskets. And so, just as that bread increased after it was broken, the Lord has now granted me the thoughts which are necessary for beginning this work, and they will be increased by His inspiration when I have begun to dispense them. As a result, I shall not only suffer no poverty of thought in this ministry of mine, but shall even exult in a remarkable abundance of ideas.

CHAPTER 2

All teaching is concerned with either *things* or *signs*. But things are learned by means of signs. I have defined a thing in the accurate sense of the word as that which is not used to *signify* something, for example, wood, stone, animal or others of this kind. But I do not include that tree which we read that Moses cast into bitter waters to take away their bitterness, nor that stone which Jacob placed under his head, nor that ram which Abraham sacrificed instead of his son. These are indeed things, but they are also symbols of other things. There are other signs whose whole usefulness consists in signifying. Words belong to this class, for no one uses words except to signify something. From this is understood what I designate as signs, namely, those things which are employed to signify something. Therefore, every sign is also a thing. For, whatever is not a thing is absolutely nothing, but not every thing is also a sign. So, in this division of things and signs, when I speak of things, I shall do so in such a way that, although some of them can be used to signify, they will not disturb the division according to which I am treating first of things and then of signs. We must keep in mind, in regard to things, that the point to be considered now is what they are, not what other thing, aside from themselves, they signify.

CHAPTER 3

There are, then, some things which are to be enjoyed, others which are to be used, others which are enjoyed and used. Those which are to be enjoyed make us happy. Those which are to be used help us as we strive for happiness and, in a certain sense, sustain us, so that we are able to arrive at and cling to those things which make us happy. But, if we who enjoy and use things, living as we do in the midst of both classes of things, strive to enjoy the things which we are supposed to use, we find our progress impeded and even now and then turned aside. As a result, fettered by affection for lesser goods, we are either retarded from gaining those things which we are to enjoy or we are even drawn away entirely from them.

CHAPTER 4

To enjoy anything means to cling to it with affection for its own sake. To use a thing is to employ what we have received for our use to obtain what we want, provided that it is right for us to want it. An unlawfully applied use ought rather to be termed an abuse. Suppose, then, we were travelers in a foreign land, who could not live in contentment except in our own native country, and if, unhappy because of that traveling abroad and desirous of ending our wretchedness, we planned to return home, it would be necessary to use some means of transportation, either by land or sea, to enable us to reach the land we were to enjoy. But, if the pleasantness of the journey and the very movement of the vehicles were to delight us and turn us aside to enjoy the things which we ought, instead, merely to use, and were to confuse us by false pleasure, we would be unwilling to end our journey quickly and would be alienated from the land whose pleasantness would make us really happy. Just so, wanderers from God on the road of this mortal life, if we wish to return to our native country where we can be happy, we must use this world, and not enjoy it, so that the 'invisible attributes' of God may be clearly seen, 'being understood through the things that are made,' that is, that through what is corporeal and temporal we may comprehend the eternal and spiritual.

CHAPTER 5

The proper object of our enjoyment, therefore, is the Father, Son, and Holy Ghost, the Same who are the Trinity, one supreme Being, accessible to all who enjoy Him, if, indeed, He is a thing and not rather the Cause of all things, or, perhaps, both Thing and Cause. It is not easy to find a term which appropriately defines such great excellence, unless it is better to say that this Trinity is one God from whom, through whom, and in whom all things exist. Thus, there are Father, Son, and Holy Ghost. Each of these individually is God. At the same time They are all one God. Each of Them individually comprises the fullness of divine substance. At the same time They are all only one Substance. The Father is neither the Son nor the Holy Ghost; the Son is neither the Father nor the Holy Ghost; the Holy Ghost is neither the Father nor the Son. The Father is only the Father; the Son, only the Son; the Holy Ghost, only the Holy Ghost. All Three have the same eternity, the same immutability, the same majesty, the same power. In the Father resides unity, in the Son equality, and in the Holy Ghost the perfect union of unity and equality. These three qualities are all one because of the Father, all equal because of the Son, and all united because of the Holy Ghost.

CHAPTER 6

Have I spoken or given utterance to anything worthy of God? On the contrary, I realize that I have done nothing but wish to speak. But, if I have spoken anything, it is not what I wanted to say. How am I aware of this, unless God is ineffable? What I have said would not have been said, if it had been ineffable. For this reason God should not be spoken of even as ineffable, because, when we say this word, we are saying something about Him. There is some contradiction of terms, since, if that is ineffable which cannot be spoken of, a thing is not ineffable which can be called ineffable. We should guard against this contradiction of terms by silence, rather than attempt to reconcile them by discussion. Yet God, although we can say nothing worthy of Him, has accepted the tribute of our human voice and has wished us to rejoice in His praise in our own language. This is the reason why He is called *Deus*. In reality, He is not recognized in the sound of those two syllables, but He causes all those who share the Latin language, when this sound reaches their ears, to ponder over His most excellent and immortal nature.

CHAPTER 7

When the one God of gods is thought of, even by those who believe in, invoke, and worship other gods 'whether in heaven or on earth,' He is considered in such a way that the very thought tries to conceive a nature which is more excellent and more sublime than all others. Men are indeed influenced by diverse goods, some by those which are concerned with the senses of the body, others by those which affect the intellectual quality of the mind. Consequently, those who have surrendered to the bodily senses think that the sky, or what they see so radiant in the sky, or the world itself is the God of gods. Or, if they attempt to go beyond the world, they visualize something luminous and conceive it as infinite or of that shape which seems most pleasing in their vague imagining. Or they think of it in the form of the human body, if they prefer that to other things. However, if they do not think there is one God of gods, but rather many or innumerable gods of equal rank, they still attribute to each one the form of body that seems most excellent in their own minds. Those who by means of their intellect strive to visualize what God is, place Him above not only all visible and corporeal natures, but even all intellectual and spiritual natures, above all changeable things. All men engage in contest over the excellence of God, and no one can be found to believe a being is God if there is any being more excellent. Hence, all men agree that He is God whom they esteem above all other things.

CHAPTER 8

Since all who reflect upon God think of a living Being, only those who think of Him as Life itself can form an opinion of God that is not unworthy and absurd. Whatever bodily shape presents itself to their minds, they determine that it is life which makes it animate or inanimate and esteem the animate above the inanimate. They realize that the living body itself—however resplendent it may be with brilliance, remarkable in size, or distinguished by its beauty—is one thing, while the life by which it is animated is another. Moreover, because of its incomparable dignity, they esteem that life above the mass which is nourished and animated by it. Then they strive to look upon life itself. If they find it to be vegetative life without feeling, such as trees have, they prefer a sentient life to it, for example, that of cattle; and in turn, to this latter they prefer intelligent life, such as that of man. When they have seen that even this life is still changeable, they are compelled to prefer something unchangeable to it, that very Life, in fact, which is not sometimes foolish and at other times wise, but is rather

Wisdom itself. For a wise mind, that is, one that has attained wisdom, was not wise before it attained it; but Wisdom Itself was never unwise, nor can It ever be. If men did not perceive this, they would not, with the utmost trust, esteem an unchangeably wise life above a changeable one. Indeed, they see that the very rule of truth, according to which they claim the unchangeable life is better, is itself unchangeable. They do not perceive this rule anywhere except beyond their own nature, since they perceive that they are changeable beings.

CHAPTER 9

No one is so shamelessly foolish as to say: 'How do you know that an unchangeably wise life should be preferred to a changeable one?' For, the very point that he is inquiring about—how I know—is universally and unchangeably evident for all to see. He who does not see this is just like a blind man in the sunlight who derives no benefit at all, even though the brightness of light, so clear and so close at hand, pours into the very sockets of his eyes. But, he who sees the light of truth and flees from it is one who has caused the keenness of his mind to become dulled through association with carnal shadows. So then, men are driven back from their native country by the contrary breezes of bad habits, as it were, and eagerly seek after inferior and less estimable things than the One which they acknowledge is better and more excellent.

CHAPTER 10

Since we are to enjoy to the full that Truth which lives without change and since, in that Truth, God the Trinity, the Author and Founder of the universe, takes counsel for the things which He has created, the mind must be cleansed in order that it may be able to look upon that light and cling to it when it has seen it. Let us consider this cleansing as a sort of traveling or sailing to our own country. We are not brought any closer to Him who is everywhere present by moving from place to place, but by a holy desire and lofty morals.

CHAPTER 11

We would not be able to do this, unless Wisdom Himself designed to share even such great weakness as ours and show us the way to live according to human nature, since we ourselves are human. But, because we act wisely when we come to Him, He was thought by proud men to have acted foolishly when He came to us. When we come to Him we grow stronger; He was regarded as weak when He came to us. But, 'the foolishness of God is wiser than men, and the weakness of God is stronger than men.' Therefore, although He Himself is our native land, He made Himself also the Way to that native land.

CHAPTER 12

Whereas He is everywhere present to the healthy and pure interior eye, He deigned to appear even to the fleshly eyes of those who have weak and unclean vision. Since, in God's wisdom, the world could not know God by 'wisdom,' it pleased God by the foolishness of preaching to save those who believe.

Therefore, He is said to have come to us, not by traveling through space, but by appearing to mortals in human flesh. He came, then, to that place where He already was, because He was in the world and the world was made by Him. But, because of their eagerness to enjoy the creature in place of the Creator, men have been conformed to this world and have been fittingly called 'the world.' Consequently, they did not know Wisdom, and, therefore, the Evangelist said: 'the world knew Him not.' And so, in God's wisdom, the world could not know God by 'wisdom.' Why, then, did He come, since He was really here, except that it pleased God by the foolishness of preaching to save those who believe?

CHAPTER 13

How did He come, except that 'the Word was made flesh, and dwelt among us'? Just as in speaking: In order that what we have in our mind may penetrate to the mind of our listener through his ears of flesh, the word which we carry in our heart becomes a sound and is called speech. Nevertheless, our thought is not changed to the same sound. Remaining entire in itself, it takes on the nature of speech, by means of which it may pene-trate his ears; yet it does not incur any deterioration in the change. Just so, the Word of God, although unchanged, was made flesh, in order that He might dwell among us.

CHAPTER 14

Just as medical care is the road to bodily health, so this Care has received sinners to heal them and make them strong again. And as physicians bind up wounds in an orderly and skillful manner, so that even a certain beauty may join the use-fulness of the bandage, so the medicine of Wisdom, by assuming humanity, accommodated Himself to our wounds, healing some by opposite remedies and others by like remedies. A physician, in treating an injury to the body, applies certain opposites, as cold to hot, wet to dry; in other cases he applies like remedies, as a round bandage to a circular wound or an oblong bandage to an oblong wound, not using the same bandage for every limb, but adapting like to like. Likewise, the Wisdom of God, in healing humanity, has employed Himself to cure it, since He is both the physician and the medicine. Therefore, because man fell through pride, He has applied humility to cure him. We were deceived by the wisdom of the serpent, but we are freed by the foolishness of God. Furthermore, just as that which was called wisdom was really foolishness in the case of those who despised God, so that which is called foolishness is wisdom for those who vanquish the devil. We abused our immortality, and, as a result, died; Christ used His mortality well, and so we live. The disorder began in the corrupted soul of a woman; salvation came from the untainted body of a woman. There is another example of the use of opposites in the fact that our vices are cured by the example of His virtues. But, it was as if He were applying like bandages to our limbs and wounds when, as a man born of a woman, He saved men deceived by a woman; as a mortal He rescued mortals; by His death He freed the dead. Instruction will unfold many other uses of contrary and like remedies in Christian medicine to those who ponder them more carefully and are not hurried away by the necessity of com-pleting a task they have undertaken.

CHAPTER 15

Indeed, our belief in the Resurrection of our Lord from the dead and His Ascension into heaven sustains our faith with great hope. For this belief shows us forcibly how willingly He who had the power to take it up again laid down His life for us. What great confidence, then, inspires the hope of the faithful when they consider what great things He who is so great suffered for men who were not yet believers. When He is expected from heaven as the Judge of the living and the dead, He strikes great fear into the negligent, with the result that they devote themselves to earnest effort and long for Him by leading a saintly life, instead of dreading His coming because of their wicked lives. What words can tell or what thought can conceive the reward which He will give at the last day, when He already has given so great a measure of His spirit for our consolation in this journey, in order that, in the midst of the adversities of this life, we may have such great trust in Him and love of Him whom we do not yet see? Moreover, He has granted to each of us the special graces requisite for the upbuilding of His Church, so that we will do what He has indicated should be done, not only without complaint, but even with joy.

CHAPTER 7

Who would not see what the Apostle was trying to say and how wisely he spoke, when he said: 'We exult in tribulations, knowing that tribulation works out endurance, and endurance, tried virtue, and tried virtue, hope. And hope does not disappoint, because the charity of God is poured forth in our hearts by the Holy Spirit who has been given to us'? Here, if anyone unlearnedly learned (if I may use the expression) were to argue that the Apostle had followed the rules of the art of rhetoric, would he not be laughed at by both learned and unlearned Christians? Nevertheless, we recognize in this passage the figure which is called *climax* in Greek, and *gradatio* in Latin, by some, since they do not wish to call it *scala* ['ladder'], when words or thoughts are joined together, one proceeding from another. Here, for example, we see 'endurance' proceeding from 'tribulation,' 'tried virtue' from 'endurance,' and 'hope' from 'tried virtue.' Here, too, we perceive another ornament of style. After certain statements completed in a single tone of expression, which our writers call *membra* and *caesa* ['clauses' and 'phrases'], while the Greeks call them *cola* and *cómmata*, there follows a rounded sentence or period which the Greeks call *periodos*, whose *membra* are held suspended by the voice of the speaker until it is completed by the last one. The first *membrum* of those preceding the period is: 'since tribulation works out endurance'; the second is: 'and endurance, tried virtue'; and the third is: 'and tried virtue, hope.' Then follows the period itself, which is completed in three *membra*. The first of these is: 'And hope does not disappoint'; the second is: 'because the charity of God is poured forth in our hearts'; and the third is: 'by the Holy Spirit who has been given to us.' These things and others like them are taught in the art of rhetoric. Therefore, just as I do not maintain that the Apostle followed the rules of rhetoric, so I do not deny that eloquence followed his wisdom.

Writing in his second Epistle to the Corinthians, he contradicts certain false apostles among the Jews who were disparaging him. Since he is forced to speak of himself, as if attributing this folly to himself, how wisely and how eloquently he speaks! He is the companion of wisdom and the leader of eloquence. The former he follows; for the latter, he leads the way, not spurning it, however, when it chooses to follow him. He says: 'I repeat, let no one think me foolish. But if so, then regard me as such, that I also may boast a little. What I am saying in this confidence of boasting, I am not speaking according to the Lord, but, as it were, in foolishness. Since many boast according to the flesh, I too will boast. For you gladly put up with fools, because you are wise yourselves! For you suffer it if a man enslaves you, if a man devours you, if a man takes from you, if a man is arrogant, if a man slaps your face! I speak to my own shame, as though we had been weak. But wherein any man is bold—I am speaking foolishly—I also am bold. Are they Hebrews? So am I! Are they Israelites? So am I! Are they offspring of Abraham? So am I! Are they ministers of Christ? I—to speak as a fool—am more: in many more labors, in prisons more frequently, in lashes above measure, often exposed to death. From the Jews five times I received forty lashes less one. Thrice I was scourged,

once I was stoned, thrice I suffered shipwreck, a night and a day
I was adrift on the sea; in journeyings often, in perils from
floods, in perils from robbers, in perils from my own nation, in
perils from the Gentiles, in perils in the city, in perils in the
wilderness, in perils in the sea, in perils from false brethren; in
labor and hardships, in many sleepless nights, in hunger and
thirst, in fastings often, in cold and nakedness. Besides those
outer things, there is my daily pressing anxiety, the care of all
the churches! Who is weak, and I am not weak? Who is made to
stumble, and I am not inflamed? If I must boast, I will boast of
the things that concern my weakness.' Attentive souls can see
how much wisdom is in these words. Even one who is deep in
sleep can observe also with what a noble flow of eloquence they
rush on.

Further, anyone who has learned about them observes
that, inserted with a most suitable variety, those *caesa,* called
cómmata by the Greeks, and the *membra* and periods of which
I spoke a little while ago, created the whole figures and expression, so to speak, of a style which charms and arouses even the
unlearned. From the place where I began to introduce this passage there are periods. The first is the smallest, that is, it has
two *membra* (periods cannot have less than two *membra,* although they may have more). The first, then, is: 'I repeat, let
no one think me foolish.' The second follows with three *membra*: 'But if so, then regard me as such, that I also may boast a
little.' The third, which comes next, has four *membra*: 'What I
am saying, in this confidence of boasting, I am not speaking
according to the Lord, but as it were in foolishness.' The fourth
has two: 'Since many boast according to the flesh, I too will
boast.' The fifth has two: 'For you gladly put up with fools,
because you are wise yourselves!' The sixth also has two: 'For
you suffer it if a man enslaves you.' Three *caesa* follow: 'If a
man devours you, if a man take from you, if a man is arrogant.'
Then come three *membra*: 'If a man slaps your face! I speak to
my own shame, as though we had been weak.' A period of three
membra follows: 'But wherein any man is bold—I am speaking
foolishly—I also am bold.' From this point on, after several
caesa have been proposed as questions, so separate *caesa* are
given back in answer; three answers to three questions: 'Are

they Hebrews? So am I! Are they Israelites? So am I! Are they offspring of Abraham? So am I!' Although the fourth *caesum* has been expressed with the same interrogation, he does not reply with the balance of another *caesum,* but of a *membrum*: 'Are they ministers of Christ? I—to speak as a fool—am more.' Then, after the form of interrogation has been properly set aside, the four following *caesa* are poured forth: 'in many more labors, in prisons more frequently, in lashes above measure, often exposed to death.' A short period is then inserted, because by the elevation of our voice we must distinguish 'From the Jews five times,' making it one *membrum* to which is joined the other: 'I received forty lashes less one.' Then he returns to *caesa* and uses three: 'Thrice I was scourged, once I was stoned, thrice I suffered shipwreck.' A *membrum* follows: 'a night and a day I was adrift on the sea.' Then fourteen *caesa* flow forth with appropriate vigor: 'in journeyings often, in perils from floods, in perils from robbers, in perils from my own nation, in perils from the Gentiles, in perils in the city, in perils in the wilderness, in perils in the sea, in perils from false brethren; in labor and hardships, in many sleepless nights, in hunger and thirst, in fastings often, in cold and nakedness.' After these he inserts a period of three *membra*: 'Besides those outer things, there is my daily pressing anxiety, the care of all the churches!' And to this we join two *membra* as a question: 'Who is weak? and I am not weak? Who is made to stumble, and I am not inflamed?' Finally, this whole passage, as if panting for breath, is completed by a period of two *membra*: 'If I must boast, I will boast of the things that concern my weakness.' After this outburst, because he rests, as it were, and makes his hearer rest by inserting a little narrative, it is impossible to describe adequately what beauty and what charm he produces. For, he continues by saying: 'The God and Father of our Lord Jesus, who is blessed forevermore, knows that I do not lie.' And then he tells briefly how he has been exposed to danger and how he escaped.

It would be tedious to recount other examples or to indicate these in other passages of the Holy Scriptures. What if I had tried to point out also the figures of speech which are taught in the art of rhetoric and are present in those passages

134

at least which I have quoted from the Apostle's eloquence? Is it not true that thoughtful men would more readily have believed that I am going to excess rather than that any students would have felt that I was meeting their needs? When all these principles are taught by masters, they are considered of great value, are purchased at a high price, and are sold with considerable display. I myself have a dread of being tainted by that ostentation while I am discussing these matters in this way. However, I must give an answer to the ill-informed men who believe that our authors should be despised not because they do not possess, but because they do not make a display of, the eloquence which those others value too highly.

Someone might think that I have selected the Apostle Paul as if he were our one eloquent speaker. For when he said: 'Even though rude in speech, but not in knowledge,' it seems as if he spoke by way of concession to his detractors, not as if he were recognizing it as true by acknowledging it. On the other hand, if he had said: 'Indeed rude in speech, but not in knowledge,' nothing else could possibly be understood. He did not hesitate to declare his knowledge openly, because without it he would not have been able to be the 'teacher of the Gentiles.' Surely, if we quote any utterance of his as a model of eloquence, we certainly quote from those Epistles which even his detractors, who were anxious that his spoken word be considered of no consequence, had to acknowledge were 'weighty and telling.' Consequently, I see that I must say something about the eloquence of the Prophets, where many points are kept hidden through a figurative manner of speaking. The more these seem to be concealed by figurative words, the more delightful they become when they have been explained. At this point I should quote something of such a nature that I shall not be compelled to explain what has been said, but only to praise the manner in which it was said. In preference to all others I shall select this from the book of the Prophet who says that he was a shepherd or herdsman, and was withdrawn from that occupation by divine Providence and sent to prophesy to the people of God. Nor shall my example be according to the Septuagint translators, who, translating also under the guidance of the Holy Ghost, seem to have altered some passages so that the attention of the reader might be the more encouraged to investigate thoroughly the spiritual meaning (for this reason, several passages of theirs are even more obscure because they are more figurative). I shall use, instead, these passages as they have been translated from Hebrew to the Latin language by the priest Jerome, a skilled interpreter of both languages.

When, then, he was reproving the wicked, the proud, the voluptuous, and those who were very careless about fraternal charity, this peasant, or this one-time peasant turned prophet, exclaimed: 'Woe to you that are wealthy in Sion, and to you that have confidence in the mountain of Samaria: ye great men, heads of the people, that go in with state into the house of Israel. Pass ye over to Chalane, and see, and go from thence into Emath the great: and go down into Geth of the Philistines, and to all the best kingdoms of these: if their border be larger than your border. You that are separated unto the evil day: and that approach to the throne of iniquity: You that sleep upon beds of ivory, and are wanton on your couches; that eat the lamb out of the flock, and the calves out of the midst of the herd: You that sing to the sound of the psaltery: they have thought themselves to have instruments of music like David: that drink wine in bowls, and anoint themselves with the best ointment: and they were not concerned for the affliction of Joseph.' Would those men who, as if they themselves were learned and eloquent, despise our prophets as illiterate and unskilled in speaking— would they have wished to express themselves otherwise, if they had been obliged to say something like this to such people— those of them, at least, who would not have wanted to act like madmen?

What more could discriminating listeners desire from this eloquence? At first, with what a roar the invective itself is hurled as against senses steeped in sleep, in order to arouse them! 'Woe to you that are wealthy in Sion, and to you that have confidence in the mountain of Samaria: ye great men, heads of the people, that go in with state into the house of Israel.' In order to show that they are ungrateful for the gifts of God, who has given them the spacious expanses of their kingdom, in that they put their trust in the mountain of Samaria, where idols are worshipped, the prophet then says: 'Pass ye over to Chalane, and see, and go from thence into Emath the great: and go down into Geth of the Philistines, and to all the best kingdoms of these: if their border be larger than your border.' Even at the same time that he says these words, his discourse is adorned, as if by lights, with the names of such places as Sion, Samaria, Chalane, Emath the great, and Geth of the Philistines. Then, the words used in these places are very appropriately varied: 'You are wealthy,' 'you have confidence,' 'pass ye over,' 'go,' and 'go down.'

Next he announces that a future captivity under a hostile king is approaching when he adds: 'You that are separated unto the evil day: and that approach to the throne of iniquity.' Then the evils of luxury are brought to mind: 'You that sleep upon beds of ivory, and are wanton on your couches; that eat the lambs out of the flock, and the calves out of the midst of the herd.' Those six *membra* formed three periods of two *membra* each. He does not say: 'You that are separated unto the evil day, that approach to the throne of iniquity, that sleep upon beds of ivory, that are wanton on your couches, that eat the lambs out of the flock, and the calves out of the midst of the herd.' If he had expressed it this way, so that each of the six *membra* began with the same pronoun repeated each time and so that each one was ended by the tone of the voice, it would certainly have been beautiful. But it has become more beautiful because the *membra* were joined in pairs to the same pronoun, and these developed three sentences: one, a prediction of the captivity: 'You that are separated unto the evil day: and that approach to the throne of iniquity'; the second pertaining to lust: 'You that sleep upon beds of ivory, and are wanton on your couches'; and the third concerning gluttony: 'that eat the lamb out of the flock, and the calves out of the midst of the herd.' The result is that it is left to the inclination of the speaker whether he will finish each one separately and make six *membra,* or whether he will raise his voice at the first, third, and fifth, and, by linking the second to the first, the fourth to the third, and the sixth to the fifth, very properly create three periods of two *membra* each; one to tell of impending disaster, the other to denounce impurity, and the third to censure intemperance.

Next, he rebukes their immoderate pleasure in the sense of hearing. When he had said: 'You that sing to the sound of the psaltery' (since music can be used with wisdom by those who are wise), he checks the vehemence of his invective with admirable beauty of style, speaking now not to them, but about them. To impress upon us that we should discriminate between the music of the wise man and the music of the voluptuous man, he does not say: 'You that sing to the sound of the psaltery and think you have instruments of music like David'; but, when he said to the licentious what they should hear: 'You that sing to the sound of psaltery,' he pointed out their ignorance to others, adding: 'They have thought themselves to have instruments of music like David: that drink wine in bowls, and anoint themselves with the best ointment.' These three are pronounced more correctly if the voice is kept raised for the first two *membra* and the period is completed with the third.

The following is now added to all the former passages: 'And they were not concerned for the affliction of Joseph.' Whether it is pronounced continuously to form one *membrum,* or it is more appropriate to keep the voice raised for 'And they were not concerned,' and, after this separation, say 'for the affliction of Joseph' to form a period of two *membra*—in any case, he did not say: 'they were not concerned for the affliction of their brother,' but with wondrous beauty used the word 'Joseph' instead of 'brother.' In this way every brother is signified by the proper name of the man whose renown among his brothers is celebrated both for the wrongs which he suffered and for the benefits which he paid in return. In fact, I do not know whether that figure by which Joseph is taken to mean every possible brother is taught by that art of rhetoric which I have learned and taught. But, it is pointless to tell anyone who does not realize it himself how beautiful it is and how it influences those who read with understanding.

Indeed, many points which apply to the rules of eloquence can be discovered in this very passage which I have used as an example. A sincere reader is not so much instructed when he carefully analyzes it as he is set on fire when he recites it with glowing feeling. For, not by human effort were these words devised; they have been poured forth from the Mind of God both wisely and eloquently, so that wisdom was not bent upon eloquence, nor did eloquence separate itself from wisdom. As some very eloquent and intelligent men could observe and maintain, if those principles which are learned in the art of oratory could not be respected, observed, and brought to these teachings, unless they were first discovered in the natural ability of orators, is it any wonder that they are discovered in those men sent by Him who creates natural abilities? Therefore, let us admit that our canonical writers and teachers were not only wise, but truly eloquent, with such an eloquence as was appropriate for persons of this kind.

CHAPTER 20

To speak more definitely, there is an example of subdued style in the Apostle Paul when he says: 'Tell me, you who desire to be under the Law, have you not heard the Law? For it is written that Abraham had two sons, the one by a slave-girl and the other by a free woman. And the son of the slave-girl was born according to the flesh, but the son of the free woman in virtue of the promise. This is said by way of allegory. For these are the two convenants: one indeed from Mount Sinai, bringing forth children unto bondage, which is Agar. For Sinai is a mountain in Arabia, which corresponds to the present Jerusalem, and is in slavery with her children. But that Jerusalem which is above is free, which is our mother,' and so on. And likewise where he reasons, saying: 'Brethren (I speak after the manner of men); yet even a man's will, once it has been ratified, no one annuls or alters. The promises were made to Abraham and to his offspring. He does not say, "And to his offsprings," as of many; but as of one, "And to thy offspring," who is Christ. Now I mean this: The Law which was made four hundred and thirty years later does not annul the covenant which was ratified by God, so as to make the promise void. For if the right to inherit be from the Law, it is no longer a promise. But God gave it to Abraham by promise.' Because it could occur to the mind of his listener to ask: 'Why, then, was the Law given, if there is no inheritance from it?' he cast this up to himself and said as if he were inquiring: 'What then was the Law?' Then, he answered: 'It was enacted on account of transgressions, being

139

delivered by angels through a mediator, until the offspring should come to whom the promise was made. Now there is no intermediary where there is only one; but God is one.' And here an objection occurred which he proposed to himself: 'Is the Law then contrary to the promises of God?' And he answered: 'By no means!' and, giving his reason, said: 'For if a law had been given that could give life, justice would truly be from the Law. But the Scripture shut up all things under sin, that by the faith of Jesus Christ the promise might be given to those who believe, and so on. And similar examples could be cited. Therefore, it is the business of teaching not only to explain obscurities and settle the difficult points of questions, but also, while this is being done, to meet other questions which might possibly occur, so that they may not make void or disprove what we are saying. Care must be taken, however, that the answer to these difficulties occurs at the same time as the question, so that we may not stir up what we are unable to remove. Further, it happens that, when other questions arising from one question and others again arising from these are investigated and answered, the effort of reasoning is drawn out to such a length that, unless the disputant has a very powerful and vigorous memory, he cannot return to the original question. However, it is very beneficial to refute whatever objection can be made, if it occurs to the mind, so that it may not present itself at a place where there will not be anyone to answer it, or that it may not occur to someone who is indeed present, but who keeps silent about it and would go away uncorrected.

However, in the words of the Apostle which follow, the style is moderate: 'Do not rebuke an elderly man, but exhort him as you would a father, and young men as brothers, elderly women as mothers, younger women as sisters'; as it is in these words: 'I exhort you, therefore, brethren, by the mercy of God, to present your bodies as a sacrifice, living, holy, pleasing to God.' Almost the entire passage in which this exhortation occurs employs the moderate style of eloquence. There is more beauty in those portions where, as if in payment of a just debt, things that belong together proceed fittingly from one another; for example: 'But we have gifts differing according to the grace that has been given us, such as prophecy to be used according

to the proportion of faith; or ministry, in ministering; or he
who teaches, in teaching; or he who exhorts, in exhorting; he
who gives, in simplicity; he who presides, with carefulness; he
who shows mercy, with cheerfulness. Let love be without
pretence. Hate what is evil, hold to what is good. Love one
another with fraternal charity, anticipating one another with
honor. Be not slothful in zeal; be fervent in spirit serving the
Lord, rejoicing in hope. Be patient in tribulation, persevering in
prayer. Share the needs of the saints, practising hospitality.
Bless those who persecute you; bless and do not curse. Rejoice
with those who rejoice; weep with those who weep. Be of one
mind towards one another.' And how beautifully all these out-
pourings are brought to a close in a period of two *membra*: 'Do
not set your mind on high things but condescend to the lowly!'
And a little farther on he says: 'Persevering unto this very end,
render to all men whatever is their due; tribute to whom tribute
is due; taxes to whom taxes are due; fear to whom fear is due;
honor to whom honor is due.' After these have been poured
forth as *membra,* they are also concluded in a period formed
from two *membra:* 'Owe no man anything except to love one
another.' And a little later he says: 'The night is far advanced;
the day is at hand. Let us therefore lay aside the works of darkness, and put on the armor of light. Let us walk becomingly as
in the day, not in revelry and drunkenness, not in debauchery
and wantonness, not in strife and jealousy. But put on the Lord
Jesus Christ, and as for the flesh, take no thought for its lusts.'
But if someone were to express the last phrase this way: *et
carnis providentiam ne in concupiscentiis feceritis* (instead of
et carnis providentiam ne feceritis in concupiscentiis), unques-
tionably he would delight the ear with a more rhythmical
ending, but the stricter translator has preferred to keep even
the order of the words. How this would sound in the Greek
language in which the Apostle spoke, those whose skill in that
language is adequate for such questions would know. However,
it seems to me that what has been translated for us in the same
word order does not run on melodiously even in that language.

Indeed, we must admit that our writers lack this adorn-
ment of style which is produced by rhythmical endings. Whether
this was done by the translators or whether, as I consider more

likely, the authors themselves intentionally shunned such ostentation, I do not venture to assert, since I confess I do not know. However, I do know that if someone skilled in this rhythm should arrange the sentence endings of those writers according to the law of harmony, which is very easily accomplished by changing certain words which have the same meanings or by changing the order of those he finds there, he would see that these divinely inspired men lacked none of those qualities which he learned to regard as important in the schools of the grammarians and rhetoricians. Furthermore, he will find many examples of great beauty of style, which are elegant in our language, to be sure, but are especially so in the original, although we discover none of these in the writings of which they are so proud. We must be careful, however, not to detract from the authority of inspired and serious thoughts while we are adding rhythm. Our prophets were so far from lacking that musical training in which this harmony of prose is learned in its entirety, that Jerome, a very learned man, mentions even the meters of some of them, at least in the Hebrew language. In order to preserve the integrity of this language in regard to words, he did not transfer these meters from the original language. I, however (to offer my own opinion, which is naturally better known to me than to others and than the opinion of others is to me), while I do not neglect these rhythmical endings in my own speech within the limits of moderation, still I am more pleased that among our own writers I find them used very seldom.

Now, the grand style of eloquence differs from this moderate style principally in the fact that it is not so much embellished with fine expressions as it is forceful because of the passionate feelings of the heart. It adopts nearly all those ornaments of style, but it does not search for them if it does not have them at hand. In fact it is driven on by its own ardor and, if it chances upon any beauty of style, carries it off and claims it, not through a concern for beauty, but because of the force of the subject matter. It is sufficient for the purpose that appropriate words conform to the ardent affection of the heart; they need not be chosen by carefulness of speech. For, if a brave man, eagerly bent upon battle, is armed with a golden and jewel-studded sword, he certainly achieves whatever he does with these weapons, not because they are costly, but because they are weapons. Yet, he is the same man and is very powerful even when 'anger provides a weapon for him as he cast about for one.' The Apostle is endeavoring to persuade us, for the sake of the preaching of the Gospel, to endure patiently all the misfortunes of this life with the consoling help to the gifts of God. It is a noble subject delivered in the grand style, and it does not lack the ornaments of eloquence. 'Behold,' he says, 'now is the acceptable time; behold, now is the day of salvation! Giving no offense to anyone, that our ministry may not be blamed. On the contrary, conducting ourselves in all circumstances as God's ministers, in much patience; in tribulations, in hardships, in distresses; in stripes, in imprisonments, in tumults; in labors, in sleepless nights, in fastings; in innocence, in knowledge, in long-suffering; in kindness, in the Holy Spirit, in unaffected love; in the word of truth, in the power of God; with the armor of justice on the right hand and on the left; in honor and dishonor, in evil report and good report; as deceivers and and yet truthful, as unknown and yet we are well known, as dying and behold, we live, as chastised but not killed, as sorrowful yet always rejoicing, as poor yet enriching many, as having nothing yet possessing all things.' See him still aflame: 'We are frank with you. O Corinthians; our heart is wide open to you' and the rest which is too long to quote.

In the same way, he urges the Romans to overcome the persecutions of this world by charity with a sure hope in the help of God. He pleads in the grand style, and also with polish, as he says: 'We know that for those who love God all things work together unto good, for those who, according to his purpose, have been called. For those whom he has foreknown he has also predestined to become conformed to the image of his Son, that he should be the firstborn among many brethren. And those whom he has predestined, them he has also called; and those whom he has called, them he has also justified, and those whom he has justified, them he has also glorified. What then shall we say to these things? If God is for us, who is against us? He who has not spared even his own Son but has delivered him for us all, how can he fail to grant us also all things with

him? Who shall make accusations against the elect of God? Is
it God who justifies? Who shall condemn? Is it Christ Jesus who
died; yes, and rose again, he who is at the right hand of God,
who also intercedes for us? Who shall separate us from the love
of Christ? Shall tribulation, or distress, or persecution, or
hunger, or nakedness, or danger, or the sword? Even as it is
written, "For Thy sake we are put to death all the day long. We
are regarded as sheep for the slaughter." But in all these things
we overcome because of him who has loved us. For I am sure
that neither death, nor life, nor angels, nor principalities, nor
things present, nor things to come, nor powers, nor height, nor
depth, nor any other creature will be able to separate us from
the love of God, which is in Christ Jesus our Lord.'

Although the whole Epistle to the Galatians was written
in the subdued style of eloquence, except in the concluding
passages where the eloquence is moderate, he inserts one
passage of such passionate feeling that, although it lacks any
ornaments of style such as are found in those I have cited as
examples, it could only be expressed in the grand style. He
says: You are observing days and months and years and seasons.
I fear for you, lest perhaps I have labored among you in vain.
Become like me, because I also have become like you, brethren,
I beseech you! You have done me no wrong. And you know
that on account of a physical infirmity I preached the gospel to
you formerly; and though I was a trial to you in my flesh, you
did not reject or despise me; but you received me as an angel of
God, even as Christ Jesus. Where then is your self-congratu-
lation? For I bear you witness that, if possible, you would have
plucked out your very eyes and given them to me. Have I then
become your enemy, because I tell you the truth? They court
you from no good motive; but they would estrange you, that
you may court them. But court the good from a good motive
always, and not only when I am present with you, my dear
children, with whom I am in labor again, until Christ is formed
in you! But I wish I could be with you now, and change my
tone, because I do not know what to make of you.' In this passage have antithetical words balanced each other, have any
words been joined to one another in a climax, or did *caesa,
membra,* or periods ring in our ears? Nevertheless, not on that

account is there any diminution in the stirring emotion with
which we feel it vibrate.

Alcuin of York
735-804

Alcuin was born in Northumbria, England, and was educated in the cathedral school of York. He became librarian and teacher there in 778. In 781, while returning from a visit to Rome, he met Charlemagne at Parma, an event that determined the rest of his life. Charlemagne secured his services for the Frankish state, and for nearly a quarter of a century he was "the schoolmaster of the empire."

As the leading scholar in the court of Charlemagne, he left his mark on the theology, the liturgy, the preaching, the educational system, and the political order of his day. In 796, though not a professed monk, he was made abbot of the monastery of St. Martin of Tours where he numbered the most distinguished men of the day among his students.

Alcuin's liturgical reforms, part of Charlemagne's strategy to unify his broad domain, introduced several items of lasting impact, e.g., the chanting of the Creed at Mass and the celebration of the feast of All Saints. His interest in editing better Latin texts of all kinds gave an impetus to activity in Frankish scriptoria. All in all, he was the major force responsible for "the Carolingian renaissance."

The migration of populations referred to as the "barbarian invasions" had taken their toll as far as earlier Christian culture was concerned. Charlemagne brought an era of relative stability after widespread chaos involving incalculable destruction. The mood of the "revival" was understandably to look back beyond the disruption, to recover what could be salvaged from the more glorious past.

This manifests itself especially in regard to the Bible. The work of Alcuin that is presented here is typical. Originality is not to be looked for. The greatest service is rendered by passing on the riches amassed in better days. Thus, the best commentary is the one that most ingeniously copies the Fathers. In the case of his commentary on Titus, Alcuin lifts entire sentences, word for word, from Jerome. On the one hand, one can appreciate the great reverence and esteem felt for the great writers of old; but on the other hand, such a renaissance was adopting a built-in limitation, accepting with resignation from the start that there was little hope of progressing beyond what had been achieved long centuries ago.

The contribution of Alcuin and his contemporaries, therefore, is to be seen chiefly in keeping alive, in passing on, what might otherwise have been permanently lost. The marvel is that they did this so well in view of what we know about the chaotic conditions of the time.

COMMENTARY ON
THE EPISTLE TO TITUS

THE TEXT

PREFACE

This letter the apostle wrote from the city of Nicopolis, which is situated on the coast of Actium, to Titus, his pupil and son in Christ, whom he had left in the island of Crete to instruct the churches. For he did not wish the Cretans, from whom the seeds of idolatry first grew, to remain in his absence in ancient error. And though he asked Titus to come to him on account of the necessity of preaching, he directs Artemas and Tychicus to come there, so that by their teaching and support the Cretans might be encouraged.

CHAPTER 1

"Paul, a servant of God, yet an apostle of Christ Jesus": In the letter to the Romans he began thus: "Paul, a servant of Christ Jesus, called an apostle." In this one, however, he says that he is a servant of God, but an apostle of Christ Jesus. If the Father and the Son are one, and he who has believed in the Son believes in the Father, the status of servant in the case of the apostle Paul and of all saints must be referred without distinction to the Father or to the Son because one God is the Father and the Son, and is to be worshiped in one condition of servant. For this is the servitude of love, not of the letter of the law which kills but of the spirit which quickens. A servant of God is one who is not a slave of sin, because "everyone who does a sin is a servant of sin."

"Yet an apostle of Jesus Christ": Paul claims great authority for himself among Christians. He uses as title the phrase "apostle of Christ," so that from the very authority of the name he may strike terror into his readers, and arouse them to respect for his preaching, indicating that all who believe in Christ should be subordinated to himself.

"According to the faith of God's chosen and their knowledge of truth": This must be taken in reference to what is said above, "Paul, a servant of God, yet an apostle of Christ Jesus."

"According to the faith of God's chosen": That is, of those who are not only called but chosen. Of the chosen themselves there is great diversity in works, opinions, and words. Therefore, he added, "according to their knowledge," that is, those who possess a knowledge of truth according to faith. That both the true faith and the knowledge of truth may agree, he added, "which is in accordance with godliness," because some truth is not in accordance with godliness, like grammar, dialectic, geometry, and arithmetic, for these arts have to do with a true knowledge of proper discourse, but it is not a knowledge of godliness. A knowledge of godliness is to be acquainted with God's law, to understand the prophets, to believe the gospel, not to be ignorant of the words of the apostles, and, the greatest good, to love God with the whole heart, with the whole mind, and with all strength. This is the truth, the understanding of which is according to godliness, and is based

"On hope of eternal life," because whoever understands it, to him it grants the reward of immortality, and though without godliness a knowledge of truth gives pleasure for the present, yet it does not have the eternity of rewards, "which God who does not lie has promised ages ago," and

"Has manifested in his time" in Christ Jesus. Yet to whom has he long ago promised it and later made it clear, except to his wisdom which was always with the Father, since he rejoiced when the world was completed and was joyful over the sons of men, and again promised to those, whoever they were, who would believe in it that they would have eternal life? Before he laid the foundations of the world, before he poured forth the seas, raised up the mountains, hung aloft the sky, established the earth beneath, this was promised by God, in whom there is no deceit—not that he can lie, if he were unwilling to break forth into words of falsity, but that he who is the Father of truth and himself truthful can have no deceit in him.

Alcuin of York

Does it seem inappropriate to discuss briefly why God is alone truthful, and every man is, in the apostle's word, called a liar? And, if I make no mistake, as He alone is said to possess immortality, though he has made the angels and many reasoning creatures to whom he has given immortality, so he alone is said to be truthful, not because the other immortals are not lovers of the truth, but because he alone is immortal and true by nature. But let the others acquire immortality and truth from his gift: it is one thing to be true and to have it by nature and of oneself, another thing to be subject to the power of the one who gives you what you possess. But we must not pass over in silence how God who does not lie has promised eternal life endless ages ago. By him, according to the story in Genesis, the world was made, and through the changes of nights and days, likewise of months and years, seasons were established, in this journey and rotation of the earth the seasons pass away and come again—and either will be or have been. Thus it is that certain of the philosophers do not think that time is present but that it is either past or future; that everything we speak, do, think, either while it takes place passes away, or if it has not yet been done is still awaited. Therefore, before these times of the world, one must believe there was an eternity of ages in which the Father with the Son and the Holy Spirit always existed, and, as I say, all eternity is a single time of God; indeed, there are countless times, since he himself is infinite who before the times exceeds all times. Not yet has our world existed six thousand years, and how many eternities and how many times before the beginnings of the centuries must one think there were in which angels, thrones, powers, and other forces served the Creator and existed, by God's order, without change and measurements of times. Before all these times which neither does speech dare to utter, nor the mind to comprehend, nor thought to touch upon in silence, God the Father promised his Word to his Wisdom that that very Wisdom of his, and the life of those who would believe, should come into the world. Pay careful attention to the text and the order of the reading, how life eternal, which God who does not lie promised eternal ages ago, is not different from God's Word.

"He manifested, in his own times, his own Word": that is, this eternal life he promised is itself his Word which in the beginning was with the Father, and God was the Word, and the Word was made flesh and dwelt among us. That this Word of God, that is, Christ himself, is life, is witnessed in another passage which says, "I am life." But life that is not short, not limited by any times, but everlasting, eternal, which has been made manifest in most recent ages through the preaching which was entrusted to Paul, the doctor and teacher of the Gentiles, that it should be proclaimed in the world and became known to men, in accordance with the command of God the Saviour, who has willed us to be saved by fulfilling what had been promised.

"In the preaching which was entrusted to me according to the command of God our Saviour": We read in The Acts of the Apostles how Paul, while hastening to Damascus, was suddenly called and how Ananias said of him, "This is my chosen vessel." And again, "Separate for me Paul and Barnabas." That they should preach Christ to the Gentiles was the command of the Saviour. The word, wisdom, and teaching in which Titus was instructing the churches of Christ, made him, of course, the apostle's own son, and separated from anything shared in by others. Let us see what follows after that:

"According to a common faith": Did he mean a faith shared by all who believed in Christ or shared only by himself and Titus? It appears to me better to take this as meaning the faith shared in by Paul and Titus than as the faith of all believers among whom, on account of the diversity of minds, faith could not be common but different.

Finally, the preface of the letter and the preface's greeting of the apostle to Titus are ended in this way:

"Grace and peace from God the Father and Christ Jesus our Saviour": This can be taken to mean either that grace and peace are from God the Father as well as from Christ Jesus, both being given by both, or grace may be taken with reference to the Father and peace with reference to the Son.

"This is why I left you in Crete, that you might correct what was lacking": It was an apostolic prerogative to lay the foundation like a wise architect, but it was the task of Titus and his other disciples to build on it. After Paul had softened the hard hearts of the Cretans by leading them to faith in Christ and had tamed them both by speech and by signs, with the result that they believed in God the Father and in Christ, he left his disciple Titus in Crete to strengthen the knowledge of the growing church, and if anything seemed to be lacking, to amend it, and he himself hastened on to other nations that again he might lay the foundation of Christ in them. They had, of course, been corrected by the apostle, yet they still needed corrections, for everything which is corrected is uncompleted.

"And that you should appoint presbyters in the cities as I directed you": There are, however, bishops who do not consider the merits of individuals but are cajoled by their entourage or are related to them by ties of kinship. From this it is clear that they who, having despised the law of the apostle, have been willing that ecclesiastical rank be conferred on anyone, not according to merit but out of favoritism, are acting against Christ, who has prescribed what sort of person should be appointed presbyter in the church through the words of his apostle in the following passages. Beyond all these the greatest evil is those who obtain clerical office through bribery: the blessed Peter, prince of apostles at the beginning of the church, strikes out terribly against these in the person of Simon Magus.

"For a bishop ought to be blameless, as a steward of God": The same man is, therefore, a presbyter who is also a bishop; and before, at the devil's instigation, there arose partisan differences of religion in the church, and among the people it was said, "I am of Paul, I am of Apollos, or I am of Cephas," churches were governed by the common counsel of the elders. But after each one thought that those whom he had baptized were his own and not Christ's, it was decided over the whole earth that one of the elders should be chosen to be placed over the others and to him the whole care of the church should belong and the seeds of schisms be destroyed. This can be proved from other letters of the same apostle, and also from The Acts of the Apostles, in which it is said that Paul called the presbyters from Ephesus, to whom afterward he said among other things, "Take heed to yourselves and to all the flock in which the Holy Spirit has made you bishops to feed the church of the Lord which he obtained with his blood." Those he called presbyters before he now calls bishops. And Peter, who got his name from the steadfastness of his faith, in his letter says, "So I exhort the presbyters among you as a fellow presbyter and witness of Christ's sufferings: feed the Lord's flock which is in your charge." Formerly every presbyter was rightly called a bishop, but now every bishop can be called a presbyter, not every presbyter a bishop, because in order to exclude the hotbeds of dissension, the whole care of the churches has been entrusted to one, as to a father who loves his children and governs those who are subject to him, not with the imperial power but with paternal piety. Let them, like sons, of each rank in the churches, show respect to their bishops. Let us see, then, what sort of presbyter or bishop should be ordained.

"If any man is blameless, the husband of one wife, having children who are believers and not open to the charge of profligacy or not slaves to sin. For a bishop ought to be blameless, as a steward of God": First, let him be a blameless steward of Christ's church of the sort which in Timothy he calls "above reproach." For how can anyone be in charge of the church and ward off evil from its midst who has rushed into a like fault? Or with what freedom can he correct a sinner when he knows that he has admitted into himself what he reproves in another. We must understand the phrase "husband of one wife" to mean that he who must be chosen to the episcopate should have a respectable marriage, that one befouled with wandering lust should not dare to take his place at God's altar. Not that we think, however, that every man who has had but one wife is better than a man who has had two, but that he can in his teaching exhort others to observe monogamy and continence who displays his own example. There are those who understand this commandment of the apostle ("husband of one wife," that is) to mean "teacher of the catholic church," not to be carried abroad through heretical errors through the brothels of the different sects. But certain people also think that this apostolic decree forbids bishops to go out from the church or from the city to a church in quest of gain. Because it is a rare man who wants to pass from a greater and a richer to a lesser and a poorer status.

"Having children who are believers and not open to the charge of profligacy or not slaves to sin": The righteous man is not thereby defiled from the faults of his children but freedom of reproving others is reserved by the apostle for the ruler of the church. How can one remove another's particle of dust from another's house if one has in the sins of one's children a beam in one's own house? For a bishop ought to be such a man as not to be afraid to reprove other people on account of his own children's faults, lest by chance some brother may quietly answer, "Why don't you take the trouble to reprove your own children?" For if the sins of his children disqualify the righteous man from the episcopate, how must more ought they to disqualify him from removing his own sins from Christ's altar? Finally, it should be said that in the Scriptures sons should be thought of as *logismos,* that is, as thoughts, but daughters as *praxeis,* that is, as works, and he now is commanding that that man should be made bishop who is keeping his thoughts and works under his own control and truly believes in Christ and is spotted by no stain of secret faults.

"A bishop, therefore, ought to be blameless, as a steward of God": Among the stewards, then, one is sought for who is found faithful and, not eating and drinking with the drunken, may strike at the servants and handmaidens of his Lord; but let him wisely await the unknown day of the Lord's coming and give meanwhile to his fellow servants the food of catholic doctrine. Let the bishop and the presbyter know that the people are not his servants but his fellow servants. For this reason let him not dominate them as common slaves but let him teach them with all love as sons.

"Not arrogant": That is, not puffed up or pleased with himself at being a bishop, but one embracing good works and seeking that which contributes to the good of most.

"Not wrathful": That is, as a leaf hanging on a branch is moved by a light wind. And nothing is really more disgraceful than a wrathful teacher; for he who at times is angry is not full of anger, but he really is called full of anger who is frequently conquered by this passion.

"Not a drunkard": But now it is enough to have said that, according to the apostle, there is profligacy in wine, and wherever there is gluttony and drunkenness, there lust rules. We are surprised that the apostle condemned drunkenness among bishops and presbyters, since in the old law there was also a commandment that priests when entering the Temple to minister to God should drink no wine at all. The Nazarites are also to abstain from all wine and strong drink, while they let their holy hair grow long.

"Not violent": This may be taken in a simple sense that he may edify the mind of his hearer to keep him from quickly stretching forth his hand to slaughter or to rush to arms; or, more subtly and better, that the bishop may do nothing to offend the minds of those who understand and see, but that he may be calm of speech, pure of character, and not destroy the one whom the moderation of his life and his words could teach.

"Not greedy for gain": Seeking for such is to think more about things present than things to come. A bishop who is desirous of being an imitator of the apostle should be content, when he has food and clothing, with only these. Let those who serve the altar live from the altar. "Let them live," he says, not "let them become rich." Up to this point the apostle's words have been prescribing what a bishop or presbyter ought not to have; now, on the contrary, what he ought to have is explained.

"But, hospitable, kind": Above everything, hospitality is prescribed for one who is to be a bishop, for if everybody wants to hear from the Gospel this: "I was a stranger and you took me in," how much more should a bishop, whose house ought to be a common guesthouse and in it those pilgrims who come should be kindly received, so that even their feet should be washed in humble duty?

"Chaste, just, holy": If laymen are ordered on account of prayer to refrain from intercourse with their wives, what should be thought of the bishop who is to offer spotless sacrifices of holy prayers daily for his sins and those of the people? For Abimelech the priest refused to give to David and his boys the display bread unless he should hear that the boys were clean from women—not only from other men's women but their own. There is as much difference between the display bread and Christ's body as between shadow and bodies, between a picture and its reality, between foreshadowings of future events and the events of which they are the foreshadowings. As, then, the virtue of hospitality, kindness, ought peculiarly to be in a bishop, so, also, chastity and, as I said, modesty are the proper marks of a priest, so that he not only should abstain from unclean acts but also [see] that the mind that is to make the body of Christ be free from unlawful touch and thought of error. A bishop ought to be just and holy, and to practice justice among the people over whom he is placed, and not to show any respect of persons in his judgment but decide justly for every person; and holy with respect to his life, so as not only to teach with words, but also to instruct the people entrusted to him by his example.

"Self-controlled, holding firm to that faithful word which is according to doctrine": It befits a bishop to be abstinent, not only in carnal desire but even in the moderation of his speech, and in particular in his thought, that he keep under control what he thinks, what he speaks, and what he does. Finally, let him acquire that "faithful word which is according to doctrine," [that] as he is in some sense the faithful word of God and worthy of every acceptance, he may also display himself in such a manner so that everything he says may be thought worthy of belief and that his words may be the rule of truth.

"So that he may be able to give instruction in sound doctrine and confute those who contradict it": That is, he may be able to comfort those who are tossed about in the tempests of this life, and through sound doctrine, that is, catholic doctrine, destroy heretical wickedness. Doctrine is called sound in opposition to doctrine that is weak and feeble. It is of such a character that it can confute freely those heretics who speak against it, whether Jews or the wise ones of this world. The higher matters, which he places on the virtues of a bishop, involve a life that is honorable, but when he says "so that he may be able to give instruction in sound doctrine and confute those who contradict it," this must be taken with reference to perfect knowledge, because if only the life of the bishop is holy, living so, he can be of profit to himself, but if he be instructed in doctrine and the word, he can also teach others, and not only teach and instruct his own, but even strike at his opponents.

"There are also many insubordinate men, empty talkers and deceivers, especially those who are of the circumcision, who ought to be confuted, who are upsetting whole houses, teaching what they ought not, for the sake of base gain": He who is to be first in the church, let him have eloquence accompanied by integrity of life. lest his works without speech be silent, and his saying blush at his wicked deeds. There are many and not a few who corrupt the good seed of God's Word with empty argumentation. They also strive to support their wicked doctrine with quotations of the Holy Scriptures twisted about. So it befits the teacher of the church diligently to learn the Holy Scriptures, so that if struck on the right cheek, he may at once turn the other toward the striker. These are the Jews of the circumcision who then tried to overthrow the nascent church of Christ and to bring in the teaching of the law, namely, circumcision and the Sabbath and other teachings from the law. Such men the teacher of the church, to whom the souls of the people have been entrusted, ought to master by means of the Scriptures and to silence them by weight of witnesses. They are upsetting, not one or a few homes, but all the families with their masters, teaching about differences of foods, when all foods are clean to the clean. But since their "god is their belly," for the sake of base gain they wish to make their own disciples, so that, as if they were schoolteachers, let them be received and honored by their followers. So every heretic who deceives men by any tricks, and is deceived, speaks what he should not for the sake of base gain. The gainer is perverse to the death of souls, not to their life. On the other hand, the one who rebukes, in accordance with the gospel, his wandering brother, and corrects him, has gained him. What can be greater gain or what can be more precious than if anyone gains a human soul for God?

"A certain one of them, a prophet of their own, has said, 'Cretans are always liars, evil beasts, lazy bellies' ": Notice that this must be said twice: what he says here: "A certain one of them, a prophet of their own, has said," is coupled with the passage above, "This is why I left you in Crete, that you might correct what was lacking," and to it refers the phrase, "A certain one of them, a prophet of their own, has said," that is, of the Cretans. Or it must be joined to the passage just preceding, "There are also many insubordinate men, empty talkers and deceivers, especially those who are of the circumcision." These many insubordinate men, empty talkers and deceivers of minds, together with those who are of the circumcision, ought to be bridled, these upsetters of whole houses, teaching what they ought not, for the sake of base gain. Of such people, that is, of those who teach for the sake of base gain, a certain one of them, a prophet of their own, has said—the phrase "a prophet of their own" should be referred, not especially to the Jews and to those particularly who are of the circumcision, but to the many who are insubordinate, empty talkers and deceivers of minds, who, of course, because they were in Crete, must be believed to be Cretans. For this verse is said to be found in the *Oracles* of the Cretan poet Epimenides, whom in the present passage, by a pun, he called a prophet. Such Christians, of course, deserve to have such prophets in the same way as there were prophets of Baal and of idols, as one reads in the books of Kings. Finally, that book from which the apostle took this bears the title of *Oracles*. Because it seems to imply some sort of divination is what, I think, the apostle looked at to see what pagan divination it should promise, and he misapplied the verse when he was writing to Titus, who was in Crete, so that he might refute the false teachers of the Cretans on the authority of one from their own island. The apostle is found to have done this same thing in other places, as in The Acts of the Apostles, finding an inscription "To an unknown God," he took from this something serviceable for his preaching.

"The testimony is true": Not the whole poem from which the testimony is taken, not the whole work, but only this testimony.

"Therefore, rebuke them harshly, that they be sound in faith, not paying attention to Jewish myths or the commands of men who turn from the truth": He says, Rebuke them harshly since they are liars and evil beasts and lazy bellies, who argue for what is untrue, who like wild animals thirst for the blood of people they have deceived, and not working in silence eat their bread, "whose god is their belly and whose glory is their shame." Such as these "rebuke that they be sound in faith," concerning which soundness of faith he speaks in the following passages: The old men are to be temperate, serious, modest, sound in faith and love and patience. Concerning this soundness of faith he writes also to Timothy, "If any man teaches otherwise and does not agree that the words of our Lord Jesus Christ are sound": He calls them sound words, and [says] that in those who keep them soundness works.

"Not paying attention to Jewish myths or the commands of men who turn from the truth": Concerning them he discusses at great length to the Galatians, and the Romans, who thought that there was a difference between foods, since some seem to be clean, some unclean. Therefore, now he continues:

"All things are clean to the clean": That is, to those who believe in Christ, and know that every creature is good and that nothing should be rejected which is received with thanksgiving.

"To the defiled, however, and to the unclean nothing is clean, but unclean is their mind and conscience": Therefore, what is unclean by nature becomes unclean to them through fault, not because something is clean or unclean, but on account of the character of the eaters. Food that is lawful and customary in the catholic church is clean to the clean, unclean to the defiled whose mind and conscience are unclean; so any unfaithful and defiled persons are not helped even by the bread of benediction or the Lord's cup, but are made even more defiled, because anyone who eats unworthily of that bread or drinks from the cup, eats and drinks to his own condemnation. So it is in us to eat either clean or unclean things, for if we are clean, the creature is clean for us; if we are unclean and unfaithful, everything becomes common for us, whether by the heresy dwelling in our hearts or by consciousness of sins.

"They profess to know God but deny it by their deeds for they are detestable, unreliable, unsound with respect to every good deed": According to what is said in Isaiah, "This people honors me with their lips, but their heart is far from me." In the way that anyone honors with lips and goes far away in his heart, so anyone who professes God in speech denies him in works. One denying God in works, having pretended to profess him, is properly detestable and profane, and one who has been persuaded without true reason, and is disobedient, is properly called unreliable. The corrupt of mind will deny Christ, not only in witnessing, but as often as we are conquered by vices and sins, and act contrary to God's commandments, so often we deny God, and, conversely, as often as we do well, we profess God and praise him.

CHAPTER 2

"Show yourself a model of good deeds": There is no use for anyone to be practiced in oratory and to have his tongue worn out in speaking, unless he teaches more by example than by word.

"In doctrine, in integrity": In "doctrine," he says, so that you may fulfill with work what you teach with your mouth. But "integrity" pertains more properly to virginity, whence another translation has "in incorruption," for virgins are called uncorrupted.

"In gravity, sound speech that cannot be censured": It is befitting that a teacher of the church have gravity, that is, good character. Reference has been made above to sound speech.

"That cannot be censured": We speak in this instance, not of anyone so eloquent or wise as to be beyond censure by anyone, but of one who has done nothing or said nothing worthy of censure, though his opponents stand ready to censure.

"So that a man from the opposite party may be afraid, having nothing bad to say against us": Let the man from the opposite party, that is, the adversary, have nothing true or resembling the truth to object to, however ready he may be to censure. This man from the opposite party can be taken to be the devil, who is the accuser of our brothers, as the Evangelist John says, who, when he has nothing evil to object to in us, blushes, and the accuser cannot accuse. For in Greek "devil" is the same as "accuser."

"Slaves to be subject to their masters, pleasing them in every respect, not contradictory, not cheating, but exhibiting good faith in every respect": Since the Lord our Saviour, who in the Gospel says, "Come to me, all of you who labor and are heavily laden and I will give you rest," thinks no condition, age, or sex foreign to blessedness, for this reason, now, the apostle establishes directions even for slaves, that is to say, when they are made a member of the church, which is Christ's body, and they pursue eternal salvation itself. And what Titus ought to teach, did teach, the old men, old women, young women, young men, above, so now he has established as directions for the slaves. First, that they be obedient to their masters in all things; in all things, however, which are not contrary to God; so that if a master gives orders which are not opposed to holy Scripture, let them be subject to their master in servitude, but if he commands what is contrary, let them obey the spirit rather than the body.

"Pleasing": This is to be taken in two senses, that is, pleasing themselves in their slavery, and also pleasing their masters, completing faithfully and in humility everything which they are ordered to do.

"Not contradictory": He says this because the worst fault in slaves is to contradict their masters and to grumble when they order anything. For if a slave must of necessity fulfill what a master orders, why should he not do this agreeably?

"Not stealing": This is another fault of slaves which Christian teaching corrects, but a thief is condemned, not only in major matters but also in lesser. In a theft, it is not what is carried off that receives the attention but the mind of the one who does the stealing. So let the slaves be subject to their masters in all things. Let them be satisfied with their state so as to bear their servitude with equanimity, not to contradict their masters, not to steal, and after that "to show good faith in all things that in all things they may adorn the doctrine of God our Saviour." For if under the masters of their flesh they are faithful in a very small matter, they will begin under the Lord to have greater matters entrusted to them. He adorns the Lord's doctrine who does those things which are products of his condition. How can anyone be faithful in God's property and in churchly duty who cannot display reliability toward a master after the flesh?

"For the grace of God our Saviour has appeared for all men, training us to renounce irreligion and worldly passions, to live soberly, uprightly, and piously in this life, awaiting our blessed hope and the coming of the glory of our great God and

Alcuin of York

Saviour Jesus Christ, who gave himself for us, to redeem us from all iniquity, and to purify a people acceptable to himself who are zealous for all good deeds": After the list of teachings for Titus, what training he ought to give the old men, the old women, the young women and the young men, finally, even the slaves, he rightly now continues: "For the grace of God the Saviour has appeared for all men." There is no other difference of free or slave, Greek or barbarian, circumcised or uncircumcised, woman or man, but with Christ, we are all one, we are all called to God's Kingdom. When we have sinned, we must be reconciled to our Father, not through our own merits but through the Saviour's grace, either because Christ himself is the living and existing grace of God the Father, and we have not been saved by our own merit, as is said in another passage, "You will save them for nothing," This grace has therefore shown forth upon all men, to "train them to renounce irreligion, worldly passions, to live soberly, uprightly, and piously in this life." What to renounce irreligion, worldly passions, is, I am sure can be understood from our explanation given above: "They profess to know God but they deny him by their deeds." Worldly passions, therefore, are what are piled up from the beginning of this life, and since they are lovers of this world, they pass away completely with the cloud of this world. Since we, however, shall live in Christ modestly and uprightly, sinning, of course, neither in body or mind, let us live piously also in this life. This piety awaits "the blessed hope and coming of the glory of the great God and our Saviour Jesus Christ." For as irreligion avoids in fear the coming of the great God, so confidently from its own work and faith piety awaits him. Where is that serpent Arius, where that sinewy snake Eunomius? The great God is called Christ the Saviour, not the firstborn or every creature, not God's Word and Wisdom, but Jesus Christ, which are the names of the One who assumed humanity. Nor are we speaking of another Jesus Christ, another Word, as the Nestorian heresy falsely alleges, but the same one both before the ages and in the ages and before the world, and through Mary—no, from Mary— we call the great God, our Saviour Jesus Christ, who gave himself for us, that by his precious blood he might redeem us from

163

all iniquity, and purify a people acceptable to himself who are zealous for good works, that is, who imitate them.

"Speak these things and exhort": It appears that the word "speak" should be referred to doctrine, and the added word "exhort" refers to comforting, but he continues further with, "Reprove with all authority," that is, whoever does not listen to doctrine and comforting is worthy of reproof and deserves to hear, "You have forgotten the comforting which God speaks to you as sons."

"Let no one disregard you": The sense is: Let no one of those who are in the church live, through your slothful action, so that he thinks himself better. What sort of edification will there be in a disciple if he takes himself to be greater than his teacher? For this reason bishops, elders, and deacons ought to be very vigilant to excel in character and speech all the people over whom they preside.

Rupert of Deutz
d. 1130

Rupert was born sometime in the last quarter of the 11th century and raised in the Benedictine abbey of St. Lawrence in Liège. He was ordained a priest around 1106 and transferred to the abbey of Siegburg. Then in 1119 or 1120 he was elected abbot of Deutz, where he remained until his death.

From an early age he wrote abundantly: poems, hymns, chronicles, biographies, biblical commentaries, and liturgies. It tells us something about the changing spirit of the age when we hear that Rupert was attacked for all this literary activity, on the grounds that the writings of the "holy fathers" ought to suffice without all these new works by unknown and insignificant people. He was also involved in disputes over his theology, one concerning the Eucharist and another concerning predestination.

Three centuries separate Rupert from Alcuin. The promise of the Carolingian renaissance did not materialize. European civilization declined to the point that some consider the 10th century the darkest age of all. But with Rupert and several of his contemporaries, it is obvious that something is afoot. Biblical interpretation is beginning to show new life. "Rupert's works show his extensive learning in the classical, Biblical, and patristic fields. Although in common with most scholars, he has a penchant for the citation of authorities, he demonstrates nonetheless a high degree of independence in his thought. His Victory of God's Word, *for instance, has some of the vast sweep of Augustine's* City of God, *but with a different and quite interesting point of view. Rupert recounts, not a tale of two cities, but a mighty warfare between the Second Person of the Trinity and the proud old serpent, a tale of incredibly powerful foes locked in an age-old struggle. The line of battle stretches from the fall of Lucifer to the final victory of the Word at the end of historical time."* *(McCracken).*

It is unnecessary to dwell upon the fact that much is still to be learned about the use of the Bible in the Middle Ages. It is a field that too little attention has yet been given to, but it is clear that we have much to learn from these men whose works have remined all too obscure. When justice is done to their achievement, the name of Rupert may well occupy a quite different position among Christian historians than has hitherto been the case.

THE VICTORY
OF GOD'S WORD

When the charge was made before Pilate concerning use of the royal title as though it were a great crime, our king, gracious and humble of heart, absolved himself with these words; "My kingship is not of this world; if my kingship were of this world, my servants would surely fight, that I might not be handed over to the Jews; but my kingship is not from here." With the same gracious lips he could have said: "If my kingship were of this world, a horse or chariot would have been brought for me, not the ass upon which I sat three days ago. Those who acclaimed me as king would have displayed accouterments of warlike weapons, not branches of olive trees. And if they should not suffice, I would have asked my Father and he would have offered just now more than twelve legions of angels." He could have said also, "After the distribution of the five loaves among five thousand men, when I became alarmed that they might seize me because of the miracle and force me to be king over them, I would not have fled from them, if it were not true that my kingship is not of this world." In reply to Pilate he could have declared these things, I say, and many others like them as arguments for his innocence who wished no harm to Caesar. He could have done so if Pilate had not been deaf and if it had not been foretold of him, "Do not pour out your words where there is no hearing." He reserved these things to be understood by us, and it is our duty to rebuke his adversaries even though they are dead, because he did not destroy human kingdoms, because he gives heavenly kingdoms, and because their own craftiness deceived them who wished to be deceived, and wickedness lied to them when they said, "We found this man forbidding tribute to be given to Caesar." He did not make himself such a king, nor did he so gainsay Caesar. Quite the contrary, he says, "Render to Caesar the things that are Caesar's, and to God the things that are God's."

10. What more shall we say? It was necessary for him to die, and the dragon so often mentioned was standing there, was dwelling there, was waiting there for him to die, because he thought that he was His doom. He thought, I say, that through death he could devour Him, could annihilate the counsel and purpose of God, so that what had been foretold might not come to pass ("He shall be the long-awaited hope of the Gentiles," and, "In him shall all nations be blessed"), which, however, he already fears, since Christ says to the Jews, "You will seek me and you will not find me; and where I am you cannot come." (He was speaking in answer to the question they were whispering to each other, "Where does this man intend to go that we shall not find him? Does he intend to go to the dispersion among the nations and teach the nations?") The psalmist sang the truth: "That dragon which thou didst form to sport in it," and the Lord himself spoke of it to blessed Job: "Will you play with him as with a bird?" Again: "Behold, his hope will disappoint him." Truly he was played with or mocked, his hope did disappoint him, since in dying Christ was devoured in vain; rather, when he was devoured, it came to pass by that death, and except through that death it could not have come to pass, for him to go to the dispersion of the nations and teach them.

Let us examine the sacraments, through which according to the promise of all nations have been and shall be blessed in him. Against that dragon we shall marvel at the magnitude of the mockery for the praise of God who formed him to jeer at Him, for when the dragon wishes to oppose, he is enslaved by God's purpose, and when he thinks that he will devour so great a Son of the blessed woman, he fulfills a very effective compliance with His plan.

11. What and how many are the chief sacraments of our salvation? Holy Baptism, the holy Eucharist of His body and blood, and the twofold gift of the Holy Spirit, one for the remission of sins, the other for the bestowal of differing and multiple graces. These *three* sacraments are the necessary means of our salvation; yet these were not to be found or were not found except through his death and resurrection. First, concerning the

sacrament of Baptism we believe and know that it flowed from his death when he was presumed to have been devoured, that is, when he was already dead. For, says the Evangelist, "when they came to Jesus and saw that he was already dead, they did not break his legs. But one of the soldiers pierced his side with a spear, and at once there came out blood and water." Redeemed by that blood, we, Jews as well as Gentiles, are washed by that water, the Jews first, then the Gentiles—or rather, the dead first, then the living. For all believers who had died since the beginning of the world and who among the dead were awaiting the blessed hope were the first to receive the fruit of this salvation. They were like catechumens who had not yet participated at the heavenly altar (that is, in the vision of the Godhead), because the wall of hostility had not yet been removed. "And so," they say, "we too were once by nature children of wrath, like the others," and, "All our righteous deeds are like a polluted garment." Then, however, washed and made clean by that torrent, they entered God's sanctuary, God's Kingdom, which is entirely holy. Since the whole church of all past ages together was baptized at that time, this sacrament has been appointed as though at the door of the same church, so that whoever thereafter wished to be incorporated in the church may be baptized on his own behalf, since the church was at once completely baptized in Christ's death. For the sacrament of Christ's death is present and effectual when water has been used and the word of the cross spoken, together with invocation of the Holy Spirit. Wherefore the apostle says, "All of us who have been baptized in Christ Jesus were baptized in his death," etc.

There was a long-lasting dispute of the holy Roman church against the practice of the Greeks who wish to require the solemn celebration of the sacrament of Baptism to take place on the feast of Epiphany on the ground that the Lord Himself was baptized by John in the waters of the Jordan on that day. The Roman church, through Leo the Great who wrote against that, demonstrates with reason that the baptism of John did not relate to the same virtue, that it was not for remission of sins but for repentance; that the baptism instituted by Christ took its origin in His death, when (as we have already observed) his side was pierced by the lance and when blood and water came forth. This sacrament, therefore, should be celebrated on the anniversary of His death and resurrection.

12. Concerning the sacrament of the Lord's body and blood, it is certain—our statement is really unnecessary—that it is indeed the special and unique commemoration of his suffering and death, and that it had and properly should have had its origin in his suffering and death. This sacrament, indeed, was established as near his death as possible, when he had already been given up to death, on the night on which he was betrayed. For us who now live and still remain, that sacrament has been preserved and transmitted wherein the advantage of his death and resurrection lies hidden under the species of bread and wine. But for those believers who have died, the food has been prepared and bestowed in a marvelous way in that very species wherein he hung on the cross, even as his soul went down to their souls in Hades and his body to their bodies, and was for three days and three nights in in the heart of the earth, in the same womb of earth where their bodies had been admitted and received.

Of this very great mystery we do not now propose to treat any longer, yet that it may not be left entirely untouched it is appropriate to say something about the reason why it is necessary to us. This was the reason: The first humans were unfaithful to God and, far more wickedly, were believers in the devil. When they did not see anything except the apple, so pleasantly sweet, fragrant, and beautiful, they believed that from it they would secure the quality of divinity; they believed the devil when he said, "It will not indeed be as God said, 'If you shall eat, you shall die the death.' But it will be as I say, 'If you shall eat, you shall be as gods.' " Over against that food, the food of death, as reason insists, it was necessary for righteousness that another food be provided, the food of life. In like manner it was necessary so that the mind might believe to be present what the eye could not see, might believe it to be truly the food and drink of participation in divinity, might believe it to be effectually the flesh and blood of Christ, although they cannot perceive the appearance of flesh and blood. By this faith, God deems that he has been satisfied by man when he believes in him not less than he formerly believed in the devil.

13. Who does not know that all we who believe receive or have received, through the death of Christ and his blood, the gift of the Holy Spirit, first for the remission of sins? For that reason, on the day when he arose from the dead, late on that same day, he, standing in the midst of his disciples, "breathed on them, and said, 'Receive the Holy Spirit.' " Then he added immediately, "Whose sins you remit, they are remitted to them." Later, on the fiftieth day, they received the second gift of the Holy Spirit for the distribution of graces, which the apostle recalled when he wrote to the Corinthians, "To one is given through the Spirit the utterance of wisdom, to another the utterance of knowledge," etc. The gifts are the kind of which it is written, "When he ascended on high he led captivity captive, he gave gifts to men." Of them the better ones are these: "He appointed some to be apostles, some prophets, some evangelists, some pastors and teachers."

These are the consolations of the Paraclete, of which He told them when he was about to go away: "Because I have said these things to you, sorrow has filled your heart. Nevertheless I tell you the truth: it is to your advantage that I go away, for if I shall not go away, the Paraclete will not come to you; but if I shall go away, I will send him to you." The phrase, "If I shall go away," is of course rightly understood as though he might have said, "If I shall ascend into heaven," or, "If I shall remove my bodily presence from you." Although they did not have to be sad about his ascension—quite the contrary, they rejoiced with great delight, as Luke recalled when he wrote, "Worshiping him they returned to Jerusalem with great joy," yet they were very sorrowful about his suffering. For "because I have said these things to you," he states, "sorrow has filled your heart." It is therefore more accurately understood that he spoke of his suffering and death when he spoke of going away, for so the Evangelist sought to make clear when he remarked: "Before the festal day of the Passover, when Jesus knew that his hour had come to depart out of this world to the Father. . . ." For did he not then first depart from this world rather than when dead and risen again he ceased to walk with men and endure earthly labors?

14. These three things had to be, and because of these his death was necessary for the nations, since these are the blessings

171

by which all nations are to be blessed in that seed which is Christ. This the great dragon did not know who thought that through death he could devour that Son, that man. He did not know, I say—that is, they over whom he presided did not know—of whom Wisdom speaks, "These things they imagined, yet erred; their own iniquity blinded them, and they knew not the mysteries of God." The apostle says, "Had they understood this (that is, the wisdom which is from God, which we impart among the mature), they would never have crucified the Lord of glory." It is absolutely true that if leviathan, the great whale which is in the sea, had known that under the flesh an iron hook was hidden, he would never have bitten that flesh with which the iron is concealed. He knew that Jesus was indeed the Christ, the Son of God, and that he had come to save the human race, but he did not know the secret hidden from the world, the plan of God's wisdom, that by the death of one the life of all should be renewed. Christ knew his own plan, but it was hidden from all the ages and indeed so inconceivable to the minds of men that the very apostles comprehended none of these things, although he discussed them privately with them (as the holy Gospels declare in a great many places), since it was not yet time for them to understand before he was glorified in the splendor of the resurrection.

15. Who, then, does understand? Who feels with deepest love what disposition was in the mind of that Son of Man when the woman so often mentioned gave birth to him, while the dragon waited so long to devour him (that is, while evil men waited to destroy his body), to blot out his name? If you can count rightly, he [the dragon] waited seven times with mouth yawning wide, he opened his savage jaws seven times. Disappointed six times, at length the seventh he seized His flesh in his jaw, but to his own hurt, for as we have said above he felt the very offensive iron in that flesh. The *first* attempt of the dragon was when, according to Matthew, cruel Herod sought the life of the new-born babe and because of him slew the infants, as already mentioned above. The *second* was when, according to Luke, he came to Nazareth, where he had grown up, and taught in the synagogue: "They rose up and put him out of the city; they led him to the brow of the hill on which their city was built, that

they might hurl him down headlong, but passing through the midst of them he went away.

The *third* was when, according to John, he fled from the presence of the Jews who mocked his statement, "Unless you shall eat the flesh of the Son of man and drink his blood, you will not have everlasting life." For truly, by saying those things, he did flee and hide himself from them, according to the title of the Thirty-third Psalm, which reads thus: "A Psalm of David, when he changed his appearance before Abimelech, who sent him away, and he departed and drummed on the doors of the city gate and spittle ran down on his beard and he was borne away in his own hands." Abimelech is the one who was earlier called Achish. Abimelech means "My Father's kingdom"; but Achish, "How is it?" What "Abimelech" therefore means signifies the Jews, whom Christ at first rightly called his Father's Kingdom. But now they are called "Achish," because they said, "How can this be?"

Wherein did He change his appearance before them? It was herein: he changed the rite of the old sacrifice into a new one. Herein also the spittle ran down his beard: when he said, "Unless you shall eat the flesh of the Son of man and drink his blood," etc., he seemed to them to be babbling childish words, and it is the habit of babies to drool. He drummed on the city gate when he preached the mystery of his Passion to a people reluctant and unwilling to listen to him, because he knew that the time would come when some would believe and open the gate. He was borne away in his own hands when, holding in his hands bread and wine, he said, "Take and eat; this is my body. . . . This is my blood of the new covenant," etc. According to "Hebrew truth," however, we read, "And he fell in a swoon in their hands."

The *fourth* persecution was when the chief Pharisees sent their servants to seize him. When the servants returned and were asked, "Why did you not bring him?" they replied, "Never did a man speak as this man speaks." Persisting in their effort to accuse him, they then brought forward a woman taken in adultery. The *fifth* persecution was when he said, "Truly, truly, I say to you, before Abraham was, I am," and they took up stones to stone him. The *sixth* was when he said, "I and the Father are one," and again they took up stones to stone him. The *seventh* and last was when they gathered the council against him and did not leave off until they had crucified him.

16. Who, I ask, understands his mild and humble spirit in such prolonged struggle with death? The psalmist says, "Blessed is the man who takes thought for the poor and destitute," whom (according to another psalm) the dragon pursued to death in Judah, in the Jewish people, as "a poor, needy, brokenhearted man." We are almost unteachable or at least slow to learn from Him who says, "Learn from me; for I am gentle and lowly in heart." We understand far less than we ought about him, poor, gentle, humble, grieving for us, wounded for us. "Look how the righteous man dies," says the prophet, "but no one lays it to heart." He also states in the psalm, "I patiently nourished one to be sorrowful with me, but there was no one."

But did not blessed Mary take it to heart, was she not at the same time afflicted, when she stood beside his cross watching him die? Yes, she took it deeply to heart, she was greviously afflicted, and (as Simeon had foretold) a sword pierced her soul. With sensitive perception and sorrow the beloved disciple also watched him dying. Although the other disciples had abandoned him and fled, they too grieved with him and sorrow filled their heart. The statements, "No one lays it to heart," and, "There was no one to be sorrowful with me," were made, not according to judgment based on reason, but according to abundance of grief, which sometimes does not allow reason. Quite properly you notice that they were expressed when those who sorrowed with him were so exceedingly few in quantity and number compared with the great crowd of those who jeered and mocked. Yet, when he says elsewhere, "I looked about, but there was no helper; I sought, but there was no one to give aid; so my own arm saved me, and my wrath helped me," that is not a similiar complaint; it is simply the affirmation of a fact that absolutely no one, even had one wished to do so, could come to his aid and help him in the battle or encounter when the prince of the world, the ancient sinner, the lord of death, came against him. For there was no one else who could say of the evil one, "He has no power over me." Nor was there anyone but him in whom there was the arm and wrath (that is, the zeal and courage) of divine nature coupled with human innocence.

17. What then? By looking for a helper was he seeking not to die, he who had come for that very purpose? As he was both God and man, so also he had two wills, one of divinity, the other humanity, in that very moment of his Passion. Humanity, of course, was naturally frightened at the taste of death and recoiled from it; the soul was possessed by natural love of the body and wished to continue in the flesh. Divinity nonetheless, by a reasonable decision, intended something else, namely, that which was necessary for the salvation of the human race; and humanity preferred the will of that nature to its own will, as in its prayer, "My Father, if it is possible, let this cup pass away from me," yet it added immediately, "nevertheless, not as I will, but as thou wilt." Or: "Nevertheless not my will, but thine, be done." It was therefore according to the decision of divinity that he looked about searching for someone to help him, but it was according to the natural sense of the flesh that he wished this very thing which holy men choose when with the apostle they say, "Not that we would be unclothed, but that we would be further clothed, that what is mortal may be swallowed up by life."

Why did he not only look about and, looking about, seek someone to aid him, but also cry with a loud voice, "Eli, Eli, lama sabachthani?" that is, "My God, my God, why hast thou forsaken me?" We interpret that cry most accurately as if he had said: "O entire fullness of divinity dwelling in me, why do you keep yourself deeply hidden, why are you silent when I am dying? Only a short time ago, when they came to arrest me, you did for a moment utter one statement, 'I am the one whom you seek,' and immediately they drew back and fell to the ground. Lately you also terrified a huge multitude by a flashing from those eyes which now grow dim in death, and what an enormous army could not do, you have done with a whip made of cords, cleansing the Temple, reminding them of that word of the prophet, 'My house shall be called a house of prayer; but you have made it a den of robbers.' Why, then, O most mighty, most powerful divinity of the Word, why have you forsaken me, your own flesh, hiding yourself within as a sword which is unwilling to leave its scabbard?"

[18-26 omitted.]

27. The hour has come of which he had spoken in a certain passage to the Jews, "The hour has come for the Son of man to be manifested." That hour, I say, has come with the proclamation of a word from the mouth of the Father, speaking thus by the voice of David: "Awake, O my glory! Awake, O psaltery and lute!" What was that psaltery and what was that lute? The very body resting in the grave was both psaltery and lute. It was the lute which the Jews broke in pieces while it was playing the sweet notes of preaching, sounding them forth on the taut string of charity. But the shattering of that lute became for it an occasion of growth, an occasion of greatest advance, for it permitted the ten-string psaltery, the sweet-sounding psaltery, to rise up, never to be broken, destined forever to give voice to praise among the peoples, to psalmody among the nations, whose strings no hand may hereafter snap, whose wooden frame no violence may henceforth be strong enough to crush. For, as the apostle says, "Christ rising from the dead dies no more; death no longer has dominion over him." This is the glory of God the Father that in his own work he boasts a great abundance of charity. "Awake, therefore, O my glory!" he exclaims. "Awake, O psaltery and lute!" Does not that soul hear this utterance of the Father, does it not discern this endeavor of the Word, is it not joined to the same Word as bride to bridegroom with an unending kiss, bound with an unrelaxing embrace? Yes, it obviously heard, it fully discerned.

All these things, indeed, of the selfsame Word it knew, it seized upon by more than wifely intuition. It therefore responded with joy, "I will awake at dawn." What is more joyful than this reply? What is readier than the heart of the one making this response? The reason is not hidden from us, since at the beginning of the psalm the psalmist spoke in his own name: "My heart is ready, O God, my heart is ready." O heart so agreeably ready, so willingly roused to undertake the command of divinity, the sweet command of the One who says, "Awake!" When the heart is ready to receive this, it thus replies, "I will awake at dawn." But was the heart prepared for this alone? No, indeed, the heart had been prepared to obey, even to die. The heart was utterly ready to give its body to those who were to beat it, its cheeks to those who were to smite them, and not to turn away its face from those who were to scorn it and spit upon it, but to endure all things unto death, even death on a cross. "Yet I did not gainsay them nor did I turn back." It was appropriate for that heart to be ready to respond, "I will awake at dawn," because it had been prepared to obey His Father, who for our sake did not spare him. Therefore, I say, the reason is not hidden from us why the beginning of the psalm thundered forth, "My heart is ready," and why he was not content to say it only once, but repeated it again and again: "My heart is ready, O God, my heart is ready."

28. Who now is that man of whom Wisdom says, "The obedient man speaks of victories"? Even if many men are or have been sons of obedience, there is only one man, one unique man, to whom there was, is, and will be no one similar or as obedient in like or equal manner. This one man alone was obedient in that, having absolutely no sin, he humbled himself unto death, even death on a cross. It is henceforth appropriate that this obedient man always speak of victories. And, behold, he does so with ceaseless, unending speech. His speech is of such a manner, very clear and loud, because it is the very evidence of his wounds to which he submitted by that obedience. His five wounds are like five tongues. For that reason he preserved in his body the scars of his wounds, that he may always speak of his victories through them as though they were tongues. To whom does he speak? First, of course, to God the Father, then to angels and to men, to all saints, to all the elect. God the Father looks, and is pleased with those noble testimonies of victories. Angels look, and are aroused to acclamations of praise and glory. Redeemed men look, and unremittingly multiply thanksgivings.

29. We affirm with the apostle and we understand his meaning when he says that father Abraham received and transmitted to his posterity the token of circumcision, the seal of the righteousness of faith. For as a believer Abraham trusted in God who said, "By your offspring all nations shall be blessed," although he had no son, although he himself was already an elderly man, and although his wife was a sterile old woman. Circumcision was the testimony of a great deed, a great seal of faith. It proclaimed to him and his descendants the victory of a great righteousness before God, reminding him of God's promise, lest,

sometime, somewhere, being displeased, he avoid offering his posterity "by which all nations shall be blessed." So long as he saw the seal of that promise, so long he declared himself to be faithful and true.

But here at the cross, behold many seals, many seals of righteousness and faith, namely, the five wounds which that obedient Man, that just and faithful Man, suffered as a condition of human salvation. The prophet himself was surely not aware of such a proposed condition: "If he shall offer his own soul for sin, he shall see a long posterity; the will of God shall prosper in his hand; he shall see that for which his soul travailed and be satisfied; by his knowledge shall the righteous one, my servant, justify many; and he shall bear their iniquities." Therefore does not just divinity rightfully award us, his offspring, the palm of justification and salvation when he sees not merely one seal or merely one wound as the seal of righteousness (as was the wound of circumcision), but five wounds of the just Man beating down whatever wrong our flesh has committed by its five senses? For in Baptism we have pleasantly endured those seals of righteousness and faith which he endured painfully. As by the testimony of one seal, circumcision, he was once expected to come and redeem men, so now by the seal of the five wounds, that is, by the seal of the cross imprinted upon our brows, he is expected to return to judge the living and the dead.

St. Thomas Aquinas
1225-1274

Thomas Aquinas taught at the University of Paris from 1256 to 1259, then spent the following decade teaching in Italy. From 1269 to 1272 he taught in Paris for the second time, and ended his teaching career in Naples the following year, 1273. The impact of that relatively brief career has been phenomenal.

Aquinas' use of the Bible has not, until quite recently, received the attention that his use of Aristotle has. Today it is being realized that his approach to the Scriptures ". . . marked a notable transition in regard to the Fathers. Before him biblical exegesis in the West relied mostly on concepts borrowed from a Middle or Neoplatonism. In the great Origenist and Augustinian schools the conceptual orientation was to exemplary and final causality. The visible world and human history were symbols of spiritual realities known through illumination . . . For Thomas human knowing is impossible without sense and imagination. Efficient and formal causality receive greater recognition. The world and history take on their own value, they are not just symbolic of a higher realm. Reason with its philosophies and sciences is clearly differentiated from faith with its mysteries."
(Matthew Lamb).

This shift in presuppositions led Aquinas to give the literal sense a much more central role. It was the only sense on which a theological argument could be based. As he says in the Summa, *"all meanings are based on one, namely, the literal sense." That is not to say that he was able to follow through consistently with this principle. Not having the advantages of the multiplicity of tools and insights provided by contemporary Biblical studies, it would be grossly anachronous to expect him to draw the full implications of his breakthrough.*

In this sense it seems just to say that Aquinas was a transitional figure. He pointed in the direction where progress could be made, once other obstacles were removed. Situating him properly in his times, Père Spicq felt justified in concluding that Thomas' commentaries on St. Paul are "the maturest fruit and the most perfect realization of medieval scholastic exegesis." It would take another six or seven centuries before there was much advance beyond them.

These commentaries are actually transcriptions of Thomas' lectures. They were recorded by his faithful companion Reginald of Piperno. There is thus no great concern for style; the effort was to capture the substance. It was stipulated in university statutes that a master had to correct such "notes" before they could be published, which Thomas presumably did. They were probably delivered sometime during his "Italian decade" between his two teaching stints in Paris.

To appreciate Aquinas' method, one should keep in mind that verse numbers had not yet been introduced into the text of the New Testament. He simply breaks the chapters up into manageable passages. What follows are five of his lectures, enough to give the general flavor of his approach. The passages he is commenting upon are: 1) Galatians 1:11-14; 2) Galatians 2:11-14; 3) Ephesians 1:1-6a; 4) Ephesians 1:11-12; and 5) Ephesians 1:13-14.

COMMENTARY ON ST. PAUL'S EPISTLES TO THE GALATIANS AND TO THE EPHESIANS

GALATIANS

CHAPTER 1

LECTURE 3

For I give you to understand, brethren, that the gospel which was preached by me is not according to man.

12 For neither did I receive it of man; nor did I learn it but by the revelation of Jesus Christ.

13 For you have heard of my conversation in time past in the Jew's religion; how that, beyond measure, I persecuted the church of God and wasted it.

14 And I made progress in the Jews' religion above many of my equals in my own nation, being more abundantly zealous for the traditions of my father.

In the foregoing the Apostle rebuked the Galatians for their fickleness of mind in so quickly setting aside the Gospel teaching; now he shows the dignity of the Gospel teaching. And concerning this he does two things:

First, he commends the authority of Gospel teaching according to itself;

Secondly, on the part both of the other apostles and himself (2:1): **Then, after fourteen years, I went up again to Jerusalem with Barnabas.**

The first part is further divided into two others, because

First, he presents his intention;
Secondly, he manifests his purpose (v. 13).

Regarding the first he does two things:

First, he proposes what he intends;
Secondly, he proves what he proposes (v. 12).

Intending, therefore, to commend the truth of the Gospel teaching, he says, **For I give you to understand, brethren . . .** As if to say: So certain am I of the Gospel's authority, that I would disbelieve not only men but even angels saying the contrary; so that if they were contrary, I would say anathema to them. And I have this certainty, because one must believe God rather than men or angels. Therefore, since I have this Gospel from God, I should and do have the greatest of certainty. Hence he says, **For I give you to understand, brethren, that the gospel which was preached by me** to you and to the other Churches is **not according to man,** i.e., not according to human nature out of tune with the divine rule or divine revelation. In this sense, **according to man** implies something evil: "For whereas there is among you envying and contention, are you not carnal, and walk according to man?" (1 Cor. 3:3). And this is the sense the Apostle takes here; hence he says, **not according to man** teaching me or sending me. As if to say: Not at all can this Gospel be had from men but from God.

That is why he adds, **For neither did I receive it of man; nor did I learn it but by the revelation of Jesus Christ,** whereby he precludes two ways of receiving. First, that he did not receive from man the authority to preach. As to this he says, **nor of man,** i.e., purely man, **did I receive it,** i.e., the authority to preach the Gospel, but of Christ: "And how shall they preach unless they be sent?" (Rom. 10:15); "I have given thee for a light of the Gentiles, for a covenant of the people" (Is. 42:6); "This man is to me a vessel of election, to carry my name before the Gentiles and kings and the children of Israel" (Ac. 9:15). Secondly, that he did not receive the science of the Gospel from man. Hence he says, **not did I learn it,** namely, the Gospel, from mere man, **but by the revelation of Jesus Christ,** i.e., by Jesus Christ showing everything clearly. "But to us, God hath revealed them" (1 Cor. 2:10); "The Lord hath opened my ear, and I do not resist" (Is. 50:5), and "The Lord has given me a learned tongue, that I should know how to uphold by word him that is weary" (Is. 50:4). Now this revelation was made to the Apostle when he was rapt into paradise, where "he heard secret words which it is not granted to man to utter" (2 Cor. 12:4).

Then when he says, **For you have heard of my conversation in time past,** he shows that he did not receive the Gospel from men, either before his conversion or after his conversion to Christ (v. 15). That he did not receive it from man before his conversion he shows both by the hatred he bore toward the faith of Christ and toward Christians, and by the zeal he had for Judaism: **And I made progress in the Jews' religion above many of my equals in my own nation** (v. 14).

He says therefore: I say that I did not receive it of man, and this is true of the time before my conversion. This, indeed, is obvious from my actions at that time and from the hatred I bore toward the faith. For you yourselves **have heard**—"But they had heard only: He who persecuted us in times past doth now preach the faith which once he impugned" (v. 23)—**of my conversation in time past,** when I was an unbeliever, **in the Jews' religion,** when I lived as a Jew. And he says, **my,** because evil we do is from ourselves, but from God is whatever good we do: "Destruction is thy own, O Israel: thy help is only in me" (Os. 13:9).

This you have heard, **how that, beyond measure,** i.e., more than others, because he bestirred not only himself to this but rulers as well. For others, when they persecuted, were possibly led to it by the rulers, but he urged even them: "Saul, as yet breathing out threatenings and slaughter against the disciples of the Lord, went to the high priest" (Ac. 9:1). Also because He did this not only in Jerusalem but in the entire region. Hence "he received letters to Damascus, that if he found any men and women of this way, he might bring them bound to Jerusalem." Therefore what is said in Genesis (49:27): "Benjamin a ravenous wolf, in the morning shall eat the prey, and in the evening shall divide the spoil," can be understood as applying to him.

I persecuted the church of God, i.e., by hunting down Christians and discomfiting them: "I am not worthy to be called an apostle, because I persecuted the church of God" (1 Cor. 15:9); **and I wasted it,** not indeed spiritually, because I was unable to turn the hearts of the faithful from their faith, but physically by inflicting bodily punishment on them and casting them into prison: "Is not this he who persecuted in Jerusalem those that called upon this name?" (Ac. 9:21); "Often have they fought against me" (Ps. 128:1).

It is plain, therefore, from the hatred he bore toward the faith of Christ before his conversion, that he did not receive the Gospel from man.

It is plain also from the love and burning zeal he had for Judaism, as to outward progress. Hence he says, **And I made progress in the Jews' religion above many of my equals in my own nation**: wherein he mentions three things that indicate how great **was** his progress. For he progressed not above a few but **above many**, not above old men incapable of progress in learning, but **my equals**, i.e., young men who were intelligent and capable of progress: "It is good for a man, when he has borne the yoke from his youth" (Lam. 3:27). Furthermore, not above equals who were foreigners and ignorant of the language, but equals **of my own nation**, i.e., Jews: "I am a Jew, brought up at the feet of Gamaliel, taught according to the truth of the law of the fathers, zealous for the law, as also all you are this day" (Ac. 22:3).

Finally, as to the inward zeal he had for the Law. Hence he says, **being more abundantly zealous**, not only for the Law, but **for the traditions of my fathers**, namely, those traditions which the Jews lawfully kept and "which the good fathers added," as is said in a Gloss. He calls these traditions his own because he treasured them as though they were his: "According to the Law, a Pharisee; according to zeal, persecuting the church of God" (Phil. 3:5).

But a question arises from the fact that the aforesaid Gloss says: "The good fathers added." For it seems that they were not good, because it is said in Deuteronomy (4:2): "You shall not add to the word I speak to you." Hence in adding traditions they acted against the command of God and so were not good. To this one may answer that this word of the Lord is taken to mean that you shall not add anything contrary or alien to the words which I shall speak. But to add certain things not contrary was lawful for them, namely, certain solemn days and the like, as was done in the time of Mordochai and of Judith, in memory of the blessings they received from God.

But against this is the rebuke addressed to them by our Lord, when He says: "You have made void the command of the Lord for the traditions of men" (Mt. 15:16). Hence those traditions were not lawful.—I answer that they are not rebuked for holding the traditions of men, but because for the sake of the traditions of men, they neglect the commands of God.

CHAPTER 2

LECTURE 3

11 But, when Cephas was come to Antioch, I withstood him to the face, because he was to be blamed.

12 For, before that some came from James, he did eat with the Gentiles; but, when they were come, he withdrew and separated himself, fearing them who were of the circumcision.

13 And to his dissimulation the rest of the Jews consented; so that Barnabas also was led by them into that dissimulation.

14 But, when I saw that they walked not uprightly unto the truth of the gospel, I said to Cephas before them all: If thou, being a Jew, livest after the manner of the Gentiles and not as the Jews do, how dost thou compel the Gentiles to live as do the Jews?

The Apostle showed above that he received nothing useful from the discussion held with the apostles; now he shows that he benefited them:

First, he shows how he helped Peter by correcting him;
Secondly, he tells what he said (v. 12).

He says, therefore: Indeed, they advantaged me nothing; rather I conferred something upon them, and especially upon Peter, because when Cephas was come to Antioch, where there was a church of the Gentiles, I withstood him to the face, i.e., openly: "Reverence not thy neighbor in his fall and refrain not to speak in the time of salvation" (Ecclus. 4:27). Or: to his face, i.e., not in secret as though detracting and fearing him, but publicly and as his equal: "Thou shalt not hate thy brother in thy heart: but reprove him openly, lest thou incur sin through him" (Lev. 19:17). This he did, because he was to be blamed.

But it might be objected: This took place after they received the grace of the Holy Spirit; but after the grace of the Holy Spirit the apostles did not sin in any way. I answer that after the grace of the Holy Spirit the apostles did not sin mortally, and this gift they had through the divine power that had strengthened them: "I have established the pillars thereof" (Ps. 74:4). Yet they sinned venially because of human frailty: "If we say that we have no sin," i.e., venial, "we deceive ourselves" (1 John 1:8).

Apropos of what is said in a certain Gloss, namely, that **I withstood him** as an adversary, the answer is that the Apostle opposed Peter in the exercise of authority, not in his authority of ruling. Therefore from the foregoing we have an example: prelates, indeed, an example of humility, that they not disdain corrections from those who are lower and subject to them; subjects have an example of zeal and freedom, that they fear not to correct their prelates, particularly if their crime is public and verges upon danger to the multitude.

Then when he says, **For, before that some came from James,** he manifests what he has said.

First, that he said he was to be blamed;
Secondly, that he rebuked Peter (v. 14).

As to the first he does three things:

First, he shows what Peter's opinion was;
Secondly, what he did (v. 11);
Thirdly, what resulted from it (v. 13).

He says therefore, as to the first point, that Peter felt that legalism ought not be observed. This he showed by the fact that **before some came,** namely, Jews zealous for the Law, **from James,** Bishop of the Church at Jerusalem, **he did eat,** namely, Peter did, **with the Gentiles,** i.e., without compunction he ate the food of Gentiles. He did this through the inspiration of the Holy Spirit Who had said to him: "That which God hath cleansed, do not thou call common," as is had in Acts (10:15), and as he himself in the following chapter said in answer to the Jews who rose up against him, because he had eaten with the uncircumcised.

What Peter did Paul now shows, saying that when he was with the Jews, **he withdrew** from the company of the faithful who had been converted from the Gentiles and adhered to the Jews alone and mingled among them. Therefore he says, **but when they were come,** namely, from Judea, Peter withdrew from the converted Gentiles **and separated himself from them.** This he did because he was **fearing them who were of the circumcision,** i.e., the Jews, not with a human or worldly fear but a fear inspired by charity, namely, lest they be scandalized, as is said in a Gloss. Hence he became to the Jews as a Jew, pretending that he felt the same as they did in their weakness. Yet he fear unreasonably, because the truth must never be set aside through fear of scandal.

What resulted from this dissimulation he mentions when he says that **to his dissimulation,** i.e., Peter's, **the rest of the Jews consented** who were at Antioch, discriminating between food and separating themselves from the Gentiles, although prior to this act of dissimulation they would not have done this. And not only they consented to Peter, but such was the effect of that dissimulation upon the hearts of the faithful, **that Barnabas also,** who along with me was a teacher of the Gentiles and had done and taught the contrary, **was led by them into that dissimulation** and withdrew from them, namely, the Gentiles. And this on account of what is said in Ecclesiasticus (10:2): "What manner of man the ruler of a city is, such also are they that dwell therein" and "as the judge of the people is himself, so also are his ministers."

Then when he says, **But, when I saw that they walked not uprightly unto the truth of the gospel, I said to Cephas before them all . . . ,** he explains what he had said concerning the rebuke with which he rebuked Peter. As to this he does three things:

First, he gives the reason for the rebuke;
Secondly, the manner of the rebuking;
Thirdly, the words of the rebuke.

The occasion of the rebuke was not slight, but just and useful, namely, the danger to the Gospel teaching. Hence he says: Thus was Peter reprehensible, but I alone, **when I saw that they,** who were doing these things, **walked not uprightly unto the truth of the gospel,** because its truth was being undone, if the Gentiles were compelled to observe the legal justifications, as will be plain below. That they were not walking uprightly is so, because in cases where danger is imminent, the truth must be preached openly and the opposite never condoned through fear of scandalizing others: "That which I tell you in the dark, speak ye in the light" (Mt. 10:27); "The way of the just is right: the path of the just is right to walk in" (Is. 26:7). The manner of the rebuke was fitting, i.e., public and plain. Hence he says, **I said to Cephas,** i.e., to Peter, before them all, because that dissimulation posed a danger to all: "Them that sin, reprove before all" (1 Tim. 5:20). This is to be understood of public sins and not of private ones, in which the procedures of fraternal charity ought to be observed.

The words of the Apostle spoke to Peter when he rebuked him, he adds, saying, **If thou, being a Jew,** by nature and race, **livest after the manner of the Gentiles and not as the Jews do,** i.e., if you observe the customs of Gentiles and not of Jews, since you know and feel that discriminating among foods is of no importance, **how dost thou compel the Gentiles,** not indeed by command, but by example of your behavior, **to live as do the Jews?** He says, **compel,** because as Pope Leo says, "Example has more force than words." Hence Paul rebukes Peter precisely because he had been instructed by God that although he had previously lived as the Jews do, he should no longer discriminate among foods: "That which God hath cleansed, do not thou call common" (Ac. 10:15). But now Peter was dissembling the opposite.

It should be noted that these words occasioned no small controversy between Jerome and Augustine and, as their writings show, they are seen to disagree on four points. First, as to the time of the legal justifications, namely, when they should have been observed. For Jerome distinguishes two periods, one before the passion of Christ and one after. Jerome's opinion is that the legal justifications were *living* before the passion of Christ, i.e., had validity, inasmuch as original sin was removed through circumcision, and God was pleased with sacrifices and victims. But after the passion they were, according to him, not only not living i.e., dead, but what is more, they were *deadly*, so that whoever observed them after the passion of Christ sinned mortally.

Augustine, on the other hand, distinguishes three periods. One period was before the passion of Christ and, in agreement with Jerome, he says that during that period the legal justifications were *living*. Another was the period immediately following the passion of Christ, before grace was promulgated (as the time of the apostles in the beginning); during this period says Augustine, the legal justifications were *dead* but not yet *deadly* to the converted Jews, so long as the ones observing them placed no hope in them. Hence the Jews observed them during that period

188

without sinning. But had they placed their trust in them when observing them after their conversion, they would have sinned mortally; because if they placed their trust in them so as to believe that they were necessary for salvation, then, as far as they were concerned, they would have been voiding the grace of Christ. Finally, he posits a third period, after the truth and grace of Christ had been proclaimed. It was during that period, he says, that they were both *dead* and *deadly* to all who observed them.

The reasoning that underlies these statements is that if the Jews had been forbidden the legal observances right after their conversion, it might have seemed that they had previously been on an equal footing with idolaters, who were immediately forbidden to worship idols, and that just as idolatry had never been good, so too the legal observances. Therefore, under the inspiration of the Holy Spirit, the legal observances were condoned for a short time for the reason given, namely, to show that the legal observances had been good in the past. Hence, says Augustine, the fact that the legal justifications were not forbidden right after the passion of Christ showed that the mother, the synagogue, was destined to be brought in honor to the grave. But whosoever did not observe them in that manner would not be honoring the mother, the synagogue, but disturbing her grave.

Secondly, the aforesaid Jerome and Augustine disagree on the observance of the legal justifications with respect to the apostles. For Jerome says that the apostles never really observed them but pretended to do so, in order to avoid scandalizing the believers who had been of the circumcision. He says that even Paul made this pretense when he fulfilled a vow in the temple at Jerusalem, as is narrated in Acts (21:26), and when he circumcised Timothy, as in Acts (16:3), and when on advice from James he observed some of the justifications, as recorded in Acts (20:20). But in so doing the apostles were not misleading the faithful, because they did not act with the intention of observing the justifications but for other reasons; for example, they rested on the Sabbath, not because it was a legal observance, but for the sake of rest. Likewise, they abstained from food legally unclean, not for the sake of observing the legal justifications but for other reasons; for example, on account of an abhorrence or something of that nature. But Augustine says that the apostles observed the legal justifications and intended to do so, but without putting their trust in them as though they were necessary for salvation. Furthermore, this was lawful for them to do, because they had been Jews. Nevertheless, they observed them before grace was proclaimed. Hence just as certain other Jews could safely observe them at that time without putting any trust in them, so too could the apostles.

Thirdly, they disagree on the sin of Peter. For Jerome says that in the dissimulation previously mentioned, Peter did not sin, because he did this from charity and, as has been said, not from mundane fear. Augustine, on the other hand, says, that he did sin—venially, however—on account of the lack of discretion he had by adhering overmuch to one side, namely, to the Jews, in order to avoid scandalizing them. But the stronger of Augustine's arguments against Jerome is that Jerome adduces on his own behalf seven doctors, four of whom, namely, Laudicens, Alexander, Origen, and Didymus, Augustine rejects as known heretics. To the other three he opposes three of his own, who held with him and his opinion, namely, Ambrose, Cyprian, and Paul himself, who plainly teaches that Peter was deserving of rebuke. Therefore, if it is unlawful to say that anything false is contained in Sacred Scripture, it will not be lawful to say that Peter was not deserving of rebuke. For this reason the opinion and statement of Augustine is the truer, because it is more in accord with the words of the Apostle.

Fourthly, they disagree on Paul's rebuke. For Jerome says that Paul did not really rebuke Peter but pretended to do so, just as Peter pretended to observe the legal justifications, i.e., just as Peter in his unwillingness to scandalize the Jews pretended to observe the justifications, so Paul, in order not to scandalize the Gentiles, feigned displeasure at Peter's action and pretended to rebuke him. This was done, as it were, by mutual consent, so that each might exercise his care over the believers subject to them. Augustine, however, just as he says that Peter really did observe the justifications, says that Paul truly rebuked him without pretense. Furthermore, Peter really sinned by observing them, because his action was a source of scandal to the Gentiles from whom he separated himself. But Paul did not sin in rebuking him, because no scandal followed from his rebuke.

190

EPHESIANS

CHAPTER 1

LECTURE 1

1 Paul, an apostle of Jesus Christ, by the will of God, to all the saints who are at Ephesus and to the faithful in Christ Jesus:

2 Grace be to you and peace, from God our Father and from the Lord Jesus Christ.

3 Blessed be the God and Father of our Lord Jesus Christ, who hath blessed us with spiritual blessings in heavenly places, in Christ;

4 As he chose us in him before the foundation of the world, that we should be holy and unspotted in his sight in charity.

5 Who hath predestinated us unto the adoption of children through Jesus Christ unto himself, according to the purpose of his will;

6a Unto the praise of the glory of his grace.

The Apostle writes this letter to the Ephesians who were Asians, coming from Asia Minor which is part of Greece. They were not initiated into the faith by the Apostle Paul but he did strengthen them in it. Even before he had met them, they had been converted, as can be gathered from Acts 19 (1): "And it came to pass, while Appollo was at Corinth, that Paul, having passed through the upper coasts, came to Ephesus and found certain disciples." Once they were converted and fortified by the Apostle, they were steadfast in the faith, not succumbing to false doctrine. Thus, they were entitled to encouragement rather than reprimand; and Paul's letter has a tone of reassurance and not of rebuke. He wrote them from the city of Rome through the deacon, Tychicus.

The Apostle's intention is to strengthen them in good habits, and spur them on to greater perfection. The method of presentation can be seen in the division of the letter:

First, the greeting, in which he shows his affection for them.

Secondly, the narrative, in which he strengthens them in good habits (1:3-3:21).

Thirdly, the exhortation, in which he urges them on
to greater perfection (4:1-6:9).
Fourthly, the conclusion of the letter, in which he for-
tifies them for the spiritual combat (6:10-24).

In the salutation, the person greeting comes first, second
those greeted, and thirdly the formula of greeting. In reference
to the first, he gives the name of the person, **Paul**; second, that
person's authority as an **Apostle of Christ**; lastly, the giver of this
authority, **by the will of God**. He says **Paul** which is a name of
humility, whereas the title of **Apostle** is one of dignity; the reason is that "he that humbleth himself shall be exalted" (Lk.
14:11; 18:14). An Apostle, I mean, **of Jesus** and not one of the
pseudo-apostles who are of Satan: "It is no great thing if his
[Satan's] ministers be transformed as the ministers of justice"
(2 Cor. 11:15). I am an apostle, he says, not by my own merits
but **by the will of God**. In many instances it is just the opposite—
"They have reigned, but not by me" (Os. 8:4).

He writes **to all the saints who are at Ephesus and to the
faithful**. Either [this could mean], I, Paul, write about morals
to those who are holy through the exercise of virtues; and about
faith to those who believe with true knowledge. Or, [it may
mean], **to the saints** who are the elders and perfect [members],
and **to the faithful** who are less experienced and imperfect. They
are said to believe **in Christ Jesus** and not in their own deeds.

He adds here the formula of greeting which indicates three
qualities which make any gift pleasing: the sufficiency of the
gift, in **grace be to you and peace**; the power of the giver, **from
God our Father**; and the excellence of the mediator, **and from
the Lord Jesus Christ**. For a gift is pleasing when what is given
is sufficient and is offered by someone in power, as a king or
prince, and is presented by a solemn messenger, for example, by
his son.

He mentions **grace** meaning justification from sin, **and peace**
which is calmness of mind, or reconciliation to God, in regard
to the freedom from punishment due to sin. May this be **to you
from God our Father** from whom every good comes: "Every
best gift and every perfect gift is from above, coming down from
the Father of lights" (Jas. 1:17). **And the Lord Jesus Christ** without whom no blessings are given. That is why nearly all the [li-

192

turgical] prayers are concluded "through our Lord Jesus Christ."
The Holy Spirit is not mentioned in the greeting formula since
he is the bond uniting Father and Son and is understood when
they are mentioned; or he is understood in the gifts appropriated
to him, grace and peace.

Then when he says **Blessed be God . . .** (v.3) in giving thanks,
he strengthens them in good, and he does this in three ways:

> First, by giving as a reason Christ, from whom they
> have receive so many gifts (Ch. 1).
> Secondly, by reason of they themselves who have been
> transformed from a former evil condition to their
> present good one (Ch. 2).
> Thirdly, because of the Apostle himself, whose minis-
> try and solicitude has confirmed them in their
> good state (Ch. 3).

The first is divided into three sections:

> First, in giving thanks he touches on blessings in a gen-
> eral way.
> Secondly, then the blessings given the Apostles in
> particular (1:8).
> Thirdly, finally the blessings especially granted to the
> Ephesians themselves (1:13).

He treats of six blessings offered generally to the human race:

> First, that of praising [God] in the certainty of future
> beatitude (1:3).
> Secondly, that of being chosen in the foreordained
> separation from those headed toward destruction
> (1:4).
> Thirdly, that of predestination in the foreordained
> community of the good, namely, of the adopted
> sons (1:5).
> Fourthly, that of becoming pleasing [to God] through
> the gift of grace (1:6b).
> Fifthly, that of being redeemed, liberated from the
> punishment of diabolical slavery (1:7a).
> Sixthly, that of being pardoned by having sin blotted
> out (1:7b).

Regarding the benefit of praise (v.3) two aspects are touched on:

First, the praise itself which should be rendered, at **Blessed be God.**

Secondly, the blessing on account of which it should be rendered, at **who hath blessed us.**

He says that God should be **blessed** or praised by you, me and others with our hearts, tongues and actions. He who is **God** by the divine essence and **Father** because of his property of generating [the Son]. The copula **and** is not placed between **God** and **Father** to designate two separate persons, for there is only one Father, but to denote what he is by his essence and what he is in relation to the Son. **Father, I say, of our Lord Jesus Christ,** that is, of the Son who is our Lord because of his divinity, and Jesus Christ according to his humanity.

God **who hath blessed us** with hope in the present while in the future he will bless us with the reality. He puts [the verb] in the past tense, instead of the future, on account of his certainty. Even though by our own merits we were cursed, he blessed us **with every spiritual blessing** both for soul and for body. For then the body will be spiritual: "It is sown a natural body: it shall rise a spiritual body" (1 Cor. 15:44). [This will occur] by a blessing enjoyed **in heavenly places,** that is, in heaven, and **in Christ** since it will be through Christ or by Christ's action: "For he himself will transform our lowly body" (Phil. 3:21).

This blessing is greatly to be desired. And this by reason of its efficient cause since **God** is the one who blesses; and by reason of its material cause since **he hath blessed us;** and because of the formal cause since he blessed us with **every spiritual blessing;** and on account of the end, he blessed us **in heavenly places.** "Behold, thus shall the man be blessed that feareth the Lord" (Ps. 127:4).

Next (v. 4), he treats of the blessing of election; he sets forth the advantages of this election because: it is free, **as he chose us in him;** it is eternal, **before the foundation of the world;** it is fruitful, **that we should be holy;** and it is gratuitous, **in charity.**

Therefore he states: He blessed us in the same way—not through our merits but from the grace of Christ—as he choose us and, separating us from those headed to destruction, freely foreordained us in him, that is, through Christ. "You have not chosen me; but I have chosen you" (Jn. 15:16). This happened before the foundation of the world, from eternity, before we came into being. "For when the children were not yet born, nor had done any good or evil, that the purpose of God according to election, might stand" (Rom. 9:11). He chose us, I say, not because we were holy—we had not yet come into existence—but that we should be holy in virtues and unspotted by vices. For election performs this twofold action of justice: "Turn away from evil and do good" (Ps. 33:15).

Saints, I assert, in his sight; interiorly in the heart where he alone can see: "the Lord beholdeth the heart" (1 Kg. 16:7). Or, in his sight may mean that we may gaze on him since the [beatific] vision, according to Augustine, is the whole of our reward. He will accomplish this, not by our merits, but in his charity; or, by our [charity] with which he formally sanctifies us.

Then (v. 5) he adds the third blessing, that of predestination in the foreordained community of those who are good. Six characteristics of predestination are sketched here. First, it is an eternal act, he hath predestinated; secondly, it has a temporal object, us; thirdly, it offers a present privilege, the adoption of children through Jesus Christ; fourthly, the result is future, unto himself; fifthly, its manner [of being realized] is gratuitous, according to the purpose of his will; sixthly, it has a fitting effect, unto the praise of the glory of his grace.

Hence he affirms that God, who hath predestinated us, has forechosen us by grace alone unto the adoption of children that we might share with the other adopted children the goods yet to come—thus he says unto the adoption of children. "For you have not received the spirit of bondage again in fear; but you have received the spirit of adoption of sons," and further on, "waiting for the adoption of the sons of God, the redemption of our body" (Rom. 8:15 & 23).

It must be through contact with fire that something starts to burn since nothing obtains a share in some reality except through whatever is that reality by its very nature. Hence the adoption of sons has to occur through the natural son. For this reason the Apostle adds **through Jesus Christ,** which is the third characteristic touched on in this blessing, namely, the mediator who draws all to himself. "God sent his Son, made of a woman, made under the law, that he might redeem them who were under the law, that we might receive the adoption of sons" (Gal. 4:4-5). This is accomplished **unto himself,** that is, inasmuch as we are conformed to him and become servants in the Spirit. "Behold what manner of charity the Father hath bestowed upon us, that we should be called and should be the sons of God," after which comes: "We know that when he shall appear we shall be like to him" (1 Jn. 3:1-2).

Here it should be noted that the likeness of the predestined to the Son of God is twofold. One is imperfect, it is [the likeness] through grace. It is called imperfect, firstly, because it only concerns the reformation of the soul. Regarding this Ephesians 4 (23-24) states: "Be renewed in the spirit of your mind, and put on the new man, who according to God is created in justice and holiness of truth." Secondly, even with the soul it retains some imperfection, "for we know in part" (1 Cor. 13:9). However, the second likeness, which will be in glory, will be perfect; both as regards the body—"He will reform the body of our lowness, made like to the body of his glory." (Phil. 3:21)—and in regard to the soul—"when that which is perfect is come, that which is in part shall be done away" (1 Cor. 13:10).

What the Apostle says, therefore, about his predestinating us unto the adoption of children can refer to the imperfect assimilation to the Son of God possessed in this life through grace. But it is more probable that it refers to the perfect assimilation to the Son of God which will exist in the fatherland. In reference to this adoption Romans 8 (23) asserts: "Even we ourselves groan within ourselves, waiting for the adoption of the sons of God."

Divine predestination is neither necessitated on God's part nor due to those who are predestined; it is rather **according to the purpose of his will.** This is the fourth characteristic which recommends the blessing to us, for it springs from pure love. Predestination, according to [how man] conceives it, presupposes

196

election, and election love. A twofold cause of this immense blessing is designated here. One is the efficient cause which is the simple will of God—according to the purpose of his will. "Therefore, he hath mercy on whom he will; and whom he will be hardeneth" (Rom. 9:18). "For of his own will hath he begotten us by the word of truth" (Jas. 1:18). Unto the praise of the glory of his grace specifies the final cause which is that we may praise and know the goodness of God. Once again this eminent blessing is recommended inasmuch as the homage [it results in] is in accord with itself. For the [efficient] cause of divine predestination is simply the will of God, while the end is a knowledge of his goodness.

Whence it should be realized that God's will in no way has a cause but is the first cause of everything else. Nevertheless, a certain motive can be assigned to it in two ways. On the part of the one willing, the motive for the divine will is his own goodness which is the object of the divine will, moving it to act. Hence, the reason for everything that God wills is his own goodness: "The Lord hath made all things for himself" (Prov. 16:4). On the side of what is willed, however, some created existent can be a motive for the divine will; for example, when he wills to crown Peter because he has fought well (cf. 2 Tim. 4:7-8). But this latter is not the cause of [God's] willing; rather it is a cause of it happening the way it did.

Nonetheless, it should be acknowledged how, in the realm of what is willed, effects are a motive for the divine will in such a way that a prior effect is the reason for a later one. But when the primary effect [i.e., the perfection of the Universe] is arrived at, no further reason can be given for that effect except the divine will. For instance, God wills that men should have hands that they might be of service to his mind; and [he wills] man to possess a mind since he wills him to be a man; and he wills man to exist for the sake of the perfection of the Universe. Now since this is what is primarily effected in creation, no further reason for the Universe can be assigned within the domain of creatures themselves; [it lies] rather within the domain of the Creator, which is the Divine Will.

In this perspective, neither can predestination find any reason on the part of the creature but only on the part of God. For there are two effects of predestination, grace and glory. Within the realm of what is willed [by God], grace can be identified as a reason for the effects which are orientated towards glory. For example, God crowned Peter because he fought well, and he did this because he was strengthened in grace. But no reason for the grace, as a primary effect, can be found on the part of man himself which would also be the reason for predestination. This would be to assert that the source of good works was in man by himself and not by grace. Such was the heretical teaching of the Pelagians who held that the source of good works exists within ourselves. Thus it is evident that the reason for predestination is the will of God alone, on account of which the Apostle says **according to the purpose of his will.**

To understand how God creates everything and wills it because of his own goodness, it should be realized that someone can work for an end in two ways. [A person may act] either in order to attain an end, as the sick take medicine to regain their health; or [he may act] out of a love of spreading the end, as a doctor will work to communicate health to others. But God needs absolutely nothing external to himself, according to Psalm 15 (2): "Thou art my God, for thou hast no need of my goods." Therefore, when it is said that God wills and performs everything on account of his own goodness, this should not be understood as though he acted in order to confer goodness on himself but rather to communicate goodness to others.

This divine goodness is properly communicated to rational creatures in order that the rational creature himself might know it. Thus, everything that God performs in reference to rational creatures is for his own praise and glory, according to Isaias 43 (7): "And everyone that calleth upon my name, I have created him for my glory: I have formed him and made him" so that he may know what goodness is, and in this knowledge praise it. The Apostle thus adds **unto the praise of the glory of his grace,** that man might realize how much God must be praised and glorified.

Nor does he say "unto the praise of justice." For justice enters into the picture only where a debt is present or is to be returned. But for man to be predestined to eternal life is not due to him—as was said, it is a grace given in perfect freedom. Nor does he simply say **of the glory**, but annexes **of his grace** as though it were of a glorious grace. And grace is just this; the greatness of grace is revealed in that it consists in the greatness of glory. [Its grandeur is shown] also in the way it is bestowed; for he gives it without any preceding merits when men are unworthy of it. "But God commendeth his charity towards us; because, when as yet we were sinners according to the time, Christ died for us"; and a little further on, "when we were enemies, we were reconciled to God by the death of his Son" (Rom. 5:8 & 10).

By now it must be clear how divine predestination neither has nor can have any cause but the will of God alone. This, in turn, reveals how the only motive for God's predestinating will is to communicate the divine goodness to others.

CHAPTER 1

LECTURE 4

11 In whom we also are called by lot, being predestinated according to the purpose of him who worketh all things according to the counsel of his will;

12 That we may be unto the praise of his glory; we who before hoped in Christ.

Previously the Apostle wrote of how he and the other Apostles received an abundance of grace from Christ (1:8). Lest anyone imagine they had it coming to them the Apostle quickly affirms that they were called by God gratuitously, not for their personal merits. This section is divided into three parts:

First, the gratuity of the [Apostolic] call.
Secondly, God's freedom in predestination (1:11b).
Thirdly, what is the end of both [vocation and predestination] (1:12).

I have indicated, he says, that grace has superabounded in us and that everything has been re-established in Christ. The same Christ **In whom we also are called by lot**, not by our own merits but by a divine choice: "Giving thanks to God the Father, who hath made us worthy to be partakers of the lot of the saints in light" (Col. 1:12) because "my lots are in thy hands" (Ps. 30:16).

To understand this it should be realized that many human events which seem to occur by fate and chance, in reality are arranged according to divine providence. Casting lots is no more than a search for divine guidance in contingent and human affairs. Augustine, commenting on Psalm 30 (16), teaches that casting lots is not an evil but a means of discovering God's will in a doubtful issue.

Nonetheless, three sins must be avoided. First, is superstition; for any religion which is shallow and immoral is superstition. The forbidden sin of superstition would be incurred when the casting of lots is performed in league with the devil. For instance, Ezechiel 21 (21) relates how: "the king of Babylon stood in the highway, at the head of two ways, seeking divination, shuffling arrows: he inquired of the idols and consulted entrails." The shuffling of the arrows is related to sortilege, and the questioning of idols belongs to superstition. Sortilege, moreover, is condemned there (Ez. 21) among sins pertaining to superstition.

Secondly, the sin of tempting God must be shunned. As long as a man can discover and accomplish by himself what he ought to do, he tempts God if he resorts to lots, or any other such method, to ascertain what he should do. Only when unavoidable threatened by situations where one is powerless by himself can a man licitly resort to [extraordinary ways of] questioning God concerning what he must do. "But as we know not what to do, we can only turn our eyes to thee" (2 Par. 20:12). Vanity is the third sin. It is committed if we inquire into futile matters not pertaining to us; for example, contingent events in the future. It is not for you to know the times or moments, which the Father hath put in his own power" (Ac. 1:7).

Relative to this [purpose for which they are cast], there are three types of lots: some are divisory, others are consultatory, while still others are divinatory.

Divisory lots are those which people cast when they are dividing an inheritance and cannot agree. Using a certain ring, slip of paper, or the like, they declare: Whoever it will fall to shall have this part of the inheritance. Such lots can be cast lawfully: "The lot suppresseth contentions: and determineth even between the mighty" (Prov. 18:18) when they wish to divide in this way.

Consultatory lots are used when someone doubts what he should do and consults God by casting lots. Jonas 1 (7) recounts how, when the great storm came upon them at sea, they cast lots to seek information from God that they might know for whose sin the tempest had occurred. This method is licit, especially in necessities and in the elections of secular rulers. Hence, men will make small wax balls called "bussuli," of which some contain slips of paper and others none. Whoever draws a "bussulus" with the paper inside has a voice in the election. This was done also, previous to the Holy Spirit's coming, in spiritual elections, evidenced in the choice of Mathias by lot (Ac. 1:26). Now that the Holy Spirit has come, however, it is no longer lawful in these elections since making use of them would be an insult to the Holy Spirit. It must be believed, after all, that the Holy Spirit will provide his Church with good pastors. After the Holy Spirit's advent, therefore, when the Apostles chose the seven deacons (cf. Ac. 6), they did not cast lots. Thus, this method is not lawful in an ecclesiastical election.

Divinatory lots augur future events reserved to the divine knowledge alone. They always are colored by vainglory, nor can they be resorted to without a sinful curiosity.

Lots, therefore, are nothing other than a questioning concerning realities whose occurrence depends on the divine will. Since grace depends on the divine will alone, the grace of divine election is termed a lot. For God, as though by lot, according to his hidden providence, calls men through an inner grace and not on account of anyone's merits.

Next, when he says **predestined according to his purpose, he** writes of the free predestination of God concerning which Romans 8 (30) deals: "And whom he predestinated, them he also called." The reason for this predestination is not our merits but the will of God alone, on account of which he adds **according to the purpose of him.** "And we know that to them that love God, all things work together unto good; to such as, according to his purpose, are called to be saints" (Rom. 8:28).

He approves of what he has predestined according to his purpose since not only this, but also everything else that God does **he worketh according to the counsel of his will.** "Whatsoever the Lord pleased he hath done, in heaven, in earth, in the sea, and in all the deeps" (Ps. 134:6). "My counsel shall stand, and all my will shall be done" (Is. 46:10). He did not say "according to his will" lest you would believe it was irrational, but **according to the counsel of his will**. This means, according to his will which arises from reason; not that reason here implies any transition in his thoughts, it rather indicates a certain and deliberate will.

Finally, he briefly mentions the end of one's predestination and vocation, namely, the praise of God. Thus he states **that we may be unto the praise of his glory, we who before hoped in Christ.** Through us, who believe in Christ, the glory of God is extolled. "The mountains and hills shall sing praise before you" (Is. 55:12). The praise of God's glory, as Ambrose remarks, occurs when many persons are won over to the faith, as a doctor's glory is in a large clientele and their cure. "Ye that fear the Lord, hope in him; and mercy shall come to you for your delight" (Ecclus. 2:9).

CHAPTER 1

LECTURE 5

13 In whom you also, after you had heard the word of truth, the gospel of your salvation, in whom also believing, you were signed with the holy Spirit of promise.

14 Who is the pledge of our inheritance, unto the redemption of acquisition, unto the praise of his glory.

Once the Apostle has enumerated the blessings offered generally to all the faithful, then those especially given the Apostles (1:8), he begins to recount those granted to the Ephesians themselves. This section is divided into two parts:

First, he sets down the favors shown them.
Secondly, he describes his feelings aroused by the favors (1:15).

The first is divided into three parts according to the three blessings granted to them:

First, the blessing of preaching.
Secondly, the blessing of conversion to the faith (1:13).
Thirdly, the blessing of justification (1:13-14).

In reference to the first point he says: Christ **in whom you also, after you had heard,** that is, by whose favor and power you have the proclamation of the **word of truth** since Christ himself has sent those who preach it to you. "How shall they believe him of whom they have not heard? And how shall they hear, without a preacher? And how shall they preach unless they be sent? . . . Faith, then, cometh by hearing; and hearing by the word of Christ" (Rom. 10:14-15, 17). They hear through the blessing of him who sends them the preachers: "Blessed are they who hear the word of God and keep it" (Lk. 11:28).

The Apostle mentions the threefold recommendation of this preached word. It is, first of all, true; a **word of truth.** Indeed, it could be nothing else since its source is Christ concerning whom John 17 (17) states: "Thy word is truth." And James 1 (18): "For of his own will hath he begotten us by the word of truth." Secondly, it is a proclamation of good news. Hence he says **the gospel:** it announces the highest good and eternal life. "Word of faith" is preeminently (*antonomastice*) applicable to the Gospel as the communication of the highest good. "How beautiful upon the mountains are the feet of him that bringeth good tidings, and that preacheth salvation. . . Get thee up upon a high mountain, thou that bringest good tidings to Sion" (Is. 52:7; 40:9). This refers to future goods. The present goods are what describe and recommend [Christian preaching] in the third place, for it saves. Thus he says **of your salvation;** if believed in, it gives salvation. "I am not ashamed of the gospel. For it is the power of God unto salvation to every one that believeth" (Rom. 1:16). "Now I make known unto you, brethren, the gospel which I preached to you, which also you have received and wherein you stand: by which also you are saved" (1 Cor. 15:1).

Regarding the blessing of conversion to the faith, he states **in whom,** namely, Christ, by whose action you **also believing, were signed.** This blessing is applied to faith since faith is necessary for those who listen. In vain would anyone listen to the word of truth if he did not believe, and the believing itself is through Christ. "By grace you are saved through faith, and that not of yourselves, for it is the gift of God" (Eph. 2:8).

Concerning the blessing of justification he mentions that **you were signed with the Holy Spirit** who was given to you.

Concerning this [Spirit] three things are said; he is a sign, the spirit of the promise, and the pledge of our inheritance.

He is a sign inasmuch as through him charity is infused into our hearts, thereby distinguishing us from those who are not the children of God. Relating to this he says **you were signed**, set apart from Satan's fold. "Grieve not the holy Spirit of God; whereby you are sealed unto the day of redemption" (Eph. 4:30). Just as men brand a mark on their own herds to differentiate them from others, so the Lord willed to seal his own flock, his people, with a spiritual sign. The Lord had the Jews as his own people in the Old Testament. "And you, my flocks, the flocks of my pastures are men" (Ez. 34:31). "And we are the people of his pasture and the sheep of his hand" (Ps. 94:7). This flock was fed on the earthly pastures of material teachings and temporal goods: "If you be willing and will harken to me, you shall eat the good things of the land" (Is. 1:19). The Lord, therefore, differentiated and set them apart from others by means of the bodily sign of circumcision. "And my covenant shall be in your flesh" (Gen. 17:13); before this it says, "You shall circumcise the flesh of your foreskin, that it may be for a sign of the covenant between me and you" (Gen. 17:11).

In the New Testament the flock he had is the Christian people: "You are now converted to the shepherd and bishop of your souls" (1 Pet. 2:25). "My sheep hear my voice, and I know them; and they follow me" (Jn. 10:27). This flock is fed on the pastures of spiritual doctrine and spiritual favors; hence the Lord differentiated it from others by a spiritual sign. This is the Holy Spirit through whom those who are of Christ are distinguished from the others who do not belong to him. But since the Holy Spirit is love, he is given to someone when that person is made a lover of God and neighbor. "The charity of God is poured forth in our hearts, by the Holy Ghost who is given to us" (Rom. 5:5). Therefore, the distinctive sign is charity which comes from the Holy Spirit: "By this shall all men know that you are my disciples, if you have love one for another" (Jn. 13:35). The Holy Spirit is he by whom we are signed.

The Spirit is described as a promise for three reasons. First, he is promised to those who believe: "I will put a new spirit within you. . . And I will give you a new spirit" (Ez. 36:26, 37:6).

Secondly, he is given with a certain promise, by the very fact that he is given to us we become the children of God. For through the Holy Spirit we are made one with Christ: "If any man have not the Spirit of God, he is none of his" (Rom. 8:9). As a result of being made adopted children of God, we have the promise of an eternal inheritance since "if sons, heirs also" (Rom. 8:17).

Thirdly, he is termed a **pledge** inasmuch as he makes us certain of the promised **inheritance**. Adopting us into the children of God, the Holy Spirit is the **Spirit of promise** who also is the seal of the promise yet to be attained.

However, as is mentioned in a Gloss, a variant reading has **who is the earnest of our inheritance**, and perhaps this is a better rendering. For a pledge differs from the object in place of which it is given, and it must be returned once he who has received the pledge obtains the object due him. An earnest, however, does not differ from the object in place of which it is given, nor is it returned since it is a partial payment of the price itself, which is not to be withdrawn but completed. God communicates charity to us as a pledge, through the Holy Spirit who is the spirit of truth and love. Hence, this is nothing else than an individual and imperfect participation in the divine charity and love; it must not be withdrawn but brought to perfection. More fittingly, therefore, it is referred to as an earnest rather than as a pledge.

Nevertheless, it can also be called a pledge. For through the Holy Spirit God grants us a variety of gifts. Some of these will remain in the fatherland, as charity which "never falleth away" (1 Cor. 13:8); while others will not last on account of their imperfection, such as faith and hope which "shall be done away" with (*ibid.*, v. 10). Hence, the Spirit is called an earnest in reference to what will remain, and a pledge with respect to what will be done away with.

He adds the purpose for which we are signed as **unto the redemption**. For when a man buys new animals and adds them to his flock, he puts a mark on them to the effect that he has purchased them. Now Christ has purchased a people from the Gentiles. "Other sheep I have that are not of this fold; them also I must bring. And they shall hear my voice; and there shall be one fold and one shepherd" (Jn. 10:16). And on them he imprints a sign of purchase: "A holy nation, a purchased people" (1 Pet. 2:9) "which he hath purchased with his own blood" (Ac. 20:28).

Christ acquired this people, not because they never were his, but because they previously belonged to him and yet, by sinning, had sold themselves into a diabolical slavery which oppressed them. So it does not simply state that he acquired them but adds **unto redemption,** as though to say: You are not strictly a new acquisition; you are re-purchased from the slavery of the devil through his blood. "You were not redeemed with corruptible things as gold or silver, from the vain manner of life handed down from your fathers: but with the precious blood of Christ" (1 Pet. 1:18-19). Christ purchased us, therefore, through a redemption; not that this added anything to God since he needs none of our goods. "And if thou do justly, what shall thou give him [God], or what shall he receive of thy hand?" (Job 35:7). The purpose for which Christ acquired us is **unto the praise of his glory,** that God himself be praised since "everyone that calleth upon my name, I have created him for my glory" (Is. 43:7).

Meister Eckhart
1260-1327

Eckhart was born in Thuringia and entered the Dominicans in Erfurt. In 1277 he was a student in Paris and before 1280 he had started studying theology in Cologne. In the years 1293-1294, as a bachelor of theology, he commented on the Sentences *of Peter Lombard in Paris. He graduated as master of theology at Paris and lectured there in 1302-1303, then he was appointed Provincial of Saxony (1303-1311). In 1311 he went back to Paris for a second regency in theology, then from 1313 to 1323 was professor of theology at Strasbourg. During this period he became very active as a preacher and spiritual director.*

In 1326 Meister Eckhart encountered serious difficulties over his doctrine. Several statements from his sermons were reported by inquisitors to the Archbishop of Cologne, and Eckhart defended himself vigorously. He appealed his case to the Holy See and left for Avignon to defend himself personally, but died before the case was finished. There have been controversies ever since about various aspects of what he taught or was thought to have taught.

In his treatment of the Prologue of John's Gospel we can see an example of the best and the worst of scholastic biblical commentary. The admirable part is the focus on the text, the persistent effort to derive from it every last insight, as it were, to squeeze it dry. In the process one might just as readily appeal to the Apostle (Paul), to Aristotle, to Augustine, or to Averroës, as to one's own light of reason. The virtually endless enumeration of aspects, some of the subtlest kind, does not sit well with contemporary tastes, but once more it must be kept in mind that the resources for more fruitful exploration were simply not yet on hand. Hebrew and Greek were largely unknown in this Latin world, and little in the way of ancillary sciences could be called upon.

In saying this, however, we must acknowledge that far too little study has as yet been devoted to the use of the Bible in the Middle Ages. As such studies advance, it will undoubtedly be necessary to modify some of our current outlooks, but certain shortcomings seem clearly to be here. People like Meister Eckhart retained a concern for the literal sense, "but only as a basis for the spiritual interpretation. First and foremost the Scriptures were a means to holiness . . . The long line of commentators who developed the spiritual senses were not only contemplatives but men of action . . . They subordinated scholarship to mysticism and to propaganda." (Beryl Smalley).

The Bible has had its ups and downs in the heart of the Church. Sometimes, especially in later ages, it was either ignored or not taken seriously enough. That is something that Eckhart can certainly not be accused of. Whether or not this type of commentary played a role in making the Bible more peripheral than it should be is an open question. But what is beyond doubt is that his intention was to make the Word of God central in the life of the Church of Christ.

COMMENTARY ON THE GOSPEL ACCORDING TO JOHN

PROLOGUE

In the beginning was the Word

A mighty eagle with great wings and long, trailing limbs, clothed in rich, variegated plumage, came into Lebanon and carried off the heart of the cedar. He tore off the top of its foliage and bore it into the land of Canaan' (Ezekiel xvii, 3-4). This refers to John the Evangelist himself, 'building his nest', the nest from which he looks forth, contemplates and preaches, 'on the heights, on steep crags and inaccessible rocks' (Job xxxix, 27-8). 'He came unto Lebanon, carried off the heart of the cedar, tore off the top of its foliage and bore it into the land of Canaan,' in that he drank of the Word itself in the bosom of the Father and proclaimed it to all who dwell on the earth, saying: 'In the beginning was the Word.' For 'he excels among the writers of the Gospels', as Augustine says, 'in the profundity of his treatment of the divine mysteries'. 'And in the image of the four living creatures' (Ezekiel i and Apocalypse iv) 'he is likened to the eagle, which flies higher than all the other birds and gazes on the sun's rays with undazzled eyes.' He it was who lay on his Master's breast at the Last Supper and pre-eminently above the rest drank from its very source in the Lord's breast the draught of heavenly wisdom; and he made it his concern to commend unto us the divinity of Christ and the mystery of the Trinity. And this is the purport of his saying: 'In the beginning was the Word.'

In his commentary upon this and other ensuing verses it is the intention of the author—as it has been indeed in all his works—to expound by means of the natural arguments of the philosophers the doctrines taught by the holy Christian faith and the Scriptures of the Old and New Testaments. 'For the invisible things of God from the creation of the world are clearly seen, being understood by the things that are made: even the eternal power'—that is to say, the Son—'and God-head'—that is, the Holy Spirit—as the Gloss on this verse states. Augustine in Book vii of his *Confessions* declares that he read the verse, 'In the beginning was the Word', and a great part of this first chapter of John's Gospel in the works of Plato. And in Book x of his *De Civitate Dei* he tells of a certain Platonist who used to say that the opening words of this chapter as far as 'There was a man sent from God' should be inscribed in letters of gold and 'displayed in the most exalted places'.

It is, moreover, the object of this work to show how the truths of natural principles, inferences and properties are clearly intimated—for him 'that hath ears to hear'—in the very words of Holy Scripture expounded with the help of these natural truths. Some comments, too, of moral significance are occasionally introduced.

CHAPTER 1

On these lines, accordingly, we have to expound the statement: 'In the beginning was the Word.' It must be pointed out in the first place that this very statement, 'In the beginning was the Word, and the Word was with God', and several of the ensuing statements are contained in the words: 'And God said, let there be light: and there was light. And God saw the light, that it was good, and He separated the light and the darkness' (Genesis, i, 3-4).

In order to make clear the meaning of this passage from 'In the beginning was the Word' down to 'There was a man sent from God', it must be pointed out in the first place that it is natural and generally true, both in divine matters, which are under discussion here, and in the world of nature and art, that whatever is produced by or issues from anything exists previously in that thing. A fig, for example, would be no more likely to issue from a fig-tree than from a vine or a pear-tree, unless it had prior existence and was previously in the fig-tree itself.

Moreover, secondly, it has prior existence in that thing like the seed in its source. This is what is expressed here by the statement: 'In the beginning was the Word.' 'The seed is the Word of God' (Luke viii, II).

Thirdly, it must be noted that whatever is produced by anything is universally its 'word', declaring, announcing and proclaiming that from which it issues. Therefore he says: 'In the beginning was the Word.'

Fourthly, it must be noted that the thing which issues is in its producer as the idea and likeness in which and in accordance with which it is produced by the producer. So the Greek text has: 'In the beginning was the Word', that is, the *Logos*, which signifies word and idea in Latin.

We have, accordingly, four considerations, namely that the thing issuing is in the producer, that it is in it as the seed is in its source, as the word is in the speaker, and that it is in it as the idea, in which and through which the product issues from the producer.

In the fifth place, however, we must realize that by the very fact of a thing's issuing from something else it is distinguished from it. Hence follows the statement: 'The Word was with God.' It does not say 'below God', nor 'it came down from God', but 'the Word was with God'. For the expression 'with God' indicates a certain measure of equality. In this connexion it should be noted that in analogical relations the product is always inferior, less, more imperfect than, and unequal to the producer, whereas in homogeneous relations it is always equal to it, not sharing the same nature but receiving it in its totality, simply and integrally and on an equal footing, from its principle.

Hence, sixthly, that which issues forth is the 'son' of the producer. For a son is one who becomes another in respect of personality but not other in nature.

From this it follows, seventhly, that the son or the word is identical with the father or principle. And so we have next: 'The Word was God.' Yet here it must be noted that, although the product in analogical relations derives from the producer, it is nevertheless below its principle, not with it. Furthermore, it is other in nature and so is not the principle itself. Yet in so far as it is in the latter, it is not other in nature nor yet in substance. A chest in the mind of an artist is not a chest but the life and intelligence of the artist, his actual concept. My purpose in mentioning this point is to bring out the implication contained in these words on the procession of the divine Persons, namely, that the same thing holds good and is found in the procession and production of every being in nature and in art.

Eighthly, it should be noted that the chest which issues or is produced externally into being nevertheless is and remains in the artist himself, just as it was from the beginning, before it became a chest, and that it continues to do so, even if it be destroyed externally. Hence follows the statement: 'This Word was in the beginning with God.' For prior to this he had said: 'In the beginning was the Word.'

Ninthly, it must be realized that the procession or production and emanation of which we speak takes place properly, primarily and above all by way of generation, a generation which is not effected with movement or in time but which is the end and terminus of movement in that it is concerned with the substance and being of a thing. Consequently it does not pass over into non-being nor does it flow into the past. That being so, it is always 'in the beginning'—so too with us, if you do away with time, sunset is sunrise—and, if it is always 'in the beginning', it is always in process of being born, of being begotten. Either never or always, since the 'beginning' or 'in the beginning' is always. And so it comes about that the Son in the Godhead, the Word 'in the beginning' is always being born, is always already born. That is what is meant by the ensuing word 'was': 'In the beginning *was* the Word.' For the Word 'was' implies three things—substance, since it is a substantive verb, the past and the imperfect. In that it is substantive, the Word is the very substance of the principle: in that it is past, it (has been and so) always *is* born: in that it is imperfect, it is always *being* born. That is why in each of the four first clauses, when John speaks of the Word, he invariably employs this word 'was' with its connotations of substance, past and imperfect.

It is to be noted tenthly that it is the property of the intellect to receive its object—its intelligible object, that is to say—not as it is in itself, as something whole, perfect and good, but in its beginnings. And this is expressed by the statements:

'In the beginning was the Word' and 'This Word was in the beginning with God'.

Note, in the eleventh place, that the 'word', the mental concept or the art itself, in the mind of the artist is the means whereby he makes everything and without which, as artist, he makes nothing. This is what is expressed in the next sentence: 'All things were made by Him and without Him nothing was made.'

Twelfthly, the chest in the mind and art of the artist is neither a chest nor is it made, but is art itself, is life, the living concept of the artist. And this is what is expressed by 'What was made in Him was life'.

Thirteenthly, the word, as idea, pertains to the rational faculty, which is proper to man. For man is a rational animal and 'mankind', as Aristotle says in Book I of his *Metaphysics*, lives 'by art and reason'. Hence not only is the word life but the life is the light of men. And this is expressed in the next phrase: 'And the life was the light of men.'

Again, fourteenthly, the word, as idea and art, shines just as much in the night as by day and illumines things inwardly hidden no less than those externally manifest. This is what is expressed by the words, 'And the light shineth in darkness'—in contrast with physical light, which is not life, nor properly speaking the light of men, and which does not shine in the night nor illumine things inwardly hidden.

Indeed it would be more correct to say that in the case of created things nothing 'shines' but their ideas. 'For the idea of a thing, which is expressed by its name, is its definition', as the philosopher says. But a definition is a means of demonstrating something, or rather a complete demonstration effecting knowledge of a thing. It is obvious, therefore, that in the case of created things nothing 'shines' save only the idea of the things. Hence the statement here that the word is 'the light of men', in other words their 'idea'. Hence too the statement, 'And the light shineth in darkness', as though to say: in the case of created things nothing shines, nothing is known, nothing effects knowledge, save the quiddity, the essential nature, of the thing itself, its definition or idea.

Fifteenthly, it must be realized that the word, the *Logos* or idea of things, is in the things, and indeed wholly in each one of them, in such a way that it is nevertheless wholly outside each, wholly within and wholly without. This is obvious in the living creature, in each species and in every single member of the various species. For that reason the idea of a thing remains completely immovable and exempt from destruction even although the thing itself be moved, changed or destroyed. Nothing, for example, is so eternal and immutable as the idea of a circle which is obliterated. For how could that which is wholly outside the circle be obliterated with the obliteration of the circle itself?

The idea, then, is 'the light shining in darkness'—that is to say in created things—yet not enclosed, intermingled or comprehended by it. And that is the Apostle's reason for adding to the words in question the statement: 'And the darkness comprehended it not.' We find the same idea stated in the *De Causis* in the words: 'The first cause governs all things without being involved in them.' The first cause of anything is its idea, the *Logos,* 'the Word in the beginning'.

We can see then how this passage, from 'in the beginning was the Word' down to 'There was a man sent from God', may be expounded by means of the ideas and properties of natural things. It is clear too that the actual words of the Evangelist, if subjected to careful scrutiny, teach us about the nature and properties of things whether in being or in operation and so in addition to establishing our faith provide us with instruction on the nature of things. For the Son of God Himself, 'the Word in the beginning', is the Idea, 'a sort of creative power charged with all living and immutable ideas, which are all one in it', as Augustine says in the last chapter of Book vi of his *De Trinitate.*

An example of all that we have been saying and of several things that we shall frequently have occasion to mention may be found in the consideration of the just man, in so far as he is just, in relation to justice which begets him.

Thus, it is obvious in the first place that the just man as such is *in* justice itself. For how could he be just, if he were outside justice, if he stood without, separated from justice?

214

Secondly, the just man is present in justice itself as the concrete in the abstract, the participant in that wherein he participates.

Thirdly, the just man is the 'word' of justice, by means of which justice declares and manifests itself. For if justice did not justify anyone, no one would know it: it would be known only to itself, as in the verses: 'No man hath seen God at any time; the only-begotten, which is in the bosom of the Father, hath Himself declared Him' (John i, 18), and 'Neither knoweth any man the Father save the Son' (Matthew xi, 27), and 'No man knoweth save he that receiveth' (Apocalypse ii, 17). It is universally true that no one knows divine perfection 'save he. that receiveth it'. Justice, therefore, is known only to itself and to the just man whom it has taken unto itself. And this is what is expressed in the dictum that the Trinity, God, is known only to Himself and to the man He has taken unto Himself. Hence the words of the Psalm: 'Blessed is the man whom Thou hast chosen and taken unto Thyself.'

Fourthly, it is clear that justice contains within itself an exemplar, which is the likeness or idea in which and according to which it forms and informs or invests every just person and everything just.

Fifthly, the just man proceeding from and begotten by justice is distinguished from it by that very fact. For nothing can beget itself. And yet the just man is not different in nature from justice, since on the one hand 'just' signifies justice alone, just as 'white' signifies the quality of whiteness alone, and on the other hand justice would not make anyone just, if its nature varied from one place to another, just as whiteness does not make anything black nor grammar anyone musical.

Sixthly, it is obvious from this that the just man is the offspring and son of justice. He is called, and actually is, the son because he becomes different in person but not in nature. 'I and my Father are one' (John x, 30): we 'are', that is to say, distinct in person, since nothing begets itself, but 'one' in nature, because otherwise justice would not beget the just man, nor the Father the Son, to become other than Himself, nor would generation in that case be homogeneous. This is what is meant by 'God was the Word'.

Now if the Father and the Son, justice and the just man, are one and the same nature, it follows, seventhly, that the just man is equal to, not less than, justice, and similarly with the Son in relationship to the Father. This is expressed by 'The Word was with God'. The term 'with' signifies equality, as we have said previously.

Again, eighthly, in begetting or justifying the just man justice does not cease to be justice nor does it cease to be the principle and idea of the just man. And this is what is meant by the statement: 'This Word was in the beginning with God.'

Ninthly, it is clear that justice and the just man as such are no more subject to movement and time than are life and light. For this reason the just man is always in process of being born from justice itself, just as he has been born from it from the beginning ever since he has been just. This is the case, too, with the genesis and persistence of light in a medium: it is continuously generated for the very reason that it does not persist continuously.

Tenthly, the just man as such is what he is, wholly and completely, from and in justice itself as his principle. This is expressed by the statement: 'In the beginning was the Word.' Furthermore, the just man, in so far as he is just, knows nothing, not even himself, save in justice. Indeed how could he know himself as a just man outside justice itself, which is in fact the principle of the just man? It is characteristic of man and of the reason to know things in their principles.

Again, in the eleventh place, it is clear that justice effects its entire operation through the medium of begotten justice. For just as nothing just could be begotten without justice, so once begotten it could not exist without begotten justice. But begotten justice itself is the 'word' of justice in its principle, the justice that gives it birth. This therefore is what is expressed by the words: 'All things were made by Him and without Him nothing was made.'

Again, twelfthly, the just man in justice itself is no longer begotten, nor is he begotten justice, but is unbegotten justice itself. And this is expressed by the statement, 'What was made' —or produced by any means of production whatsoever—'in Him was life', i.e. 'a beginning without beginning'. For only that which is without a beginning lives in the true sense of the word. Everything that has the source or beginning of its operation in something else, other than itself, does not live in the true sense of the word.

Moreover, thirteenthly, the just man in justice itself, his principle, by the very fact of being unbegotten, 'a beginning without beginning', and life, is also light. For every single thing is light and is luminous in its first principles. All knowledge of things is effected through and in their first principles and, until it is reduced to these principles, it is always obscure, dark and gloomy, since it involves the fear that the alternative view may be correct. But the proof, or syllogism, which enables us to know without fear and not just as a matter of opinion, is derived from the appropriate principles. And this is expressed here by the statement: 'The life was the light of men.' He says 'men', perhaps because man obtains his knowledge from things which come later in the order of being and proceeds to principles by the exercise of reason. This is not the case with higher intellectual creatures. And this is perhaps implied by the next phrase: 'The light shineth in darkness.' For every created thing is tainted with the shadow of nothingness. 'God' alone 'is light, and in Him is no darkness at all'. 'The light in darkness', accordingly, is knowledge *a posteriori*, knowledge in and through an image.

Or to consider the question from a different standpoint: it is universally the case that the origin is the light of that which it originates, the superior the light of its inferior. Conversely, the thing originated and inferior, by the very fact that it is inferior and later, as having its being from another, is in itself darkness, the darkness of privation or negation—of privation, that is to say, in the realm of the transient and corporeal, of negation in the spiritual realm. This, then, is what is meant by the words: 'The light shineth in darkness.' But as the inferior is never the equal of its superior, the statement is followed by the words: 'And the darkness comprehended it not.'

For the just man, whom we are discussing now by way of example, considered in himself or for what he is in himself, is not light. Hence the statement which is made later about John the Baptist himself, who was assuredly a just man: 'He was not that light.' And this is the fourteenth point, that the just man or that which is just, being dark in itself, does not shine. In justice itself, however, which is its principle, it does shine, and justice in turn shines in it, although by reason of its inferiority it does not comprehend justice.

Fifteenthly, it is clear that justice is present in its entirety in every just man. For half of justice is not justice. But if it is entire in every just man, it is also entirely outside every just man and everything just. And this is implied by the statement: 'The darkness comprehended it not.'

A great many passages in the Scriptures can be expounded in accordance with the foregoing remarks, particularly those referring to the only-begotten Son of God—as for example that He is 'the image of God'.

An image in so far as it is an image, receives nothing of its own from the subject in which it exists but receives its whole being from the object of which it is the image.

Secondly, it receives its being from the object alone.

Thirdly, it receives the whole being of the object in accordance with all that makes it an exemplar. For if an image received anything from something else or if it failed to receive any feature of its exemplar, it would no longer be an image of that thing but of something else.

Hence it is clear, fourthly, that the image of anything is unique in itself and refers only to one thing. There in God the Son is unique and is the Son of one alone, namely the Father.

Fifthly, it is clear from what has been said that the image is in its exemplar, since there it receives its whole being. And conversely, the exemplar, in so far as it is an exemplar, is in its image by virtue of the fact that the image contains within itself the whole being of the exemplar. 'I am in the Father and the Father is in Me' (John xiv, II).

Furthermore, it follows sixthly that the image and that of which it is an image, in so far as they are such, are one. 'I and the Father are one' (John x, 30). He uses the plural 'are' inasmuch as the exemplar is expressive or generative, the image expressed or begotten, but the singular 'one' inasmuch as the whole being of the one is in the other and nothing alien is to be found in them.

Again, seventhly, such expression or generation of an image is a sort of formal emanation. Hence the Commentator in the second book of *De Anima* maintains that the production of a visible image in the sense of sight has no need of external light, either for the visible object, which multiplies itself of its own accord, or even for the sense of sight, which automatically receives the image of the visible object, but needs it only for the transmitting medium.

Eighthly, the image and the exemplar are coeval—and this is implied by the statement, 'The Word (the image) was in the beginning with God'—so that the exemplar cannot be understood without the image nor the image without the exemplar. 'He that seeth Me, seeth also My Father' (John xiv, 9).

Further, ninthly, no one knows the image save the exemplar, nor does anyone know the exemplar save the image. 'No man knoweth the Son but the Father; neither knoweth any man the Father save the Son' (Matthew xi, 27). The reason is that their being is one and that neither has aught alien to the other. The principles of being and knowing are the same and nothing is known through anything alien to itself.

The foregoing and many similar conclusions emerge clearly from a comparison of the just with justice, the being with its act of existing, the good with goodness and, in general, the concrete with its corresponding abstract.

These statements about the image, however, are clearly resumed in the seventh chapter of the Book of Wisdom, where it is said of Wisdom, or the Word of God, that she is 'an unspotted mirror', 'a pure emanation of God'. Also that she is 'the image of His goodness' and that 'no defiled thing entereth into her'. Also that she is 'the breath of the power of God' and 'the brightness of everlasting light'.

These considerations, as we have said above, will also serve to explain almost everything that is written concerning the divinity of the Son.

This, then, should suffice for the present as one way of expounding the passage from 'In the beginning was the Word' as far as 'There was a man sent from God'.

Secondly: to understand the statement, 'In the beginning was the Word' one should know that Augustine in his *Liber lxxxiii Quaestionum,* in the chapter entitled 'Of the Word of God', writes as follows: ' "In the beginning was the Word." The Greek word *logos* signifies in Latin "idea" as well as "word". But in this context it is better to translate it as "word" in order to bring out its reference not only to the Father but to all that has been made through the Word, by its operative power. The use of the term "idea", however, is quite appropriate even if nothing is made by its agency.' Thus far Augustine. It is clearly in keeping with this that the science which teaches us to formulate ideas in the individual sciences and about individual things is called 'logic', from *logos* (idea). Again logic is also called the science of correct speech, because *logos* means speech or word.

Secondly, it should be noted that 'idea' is taken in a double sense. For there is the idea received or abstracted by the intellect from things, the idea in this case being subsequent to the things from which it is abstracted. There is also an idea which is prior to things, the cause and idea of the things, which is indicated by the definition and is grasped by the intellect in the innermost ground of the things themselves. The latter is the idea now under discussion. Therefore it is said that the *logos,* that is, the idea, is in the beginning. 'In the beginning', he says, 'was the Word.'

Following on these preliminary observations it must be realized that every agent, whether in nature or in art, effects its own likeness and therefore always bears within itself that which it makes its effect resemble. That is the principle in virtue of which the agent acts, for otherwise it would act in a haphazard way and not by design. To take an example, the architect of a house, in so far as he is an architect, has within himself, in his own mind, the form of the house, upon which he models the external house. The form is the principle by means of which the architect operates and produces externally in the appropriate material and is the word whereby he utters and expresses himself and all that is proper to him as a house-builder. Similarly in nature a hot body, such as fire, assimilates to itself anything which responds to heat, heat being the principle in virtue of which fire operates, the word whereby it utters, speaks or manifests itself in so far as it is hot. Now if the architect were

220

to build a house of his own substance, in so far as he is a man, this particular man, then the external house, his effect, would be the word whereby he uttered himself, his substance, his entire being as man and as this particular man. His effect, too, the external house, would be in his substance and so, in consequence, would actually be his substance, just as at present it is the effect of his mental image of the house, of his art, and indeed is art itself, differentiated only by certain factors alien to the form of the house, such as material, place, time and the like. This is implied by the statements, 'In the beginning was the Word, and the Word was God' and 'What was made in Him was life'.

Further it should be noted that it is quite otherwise with the effect in the case of a proximate and homogeneous cause, for example with fire in the case of fire, where the principle, namely the generating fire, possesses indeed the form of the fire generated but not the idea of fire. For bodily nature as such does not distinguish between the thing and the idea, since it does not know the idea, which is only received and known by a rational or intellectual being. Hence, in the case of the intellect, its effect in itself is not only word, but word and idea combined, the twofold connotation of *logos* mentioned above. And so we find it stated, most significantly, that 'in the beginning was the *Logos*' that it was with God', that 'it was God', and fourthly, that 'it was in the beginning with God'. For the idea is certainly *in* the primal intellect properly speaking: and it is '*with* God', that is to say in every intellectual being that is close to Him, that is His image or is made after His image, that is 'God's offspring' (Acts xvii, 29). Or (it may be said to be) *with* Him, because He always knows in act and in knowing begets the idea; and the idea which His knowing begets is God Himself. 'The Word was God' and 'this was in the beginning with God', because He has always known and has always begotten the Son. Augustine says: 'If He has always been the Father, He has always had the Son.' Or again, 'it was from the beginning with God', because He always begets in acts, as He 'was'—that is, as He has begotten—'from the beginning': it is a case of either always or never, since end and beginning are here identical, as was said above. And such an agent, namely the principle in which resides the *logos* or idea, is an essential agent bearing its effect previously within itself in nobler mode and extending its causal efficacy over the entire species.

'In the beginning was the Word.' For our third exposition of these words we must note that in created things the idea of each thing is universally its principle and is the cause of all the properties and qualities found in it. Hence the Commentator on Book vii of the *Metaphysics* declares that the ancients were always greatly exercised by the problem of the essence of things, since once this is known the cause of everything, that is of everything in the thing itself, is also known. For the principles of a substance, which are indicated by the terms of its definition, which is the idea of a thing, indicates in respect of the subject *what* it is and in respect of its qualities the reason *why* they are, and is a means of demonstrating or a complete demonstration effecting knowledge. On these lines, therefore, one can expound the words, 'In the beginning was the Logos', that is, the idea.

Further, for our fourth exposition of the text, 'in the beginning was the Word', it must be noted that the Word or the Son in God has four properties. First, He is innermost: 'Receive the engrafted word' (James i, 21). Secondly, He is the firstborn of all creation: 'the image of the invisible God, the firstborn of every creature' (Colossians i, 15). Thirdly, He is always being born and always is born, as has been explained above. Fourthly, He issues from the Father by way of intellect, as the Holy Spirit by way of Love.

And this is what is declared in the text, 'in the beginning was the Word'. 'In' refers to the first of these properties, 'beginning' to the second, 'was', in that it is a substantive verb in the imperfect tense, to the third, and 'the Word' to the fourth, since the Word is the idea and idea pertains to the intellect, whose function it is to apprehend one thing under a diversity of concepts, to distinguish those things which are one in nature and in being and to apprehend somehow the order whereby one thing is prior to another or one person derived from another.

In this connexion it must be clearly noted that intellect in God especially, and perhaps in Him alone, as the first principle of all things, is entirely and essentially intellect, absolutely pure

222

intelligence. In Him indeed reality and intellect are the same. Therefore 'the relations which follow the operations of the intellect' in God are real. And so 'the Word', or Son, 'which proceeds in intellectual mode' from the Father, 'is not just a relationship of idea but of reality, since both intellect and idea are actual realities, or rather constitute one actual reality'. Hence Augustine too says: 'The realities which make us blessed are the Father, the Son and the Holy Spirit.'

With reference to the first of the aforementioned points, denoted by the preposition 'in', note that it is proper to God and to everything divine, in so far as they are divine, to be within, to be innermost. This is evident from the first proposition of *De Causis,* especially in the commentary. It is also evident in God's first external effect, which is being, the innermost thing of all, according to the words of Augustine: 'Thou wast within and I without.' It is evident thirdly in the powers of the soul which are the more inward the more divine and perfect they are.

The second main point, expressed by the word 'beginning', is clear from what has been said above, for the first and innermost property of everything is its idea. But the word is the Logos or idea.

We have already discussed the third and fourth points denoted by 'was' and 'the Word'.

This, then, is the meaning of the text: 'In the beginning was the Word.'

Again, fifthly: 'In the beginning was the Word.' In the literal sense the Evangelist means that in the Deity there is a personal emanation and generation of the Son from the Father. In this respect the New Testament differs from the Old, since in the latter there is no explicit reference to the emanation of the Persons, whereas the New Testament speaks everywhere of the Son, both with regard to His divinity and His humanity.

So far as concerns His divinity, four points are noted in these words concerning the Son of God in relation to the Father. Firstly, He is consubstantial with the Father, as is shown by the statement that He is in the Father: 'In the beginning was the Word.' For all that is in the Father is consubstantial with the Father. The second point is that there is a personal distinction between them, as is clear from the statement: 'The Word was with God.' The third is their absolute unity in being and nature, a unity which does not even admit of parts in the idea or definition, such as genus and difference. This point is made in the statement: 'The Word was God.' The fourth is the co-eternity of the Son with the Father: 'This Word was in the beginning with God.'

From this it is clear that the emanation of the Son or the Word from the Father is personal. 'The Word, however, must have breath or spirit, for even our own word cannot dispense with breath', as John of Damascus says. So the distinction of the three Persons in God is clearly referred to here.

And since the effect is always the expression and representation or 'word' of its principle, it follows that the foregoing words, 'In the beginning was the Word and the Word was with God and the Word was God. The same was in the beginning with God', can be expounded in a sixth way as applying to every work of nature and art.

It is obvious in the first place that the form of any shape and the image of that which he paints externally on the wall, is in the painter as an indwelling form. This is what is meant here by: 'In the beginning was the Word.'

Secondly, the image must be with him as an exemplar in accordance with which and by reference to which he executes his work. 'It does not matter', declares Seneca in one of his *Epistles,* 'whether he has an external model to which he can refer or an internal one which he imagines to himself.' This is expressed here by: 'The Word was with God.'

Thirdly, the image depicted in the mind of the painter is the art itself, in virtue of which the painter is the principle of the painted image. This is expressed by 'God was the Word', that is to say the principle or cause of the effect in a relationship similar to that existing between the bath in the soul and the material bath, as the Commentator says, or the figure in the mind and the figure on the wall.

Again, fourthly, it is obvious that Polycletus, to use an instance cited by the Philosopher, is not the source or principle of a statue before he acquires the art of sculpture, nor can he be such if he ceases to possess this art. It is clear, therefore, that from the start, once he has become an artist and as long as he is an artist capable of creative work, art remains with him. This is the meaning of 'The Word was in the beginning with God', that is, the art with the artist, coeval with him, as the Son is with the Father in God. I have dealt with this point in my remarks on the saying, 'He saw three and worshipped one', in my second Genesis Commentary.

Again, seventhly: 'In the beginning was the Word.' It should be noted that there are four natural conditions for any essential principle. First, that the thing originated by it be contained in it as the effect is contained in the cause. This is expressed by the statement: 'It was in the beginning.' Secondly, that the thing originated should not merely be in it but should have a prior and more exalted existence in it than it has in itself. Thirdly, that the principle itself is always pure intellect, in which there is no being other than understanding, having, as Anaxagoras says in the third book of Aristotle's *De Anima*, nothing in common with anything. The fourth condition is that in the principle and with it the effect is coeval in power with the principle.

The last three points are indicated by the expression, 'the Word', that is, the idea. For what the effect possesses formally, the idea not only possesses but possesses in a prior and more exalted way since it does so virtually. Again the idea is also in the intellect, is formed by understanding and is nothing but understanding. Furthermore it is coeval with the intellect, since it is understanding itself and the intellect itself. This is expressed by the ensuing words: 'The Word was with God, and God was the Word. The same was in the beginning with God.'

Now it should be noted that the foregoing words have been expounded in many ways to this end, that the reader may select from them now one, now another according to taste, as it suits him. This method of expounding the same thing in many ways I also follow in my numerous commentaries.

There still remains, however, a question about this statement: 'In the beginning was the Word.' For as the first property of the Word or the Son in God seems to be that He was begotten by the Father, why does it say 'In the beginning was the

Word', and not 'From the beginning'? It seems that there are manifold reasons.

The first is that the word or the art remains in the artist, even although it issues forth in the work. The second reason is that it is proper to that which is divine to be indwelling and to be innermost. The third reason is that the Son has been born from the Father from the beginning in such a way that He is nevertheless always being born. The fourth reason is that it is the property of reason to apprehend things themselves in their principles. All these four points have been demonstrated above.

The fifth reason is that the Word itself, the exemplar of created things, is not something external to which God must refer, as is the case with us in the relationship between the picture of a wall and the painter, who refers to the exemplar of the actual wall, but is the Father Himself. 'In the beginning', he says, 'was the Word.' This is what Boethius says in the third book of his *De Consolatione Philosophiae,* addressing God:

'No external causes compelled Thee to fashion
The creation of fluid matter, but the inherent
Form of the highest goodness.'

In this connexion, however, it is better to point out that inspection of the external exemplar never gives rise to the work of the artist unless it receives the idea of the inherent form. Otherwise the amateur would make as good a picture as the expert since both see the external exemplar equally well. Therefore the work that is 'with', 'outside' and 'above' the artist must become the work that is 'in' him, taking form within him, in other words, to the end that he may produce a work of art, in accordance with the verse, 'The Holy Ghost shall come upon Thee' (Luke i, 35), that is, so that the 'above' may become 'in'. And this is what is meant by the phrase, 'In the beginning was' and the ensuing statement, 'And the Word was with God': the first expresses the formal cause, which is *in* the Father, the second the form or cause operating in the exemplar, that is, *with* the Father.

The sixth reason or cause why it is preferable to say that the Word or Son is 'in' rather than 'from' the Father or the beginning is that the word 'from' denotes the efficient cause or makes known and denotes the property of that which produces the effect, whereas 'in' shows the nature of the final cause. Now God, although He is the efficient and the final cause alike of all created things, is nevertheless much more truly, previously and properly the final cause of everything that is caused, which according to the statement of the Philosopher 'produces motion as that which is loved'. He also says that the end is the first cause in causation, and this is appropriate for the First, namely God, who is simply the first cause. Moreover, the efficient cause acts only with a view to the end and is moved by the end and on account of the end. Consequently it is 'a moved mover' and comes second in the order of causality. But this is not properly true of God. I have dealt exhaustively with this question in the treatise *Concerning the End*. This, then, is why the text says, 'In the beginning', that is to say, in the Father, 'was the Word' and not 'from the beginning' or 'from the Father'.

From the foregoing then it is to be noted that things are brought into being virtually by their end but formally by the efficient agent, hence more fundamentally, earlier and in more noble mode by the end than by the effective agent. So, too, liberty is in the will but depends on the reason and the intellect. And again, the power of generation which resides in God belongs directly and more originally to the essence than to the relation, which is paternity.

'In the beginning was the Word.' It must be noted that every effect has its being more truly and more nobly in its cause, but only in the first cause does it have being simply and absolutely. This is what is meant by: 'In the beginning was.' For in every cause short of God its effect has this or that being, just as the cause itself *is* this or that being. In God alone, however, who is pure being, every effect has its being, the fact that it is, in accordance with the words, 'All things were made by Him', as they are explained below.

But it is noteworthy that the Son in the Father is the Word, that is, the idea, which was not made. The same Son, however, is in the world no longer according to the property of the word or the idea and the knowing intellect but according to the property of being. This is why the world was made by Him but did not know Him. And this is the meaning of 'in the beginning', that is to say, in the Father, 'was the Word', whereas below it says, 'He was in the world and the world was made by Him and the world knew Him not'; and later, in the seventeenth chapter: 'O righteous Father, the world hath not known Thee but I have known Thee.'

'In the beginning was the Word.' It should be noted that all things in the universe were not simply nothing 'before the foundation of the world' but had a certain virtual being, as I have pointed out in my remarks on the verse, 'God saw the light that it was good' (Genesis i). This is expressed here by the words, 'In the beginning', that is to say, before the foundation of the world, 'was the Word', the effect in its primordial, essential and original cause.

In addition he wishes to say and to teach that there is another beginning of things, which is higher than nature, namely the intellect, which orders the separate natural things towards specific ends. And this is what is meant here by 'in the beginning was the word', that is, the idea, which pertains to intellect and to knowledge.

'In the beginning was the Word, and the Word was with God, and God was the Word. The same was in the beginning with God.' According to Augustine, in the sixth chapter of Book viii of the *De Trinitate,* justice or the just soul is not seen in the soul as though it were something imaginary existing outside the soul itself or in the same way as one sees (with the mind's eye) something not actually present to the sight such as Carthage or Alexandria. It is seen, it is true, in the soul as something which is present to it, yet (the soul) stands as it were outside, apart from justice itself, resembling it in some respect but still not quite attaining unto it. It strives, nevertheless, to attain to justice somehow, to grasp it, to enter into it, so that it may become one with justice and justice one with it. And this is achieved 'by adhering to this very form, so that it may take its form therefrom and be itself a just soul'. 'And how else could it adhere to that form (which is justice) except by loving justice?'

Careful examination of the foregoing remarks by Augustine bears out what Aristotle says in Book II of the *Posterior Analytics* that 'the questions (we ask) are equal in number to the things we truly know'. Now the following questions may be asked about things: whether they are, of what nature they are, what they are, and why. The four sentences we have here are the answers to these questions, taken in order. In the statement: 'In the beginning was the Word', you have the fact that it is, since he uses the word 'was'. The nature of the Word is pointed out in the ensuing statement: 'And the Word was with God', as will be made clear below. What it is is expressed next by: 'God was the Word.' The reason why is shown in the statement: 'The same was in the beginning with God.'

To give an example: when it is said that justice is a certain rightness whereby every man receives his due, some who stand without and afar off in the region of unlikeness, 'hearing they hear not, neither do they understand' (Matthew xiii, 13). These are the idols of whom it is said in the Psalms: 'They have ears and will not hear.' Hence in Matthew, in the chapter just quoted, it says: 'Who hath ears to hear, let him hear.'

Another, considering in his mind what he has heard and attracted towards justice, feels a sensation of sweetness in his heart. He knows now what the Word is like, since the Word is good and sweet: 'such is my beloved and he is my friend' (Canticles v, 16). For that which is loved affects the lover. Augustine says: 'Thou art like what thou lovest.' This is what is meant by the statement: 'And the Word was with God.' He says 'with', meaning near and affecting. 'Thou art near, O Lord, and all Thy ways are truth' (Psalms). For the soul desires nothing more strongly than truth, as Augustine says in the *Homilies*. And in the tenth book of the *Confessions* he says: 'Truth is so loved that those who love anything else wish the thing they love to be the truth.' So the man who is affected by the Word, which is truth, knows of what nature it is, since it is sweet, but does not yet know what it is and still seeks to discover what it is.

In the tenth book of the *Confessions* Augustine says: 'Thou dost admit me inwardly into a very unusual emotion, a sort of sweetness.' And Hugh of St. Victor inquires, speaking in the person of the soul: 'What is the sweetness that is wont from time to time to touch me and to affect me so violently and so deliciously that I begin somehow to be wholly estranged from myself and rapt away I know not whither. For suddenly I am renewed and wholly transformed, and I begin to have a sense of well-being greater than I can express. My consciousness is enlivened, all the misery of bygone sorrows is forgotten, my spirit exults, my intellect is fortified, my heart is illumined and my longings satisfied. Already I perceive myself to be elsewhere, I know not where, and I hold, as it were, something in an embrace of love, without knowing what it is.'

To the question what it is the third statement provides an answer: 'And God was the Word.' For the just man, the 'word' of justice is justice itself, as we read later in the tenth chapter of John: 'I and the Father are one.' For the just man denotes justice alone, as has been stated above.

The reason why the Word is we are taught in the next verse: 'The same was in the beginning with God.' For the end is universally the same as the beginning. It has no 'why' or 'wherefore' but is itself the 'why' of and for all things: 'I am the beginning and the end' (Apocalypse i, 8). The same is true of every beginning and everything originated in art and nature, yet to a greater or lesser degree according as one thing is more truly a beginning than another.

'In the beginning was the Word.' In the moral sphere we are taught that the beginning of all our striving and activity must be God, since 'in the beginning was the Word, and God was the Word'. Furthermore, if you wish to know whether all your inner and outer activity is divine or not, and whether it is the operation of God within you and has been done by Him, then consider whether the end of your striving is God. If it is, the action is divine, because the beginning and the end are the same, namely God.

We are taught, moreover, that our work must be rational and conform to the dictates and order of reason, which initiates the work. For it says: 'In the beginning was the Word', that is to say, reason: 'your reasonable service' (Romans xii, I), and 'reasonable without guile' (I Peter ii, 2). And Dionysius in the fourth chapter of *The Divine Names* says that man's good consists in rational being whereas evil is 'contrary to reason'. And in the first book of Aristotle's *Metaphysics* it is said that mankind lives by art and reason. This is what is said in the Psalms: 'There be many that say: Who will show us any good?' And the answer is given: 'The light of thy countenance is stamped upon us, O Lord', as though to say: the reason which is imprinted on us from God's countenance is that which shows us what is good. For that which is done in accordance with reason is well done, is rightly done and is good. It proceeds from the countenance of God, according to the words: 'Let my judgement come forth from thy countenance.' And Augustine in his *De Libero Arbitrio* teaches that every law is just and good by the very fact that it issues from the countenance of God but evil and unjust if it does not issue therefrom.

All things were made by Him

Note: he does not deny that there are other causes of things but he means that the effect does not have its being from any of the other causes, but from God alone. Hence Augustine in the first book of the *Confessions* addresses God with these words: 'There is no vein, by which life and being flows into us, derived from any source other than Thy workmanship, O Lord, for Thou art life and being in the highest degree.' The reason, therefore, for the statement that all things were made by God is that everything produces its own like and nothing acts beyond its own species. But everything short of God is this or that being, not absolute being or existence. That is proper to the First Cause alone, which is God.

Secondly, it is to be noted that the phrase 'all things' applies only to beings. Sin, however, and evil in general are not beings. Consequently they were not made by Him but without Him. This is the meaning of the next statement, 'without Him nothing was made'—that is to say, according to Augustine, sin or evil. Here we are told: 'All things were made by Him.' For evil things are not, neither are they made, because they have not been effected nor are they effects but rather defects of some kind of being.

Note, thirdly, that the expression 'all things' implies division and number, and consequently neither the Son nor the Holy Spirit is included under 'all things', nor anything divine, so far as it is divine.

Fourthly, although various things are produced or made by various secondary causes, each and every thing, whether produced by nature or by art, has its being or the fact that it is immediately from God alone, so that the text may be rearranged to read: 'All things made are by Him.' Hence it follows that 'without Him nothing was made', that is to say, everything made by anyone is nothing without Him. For it is evident that everything that is without being is nothing. For how could it *be* without being? But all being and the being of all things is from God alone, as was said above.

Jacques Benigne Bossuet
1627-1704

Bossuet was born in Dijon, France, and began his studies at the Jesuit college there. He went to Paris in 1642 to continue his studies at the Collège de Navarre. He prepared for the priesthood under Vincent de Paul and was ordained in 1652, the same year that he received his doctorate in theology. The next seven years were spent in Metz, preaching, studying the Bible, and engaging in discussions with Protestants. In 1659 he returned to Paris as a preacher, then in 1670 he was named bishop of Condom and was elected to the French Academy. He resigned his bishopric to become tutor to the Dauphin until the latter's marriage in 1681. He was then assigned as bishop of Meaux, where he resided as much as possible, but was often called to Paris for consultation. After 1700 poor health curtailed his activities, but he continued to dictate his thoughts to his secretary from his bed, until his death.

One of the great orators of Western history, Bossuet was known as "the voice of France" in the days of Louis XIV. He was a staunch defender of the theory of the divine right of kings, a believer in absolutist authority in affairs of both Church and State. His historical writing rested on a unitary vision of God's Providence working directly in history, ordering events through the Incarnation, with the Church playing the crucial role. This "philosophy of history" found expression in his Discourse on

Universal History *(1681) which he considered his most important work and which he was revising for the third time at the time of his death. His* History of the Variations of the Protestant Churches *(1688) took its place in the front ranks of Catholic polemics for the next century and a half.*

One could easily make the case that, instead of Bossuet, the one who should be included here is Richard Simon, his contemporary who is recognized today as the founder of modern Biblical criticism. His Critical History of the Old Testament *appeared in 1678 and caused a scandal by its advanced views. Simon, e.g., asked how Moses could have written Deuteronomy since his death and burial are described in it. Bossuet was horrified that a Catholic priest could publicly ask such an embarrassing question. He was a ruthless foe of any innovations in interpreting the Bible, and the fact is that, sad as it seems today, he prevailed. For three centuries Bossuet stifled Simon.*

So, we include him here as one of those responsible for and representative of the way the Bible was used in the Catholic Church during those three centuries, until historical criticism finally won acceptance. It will be seen that things were not quite as bleak as they are sometimes painted. Bossuet's panegyric on St. Paul, the 1657 work that is included here, has its own power and beauty. It undoubtedly reached the hearts and affected the lives of those to whom it was addressed. If his scholarship did not measure up to that of Simon, nonetheless his pastoral concern knew how to find strength and richness in the Scriptures. The Bible, as the Book of the Church, has not always been used in the most effective or congruous manner, but that is a statement about the human condition rather than about the Bible. Rather than simply lamenting the plight of Simon and the rigidity of Bossuet, it might prove more fruitful to ponder what factors accounted for the mentalities that found expression in each.

PANEGYRICS OF THE SAINTS

"I take pleasure in my infirmities; for when I am weak, then
am I powerful" (2 Cor. xii. 10)

R ealising how great is the task I have undertaken in proposing to myself to pronounce the panegyric of the
mightiest of preachers and most zealous of Apostles, I
must own that my heart almost fails me. When I recall to mind
the multitude of souls saved by St. Paul's ministry, the labours
endured by him, the mysteries he revealed, the innumerable
examples which he has left us of a most ardent charity, the subject appears to me so vast, so sublime, so majestic, that my mind
is perplexed, not knowing how far to venture along this wide,
this almost limitless path outstretched before me, or how much
I may dare to attempt of these heights rising above me, or what
to choose out of this rich abundance of material for my praises;
till at last I am inclined to persuade myself that not even an
Angel would suffice to laud and glorify this man who was once
rapt to the third heaven.

Amid so many splendid achievements and extraordinary
circumstances which claim my attention as I consider the life's
history of this great teacher of the Gentiles, do not be surprised
if, leaving aside his miracles and lofty revelations and that Divine
wisdom in his writings which is truly worthy of the third heaven,
and many another subject which would fill your minds with
noble and beautiful ideas, I confine myself to dwelling upon his
infirmities and asking you to concentrate your attention upon
them. And I do this because if I am to preach St. Paul to you, I
must enter into his spirit and try to feel as he felt. Having heard
him so passionately assert that he glories in nothing but his
weakness, and that his strength lies in his infirmity, I who am
about to pronounce his panegyric must try to show you what

was this all-powerful weakness by means of which he established the Church, overthrew human wisdom, and led captive men's reason and imagination to the obedience of Jesus Christ.

Let us, then, first of all enter into the spirit of his words; let us examine and explain the reasons which made St. Paul believe himself to be strong only in his weakness. The Apostle was thinking of his God annihilated for the love of man; he knew that although this immense world and all that it contains was made by the word of His Power, yet He has also made a new world, a world purchased with His Blood and regenerated by His Death, namely, His Holy Church, which is the work of His weakness. That is what St. Paul is considering; and, after those great thoughts, he turns his eyes upon himself. Then it is that he is filled with wonder and admiration at his vocation: he sees himself called to be the Preacher of the Gentiles; he sees that the Church is to be formed out of those pagan nations whose Apostle he is ordained to be, and consequently he sees that he is to be the chief co-operator with Jesus Christ in the establishment of the Church.

And now what method will he adopt for the prosecution of this great enterprise to which Providence calls him? Does he think that he will achieve it by might and force? Well, besides the fact that his own strength and powers were inadequate, the Holy Ghost made him understand that it was the will of the Eternal Father that this Divine work was to be accomplished by weakness. *The weak things of the world, he says, hath God chosen to confound the strong* (I Cor. i. 27). Therefore there is nothing left for him to do but to consecrate to the Saviour a submissive and obedient weakness, and to acknowledge his infirmity, so as to be the worthy minister of that God Who, being so strong by nature, made Himself weak for our salvation. That then is why he looks upon himself as a useless instrument, destitute of all strength and ability except that which comes to him from the hand of his Divine Master; and that is why he exults in his infirmity, and, while confessing himself to be weak, he has the daring to declare that he is powerful.

But, in order to convince ourselves of the truth of what this great Apostle asserts, we must see how he discharged three important functions of the ministry entrusted to him. For it is not now my intention to consider St. Paul in his private life, but rather in the various phases of his Apostleship, which I will reduce under three heads: first, his preaching; second, his warfare; and third, his ecclesiastical government.

And (difficult though it is to believe it), whether he preaches, combats, or governs, he is everywhere weak. Most assuredly he is weak in his preaching, since that preaching lacks the fashionable artifices of oratory and is devoid of all the skilful subtleties of philosophy: *Not in the persuasive words of human wisdom* (I Cor. ii. 4). Again, it is equally clear that he is weak in conflict, for when he is attacked on all sides, he offers no resistance to his enemies and abandons himself to their violence: *We are accounted as sheep for the slaughter* (Rom. viii. 36). But perhaps among his brethren, where he occupies a position in which the grace of the Apostleship and the authority of ecclesiastical government give him so high a rank, perhaps there St. Paul will appear stronger? No; on the contrary, it is just there that we find him at his weakest. He remembers that he is the disciple of a Master Who says that He is not come to be ministered but to minister (Matt. xx. 28); and this is why he only governs the faithful by charity, laying no yoke of proud imperious authority upon their shoulders, but accounting himself as weak as they are: *To the weak I became weak, and the servant of all* (I Cor. ix. 19, 22). He is then weak at all times, in all places; weak in his preaching, weak in his warfare, and weak in his government of the Church. And, what is most astonishing of all, it is in the midst of so much weakness that he tells us, with the boldness of a conqueror, that he is strong, that he is powerful, that he is invincible: *When I am weak, then am I strong.*

Ah! do you not see what it is that gives him this audacity? It is his consciousness that he is the minister of that God Who in making Himself weak lost none of His almighty power. Full of this sublime thought, he sees his own weakness rising superior to all else. He believes that his preaching will persuade men because there is no strength in it to persuade; he believes that in combat he will always get the upper hand because he has no weapons with which to defend himself; he believes that he will be able to do everything with his brethren in ecclesiastical government, because he will abase himself at their very feet and make himself the slave of all by the servitude of charity. So true is it that he is everywhere strong just where he is weak; since all the strength of persuasion lies in the very plainness of his preaching; since he only hopes to conquer by suffering; since he bases all the authority of his ministry upon his own servitude. Here are three infirmities in which I hope to show you the power of the great Apostle. Let us consider first the triumphant weakness of his absolutely simple preaching.

THE PERSUASIVENESS OF SIMPLICITY

What a subject for our consideration! I am going to show you what the wise and the great of antiquity longed to see: St. Paul preaching Jesus Christ to the world, and converting hardened sinners by his Divine preaching. But do not expect from this heavenly preacher any of those flowers of rhetoric with which human eloquence delights to adorn itself. This great preacher is too grave and serious to look about him for any such flimsy ornaments; or, rather, he is too passionately in love with the glorious lowliness of Christianity to be willing to corrupt the simplicity of the Gospel of Jesus Christ by borrowing any of the tawdry embellishments of poor human oratory. But in order that you may have some idea of this great Apostle destined by Providence to confound by his preaching the wisdom of this world, listen to the description of himself which he gives us in his First Epistle to the Corinthians.

There are, generally speaking, three things which contribute to make an orator agreeable and successful: the personality of the speaker, the beauty of the subject which he treats, and the skilful manner in which he handles it. The reason of this is evident. Esteem for the orator secures for him the attention and goodwill of his hearers; beautiful thoughts and ideas are food for the mind; and the art of explaining them with ability and gracefully, makes them acceptable to the taste and intellect of men. It is however very certain, from the description given of himself by St. Paul, that he possessed none of these advantages.

In the first place, as regards his exterior, he confesses that there was nothing dignified or striking in his appearance or deportment: *His bodily presence is weak* (2 Cor. x. 10). And if you consider his condition in life, he was poor, looked down upon, and was obliged to earn his livelihood by tent-making. Hence he says to the Corinthians: *I have been among you with much fear and many infirmities* (I Cor. ii. 3); so we gather that his personal appearance was not prepossessing. Ah, what sort of a preacher is this to convert the nations?

But perhaps his teaching will be so agreeable, so beautiful, as to gain some credit for this man, repulsive though he seems to be? No, it is nothing of the sort. He says that he knows nothing else but his Crucified Master: *I judged not myself to know anything among you, but Jesus Christ and Him crucified;* that is to say, that he knows nothing but what will shock, will scandalise, will appear to his audience to be folly and extravagance. How then can he hope to persuade them? But, mighty Apostle, if the doctrine you preach is so strange, so difficult, try at least to clothe it in elegant language, hide the face of your repellent Gospel with the flowers of rhetoric, soften its austerity by the charms of your eloquence. God forbid, replies the holy Apostle, that I should mix human wisdom with the wisdom of the Son of God! It is my Master's will that my words should be no less rude and unpolished than my teaching appears to be incredible: *Not in the persuasive words of human wisdom.* And here we must pause for a moment, trying to raise our minds and thoughts to the consideration of the secrets of Providence, and of the reasons which induced (if we may venture to use the word) the Eternal Father to choose this preacher, without eloquence, without charm of voice or appearance, to carry throughout the universe, to Romans and Greeks and Barbarians, to great and small, even to kings, the Gospel of Jesus Christ.

Listen to St. Paul's own words, which may help you to penetrate this great mystery. He has been representing to the Corinthians the extreme simplicity of his preaching, and he goes on to give them this admirable reason for such simplicity: *We are preaching to you a wisdom which is hidden, which none of the princes of this world have ever known.* What is this hidden wisdom? It is Jesus Christ Himself. He is indeed the Wisdom of the Father; but He is An Incarnate Wisdom, Who having of His own free will wrapped Himself in the infirmity of flesh, has hidden Himself from the great ones of the earth through the thickness of this veil. It is, then, a hidden wisdom, and upon that the Apostle's reasoning is based. Do not, he tells us, be surprised if, when I preach to you a hidden wisdom, my sermons are not aglow with sparkling eloquence. This astonishing weakness which is as it were a setting inseparable from my preaching, is a consequence of that self-abasement by which my Saviour extinguished Himself; and as He was lowly in His own person, He wishes likewise to be lowly also in His Gospel.

Do not, then, expect that the Apostle will delight your ears with tuneful cadences or that he will fascinate men's minds by indulging in idle fancies and vain speculations. Listen to what he says himself: *We preach a hidden wisdom; we preach a Crucified God.* Do not let us seek for any of the vain things of earth to adorn the message of the Eternal God, Who despises and rejects all that the world calls brilliant. If our plainness offends the proud, let them know that we covet their disdain, that Jesus Christ scorns their insolent pomp and pretentiousness and that He only wants to be known by the humble. Let us then bring ourselves and our preaching down to the level of these humble souls, so that both we and it may have some share, however small, in the humiliation of the Cross, and be worthy of that God Who only desires to conquer by weakness.

It is for these well-grounded reasons that St. Paul rejects all the tricks of rhetoric. His discourses, far from flowing with that agreeable, even harmony which we admire in the orators of Greece and Rome, appear unequal and unfinished to those who do not study them deeply; and the fastidious and critical who boast of their own refined taste, are repelled by the harshness of his irregular style. But let it not be so with us. The language of the Apostle is indeed simple, but all his thoughts are Divine. If he is unacquainted with rhetoric, if he disdains philosophy, Jesus Christ stands to him in the place of all that. The name of Christ which he has continually on his lips, the mysteries of the Gospel which he so divinely announces, make him all-powerful in his simplicity. Yes, this man, so ignorant of the art of the polished speaker, will go, with his rugged speech and his foreign phrase and accent, into Greece, the mother of philosophers and orators, and in spite of the world's resistance, will establish there more churches than Plato gained disciples by that eloquence which was thought divine. St. Paul will preach Jesus Christ in Athens, and the most learned of her senators will pass from the Areopagus into the school of this barbarian. He will pursue his triumph; he will lay prostrate at the feet of Jesus the majesty of the Roman fasces, in the person of a proconsul, and he will cause the very judges, before whom he is arraigned, to quake on their tribunals. Rome herself shall hear his voice, and the day will come when this city, this mistress of the world, will esteem herself more honoured by a letter addressed by him to her citizens, than by all the languages which she has heard from her Cicero.

And how, Christians, how happens all this? It is that Paul has means of persuasion which Greece does not teach and which Rome has not learned. A supernatural power, which exalts that which the haughty despise, mingles with the august simplicity of his language, and breathes in every word he utters. Hence it is that in his amazing Epistles we feel some subtle charm, a certain superhuman force, which does not flatter the taste and tickle the ear, but which grips and stirs the soul, leading captive the understanding and going straight to the heart. Just as a mighty river retains, when flowing through the plain, all that violent and impetuous force which it had acquired in the mountains whence it derived its source, so does this Divine virtue that resides in St. Paul's Epistles preserve undiminished, even in the plainness of his style, all the vigour and power which it brings from the Heaven whence it has descended.

It was by this Divine virtue that the simplicity of the Apostle vanquished all things. By it he overturned idols, set up the Cross of Jesus, and persuaded thousands to die in defence of its glory. This Divine virtue it was that in his marvellous Epistles revealed such deep secrets and transcendent mysteries that some of the sublimest intellects, after long indulgence in the wildest speculations and the most-far-reaching flights of philosophy, came fluttering down from those giddy heights, to which they fancied themselves to have ascended, in order to lisp in the school of Jesus Christ under the instruction of St. Paul.

But, Great Apostle, this Divine simplicity of yours, which has confounded human wisdom, is not enough. The plainness of your preaching has, it is true, persuaded men; but now human power comes to the help of false wisdom. Persecutors are rising up against you: you must prepare for combat.

THE STRENGTH OF WEAKNESS

It is one of the counsels of Providence that words alone do not suffice to proclaim Jesus Christ: something more violent and forcible is needed to reach the minds and hearts of a hardened world. That world must be spoken to, stirred, roused by wounds and blood, and the Christian religion must conquer its stubborn resistance by suffering and death. It is this truth, this persuasive power of blood shed for the Son of God, which I must now make clear to you from the example of the great Apostle; and to do so I must go back to the beginning.

It appears then that although the word of the Saviour of souls had its own Divine efficacy, yet its chief power of persuasion was to be found in His Precious Blood. For we know that the Son of God, much though He preached while on earth, had always but few followers, and that it was not till after His Death that the people flocked to hear from other lips the teaching of the Divine Master. What is this new miracle? Despised and rejected during the whole course of His life, He only begins to reign after His death. His most Divine words which ought to have drawn men to Him in loving reverence, only nailed Him to the shameful Cross, and the shame of that Cross, which would, as we might have thought, have covered His disciples with eternal confusion, made the truths of His Gospel adored throughout the whole universe. Is not this to teach us that His Cross, and not His words, was to move the hardened hearts of men, and that His power of persuasion lay in His Precious Blood that was poured out and in His Sacred Wounds?

The reason of so great a mystery would deserve much thoughtful consideration. But let me just say in a few words that the Son of God became incarnate in order to make His word carry in two different directions: He was to speak to Earth, and He was also to speak to Heaven. He had to speak to Earth by His Divine teaching; but He had also to speak to Heaven, by the outpouring of His Precious Blood which was to appease the wrath of God by expiating the sins of the world. That is why St. Paul says that the *Blood of Jesus speaketh to better purpose than that of Abel* (Heb. xii. 24); since the blood of Abel cries aloud for vengeance, but the Precious Blood of our Saviour for mercy and pardon. Jesus Christ was then compelled to speak to His Eternal Father as well as to men, to Heaven as well as to Earth.

Here, however, we must pause to consider one of the secrets of Divine Providence. And it is this: that it was necessary that Heaven should be thus approached by our Blessed Lord in order that Earth might be persuaded. And why? Because Divine grace which is to soften the hearts of men, must be sent down from Heaven. For instance: it is quite useless for you to sow your seed on arid, parched ground; you will gather but little fruit when the time of harvest comes, unless before then the rain from Heaven descends to fertilise the soil. So it is to a great extent with the truth which I am now expounding. When our Saviour spoke to men, He was the Sower scattering seed upon the earth, and that ungrateful, barren soil yielded Him in return but few followers. He must needs then speak to His Father, His Blood must cry aloud to Heaven. This being done, grace will come down in plenteous showers, our land will be fruitful and productive; then Heaven, reconciled and appeased, will without difficulty persuade men; and the word spoken by the Divine Sower will, like good seed, bear fruit throughout the universe. Hence it is that He Himself says: *I, if I be lifted up from the Earth, will draw all things to Myself* (John xii. 32); showing us by these words that His strength was in His Cross, and that His Blood would be the means of drawing the world to Him.

Taking that truth then for granted, I cannot wonder that the Church should have been established by means of persecution. Give your blood, blessed Apostle; your Master will give to it a voice capable of moving Heaven and Earth. Since He has taught you that His strength lies in His Cross, carry that Cross, conquering and all-powerful, throughout the length and breadth of the world; but carry it not chiselled in lifeless marble or wrought in cold metal, carry it on your own body, and then abandon that body to the fury of the tyrant, that on it may be imprinted a living image of the Crucified Jesus.

That is what St. Paul is going to do. He will go forth presently into all lands to carry (as he himself says) *the Passion and Death of Jesus manifested in his own body* (2 Cor. iv. 10). And this perhaps is why, in writing to the Colossians, he makes use of these strange words: *I fill up those things that are wanting of the sufferings of Christ* (Col. i. 24). But what are you telling us, O great Apostle? Can anything be wanting in the priceless, the infinite value of your Divine Master's sufferings? No, St. Paul has no such thought. He knows well that nothing can be wanting as regards their worth and perfection; but what he means and says elsewhere is that Jesus Christ suffered only in Jerusalem, and as all His power is in His Cross, it is necessary that He should suffer in all parts of the world, that He may attract all hearts, all souls to Himself. This is what the Apostle desired to accomplish. The Jews have seen the Cross of his Master, he would show it then also to the Gentiles, whose preacher he is. With this thought and intent he journeys therefore from East to West, from Jerusalem to Rome, bearing everywhere upon his shoulders the Cross of Christ and filling up the measure of His sufferings, finding everywhere new persecutions and distresses awaiting him, making everywhere new converts to the Faith, scattering far and wide the good seed of the Gospel, and, like his beloved Master, watering that seed with his own blood.

We speak of his sufferings. Yes, truly, wherever he goes these await him; it must be so, since he is always bearing the Cross of Jesus. For thirty years he knows no rest, passing from one labour to another. New dangers meet him on every hand: shipwrecks on sea, ambushes laid for him on land; hatred among the Gentiles, rage and contempt among the Jews; calumny before every tribunal, persecutions in every city; even in the Church and in his own household false brethren who betray him; now stoned and left for dead, now beaten and almost torn to pieces by the multitude; he *dies daily* for the Son of God (I Cor. xv. 31). All along the great Apostle's journeyings the way is marked out by his blood and by the conversions he has made; these two sign-posts are always side by side and show us the direction taken by his weary feet. Well indeed may we apply to him the beautiful words of Tertullian: "His wounds are his conquering weapons; every scar is hidden by a crown; the more blood he sheds from his own veins, the more palms are given to him; the more cruel and violent are the blows rained upon him, the more are the victories which he gains."

This is why Jesus the Saviour of the world, when He would cast down prostrate at His sacred feet the imperial majesty of

---

Rome, sent thither the most illustrious of all His captains, the mighty Apostle of the Gentiles. But, for the founding of that glorious Church, which was destined by Divine Providence to be the Mother of all other Christian Churches, more blood than St. Paul had even yet shed was needed. He must pour out every drop that flowed through his veins; he must die a martyr's death, as we know that he did at the hands of Nero.

And now if I were to attempt to tell you of all the triumphs of that glorious death, of what courage it gave to the long train of martyrs following in his footsteps, of how the Christian Faith grew and flourished on the soil watered by his blood, of the strength and stability which it gave to that spiritual Empire which was to be established at Rome and which was destined to surpass so far in majesty and power that of the Caesars; if (I say) I were to try to give you a just idea of these marvels, time and speech would fail me. But I have surely said enough to make us all love and adore the Cross, if only our softness, our love of ease, our fear of pain or of even discomfort, does not make that Cross repellent to us. O holy Cross, which gave victory to Paul and made his weakness all-powerful, our voluptuous age cannot endure your hardness. No one now is ready to say with the great Apostle: *I take pleasure only in my sufferings, and I am strong only in my infirmities.* We, alas! wish to be powerful in the world, and that is why we are weak in the things that belong to Jesus Christ; and the love of the Cross of Jesus having died out among the faithful, all Christian strength has dwindled away. But my thoughts on this vast subject are too many for words, and besides I must come to the consideration of St. Paul's infirmity as exhibited in his government of the Church.

THE POWER OF CHARITY

Will you believe it, that the Church of Jesus Christ is governed by weakness; that the authority of its pastors is upheld by infirmity; that the great Apostle St. Paul, who rules with so much firmness, who threatens the obstinate so boldly, who judges sinners so unsparingly, and who sustains the dignity of his office so rigidly, can be weak among the faithful, and that it is in truth this Divine weakness which makes him powerful in the Church?

This may perhaps seen incredible, yet it is a doctrine which he himself has taught us and which I will in few words explain.

You must, in the first place, bear in mind that the spiritual dominion which the Son of God gives to His Church is not like that of earthly kings. It has not that terrible majesty, it has not that disdainful pomp, it has not that proud imperiousness of spirit with which the princes of this world are puffed up. *The Kings of the Gentiles lord it over them,* says the Son of God in His Gospel; *but it is not so with you, where the greatest among you must be as the least, and the leader as he that serveth* (Luke xxii. 25-26).

This doctrine is based upon the fact that the Divine Empire of the Church is founded on charity. For this charity can take all sorts of different forms. It commands in pastors, it obeys in the people; but whether it commands or whether it obeys, it ever retains its characteristic properties: it is always charity, always gentle, always patient, always tender and sympathetic; never proud or ambitious.

Ecclesiastical government, then, being based upon and supported by charity, has nothing in it of domineering or over-bearing; its commands are reasonable, its authority calm and sweet. It is not so much that it dominates the lives of men, as that it guides and orders them with all the wise discretion of a far-reaching fraternal love.

This charity of the Church, however, which protects and leads the people of God, does even more than that. Instead of setting itself up on a pinnacle so as to make its authority highly esteemed, it believes that in order to govern it must abase itself and become weak that it may share the infirmities of its people. For that is what Jesus Christ, its great Exemplar, did: coming to reign over men, He condescended to take upon Himself their infirmities; and the Apostles, as well as all the pastors of the faithful, must after His Divine example do the same, that so sharing the weaknesses and distresses of their flock, they may be able to sympathise with them and to help the infirm to bear their infirmities. We see how truly St. Paul, making himself the servant of all, exercised his authority in this manner.

Truly only a heart of stone could fail to be touched by the infirmities with which the Apostle's charity almost overwhemed

him! If he saw any member of his flock in affliction, he was
afflicted with him. If he saw any who were so ignorant and simple that they needed the food of children, he gave it to them. If
he saw sinners whose hearts were touched by penitence, he wept
with them so as to share their contrition; or if he saw that they
were still hardened in their guilt, he wept even more bitterly over
their blindness. The blows, the wounds, the contumely inflicted
upon any of the faithful, were felt by him as if they had been
inflicted upon himself, so that he cries out: *Who is weak, and I
am not weak? who is scandalised, and I am not on fire?* Therefore when I consider the brilliant light of his sanctity and his
inspired wisdom illuminating the whole Church, while at the
same time he is a prey to all the sufferings, persecutions, afflictions of that Church's members, I often find myself picturing
him to myself as the heart of that Mystical Body; and just as the
members of the human body, as they draw from the heart all
their strength, by means of some subtle communication make
that heart instantly feel any suffering or ill by which they are
attacked, as though to warn it of their need of its assistance, so
too do all the ills which afflict the Church reflect themselves
upon the holy Apostle, soliciting his compassionate charity to
come to the help of the infirm: *Who is weak and I am not weak?*

But I go a step further, and learn from St. Chrysostom that
St. Paul is not only the heart of the Church, but that "he is
afflicted over the sufferings of each and all of its members as if
he himself in his own single person were the whole Church."
Would that time permitted me to enter more deeply into this
profound thought, and to show the full extent of this charity
which never permits St. Paul to shut himself up in himself, which
makes him permeate the whole body of the Church, merging
his very existence in that of its members, so that he lives in them
and suffers in them. There (if we understand him rightly) is the
filling up of the cup of the Apostle's infirmities.

Great St. Paul, I have been meditating upon all the details
of your life, upon your infirmities in the midst of persecutions;
but none of these is to be compared to the sufferings brought
upon you by your charity for your brethren. In your persecutions
you had only your own infirmities to bear; here, you are laden,
weighed down with those of others. In your persecutions you

suffered at the hands of your enemies; here you are afflicted at the hands of your brethren, whose needs and distresses are unceasingly pressing upon you. In your persecutions, your charity strengthened and supported you in every attack made upon you by your enemeies; here, on the contrary, it is your charity that overwhelms you. In your persecutions you could only be assailed in one place at a time; here, the whole world unites in falling upon you and you have to bear its crushing weight.

This it is then in which the Apostle glories. This makes him cry out joyfully: *When I am weak, then am I strong.* And how great is this strength of Paul, who voluntarily makes himself weak that he may support the weak; who shares their infirmities that he may help them to carry the burden; who by charity stoops down to the very ground to put them on his shoulders and lift them with himself to Heaven; who makes himself the servant of all, that he may win all for his Divine Master! Is not this to govern the Church in a manner worthy of an Apostle? Is not this to imitate Jesus Christ Himself, by Whose afflictions we are strengthened and by Whose stripes we are healed?

Christians, will you not imitate this great Apostle? There are in the Church so many weak who have to be borne with and made strong, so many ignorant to be instructed, so many poor to be relieved! My brother, enkindle your zeal: that man who has hated and maligned you, is an infirm brother whom you must heal. But his hatred is inveterate: then his sickness is the more grievous. But (you will say) his conduct towards you has been atrociously offensive: bear with his weakness, really it is only himself he has harmed; compassionate him in the evil he has done to himself, and forget the injury he has wished to do to you. Open your arms to him, gain your brother.

Also, Christians, close not your eyes to the temporal necessities of the many poor who cry out to you. Sympathise with them and aid them in their need. Support them in their poverty and helplessness; and they will plead in support of you before their Heavenly Father, Who will recompense you.

John Henry Newman
1801-1890

Newman was born in London and educated at Oxford. In the 1830s he became the prime mover in the Oxford Movement that advocated restoring the Church of England to the Church of the first five centuries. The resulting controversies led him to withdraw and in 1845 he was received into the Roman Catholic Church. That same year he published his Essay on the Development of Christian Doctrine. *He went to Rome to be ordained a priest and in 1848 founded the Birmingham Oratory.*

When challenged by Charles Kingsley in 1864 to demonstrate the sincerity of his conversion, Newman responded by writing his famous Apologia Pro Vita Sua. *Another major theological work, dealing with the problem of faith and certainty, his* Grammar of Assent, *came out in 1870. In 1879 the new Pope, Leo XIII, bestowed the red hat of Cardinal upon him.*

Newman was too subtle a thinker not to be involved in controversy. He had an innate sense for the Scholastic axiom that "the truth consists in distinctions." In 1884, after reading some observations that Renan's defection from the Catholic Church was due to his biblical studies, Newman took up his pen and wrote the article which is reprinted here, "On the Inspiration of Scripture." An Irish cleric, John Healy, dashed off a blistering attack on the article and a battle royal was on. The events of the next few decades resulted in Newman's name being listed in

THE CATHOLIC TRADITION: Sacred Scripture

Latin theology manuals as one who maintained an inadequate view of inspiration.

The atmosphere of the anti-Modernist crisis accounts for this unfortunate development. It "had the unhappy effect of allowing persons of a certain mentality to put forward a Catholic variety of fundamentalism as the only orthodoxy. In this period Newman's unsystematic and somewhat unusually expressed account of inspiration was inevitably misunderstood, misrepresented and prevented from bearing the fruit of the seeds it contained." But, as a result of Vatican II, "it is Newman, not Healy or Newman's critics in the period following him, whom the Council has vindicated." (R. Murray, SJ).

The fundamentalist, Catholic or Protestant, it has often been observed, approaches the Bible in a "Monophysite" fashion, thinking of it only and entirely as God's word. This leads to such outlandish and irrational attitudes that an unbridgeable chasm is fixed between the Bible and any other literature or history. Newman's most significant feature was his "Incarnationalism." With the Bible as with Jesus Himself the full human reality had to be maintained or Christian faith was caricatured. God did not replace the human; He embraced the human.

The current renewal of appreciation for the thought of John Henry Newman ought not to be misunderstood. No one is suggesting that his formulations of a century ago are complete and adequate for today. But in the broadened perspective of the post-Vatican II era, it is impossible to deny that Newman was ahead of his time and was moving in the direction that would prove most fruitful nearly a century later.

ON THE INSPIRATION
OF SCRIPTURE

ESSAY I

INSPIRATION IN ITS RELATION TO REVELATION

I t has lately been asked, what answer do we Catholics
give to the allegation urged against us by men of the
day, to the effect that we demand of our converts
an assent to views and interpretations of Scripture which
modern science and historical research have utterly discredited.

As this alleged obligation is confidently maintained against
us, and with an array of instances in support of it, I think it
should be either denied or defended; and the best mode perhaps of doing, whether the one or the other, will be, instead of
merely dealing with the particular instances adduced in proof,
to state what we really do hold as regards Holy Scripture, and
what a Catholic is bound to believe. This I propose now to do,
and in doing it, I beg it to be understood that my statements
are simply my own, and involve no responsibility of any one
besides myself.

A recent work of M. Renan's is one of those publications
which have suggested or occasioned this adverse criticism upon
our intellectual position. That author's abandonment of Catholicism seems (according to a late article in a journal of high
reputation) in no small measure to have come about by his
study of the Biblical text, especially that of the Old Testament.
'He explains,' says the article, 'that the Roman Catholic Church
admits no compromise on questions of Biblical criticism and
history' . . . even though 'the Book of Judith is an historical
impossibility. Hence the undoubted fact that the Roman
Catholic Church . . . insists on its members believing . . . a
great deal more is pure criticism and pure history than the
strictest Protestants exact from their pupils or flocks.' Should,
then, a doubting Anglican contemplate becoming Catholic by
way of attaining intellectual peace, 'if his doubts turn on

history and criticism, he will find the little finger of the Catholic Church thicker than the loins of Protestantism'.

The serious question, then, which this article calls on us to consider, is, whether it is 'an undoubted fact', as therein stated, that the Catholic Church does 'insist' on her children's acceptance of certain Scripture informations on matters of fact in defiance of criticism and history. And my first duty on setting out is to determine the meaning of that vague word 'insists', which I shall use in the only sense in which a Catholic can consent to use it.

I allow, then, that the Church, certainly, does 'insist', when she speaks dogmatically, nay, or rather she more than insists, she obliges; she obliges us to an internal assent to that which she proposes to us. So far I admit, or rather maintain. And I admit that she obliges us in a most forcible and effective manner, that is, by the penalty of forfeiting communion with her, if we refuse our internal assent to her word. We cannot be real Catholics, if we do not from our heart accept the matters which she puts forward as divine and true. This is plain.

Next, to what does the Church oblige us? and what is her warrant for doing so? I answer: The matters which she can oblige us to accept with an internal assent are the matters contained in that Revelation of Truth, written or unwritten, which came to the world from our Lord and His Apostles; and this claim on our faith in her decisions as to the matter of that Revelation rests on her being the divinely-appointed representative of the Apostles, and the expounder of their words; so that whatever she categorically delivers about their formal acts, or their writings or their teaching, is an Apostolic deliverance. I repeat, the only sense in which the Church 'insists' on any statement, Biblical or other, the only reason of her so insisting, is that that statement is part of the original Revelation, and therefore must be unconditionally accepted,—else, that Revelation is not, as a revelation, accepted at all.

The question then which I have to answer is: *What*, in matter of fact, has the Church (or the Pope), as the representative of God, said about Scripture, which, as being Apostolic, unerring Truth, is obligatory on our faith—that is, is *de fide*?

John Henry Newman

Many truths may be predicated about Scripture and its contents which are not obligatory on our faith, viz., such as are private conclusions from premisses, or are the *dicta* of theologians: such as about the author of the Book of Job, or the dates of St Paul's Epistles. These are not obligatory upon us, because they are not the subjects of *ex cathedrâ* utterances of a General Council. Opinions of this sort may be true or not true, and lie open for acceptance or rejection, since no divine utterance has ever been granted to us about them, or is likely to be granted. We are not bound to believe what St. Jerome said or inferred about Scripture; nor what St. Augustine, or St. Thomas, or Cardinal Caietan, or Fr Perrone has said; but what the Church has enunciated, what the Councils, what the Pope, has determined. We are not bound to accept with an absolute faith what is not an Ecumenical dogma, or the equivalent of dogma (*vide infra,* § 17), that is, what is not *de fide;* such judgments, however powerfully enunciated, we may without loss of communion doubt, we may refuse to accept. This is what we must especially bear in mind, when we handle such objections as M. Renan's. We must not confuse what is indisputable as well as true, with what may indeed be true, yet is disputable. And this is to be received, not only as against such criticisms as are to be met with in the publications of the day.

I must make one concession to him. In certain cases there may be a duty of silence, when there is no obligation of belief. Here no question of faith comes in. We will suppose that a novel opinion about Scripture or its contents is well grounded, and that a received opinion is open to doubt, in a case in which the Church has hitherto decided nothing, so that a new question needs a new answer: here, to profess the new opinion may be abstractedly permissible, but is not always permissible in practice. The novelty may be so startling as to require a full certainty that it is true; it may be so strange as to raise the question whether it will not unsettle ill-educated minds,—that is, though the statement is not an offence against faith, still it may be an offence against charity. It need not be heretical, yet at a particular time or place it may be so contrary to the prevalent opinion in the Catholic body, as in Galileo's case, that zeal for the supremacy of the Divine Word, deference to existing authorities, charity towards the weak and ignorant, and distrust of self, should keep a man from being impetuous or careless in circulating what nevertheless he holds to be true, and what, if indeed asked about, he cannot deny. The household of God has claims upon our tenderness in such matters which criticism and history have not.

For myself, I have no call or wish at all to write in behalf of such persons as think it a love of truth to have no 'love of the brethren'. I am indeed desirous of investigating for its own sake the limit of free thought consistently with the claims upon us of Holy Scripture; still, my especial interest in the inquiry is from my desire to assist those religious sons of the Church who are engaged in Biblical criticism and its attendant studies, and have a conscientious fear of transgressing the rule of faith; men who wish to ascertain how far their religion puts them under obligations and restrictions in their reasonings and inferences on such subjects,—what conclusions may, and what may not, be held without interfering with that internal assent which, if they would be Catholics, they are bound to give to the written Word of God. I do but contemplate the inward peace of religious Catholics in their own persons. Of course those who begin without belief in the religious aspect of the universe, are not likely to be brought to such belief by studying it merely on its secular side.

Here, then, the main question before us being what it is that a Catholic is free to hold about Scripture in general, or about its separate portions, or its statements, without compromising his firm inward assent to the dogmas of the Church, that is, to the *de fide* enunciations of Popes and Councils, we have first of all to inquire how many, and what, those dogmas are.

I answer that there are two such dogmas; one relates to the authority of Scripture, the other to its interpretation. As to the authority of Scripture, we hold it to be, in all matters of faith and morals, divinely inspired throughout; as to its interpretation, we hold that the Church is, in faith and morals, the one infallible expounder of that inspired text.

I begin with the question of its inspiration.

John Henry Newman

The books which constitute the canon of Scripture, or the Canonical books, are enumerated by the Tridentine Council, as we find them in the first page of our Catholic Bibles; and are in that Ecumenical Council's decree spoken of by implication as the work of inspired men. The Vatican Council speaks more distinctly, saying that the entire books, with all their parts, are divinely inspired, and adding an anathema upon impugners of this its definition.

There is another dogmatic phrase used by the Councils of Florence and Trent to denote the inspiration of Scripture, viz., 'Deus *unus et idem* utriusque Testamenti Auctor'. Since this left room for holding that by the word 'Testamentum' was meant 'Dispensation', as it seems to have meant in former Councils from the date of Irenæus, and as St Paul uses the word in his Epistle to the Hebrews, the Vatican Council has expressly defined that the concrete *libri* themselves of the Old and New Testament 'Deum habent Auctorem'.

There is a further question, which is still left in some ambiguity, the meaning of the word 'Auctor'. 'Auctor' is not identical with the English word 'Author'. Allowing that there are instances to be found in classical Latin in which 'auctores' may be translated 'authors', instances in which it even seems to mean 'writers', it more naturally means 'authorities'. Its proper sense is 'originator', 'inventor', 'founder', 'primary cause'; (thus St Paul speaks of our Lord as 'Auctor salutis', 'Auctor fidei';) on the other hand, that it was the inspired penmen who were the 'writers' of their respective works seems asserted by St John and St Luke, and, I may say, in every paragraph of St Paul's Epistles. In St John we read, 'This is the disciple who testifies of these things, and has *written* these things,' and St Luke says, 'I have thought it good to *write* to thee,' etc. However, if any one prefers to construe 'auctor' as 'author', or writer, let it be so—only, then there will be two writers of the Scriptures, the divine and the human.

And now comes the important question, in what respect are the Canonical books inspired? It cannot be in every respect, unless we are bound *de fide* to believe that 'terra in æternum stat', and that heaven is above us, and that there are no antipodes. And it seems unworthy of Divine Greatness, that the

255

Almighty should in His revelation of Himself to us, undertake mere secular duties, and assume the office of a narrator, as such, or an historian, or geographer, except so far as the secular matters bear directly upon the revealed truth. The Councils of Trent and the Vatican fulfil this anticipation; they tell us distinctly the object and the promise of Scripture inspiration. They specify 'faith and moral conduct' as the drift of that teaching which has the guarantee of inspiration. What we need, and what is given us, is not how to educate ourselves for this life; we have abundant natural gifts for human society, and for the advantages which it secures; but our great want is how to demean ourselves in thought and deed towards our Maker, and how to gain reliable information on this urgent necessity.

Accordingly, four times does the Tridentine Council insist upon 'faith and morality' as the scope of inspired teaching. It declares that the 'Gospel' is 'the Fount of all *saving truth* and all *instruction in morals*', that in the written books and in the unwritten traditions, the Holy Spirit dictating, this *truth* and *instruction* are contained. Then it speaks of the books and traditions, 'relating whether to *faith* or to *morals*', and afterwards of 'the confirmation of *dogmas* and establishment of *morals*'. Lastly, it warns the Christian people, 'in matters of *faith* and *morals*', against distorting Scripture into a sense of their own.

In like manner the Vatican Council pronounces that Supernatural Revelation consists 'in rebus divinis', and is *contained* 'in libris scriptis et sine scripto traditionibus'; and it also speaks of 'petulantia ingenia' advancing wrong interpretations of Scripture 'in rebus *fidei* et *morum* ad ædificationem *doctrinæ* Christianæ pertinentium.'

But while the Councils, as has been shown, lay down so emphatically the inspiration of Scripture in respect to 'faith and morals', it is remarkable that they do not say a word directly as to its inspiration in matters of fact. Yet are we therefore to conclude that the record of facts in Scripture does not come under the guarantee of its inspiration? we are not so to conclude, and for this plain reason:—the sacred narrative, carried on through so many ages, what is it but the very matter of our faith, and rule of our obedience? what but that narrative itself is the supernatural teaching, in order to which inspiration is given? What is the whole history, as it is traced out in Scripture from Genesis to Esdras, and thence on to the end of the Acts of the Apostles, what is it but a manifestation of Divine Providence, on the one hand interpretative (on a large scale and with analogical applications) of universal history, and on the other preparatory (typical and predictive) of the Evangelical Dispensation? Its pages breathe of providence and grace, of our Lord, and of His work and teaching, from beginning to end. It views facts in those relations in which neither ancients, such as the Greek and Latin classical historians, nor moderns, such as Niebuhr, Grote, Ewald, or Michelet, can view them. In this point of view it has God for its author, even though the finger of God traced no words but the Decalogue. Such is the claim of Bible history in its substantial fulness to be accepted *de fide* as true. In this point of view, Scripture is inspired, not only in faith and morals, but in all its parts which bear on faith, including matters of fact.

But what has been said leads to another serious question. It is easy to imagine a Code of Laws inspired, or a formal prophecy, or a Hymn, or a Creed, or a collection of Proverbs. Such works may be short, precise, and homogeneous; but inspiration on the one hand, and on the other a document, multiform and copious in its contents, as the Bible is, are at first sight incompatible ideas, and destructive of each other. How are we practically to combine the indubitable fact of a divine superintendence with the indubitable fact of a collection of such various writings?

Surely then, if the revelations and lessons in Scripture are addressed to us personally and practically, the presence among us of a formal judge and standing expositor of its words, is imperative. It is antecedently unreasonable to 'speech was, not in the persuasive words of human wisdom, so obscure, the outcome of so many minds, times, and places, should be given us from above without the safeguard of some authority; as if it could possibly, from the nature of the case, interpret itself. Its inspiration does but guarantee its truth, not its interpretation. How are private readers satisfactorily to distinguish what is didactic and what is historical, what is fact and what is vision, what is allegorical and what is literal, what is idiomatic and what is grammatical, what is enunciated formally and what occurs *obiter,* what is only of temporary and what is of lasting obligation? Such is our natural anticipation, and it is only too exactly justified in the events of the last three centuries, in the many countries where private judgment on the text of Scripture has prevailed. The gift of inspiration requires as its complement the gift of infallibility.

Where then is this gift lodged, which is so necessary for the due use of the written word of God? Thus we are introduced to the second dogma in respect to Holy Scripture taught by the Catholic Religion. The first is that Scripture is inspired, the second, that the Church is the infallible interpreter of that inspiration.

That the Church, and therefore the Pope, is that Interpreter is defined in the following words:—

First by the Council of Trent: 'Nemo suâ prudentiâ innixus, in rebus fidei et morum and ædificationem doctrinæ Christianæ pertinentium, Sacram Scripturam ad suos sensus contorquens, contra eum sensum quem tenuit et tenet Sancta Mater Ecclesia, cujus est judicare de vero sensu et interpretatione Scripturarum Sanctarum, aut etiam contra unanimem consensum Patrum, ipsam Scripturam Sacram interpretari audeat.'

Secondly by the Council of the Vatican: 'Nos, idem Decretum [Tridentinum] renovantes, hanc illius mentem esse declaramus, ut in rebus fidei et morum and ædificationem doctrinæ Christianæ pertinentium, is pro vero sensu Sacræ Scripturæ habendus sit, quem tenuit et tenet Sancta Mater Ecclesia, cujus est judicare de vero sensu et interpretatione Scripturarum Sanctarum,' etc.

Since, then, there is in the Church an authority, divinely appointed and plenary, for judgment and for appeal in questions of Scripture interpretation, in matters of faith and morals, therefore, by the very force of the words, there is one such authority, and only one.

Again, it follows hence, that, when the legitimate authority has spoken, to resist its interpretation is a sin against the faith, and an act of heresy.

John Henry Newman

And from this again it follows, that, till the Infallible Authority formally interprets a passage of Scripture, there is nothing heretical in advocating a contrary interpretation, provided of course there is nothing in the act intrinsically inconsistent with the faith, or the *pietas fidei,* nothing of contempt or rebellion, nothing temerarious, nothing offensive or scandalous, in the manner of acting or the circumstances of the case. I repeat, I am all along inquiring what Scripture, by reason of its literal text, obliges us to believe. An original view about Scripture or its parts may be as little contrary to the mind of the Church about it, as it need be an offence against its inspiration.

The proviso, however, or condition, which I have just made, must carefully be kept in mind. Doubtless, a certain interpretation of a doctrinal text may be so strongly supported by the Fathers, so continuous and universal, and so cognate and connatural with the Church's teaching, that it is virtually or practically as dogmatic as if it were a formal judgment delivered on appeal by the Holy See, and cannot be disputed except as the Church or Holy See opens its wording or its conditions. Hence the Vatican Council says, 'Fide divinâ et Catholicâ ea omnia credenda sunt, quæ in verbo Dei scripto vel tradito continentur, vel ab Ecclesiâ sive solemni judicio, sive *ordinario et universali magisterio,* tanquam divinitus revelata, credenda proponuntur.' And I repeat, that, though the Fathers were not inspired, yet their united testimony is of supreme authority; at the same time, since no Canon or List has been determined of the Fathers, the practical rule of duty is obedience to the voice of the Church.

Such then is the answer which I make to the main question which has led to my writing. I asked what obligation of duty lay upon the Catholic scholar or man of science as regards his critical treatment of the text and the matter of Holy Scripture. And now I say that it is his duty, first, never to forget that what he is handling is the Word of God, which, by reason of the difficulty of always drawing the line between what is human and what is divine, cannot be put on the level of other books, as it is now the fashion to do, but has the nature of a Sacrament, which is outward and inward, and a channel of supernatural grace; and secondly, that, in what he writes upon it, or its separate books, he is bound to submit himself internally, and to profess to submit himself, in all that relates to faith and morals, to the definite teaching of Holy Church.

This being laid down, let me go on to consider some of the criticial distinctions and conclusions which are consistent with a faithful observance of these obligations.

Are the books or are the writers inspired? I answer, Both. The Council of Trent says the writers, 'ab ipsis Apostolis, Spiritu Sancto dictante'; the Vatican says the books, 'si quis libros integros etc. divinitus inspiratos esse negaverit, anathema sit.' Of course the Vatican decision is *de fide,* but it cannot annul the Tridentine. Both decrees are dogmatic truths. The Tridentine teaches us that the Divine Inspirer, inasmuch as He acted on the writer, acted, not immediately on the books themselves, but through the men who wrote them. The books are inspired, because the writers were inspired to write them. They are not inspired books, unless they came from inspired men.

There is one instance in Scripture of Divine Inspiration without a human medium: the Decalogue was written by the very finger of God. He wrote the Law upon the stone tables Himself. It has been thought that the Urim and Thummim was another instance of the immediate inspiration of a material substance; but anyhow such instances are exceptional; certainly, as regards Scripture, which alone concerns us here, there always have been two minds in the process of inspiration, a divine *Auctor,* and a human *Scriptor;* and various important consequences follow from this appointment.

If there be at once a divine and a human mind cooperating in the formation of the sacred text, it is not surprising if there often be a double sense in that text, and (with obvious exceptions) never certain that there is not.

Thus Sara had her human and literal meaning in her words, 'Cast out the bondwoman and her son', etc.; but we know from St Paul that those words were inspired by the Holy Ghost to convey a spiritual meaning. Abraham, too, on the Mount, when his son asked him whence was to come the victim for the sacrifice which his father was about to offer, answered

'God will provide'; and he showed his own sense of his words afterwards, when he took the ram which was caught in the briars, and offered it as a holocaust. Yet those words were a solemn prophecy.

And is it extravagant to say, that, even in the case of men who have no pretension to be prophets or servants of God, He may by their means give us great maxims and lessons, which the speakers little thought they were delivering? as in the case of the Architriclinus in the marriage feast, who spoke of the bridegroom as having 'kept the good wine until now'; words which it was needless for St John to record, unless they had a mystical meaning.

Such instances raise the question whether the Scripture saints and prophets always understood the higher and divine sense of their words. As to Abraham, this will be answered in the affirmative; but I do not see reason for thinking that Sara was equally favoured. Nor is her case solitary; Caiphas, as high priest, spoke a divine truth by virtue of his office, little thinking of it, when he said that 'one man must die for the people'; and St Peter at Joppa at first did not see beyond a literal sense in his vision, though he knew that there was a higher sense, which in God's good time would be revealed to him.

And hence there is no difficulty in supposing that the Prophet Osee, though inspired, knew only his own literal sense of the words which he transmitted to posterity, 'I have called my Son out of Egypt', the further prophetic meaning of them being declared by St Matthew in his gospel. And such a divine sense would be both concurrent with, and confirmed by, that antecedent belief which prevailed among the Jews in St Matthew's time, that their sacred books were in great measure typical, with an evangelical bearing, though as yet they might not know what those books contained in prospect.

Nor is it *de fide* (for that alone with a view to Catholic Biblicists I am considering) that inspired men, at the time when they speak from inspiration, should always know that the Divine Spirit is visiting them.

The Psalms are inspired; but, when David, in the outpouring of his deep contrition, disburdened himself before his God in the words of the *Miserere* could he, possibly, while uttering them, have been directly conscious that every word he uttered was not simply his, but another's? Did he not think that he was personally asking forgiveness and spiritual help? Doubt again seems incompatible with a consciousness of being inspired. But Father Patrizi, while reconciling two Evangelists in a passage of their narratives, says, if I understand him rightly (ii, p. 405), that though we admit that there were some things about which inspired writers doubted, this does not imply that inspiration allowed them to state what is doubtful as certain, but only it did not hinder them from stating things with a doubt on their minds about them; but how can the All-knowing Spirit doubt? or how can an inspired man doubt, if he is conscious of his inspiration?

And again, how can a man whose hand is guided by the Holy Spirit, and who knows it, make apologies for his style of writing, as if deficient in literary exactness and finish? If then the writer of Ecclesiasticus, at the very time that he wrote his Prologue, was not only inspired, but conscious of his inspiration, how could he have entreated his readers to 'come with benevolence', and to make excuse for his 'coming short in the composition of words'? Surely, if at the very time he wrote he had known it, he would, like other inspired men, have said, 'Thus saith the Lord,' or what was equivalent to it.

The same remark applies to the writer of the second book of Machabees, who ends his narrative by saying, 'If I have done well, it is what I desired, but if not so perfectly, it must be pardoned me.' What a contrast to St Paul, who, speaking of his inspiration (1 Cor. vii, 40) and of his 'weakness and fear' (*ibid.* ii, 4), does so in order to *boast* that his 'speech was, not in the persuasive words of human wisdom, but in the showing of the Spirit and of power'. The historian of the Machabees would have surely adopted a like tone of 'glorying', had he had at the time a like consciousness of his divine gift.

Again, it follows from there being two agencies, divine grace and human intelligence, co-operating in the production of the Scriptures, that, whereas, if they were written, as in the Decalogue, by the immediate finger of God, every word of them must be His and His only; on the contrary, if they are man's writing, informed and quickened by the presence of the Holy

Ghost, they admit, should it so happen, of being composed of outlying materials, which have passed through the minds and from the fingers of inspired penmen, and are known to be inspired on the ground that those who were the immediate editors, as they may be called, were inspired.

For an example of this we are supplied by the writer of the second book of Machabees, to which reference has already been made. 'All such things,' says the writer, 'as have been comprised in five books by Jason of Cyrene, we have attempted to abridge in one book.' Here we have the human aspect of an inspired work. Jason need not, the writer of the second book of Machabees must, have been inspired.

Again; St Luke's Gospel is inspired, as having gone through and come forth from an inspired mind; but the extrinsic sources of his narrative were not necessarily all inspired, any more than was Jason of Cyrene; yet such sources there were, for, in contrast with the testimony of the actual eye-witnesses of the events which he records, he says of himself that he wrote after a careful inquiry, 'according as *they* delivered them to us, who from the beginning were eye-witnesses and ministers of the word'; as to himself, he had but 'diligently attained to all things from the beginning'. Here it was not the original statements, but his edition of them, which needed to be inspired.

Hence we have no reason to be surprised, nor is it against the faith to hold, that a canonical book may be composed, not only from, but even of, pre-existing documents, it being always borne in mind, as a necessary condition, that an inspired mind has exercised a supreme and an ultimate judgment on the work, determining what was to be selected and embodied in it, in order to its truth in all 'matters of faith and morals pertaining to the edification of Christian doctrine', and its unadulterated truth.

Thus Moses may have incorporated in his manuscript as much from foreign documents as is commonly maintained by the critical school; yet the existing Pentateuch, with the miracles which it contains, may still (from that personal inspiration which belongs to a prophet) have flowed from his mind and hand on to his composition. He new-made and authenticated what till then was no matter of faith.

This being considered, it follows that a book may be, and may be accepted as, inspired, though not a word of it is an original document. Such is almost the case with the first book of Esdras. A learned writer in a publication of the day says: 'It consists of the contemporary historical journals, kept from time to time by the prophets or other authorised persons, who were eye-witnesses for the most part of what they record, and whose several narratives were afterwards strung together, and either abridged or added to, as the case required, by a later hand, of course an inspired hand.'

And in like manner the Chaldee and Greek portions of the book of Daniel, even though not written by Daniel, may be, and we believe are, written by penmen inspired in matters of faith and morals; and so much, and nothing beyond, does the Church 'oblige' us to believe.

I have said that the Chaldee, as well as the Hebrew portion of Daniel, requires, in order to its inspiration, not that it should be Daniel's writing, but that its writer, whoever he was, should be inspired. This leads me to the question whether inspiration requires and implies that the book inspired should, in its form and matter, be homogeneous, and all its parts belong to each other. Certainly not. The Book of Psalms is the obvious instance destructive of any such idea. What it really requires is an inspired Editor; that is, an inspired mind, authoritative in faith and morals, from whose fingers the sacred text passed. I believe it is allowed generally that, at the date of the captivity and under the persecution of Antiochus, the books of Scripture and the sacred text suffered much loss and injury. Originally the Psalms seem to have consisted of five books, of which only a portion, perhaps the first and second, were David's. That arrangement is now broken up, and the Council of Trent was so impressed with the difficulty of their authorship, that, in its formal decree respecting the Canon, instead of calling the collection 'David's Psalms,' as was usual, they called it the 'Psalterium Davidicum,' thereby meaning to imply, that, although canonical and inspired and in spiritual fellowship and relationship with those of 'the choice Psalmist of Israel,' the whole collection is not therefore necessarily the writing of David.

John Henry Newman

And as the name of David, though not really applicable to every Psalm, nevertheless protected and sanctioned them all, so the appendices which conclude the book of Daniel, Susanna and Bel, though not belonging to the main history, come under the shadow of that Divine Presence, which primarily rests on what goes before.

And so again, whether or not the last verses of St Mark's, and two portions of St John's Gospel, belong to those Evangelists respectively, matters not as regards their inspiration; for the Church has recognised them as portions of that sacred narrative which precedes or embraces them.

Nor does it matter, whether one or two Isaiahs wrote the book which bears that Prophet's name; the Church, without settling this point, pronounces it inspired in respect of faith and morals, both Isaiahs being inspired; and, if this be assured to us, all other questions are irrelevant and unnecessary.

Nor do the Councils forbid our holding that there are interpolations or additions in the sacred text, say, the last chapter of the Pentateuch, provided they are held to come from an inspired penman, such as Esdras, and are thereby authoritative in faith and morals.

From what has been last said it follows, that the titles of the Canonical books, and their ascription to definite authors, either do not come under their inspiration, or need not be accepted literally.

For instance: the Epistle to the Hebrews is said in our Bibles to be the writing of St Paul, and so virtually it is, and to deny that it is so in any sense might be temerarious; but its authorship is not a matter of faith as its inspiration is, but an acceptance of received opinion, and because to no other writer can it be so well assigned.

Again, the 89th Psalm has for its title 'A Prayer of Moses', yet that has not hindered a succession of Catholic writers, from Athanasius to Bellarmine, from denying it to be his.

Again, the Book of Wisdom professes (*e. g.*, chs. vii and ix) to be written by Solomon; yet our Bibles say, 'It is written in the *person* of Solomon,' and 'it is uncertain who was the writer'; and St Augustine, whose authority had so much influence in the settlement of the Canon, speaking of Wisdom and Ecclesiasticus, says: 'The two books, by reason of a certain similarity of style, are usually called Solomon's though the more learned have no doubt they do not belong to him.' (Martin. *Pref. to Wisdom and Eccl.;* Aug. *Opp.* t. iii, p. 733.)

If these instances hold, they are precedents for saying that it is no sin against the faith (for of such I have all along been speaking), nor indeed, if done conscientiously and on reasonable grounds, any sin, to hold that Ecclesiastes is not the writing of Solomon, in spite of its opening with a profession of being his; and that first, because that profession is a heading, not a portion of the book, secondly, because, even though it be part of the book, a like profession is made in the Book of Wisdom, without its being a proof that 'Wisdom' is Solomon's; and thirdly, because such a profession may well be considered a prosopopœia not so difficult to understand as that of the Angel Raphael, when he called himself 'the Son of the great Ananias'.

On this subject Melchior Canus says: 'It does not much matter to the Catholic Faith that a book was written by this or that writer, so long as the Spirit of God is believed to be the Author of it; which Gregory delivers and explains in his Preface to Job, "It matters not," he says, "with what pen the King has written His letter, if it be true that He has written it." ' (*Loc. Th.* p. 44.)

I say then of the Book of Ecclesiastes, its authorship is one of those questions which still lie in the hands of the Church. If the Church formally declared that it was written by Solomon, I consider that, in accordance with its heading (and, as implied in what follows, as in 'Wisdom',) we should be bound, recollecting that she has the gift of judging 'de vero sensu et interpretatione Scripturarum Sanctarum', to accept such a decree as a matter of faith; and in like manner, in spite of its heading, we should be bound to accept a contrary decree, if made to the effect that the book was not Solomon's. At present, as the Church (or Pope) has not pronounced on one side or on the other, I conceive that, till a decision comes from Rome, either opinion is open to the Catholic without any impeachment of his faith.

John Henry Newman

And here I am led on to inquire whether *obiter dicta* are conceivable in an inspired document. We know that they are held to exist, and even required, in treating of the dogmatic utterances of Popes, but are they compatible with inspiration? The common opinion is that they are not. Professor Lamy thus writes about them, in the form of an objection: 'Many minute matters occur in the sacred writers which have regard only to human feebleness and the natural necessities of life, and by no means require inspiration, since they can otherwise be perfectly well known, and seem scarcely worthy of the Holy Spirit, as for instance what is said of the dog of Tobias, St Paul's *penula*, and the salutations at the end of the Epistles.' Neither he nor Fr Patrizi allow of these exceptions; but Fr Patrizi, as Lamy quotes him, 'damnare non audet eos qui hæc tenerent', [viz., exceptions,] and he himself, by keeping silence, seems unable to condemn them either.

By *obiter dicta* in Scripture I also mean such statements as we find in the Book of Judith, that Nabuchodonosor was King of Nineve. Now it is in favour of there being such unauthoritative *obiter dicta*, that, unlike those which occur in dogmatic utterances of Popes and Councils, they are, in Scripture, not doctrinal, but mere unimportant statements of fact; whereas those of Popes and Councils may relate to faith and morals, and are said to be uttered *obiter*, because they are not contained within the scope of the formal definition, and imply no intention of binding the consciences of the faithful. There does not then seem any serious difficulty in admitting their existence in Scripture. Let it be observed, its miracles are doctrinal facts, and in no sense of the phrase can be considered *obiter dicta*.

It may be questioned, too, whether the absence of chronological sequence might not be represented as an infringement of plenary inspiration more serious than the *obiter dicta* of which I have been speaking. Yet St Matthew is admitted by approved commentators to be unsolicitous as to order of time. So says Fr Patrizi (*De Evang.* lib. ii, p. 1), viz., 'Matthæum de observando temporis ordine minime sollicitum esse'. He gives instances, and then repeats 'Matthew did not observe order of time'. If such absence of order is compatible with inspiration in St Matthew, as it is, it might be consistent with inspiration in parts of the Old Testament, supposing they are open to re-arrangement in chronology. Does not this teach us to fall back upon the decision of the Councils that 'faith and morals pertaining to the edification of Christian doctrine' are the scope, the true scope, of inspiration? And is not the Holy See the judge given us for determining what is for edification and what is not?

There is another practical exception to the ideal continuity of Scripture inspiration in mere matters of fact, and that is the multitude of various manuscript readings which surround the sacred text. Unless we have the text as inspired men wrote it, we have not the divine gift in its fulness, and as far as we have no certainty which out of many is the true reading, so far, wherever the sense is affected, we are in the same difficulty as may be the consequence of an *obiter dictum*. Yet, in spite of this danger, even cautious theologians do not hesitate to apply the gratuitous hypothesis of errors in transcription as a means of accounting for such statements of fact as they feel to need an explanation. Thus Fr Patrizi, not favouring the order of our Lord's three temptations in the desert, as given by St Luke, attributes it to the mistake of the transcribers. 'I have no doubt at all,' he says, 'that it is to be attributed, not to Luke himself, but to his transcribers' (*ibid.* p. 5); and again, he says that it is owing 'vitio librariorum' (p. 394). If I recollect rightly, Melchior Canus has recourse to the 'fault of transcribers' also. Indeed it is commonly urged in controversy (*vide* Lamy, i. p. 31).

I do not here go on to treat of the special instance urged against us by M. Renan, drawn from the Book of Judith, because I have wished to lay down principles, and next, because his charge can neither be proved nor refuted just now, while the strange discoveries are in progress about Assyrian and Persian history by means of the cuneiform inscriptions. When the need comes, the Church, or the Holy See, will interpret the sacred book for us.

I conclude by reminding the reader that in these remarks I have been concerned only with the question—what have Catholics to hold and profess *de fide* about Scripture? that is, what it is the Church 'insists' on their holding; and next, by unreservedly submitting what I have written to the judgment of the Holy See, being more desirous that the question should be satisfactorily answered, than that my own answer should prove to be in every respect the right one.

Marie Joseph Lagrange
1855-1938

Lagrange was born in Bourg-en-Bresse in France and attended the minor seminary in Autun. He studied law in Paris, receiving a doctorate in 1878, and joined the Dominicans in the following year. He studied theology in Salamanca, Spain, and was ordained at Zamora in 1883. After teaching history and philosophy for four years at Salamanca and Toulouse, he went to the University of Vienna to do oriental studies. Two years later he journeyed to Jerusalem to set up a Biblical school. The Ecole Biblique *opened in the fall of 1890 and the* Revue Biblique *began publication in 1892, marking a new era in Catholic biblical scholarship.*

Lagrange read a paper on the sources of the Pentateuch at an international congress held in Fribourg, Switzerland, in 1897. Ten years of bitter criticism followed, as he was caught in the turbulence of the Modernist crisis. From 1907 he restricted himself to the New Testament. In the 1920s he brought out commentaries on Luke, Matthew, and John, then in 1928 his most popular work appeared, The Gospel of Jesus Christ. *Two years earlier he had published a synopsis of the Gospels, and his intention now, as he explains in the preface, was to present "little more than a rapid commentary on the* Synopsis *along with a few historical observations." His confrères, members of the*

English Dominican province, brought out the English translation less than two months before Lagrange's death in 1938.

R. T. A. Murphy observes that Lagrange "restored prestige to Catholic scholarship and almost alone lifted Catholic Biblical studies out of mediocrity." One cannot help wondering how much more he might have accomplished if he had not been hounded by lesser men who lacked his vision. Since he died five years before Pius XII's Divino Afflante Spiritu, he did not even have the consolation of knowing that better days were coming.

Amidst all the negative events of the 1890s, the opening of the Ecole Biblique in Jerusalem is looked back upon as a most important counterevent. No one could have foreseen, for instance, that in little more than a half-century that institution would be responsible for the appearance of the Jerusalem Bible, hailed at the time as "the greatest translation of the Bible ever made into any language." If Lagrange had given up, and he had every reason to, the state of Catholic Biblical studies today could hardly have been reached. His acceptance of modern historical-critical methods, balanced by his firm theological grasp of the tradition, made him a model for subsequent generations.

His book, since it is commenting on his Synopsis, follows Luke's outline. Thus, in the selection that follows, the first section is his commentary on Luke's prologue. This is followed by his treatment of the Resurrection narratives. These few pages are hardly adequate, but are simply meant to allow one to sense the richness, the simplicity, and the awe which Père Lagrange brought to or derived from the text. Great progress of many technical kinds has been made in the intervening half-century, but there is still no way to surpass the kind of spirit with which he read and meditated on the Gospel of Jesus Christ.

THE GOSPEL OF JESUS CHRIST

PROLOGUE OF THE GOSPEL (2)

Luke i, 1-4.

Both the gospels of St. Matthew and St. Mark open without any prologue; and the prologue which we find at the beginning of St. John's gospel is not an author's preface. It is a theological statement which presents to us the doctrine concerning the Son of God from a special point of view: we shall not deal with it, therefore, until we reach the end of this book. There remains the short preface of St. Luke's gospel; it is very enlightening, but we cannot help wishing that it were more explicit.

A custom had grown up among the Greeks of dedicating literary works to some distinguished personage, a custom followed by Jewish writers. Luke addresses his little book to Theophilus, a certain Christian distinguished by the title of 'Excellent,' but otherwise unknown to us. A few years later Josephus, as a Jew writing on things Jewish for Roman readers, thought it advisable to insist at some length on his impartiality. But Luke, following the example of Polybius, thought that his impartiality might be taken for granted, and considered it enough to point out that his aim was to show for his noble friend's benefit the solid truth of what he had been taught. He thus confesses that his purpose is (to use the current term) apologetic, just as St. John states quite frankly in his own case: 'But these (miracles) are written that you may believe that Jesus is the Christ, the Son of God.'

Now only too often apologists have a bad name. They are accused of being like certain lawyers, not over-nice in their choice of an argument so long as it gets home: of being ready, for instance, to use even bad arguments on people of little discernment likely to be convinced by them. But Luke aspires to be an historian worthy of the name and to convince men who are well able to judge. And, moreover, the very nobility of the cause which it is a writer's ambition to serve puts upon him the obligation of making use only of such facts as are beyond dispute. This means that he must have recourse to none but unimpeachable witnesses. And this, indeed, is what Luke professes to do. Ever since he was first associated with the preaching of the gospel, he had made it his business to get at the facts. This was all the more easy for him, inasmuch as he was, owing to his apostolic work, in constant touch with the very people who had been eyewitnesses from the beginning— with the Apostles, that is, and the first disciples. Now these Apostles and disciples preached first of all among the Jews who had just condemned Jesus on false testimony; their own witness, they claimed, was true. Could they, then, have put forward anything untrue without being at once contradicted by fiercely hostile opponents? People sitting round the fire-side at night are content to listen even to the most fanciful of stories if only they are interesting; such things blend with their mood and while away a pleasant hour. But the disciples of Jesus were hardy enough to carry on a work which the leaders of the nation had condemned as subversive of the religion of their fathers. There was one temptation to which the disciples might have seemed in danger of succumbing, from a desire to make their message more acceptable: the temptation, namely, to modify certain features, to portray Jesus as submissive to the Law, deferential to the rabbis, respectful towards the priests. But, far from yielding to it, they gave a faithful account of the very words and deeds for which He had been condemned, and thereby showed themselves absolutely trustworthy. It was precisely this fidelity to the facts which caused their testimony to be instantly punished with imprisonment. Luke had been present more than once when this same testimony had been received with furious outbursts of hatred, though the facts no one had dared to deny. So he was sure of the truth of the story he was about to tell once more. For he was not the first to tell it: those facts, which had proved for so many men the source of a new life, had been related by many before him. He mentions no names, however. Tradition gives those of St. Matthew and St. Mark; scholars conjecture others. How do these writers stand to one another? How are we to make up for St. Luke's silence about them?

The fact is that, however soon writing may have been used in the service of the Christian Faith, it must have been preceded by the oral teaching which it recorded and preserved at least in part: for in a new doctrine there are often a certain number of points which it may seem advisable to transmit only by word of mouth, at any rate in the beginning. Moreover, if a doctrine is to win men, they must be told something of the personality and doings of the one who gave it to the world. Now it was a first principle with the Jews that any doctrine, if it was to be accepted, must be put forward as from God and be confirmed by miracles: unless it were merely an exhortation to keep the Law. The oral teaching, or catechesis as we call it, comprised therefore a general view of Jesus' preaching and an account of the deeds which proved its authority. The first teacher of this catechesis was naturally the man who had been most closely associated with the Master's work, His companion on His journeys, the undisputed head of His disciples, Simon Peter. It was he who delivered the first discourse upon these lines—the first gospel, so to say. He had already decided that the two extreme points of the catechesis should be the baptism of John and the ascension of Jesus into heaven, and between these two points he would pick out the most significant incidents and the most characteristic utterances, relating them with all the authority of an eyewitness. With the subject-matter thus defined, the main lines of the gospel had now been fixed.

Among the disciples there was one accustomed to the art of writing, Levi, once a publican or tax-gatherer, now an Apostle under the name of Matthew. He had learned how to pack his thoughts into clear and striking phrases, presenting his arguments with the same decision that he had formerly shown when he presented his claims for custom-dues. He took the facts that Peter had related in so spontaneous a way about Jesus of Nazareth and, in the light of proofs drawn from the Old Testament, showed that Jesus was the expected Messiah, the promulgator of a moral law which was the Old Law perfected through charity. Something of the charm and vividness found in the original narrative of the various episodes of Jesus' life was thus sacrificed to their value as proofs, but on the other hand one advantage was gained. Matthew wrote in Aramaic, Jesus' mother tongue; hence in his gospel the words of our Saviour, which the Apostle for the most part gathered into five long composite discourses, not only keep their primitive meaning but also remain in their original language.

It is likely enough that other disciples too had set down in writing various incidents, the memory of which they particularly cherished. Jesus' Passion was a sacred memory common to them all, and it was probably the first event to be narrated and the first to be put in writing.

Meanwhile Peter had gone to Rome, where he set up his see as head of the Church. There he went on with his catecheses, speaking, as always, ardently and naturally, lingering lovingly over the details still fresh in his memory, reproducing vividly the impression these had made on him when first they moved his soul. Was this freshness of impression, was this faithful reflection of the reality to pass away with him? His hearers begged his disciple, St. Mark, to put into writing these various episodes as related by St. Peter. This he did, but without giving much place to Jesus' sayings, either because St. Peter did not insist so much on this point, or because Matthew's admirable composite discourses had already given what was necessary.

St. Matthew, being specially intent on furnishing the proof of Jesus' messiahship, had paid little heed to the order of the events. St. Mark's order was more probable, and to St. Luke it appeared almost completely satisfactory. He himself had not followed Jesus but was only a disciple of the Apostles, and he could not have found a surer guide than the man entrusted with the catecheses of St. Peter. He therefore took over into his own work nearly all that was contained in the second gospel, generally keeping as well the same sequence of events. Nevertheless he was conscious that, in the matter of order, he had improved on that of his predecessor, having made this more definitely his aim and having gone about to seek information on the point; does he not undertake 'to write in order'? It is to be remembered, however, that with the ancient historians, for whom history was an art, order did not necessarily mean purely chronological order such as is adopted by primitive annalists.

Marie Joseph Lagrange

Along with the events Luke chose to give some discourses, and—since he attached great importance to putting everything in its place—he distributed them here and there in their proper setting, thereby running the risk of losing the harmonious unity which St. Matthew gives to the long discourses in his gospel. It. is probable that Greek-speaking disciples had, quite early, translated the Aramaic gospel of St. Matthew, or at least some of the discourses in it, being more affected by the eternal principles contained in the utterances of Jesus than by his controversy with the Pharisees. St. Luke may thus have read these discourses, and yet not have known the rest of the gospel; in any case, Matthew's facts and order and his grouping of the sayings had little influence on him.

In Mark—and in Matthew, if he knew the whole of it—Luke would find proof of a considerable gap. Mark is not unaware of the fact that Jesus had preached in Judæa, but he chooses to restrict himself to Galilee; according to his narrative, Jesus leaves the lake-side *en route* for Jericho only just before the last week of his life: Luke got to know, perhaps from disciples he met at Cæsarea, perhaps from Joanna, the wife of Chusa, mentioned by him alone and on two different occasions, what had happened during a mission of Jesus in Judæa covering several months. And he has given an account of it, but place, occasion, characters, no longer stand out as they would in an account by St. Peter: though the latter, of course, being Galilean born and bred, was not altogether at home in Judæa, and he may not have been present during the whole of the journey. Hence in this whole section, peculiar to St. Luke and of priceless worth, we do not get the details that characterize the story of the lake-side.

St. Luke's prologue contains no reference to the fourth gospel, written later by John, the son of Zebedee, the disciple whom Jesus loved. He too chose to tell once more the story of the gospel, and sure in his knowledge of the inmost thought of One whose heart had been opened to him, he composed what the ancient Fathers called 'the spiritual gospel.' He was certainly acquainted with the three gospels of Matthew, Mark, and Luke, but his work is not a series of notes upon these, nor is it meant simply to supplement them. He followed his own course, but at the same time avoided repeating what everyone knew, except where the repetition was necessary to the plan of his own work; and then he gives it in his own way and according to his own reminiscences. He made a point of being more precise about times and places; thus it is to him that we owe our knowledge of a number of places existing in Palestine in the time of Jesus; our knowledge, too, that the ministry of Jesus lasted two years and a few months, and that He preached at Jerusalem at each of the great feasts, the Pasch, Pentecost, Tabernacles, and the Dedication.

We have already spoken of the translation of the Aramaic gospel of St. Matthew into Greek. The translator did not keep slavishly to the original, but gave the substance of it; as regards some details, at least, he was probably influenced by the gospel of St. Mark.

The exact date of the gospels is uncertain. St. Mark and the Greek St. Matthew were certainly written before A.D. 70, the date of the destruction of Jerusalem: St. Mark, and the Aramaic St. Matthew at least, probably much before. St. Luke, who made use of St. Mark, wrote his gospel before the Acts of the Apostles, which he had finished by A.D. 67, the year of St. Paul's martyrdom, or perhaps a little earlier.

It is with the aid of these four gospels that we shall follow the course of the life of our Saviour, Jesus Christ, and we shall strive to show the harmony that exists between them, without in any way toning down their individual characteristics.

CHAPTER I

THE GOSPEL OF THE DIVINE AND HUMAN ORIGINS OF JESUS

The good tidings.

Gospel means good tidings. In the beginning the good tidings were those announced by Jesus, and by John before Him, in the words: The kingdom of God is at hand. When His disciples understood that these good tidings had become a reality in the person of Jesus, in His death and resurrection for man's salvation, the meaning of the word gospel became more definite: the good tidings signified the doctrine of Jesus, the doctrine taught by Him and about Him, which the Apostles were publishing abroad and calling on Jews first, and then Gentiles, to accept.

Hence St. Paul, who was perhaps the first to use the word, speaks of preaching 'the gospel,' meaning by that the salvation which is in Jesus, in virtue of His Passion, for those who believe in Him. The other Apostles, who had been witnesses of our Saviour's life as He actually lived it, and St. Peter most of all, dwelt on the different details of that life, on His words and His miracles, and on all that was comprised under the gospel. We have already seen that, as planned by St. Peter, it began with the baptism of John and ended with the Resurrection and Ascension. This was also the meaning of the term for Peter's disciple, St. Mark.

To make the gospel begin further back might well seem to them unnecessary. The facts relating to our Saviour's infancy had not become known to the world, nor had the growth of faith in the mind of the disciples been in any way due to those facts. During that period Jesus went by the name of Joseph's son from Nazareth. Seemingly, these facts could be left out of account by one who wished simply to get a good idea of the impression Jesus' words and deeds produced on the Jews, and to carry his thoughts back to those early days so as to experience for himself the effect of those words and deeds. The attempt has even been made to regard these facts of the Infancy not as things which played a part in the genesis of the disciples' faith, but as inferences drawn later on from Christian belief after that belief had been formed by the Saviour's public ministry alone. But the truth is that Christians have never admitted any doubt upon the point; nor is there any doubt, though we do not know precisely when these facts came to the knowledge of the Apostles. Accordingly, when St. Matthew, in order to help converted Jews and to resist the attacks of unbelieving Jews, designed to furnish solid proof that Jesus was really the Messiah, he judged it opportune to go right back to his origin. He proved by a genealogy that He was really a descendant of David; he showed that the manner of His birth, that is to say a supernatural conception such as befitted one who was the Son of God, had been foretold by the Scriptures, which had also foretold His birth at Bethlehem and His life at Nazareth.

Then St. Luke, coming after St. Mark, decided that he would include in his gospel an orderly account of the events of the Infancy. It is only during these last few years that we have come fully to understand how these events really form part of the gospel, nay, are the gospel itself if we take the word in its earlier Christian sense. That is to say, with our fuller knowledge of the world of his time, we realize how very opportune Luke's narrative must have been. The noun 'gospel' (εὐαγγέλιον) he never uses; but twice in his story of the Infancy he has the verb 'to evangelize' (to announce the good tidings); and we now know that it was precisely here that the usage of the time made it a peculiarly appropriate word.

A custom had grown up in the East of giving to sovereigns the title of Saviour or God Saviour, and by that very fact an all-important significance was attached to their birth; for if a sovereign was entitled to be called a god it could only be because of his divine origin, and this divine origin was consecrated and made manifest to all men by means of his birth. Already as early as the year 238 B.C., the birth of King Ptolemy had been described as the day on which all mankind began to receive many benefits. In the case of Antiochus of Commagene (from 69 to about 34 B.C.) his birth and coronation were said to be divine epiphanies or, as we say, manifestations. It was about the same time that Virgil was making known to the world that a ruler was to appear who should restore the golden age, the beginnings of which were to be found in a childhood that was miraculous. Finally, in the year 9 B.C., Paulus Fabius Maximus, the proconsul of Roman Asia, made a proposal to the people of his province that they should count the birthday of Augustus as their New Year's Day. In his proclamation he said: 'It is a question whether we receive more pleasure or more profit from the birthday of the most divine Cæsar, for it is a day that might well be compared to the beginning of everything—if not the beginning of all being, at all events the source of all our benefit. For this day has restored all that was in decay and all that had fallen into misfortune; and a new appearance has been put upon the entire world, which would have perished but for the birth of Cæsar who is the blessing of all men.' Note that it is precisely the birthday of Cæsar Augustus which gives to the world the beginning of good tidings, or εὐαγγέλια (gospels) as the Greek puts it. And when a prince succeeded to the throne, his accession was looked on as a second and further announcement of good tidings: thus, when Nero came to the imperial throne in the year 54, he was proclaimed to the world as the hope of all prosperity and the good genius of the universe.

Is it St. Luke's intention, then, to imitate the official protocol? Perhaps; but if he does so it is with a tremendous difference. It was rather his intention to accept the challenge thrown down by these proud monarchs or by their flattering courtiers when he claimed the title of Saviour for a Child born in a crib, a Child who at that time had few to pay Him homage. And events have proved that Luke was in the right, for it is from the birth-day of Jesus that we count this new era, the Christian era, which, by contrast with that unknown time when the world first came into being, is like a new creation. Men have not begun to count time, as the proconsul desired, from the birth-day of Augustus, who did no more than restore a social order that has long since passed away.

The gospel, therefore, in the strictest sense of that word, ought to commence with the supernatural conception of Jesus. It was by His public mission that He proved His dignity as Son of God; but it was at the moment of His Incarnation that the Son of God became the Saviour who dwelt amongst us. Wherefore, St. John, who goes into no detail about the childhood of Jesus, has been careful to point out His divine origin right from the opening of the fourth gospel.

The gospel of the Infancy may not have furnished the Jews who listened to Jesus with any motive for belief; nevertheless it provides for us a marvellous light and is a source of delight for all devout and contemplative souls. The very beauty of that mysterious harmony which exists between God's preparation of His design and its execution is itself a motive of faith. It might be said that the Infancy Narrative teaches nothing more than Jesus is both Son of God and truly man: but is that nothing? Indeed we might almost say that, in His infancy, He is more truly man than at any time during the remainder of His life: that is why Marcion, who would believe only in a heavenly Christ, held the crib and the swaddling clothes in horror. But we mean that He is more human because He is weaker, a mere Child in His Mother's arms, dependent on her and fed at her breast. He works no miracles, for miracles are meant to serve as confirmations of doctrine, and the time for teachings has not yet arrived. Indeed the supernatural is here altogether concealed except for the angelic apparitions, and these are only necessary for the purpose of making known the good tidings to a little chosen group. Mary has to be informed so that she may give her consent: Joseph has to play his part in God's designs: a few shepherds, who stand for the whole of Israel, have to receive the news that a Saviour is born to them.

Therefore St. Luke, convinced as he is of the supreme importance of these facts, begins at once to appeal to those testimonies which, as he guarantees to Theophilus, are trustworthy. He makes two reserved, but quite clear allusions in the course of his narrative which give the reader to understand that the Mother of Jesus herself is the source from which the disciples learnt the most intimate secrets of those humble beginnings, which St. Luke has not been afraid to link up with the most important events of the time.

CHAPTER VII

THE RESURRECTION, APPARITIONS, AND ASCENSION OF CHRIST

None of the evangelists has told us a single word of the actual resurrection of Jesus. A great artist, Francois Rude, has carved Napoleon in stone rising from the bed of his tomb and awakening to glory; but the gospels have made no attempt to picture how Christ's bruised and wounded body thrilled once more at the touch of His soul. That human body of His, by which the Son of God had subjected Himself to the law of suffering, was now transfigured by glorious beatitude, while the Father's voice declared in His eternal day: 'Thou art My Son, this day have I begotten Thee,' and the Son gave thanks to His Father for having given Him the nations for an inheritance. All these things transcend the power of human words to describe and remain hidden in the secret counsels of God.

This discretion manifested by the evangelists is certainly a strong recommendation of the value of their testimony. They

bore witness to what was seen upon earth: first that the tomb
was found empty, then that Christ was seen alive with a body
that shared the glory of His soul, but truly His own body. They
do not tell us where His soul had been in the meantime, while
it was separated from that most sacred body. But the first
epistle of St. Peter gives us an indication—and Christ's words to
the good thief already gave us an inkling of it—when it says that
Jesus had gone to preach 'to those spirits that were in prison'.
Tradition expresses this as the descent of Christ into hell,
meaning by hell the abode of the dead where the just men of
old awaited the blessing of redemption. Afterwards His soul
rejoined His body, and that body, now animated by a more
perfect life than before, was enabled to come forth from the
tomb without breaking the seals fixed there by His now powerless enemies, after the manner in which, as a child, He had come
forth from His Mother's womb. Yet it was only fitting that the
empty tomb should not remain closed, and St. Matthew tells
us that an angel of the Lord shook the earth and rolled away
the stone on which he sat in triumph: 'His countenance was as
lightning and his raiment white as snow.' At that sound the
guards awoke; at that sight they trembled with terror and,
though motionless at first with astonishment, took to flight.

The tomb found empty

Luke xxiv, 1-12; Mark xvi, 1-8; Matt. xxviii, 1-8;
John xx, 1-10.

The four evangelists relate, each in his own way, how the
tomb of Jesus was found empty, to the great astonishment of
Christ's friends. St. Matthew and St. Mark are the most alike.
St. Luke is usually closer to St. Mark. As for St. John, he goes
his own way, but is in agreement with St. Luke concerning the
search made by St. Peter. The difficulty of harmonizing the
four accounts has been greatly exaggerated. Nothing is more
simple provided we do not stick at unimportant details, provided also we pay attention to the way in which each gospel
was composed.

The Sabbath had ended at sunset on Saturday evening,
and with it the prescribed rest of the day of the Pasch. The
feast lasted eight days, but only the first and last were days

of rest. However the women devoted to Jesus did not leave the house where they were probably together until the next morning, but they went out very early. According to St. Mark, they were Mary of Magdala, Mary the mother of James, and Salome. Instead of Salome St. Luke names Joanna, of whom he alone has told us; whilst St. Matthew only mentions Mary of Magdala and the other Mary. None of the evangelists intended to mention all the women there; each followed his own information without seeking to be in harmony with the others. But it will be observed that Mary of Magdala always heads the list. St. John speaks only of her.

To restore the harmony of events we need only suppose that Mary Magdalen, the most eager of all the group, went straight to the tomb. The other women, according to St. Luke, would appear to have already had spices and perfumed oil ready since Friday evening. But is it likely that they would have had a store of these in their temporary lodging? Probably St. Luke has, in accordance with his method, dealt at once with all that concerned the burial and thus anticipated what St. Mark has placed after the Sabbath, that is, the purchase of the spices. We may well imagine that the women, who had gone out very early when it was still dark, would have lost a great deal of time in getting the shops opened to buy these spices; and so, according to St. Mark, they did not arrive within sight of the sepulchre until after sunrise. Magdalen must have preceded them, since it was still nearly dark when she discovered that the stone had been taken away, in other words, rolled back so that the tomb was open. The guards had disappeared, but she was not surprised at that, for she did not know they had been posted there. By peeping within she saw that the body had disappeared, but she saw no angel, for Jesus intended to tell her Himself. In her extreme anxiety, dreading the thought of some profanation of the adorable body of Jesus, she immediately set off to run back, going straight to Simon Peter and the disciple whom Jesus loved. Quite beside herself, she did not hesitate to declare: 'They have taken away the Lord out of the sepulchre, and we know not where they have laid Him.' She says 'we,' ascribing her conviction also to the women who had started out with her, but who only at that moment were arriving at the tomb.

These women had gone to the tomb at the bidding of their generous hearts, only realizing the difficulty that lay before them as they went along. They knew nothing about the guards. How were they to get into the tomb to anoint the body of Jesus? The heavy mill-stone which closed the entrance would be an insuperable obstacle, for they were not strong enough to roll it back; even a man would need a crow-bar, but they had no hopes of finding a willing helper at that early hour. Such were the anxious thoughts they exchanged when they arrived and found the stone already rolled away. Their joy was great, for the stone 'was very large.' They therefore entered the tomb and found the body was gone. Deep was their astonishment. So it was not the disciples who had rolled back the stone, for they would not have profaned the body by disturbing the sacred rest of the dead. Then they saw a young man seated on their right upon the stone ledge, clothed in a white garment. They cast their eyes to the ground in fear. The young man said: 'Be not affrighted. You seek Jesus of Nazareth, who was crucified; He is risen, He is not here. Behold the place where they laid Him. But go and tell His disciples and Peter that He goeth before you into Galilee; there you shall see Him, as He told you.' According to St. Mark, the holy women fled and said nothing to anybody, so frightened were they. After all, that is quite natural: and they must have feared they would not be believed. No doubt they thought better of it, for St. Luke and St. Matthew relate very briefly that they gave their message to the Apostles; all that must have taken some time and have been accompanied by certain incidents.

St. Mark, who excels in relating the unexpected, would have given us information about this, had not the thread of his discourse been broken at that very point. When his gospel was finished, whether by him or someone else, the gap was not filled up.

The Apostles might have thought they would be demeaning themselves if they gave credence to women's gossip. However, St. Luke tells us how Peter, who had to be informed first for he was still the leader, ran to the tomb which he found empty: he saw nothing but the linen cloths, a fact which made him think.

This incident St. John has related in detail, for he himself took part in that anxious search, describing himself as the 'other disciple whom Jesus loved.' Peter and he were probably together when Mary of Magdala brought them the disastrous news of the removal of the body. They set out at once, and in their great excitement, they both ran. John, the younger, ran faster than Peter and therefore reached the sepulchre first. But he did not enter, surely out of respect for his companion. He merely stooped and, looking beyond the little antechamber, saw the linen cloths lying there. Peter, who followed him, entered boldly into the tomb itself. He, too, saw the cloths and saw them more plainly; their presence was proof that the body had not been removed, for it would have been taken clothed as it was. And a still more surprising thing was this: the linen that had been put round the head was not lying untidily among the cloths, but folded up and laid aside by itself. The other disciple entered and saw the same thing. Both of them, startled and thoughtful, were silent and said nothing to one another of what they thought. St. John only says that from this time he believed that Jesus had risen again, and this was surely St. Peter's conviction too. Up to that moment they had not understood from the Scriptures that Christ was to rise again, though He Himself had foretold it to all His Apostles. But the occurrence seemed to them so improbable that only the obvious fact had the power to convince them, and then it dawned upon them that this was the predicted fulfilment of the Messiah's final consecration.

Apparitions of Christ in Judæa

Luke xxiv, 13-43; Mark xvi, 9-14; Matt. xxviii, 9-15;
John xx, 11-29.

Pious children of the Church entertain no doubt that the newly risen Saviour appeared first of all to His most holy Mother. She had fed Him at her breast, she had guided Him in His childhood's years, she had, so to say, introduced Him to the world at the marriage feast of Cana, and beyond that she hardly appears again in the gospel until she stands at the foot of the cross. But to her alone with Joseph Jesus had devoted the thirty years of His hidden life, and would He not have reserved for her alone also the first moments of His new life that was hidden in God? That was no concern of the gospel's spread through the world, for Mary belongs to an order that transcends this world, an order where as the Mother of Jesus she is associated with the Father in His paternity of Jesus. Let us therefore submit ourselves to that disposition of things which has been willed by the Holy Ghost, and leave this first appearance of the risen Christ to be meditated on by contemplative souls. We may be sure that it had none of those features, which appeal so much to our emotions, found in Christ's manifestation of Himself to Mary of Magdala.

The two disciples most beloved of the Lord had now returned home, as one of them informs us; but Mary Magdalen did not go away. She had been the last to leave the cross and the sepulchre; she was the first to come back to the tomb which she had found empty. Now she could not tear herself away from it, but stayed outside and wept. After a while she determined to look again and, entering the antechamber of the tomb, she stooped and peered into the burial chamber as though she might have gathered some information from this fresh glance. It was then that she saw two angels clothed in white, seated one at the head and the other at the foot of the rock shelf on which the body of Jesus had been laid. They said to her: 'Woman, why weepest thou?' She failed to recognize that they were angels, for would not angels have known why she was weeping? She replied, therefore: 'Because they have taken away my Lord, and I know not where they have laid Him.' She does not catch sight of the burial garments, nor does she feel alarm at seeing these strangers; at present, all is emptiness and nothingness for her. She stoops again, this time in order to leave the tomb and go elsewhere to seek Jesus. Then she perceives Him, but without recognizing Him or even paying attention to Him, for she is thinking only of that beloved body which she desires to anoint with precious oil, and which she fears is now in profane hands. Jesus says to her: 'Woman, why weepest thou? Whom seekest thou?' Under the impression that He is the guardian of the place, someone she does not know, perhaps one who does not believe in Jesus, and that He must know what has happened to the body of her Lord and consequently ought to understand her·

distress, she says to Him: 'If thou hast taken Him hence, tell me where thou hast laid Him and I will take Him away.'

It is hardly surprising that she set out to come to the sepulchre without giving a thought to the stone which closed it, for all her thoughts and desires are concentrated on Jesus and on Him alone. She is determined to find Him. Then she hears the voice that goes straight to her heart and takes the veil from her eyes, addressing her by her familiar name in her own mother tongue: 'Miriam!' Straightway she returns the cry: 'Rabbouni! My Master!' and Magdalen is at the feet of Jesus, still weeping, but now for very joy. Now she is in the place of her desire, where she desires to remain so that she may continue to pour out her love. But this was not the time for the sinner to shed tears on the Saviour's feet. Jesus now belonged to the world above, and although He had not yet ascended to His Father, that would take place before long and it was necessary that He should warn His disciples of the fact. This is apparently the meaning of the words: 'Do not touch Me, for I am not yet ascended to My Father, but go to My brethren and say to them: I ascend to My Father and your Father, to My God and your God.' At that moment Mary Magdalen was consecrated to the office of Apostle of the Apostles. She obeys, like those who tear themselves from converse with their Master in order to go and announce the good tidings, and tells the Apostles: 'I have seen the Lord.' But they would not believe her. We do not even learn that any of the disciples, apart from Peter and John, showed any eagerness to verify what the women had said.

Other witnesses of the empty tomb were the guards, who fled when the stone was rolled away. There were not many of them, three or four at the most, and they were not a little bewildered by their experience. When day broke and the city had resumed its daily life the unfortunate men could no longer escape the duty of reporting the event. It was the priests from whom they had received their commission, and it was to the priests that they went to report. The position was embarrassing. Even if the guards had been lacking in vigilance, there was no question of their sincerity; it could not be supposed that these Roman soldiers had been spirited out of the way. To punish them would be to provoke protests on their part. What could

they have done in face of supernatural intervention? In pro-
testing thus the soldiers would merely have spread abroad the
rumour that the Jewish leaders precisely wished to prevent, and
such a rumour as would be considered no mere conjecture since
it was based on evidence provided by the guards. Therefore it
seemed the most prudent course to persuade them to say that
they had seen nothing, for the only plausible hypothesis open
to adoption by the enemies of Jesus was that His disciples had
removed the body. A number of the members of the Sanhedrin
came to the decision that money should be given to the guards
in order to induce them to spread this story in their own name.
If Pilate showed any inclination to hold an enquiry and punish
the offenders, it would be possible to pacify him, since he had
left the matter in the hands of the priests. But it was obvious
that the guards could not affirm that they had seen the disciples
taking away the body while they themselves were asleep. They
would have to admit that they had fallen asleep and that the
disciples had taken advantage of their neglect, for none but the
disciples could have done the deed. Such was doubtless the
solution adopted by many of the Jews when hard pressed about
the disappearance of the body of Christ.

At Jerusalem the second day of the Paschal festival was
spent in general rejoicing; in the midst of this the disciples alone
remained sorrowful, for they did not dare to believe what they
looked on as idle tales of the holy women. Two of them made
up their minds to return home to their native village; all their
hopes were dashed, for although one or two disciples had tried
to verify the women's report and had indeed found the tomb
empty, yet the Master Himself they had not seen at all. And
what sort of state would the body be in after three days? We
know from St. Luke that one of these two was named Cleophas,
and that they were making for the village of Emmaus which was
about sixty stades (or furlongs) from Jerusalem. Whilst they
were talking sadly together, discussing the terrible incidents of
the past few days, suddenly Jesus appeared alongside them as
though He were a traveller wishing to join them since He was
walking in the same direction. They did not recognize Him;
even His voice seemed that of a stranger, the more especially as
He enquired what was the matter they were discussing. Surely,

thought they, He must be the only pilgrim at Jerusalem who had failed to hear of the great event: how Jesus of Nazareth had gained the reputation of a prophet mighty in word and deed, and how the chief priests and magistrates had delivered Him up to be condemned to death, and thus had caused Him to be crucified. It was already the third day since these things had taken place. Moreover, certain women belonging to the group of those who believed in Jesus had found His tomb empty and declared that they had seen a vision of angels who told them that He was alive. But the disciples, who alone could be accepted as serious witnesses, had not seen Him. The two pilgrims apparently know nothing of Christ's appearance to Magdalen, or else they refuse to give any credit to her story.

Jesus allowed them to talk on without saying to them: 'It is I,' preferring to teach them once more that lesson in face of which His friends had always been reluctant to believe. Was it not necessary—and the Scriptures bore witness to it—that the Christ should suffer before entering into His glory? That truth followed especially from the prophecy of Isaias concerning the suffering servant of Jahweh, but the risen Christ deigned to explain to them all the Scriptures which spoke of Him, both in the Law of Moses and in the Prophets. By this time they had approached the village to which the two disciples were directing their steps. Jesus kept straight ahead without seeming to observe that they were preparing to take a path leading off the high road. But the charitable pair, enraptured by this explanation of the Scriptures which had opened up a new world for them, were unwilling so soon to lose such a companion. They must have been walking for more than three hours and the day was drawing in. Why should He not spend the night with them? Naturally they make the most of the lateness of the hour, but at any rate it must have been at least three o'clock in the afternoon. They brought their guest in and the evening meal was prepared, whereupon He reclined with them at the table. Then Jesus, whose striking air of authority they had already perceived, took bread into His hands, uttered a blessing, broke the bread, and gave it to them. Their eyes were opened and they recognized Him; but immediately He vanished. Then they

said to one another: 'Was not our heart burning within us whilst
He spoke in the way and opened to us the Scripture?'

Many have thought that their hearts were burning most of
all because they had eaten bread that had been changed into the
Body of the Lord; but there is nothing to show that Christ
spoke on this occasion the words of consecration. He was only
taking ordinary food with his disciples. Why should such a
privilege have been granted to these two who, not being of
the Twelve, had not been initiated with them into the deed
performed by Jesus during the Last Supper? Had their eyes
been opened while they were eating, St. Luke would not have
told us that they recognized Jesus at the breaking of bread,
and consequently before they began to eat. Hence we are not
to take this expression to mean the Eucharist.

It would seem that the two disciples, at first startled and
then carried away by joy, did not even stop to finish their meal.
They must spread the good news as quickly as possible. It was
the beginning of a new gospel. Returning to Jerusalem, they
found the eleven Apostles reunited along with a few companions, these also under the influence of strong emotion. Before the two new arrivals had time to speak the apostles explained why they were gathered together at so late an hour:
'The Lord is risen indeed and hath appeared to Simon.' It was
right that the chief of the Apostles, Simon Peter, should be the
first of the disciples to behold Him who was the Master of them
all. St. Paul, too, remarked on this. The fact provided proof that
Peter's denials of his Master had been pardoned, his position of
pre-eminence maintained and thus consecrated. Cleophas and
his companion narrated their experience and told how they had
recognized the Lord in the breaking of bread.

The great day of the Resurrection was now drawing to a
close, but before it ended Jesus manifested Himself to that
faithful group, now all impatience to feast their eyes on Him.
Yet when they suddenly saw Him in the midst of them before
they had heard any knocking on the doors, which were shut
fast for fear of the Jews, their first movement was an emotion
of holy fear. They recognized Jesus, but thought that they were
seeing a spirit. Then He said to them: 'Why are you troubled?

Peace be to you!' at the same time showing them His hands and feet which had been nailed to the cross, and His side pierced with the lance. St. Luke, a physician and a good psychologist, who knew the value of material details, adds that excess of joy disturbed their powers of judgement, doubtless because they were afraid lest they might be deceiving themselves into be-lieving that they were actually seeing what they so much desired to see. But Our Lord knew that better than St. Luke, and He now used the most familiar of the ordinary realities of daily life in order to calm and enlighten their minds. He asked them if they had anything they could give Him to eat, and before their eyes He ate a little broiled fish; not that He was restored to the normal life of growth and decline, but solely in order to prove to them the reality of His resurrection.

Having thus been fully convinced and restored to them-selves, they stood awaiting some fresh word from their Master. Then they heard Him say again: 'Peace be to you,' and this time peace was already regained. Following that came the mission, the majestic command that threw the world open to them: 'As the Father hath sent Me, I also send you,' and He breathed upon them, saying: 'Receive ye the Holy Ghost. Whose sins you shall forgive, they are forgiven; and whose sins you shall retain, they are retained.' This is not the great manifestation of the Spirit that He had promised them on the evening of the Last Supper—that will come in due time; but now, immediately after His resurrection, He is forming them into a spiritual govern-ment. From henceforth they have authority over the souls of men, an authority that will be especially exercised in forgiving their sins, in God's name, of course, or else in refusing to for-give owing to the bad disposition of the sinner; for where there is sincere repentance God always forgives. Those who are to be the dispensers of this divine pardon must be the judges of the cases proposed; hence they must be informed of these cases. Therefore the Church has rightly seen in this action of Christ, and in these memorable words, the institution of the Sacrament of Penance.

Now that He was risen Jesus was no longer to live with His disciples as in former days; His appearances were to be merely exceptional. Neither St. John, nor on this occasion St. Luke, found any need to say that He vanished after His manifestation on the Sunday of the Resurrection. That great day has become the real Paschal festival for the Christian faithful.

Thomas, one of the Apostles, was not present with the rest that evening. In all probability he had been summoned like the others after Christ's appearance to Peter, but it seems that he thought fit not to come because he did not believe Peter any more than the others had believed the women. He even refused to give credence to the witness of all his brethren.

Our own age is not much disposed to believe in miracles; not that it is any the less credulous for that, particularly when things are put forward in the name of 'Science.' Renan showed his cleverness in asserting, as though it were a fact, that he had seen for himself in the East that Orientals are always on the watch for the intervention of the super natural and ready to believe it with eagerness. But the fact is that the Jews were no more of that disposition in the time of Our Lord than they are in our own day. From the sublime heights to which they had relegated God, transcendent in all his majesty, they did not allow Him to interfere with things mundane except to keep the world in its regular course. Thus during the whole life of Jesus the Apostles seemed little susceptible to things of the super-natural order. They had expected, of course, the great mani-festation of the Messiah, and it had not come. The Passion, the very notion of which they rejected, had unsettled their confidence; and as they had failed to understand the words of Jesus on this point, the glorious triumph of the Resurrection had not been looked for. After they had been convinced by the event itself Thomas still refused to yield. The disciples, he thought, had surely been the victims of an hallucination; all they had seen was a ghost. And when they objected that they had seen the wounds of the Crucified, he replied that in a mat-ter like that it was not enough to see: you must touch. And for that he would trust nobody but himself: 'Except I shall see in His hands the print of the nails, and put my finger into the place of the nails, and put my hand into His side, I will not believe.'

Let us learn to be as gentle with doubters as Christ was. First He left Thomas to his obstinate denials for seven days.

The Apostles had seen Christ in Jerusalem and were in no hurry to return to Galilee. They met together again on the eighth day, perhaps for a last prayer together, perhaps to arrange for the journey to Galilee. The doors were shut, when suddenly Jesus stood again in their midst: 'Peace be to you!' Then He said to Thomas: 'Put in thy finger here and see my hands, and bring hither thy hand and put it into my side; and be not faithless, but believing.' Did Thomas allow Christ to take his hand and guide it to the wound in His side, or did he abandon his logic and surrender to the evidence of his senses? From him, the unbeliever, came the first explicit act of faith in the divinity of the risen Christ when he cried out: 'My Lord and my God!' To that Jesus replied with a smile of forgiveness: 'Thou believest now that thou hast seen?' That was not very surprising or praiseworthy. 'Blessed are they that have not seen and have believed!'

This was precisely where Thomas had been at fault. He had gone too far in refusing to believe in his Master's resurrection on the evidence of his brethren whose sincerity he already knew. Jesus pointed this out. Thomas had wanted to see the body of his risen Lord with his own eyes; when once he had seen it, there was no longer any need for him to rely upon others for the truth of the Resurrection. But, as St. Gregory has so well pointed out, when he saw the glorified Humanity he believed in the Divinity of Christ, and that is the real act of faith. That act required then, as it requires now, an assent of the mind to a truth revealed by Christ Himself, and consequently by God. Such an assent was easier for the Apostles, because what Jesus had affirmed was confirmed by His resurrection. Nevertheless, they were more blessed in believing in His Divinity than in enjoying the visible presence of His Humanity. That happy blessedness, which is a foretaste of eternal beatitude, is also the portion of those who believe without having experienced the consolation enjoyed by the Apostles. Moreover, that promise of Christ must never be forgotten, in which He assured us that we shall never lack His presence within us, where He is joined by the Father and the Holy Ghost, a presence which makes faith easier and sweeter.

Marie Joseph Lagrange

Before leaving Jerusalem with the Apostles, let us first observe that the gospel accounts of the Resurrection present no difficulty except for those reluctant to accept the very fact of the Resurrection, a reluctance already manifested by Thomas. The testimonies to that fact are in an excellent position: not only do they agree about the fact, but also about all the important points concerning it, though each of the different testimonies shows appreciable differences which prove that the authors of the different accounts each followed his own plan, without any preoccupation about not deviating from the other accounts, and still more without any dependence on them. Here even St. Luke, who is usually so faithful to St. Mark, shows complete independence. The comings and goings during the visits to the empty tomb, the appearances of the risen Christ, all fit easily into a consecutive narrative, given the sole condition that, when St. Matthew mentions the holy women, he attributes to the whole group that which belongs to Mary of Magdala alone. It is unnecessary to point out that it is not unusual to interpret statements in this way in all histories that are composed from various sources. Nor does such a procedure on the part of the evangelists call for any objection to be raised on the score of the dogma of inspiration; and, in any case, those who do not accept that dogma have no right to raise such an objection, in order to provide a basis for their doubts concerning the truth of a fact that is thoroughly well attested.

No; the only real difficulty—and in truth it is one that is plain enough—is this: when the angels appeared to the holy women they appointed a meeting-place in the name of Jesus, where He was to be seen by the disciples. The place was in Galilee; but He had the intention all the time of meeting them in Jerusalem. Even if we learned this from one and the same author, we still could not absolutely say that he had contradicted himself, for there is no contradiction in the idea that Jesus was to appear in both places; but we should have to say that the author had composed his narrative in a very clumsy fashion, as though he were ignorant of what he was leading up to. But it is not the case that this apparent contradiction is found in one and the same author, although it would be the case if the whole of St. Mark's last chapter had been written all in one piece. But here the critics render us a signal service by the way in which, with a rational comprehension of the literary problem, they have proved that St. Mark's original work ended at the eighth verse of his last chapter. The remaining verses of that sixteenth chapter were written later by another hand, or by St. Mark's own hand if we prefer that opinion, and contain only a summary of what is related by other evangelists. The summary is connected more or less skilfully with what precedes it and must be accepted as strictly true, since it was written under the inspiration of the Holy Ghost in order to complete a book that is of sacred character; but, this being the case, it ought not to be judged according to the strict laws that are applied to a work written by a single author, or composed by him as a single whole. Hence, if there be literary inconsistency between the conclusion and the rest of the gospel of St. Mark, that ought not to be used as an argument against the consistency of the facts there narrated.

St. Mark, then, gives Galilee as the place where the disciples are to meet Christ; and, indeed, the last apparition narrated in his gospel ought to be put on a parallel with the last one mentioned by St. Matthew, which was certainly in Galilee. St. Matthew's narrative is altogether coherent: the meeting-place is appointed for Galilee and the appointment is there kept. St. Luke makes no mention of any appearances in Galilee, and this is quite in conformity with his plan which gives much more importance to Judæa than the accounts of St. Matthew and St. Mark; moreover, he had the intention of making his narrative of the preaching of the Apostles begin from Jerusalem in the second volume he was to write, the Acts of the Apostles. It would have been a remarkable want of literary skill to have related an account of the meeting in Galilee; he therefore abstained from doing so. Will it be maintained by anyone that such an example of literary method is tantamount to a denial that there took place any apparitions in Galilee? St. John mentions apparitions first in Jerusalem and then in Galilee; consequently he also makes no mention of the appointment of a meeting place in Galilee.

The much-repeated objection of the critics, then, comes to this: does it not seem that St. Matthew and St. Mark invent this meeting-place in Galilee appointed by the angels in order to prepare for Christ's appearance there, which is the only appearance they could mention? It was as much as to say: 'You will see Jesus again, do not doubt, in Galilee, where you followed Him and lived with Him.' We will go so far as to ask whether the most scrupulous of historians would be led to call the historicity of a fact into question if he actually met with such a literary manipulation of sources, supposing that Matthew and Mark really did act in the manner described by the objection. It would have been a completely harmless proceeding. All the same, the evangelists had no need of it; it was perfectly natural for the Apostles to go back to Galilee.

Only one other difficulty remains to be solved. Why did not St. Matthew make any mention of the apparitions at Jerusalem? Was it because he knew nothing about them? That is as good as to demand why he said nothing about the long mission of Jesus in Judæa narrated by St. Luke, about Martha and Mary, about Zachæus the publican, and so on. The fact is that as he had put practically the whole of Christ's preaching by the shores of the lake of Galilee, he felt it necessary to put the supernatural termination of his gospel there also. Forming a link between St. Matthew the Galilæan and St. Luke, who was preparing to take the gospel from Jerusalem to Rome, comes St. John, who is fuller than either; he relates the apparitions at Jerusalem, those which were chiefly necessary to convince and reassure the Apostles, along with one of the apparitions in Galilee, which were intended to link their minds to the memories of the past.

Pope Pius XII
1876-1958

Eugenio Pacelli was ordained in 1899, became Papal secretary of state in 1929, and was elected Pope in 1939. He was an intellectual, a scholar, a diplomat, and a linguist. His energetic use of his many gifts in the service of the Church brought him the respect of all.

Divino Afflante Spiritu, *the encyclical letter issued on September 30, 1943, on "The Most Opportune Way to Promote Biblical Studies," is one of the most memorable and influential of all the documents coming from Pius XII. Augustin Bea, the German Jesuit Rector of the Pontifical Biblical Institute, had a large hand in its preparation. It was issued to mark the 50th anniversary of Leo XIII's* Providentissimus Deus. *That half-century had been bleak indeed for Catholics involved in Biblical studies, due largely to the complications of the Modernist crisis under Pius X. It is against this backdrop that the true significance of the encyclical is best appreciated.*

Speaking of that work, James Burtchaell observes that "Bea's importance lies not in the freshness of his scholarship. There is nothing . . . in the encyclical he drafted that would not have been conservative and commonplace to the more thoughtful savants back in 1900. What he did do was help the reigning pontiff to smile upon biblical scholars for the first time in four decades. It is the change of climate, the Roman thaw of 1943, that marks the end of incomparably sterile years and invites a spring of biblical studies."

In view of his own formation and his early immersion in curial politics, it is simply amazing that Pius XII should have opened the way for modern biblical studies with all of their impact on the Church. There were still die-hard professors in Roman universities twenty years later who considered the encyclical heretical.

Among the shifts in emphasis stemming from the encyclical, several had immediate and noteworthy consequences. 1) The original texts, not the Latin Vulgate, were henceforth to be the focus of attention in both translation and interpretation. 2) Principal concern was to be directed toward the literal sense. 3) The crucial role of literary forms was to be given proper consideration. 4) All manner of sub-sciences were to be used to establish solidly both text and context.

*The agenda thus set for Catholic scholars promoted intense activity so that the state of scholarship at the end of Pius XII's reign was hardly recognizable in comparison to the scene at the start. Even though he would never have called Vatican II, the irony is that no Vatican II would have been possible without him. His three great encyclicals on the Church (*Mystici Corporis*), the Bible (*Divino Afflante Spiritu*), and the Liturgy (*Mediator Dei) prepared the way for the fuller fruition that took place under the direction of John XXIII and Paul VI.*

DIVINO AFFLANTE SPIRITU

Inspired by the Divine Spirit, the Sacred Writers composed those books, which God, in His paternal charity towards the human race, deigned to bestow on them in order "to teach, to reprove, to correct, to instruct in justice: that the man of God may be perfect, furnished to every good work. This heaven-sent treasure Holy Church considers as the most precious source of doctrine on faith and morals. No wonder, therefore, that as she received it intact from the hands of the Apostles, so she kept it with all care, defended it from every false and perverse interpretation and used it diligently as an instrument for securing the eternal salvation of souls, as almost countless documents in every age strikingly bear witness. In more recent times, however, since the divine and the correct interpretation of the Sacred Writings have been very specially called in question, the Church has with even greater zeal and care undertaken their defense and protection. The sacred Council of Trent ordained by solemn decree that "the entire books with all their parts, as they have been wont to be read in the Catholic Church and are contained in the old vulgate Latin edition, are to be held sacred and canonical." In our own time the Vatican Council, with the object of condemning false doctrines regarding inspiration, declared that these same books were to be regarded by the Church as sacred and canonical "not because, having been composed by human industry, they were afterwards approved by her authority, nor merely because they contain revelation without error, but because, having been written under the inspiration of the Holy Spirit, they have God for their author, and as such were handed down to the Church herself." When, subsequently, some Catholic writers, in spite of this solemn definition of Catholic doctrine, by which such divine authority is claimed for the "entire books with all their parts" as to secure freedom from any error whatsoever, ventured to restrict the truth of Sacred Scripture solely to matters of faith and morals, and to regard other matters, whether in the domain of physical science or history, as "obiter dicta" and—as they contended—in no wise connected with faith, Our Predecessor of immortal memory, Leo XIII, in the Encyclical Letter *Providentissimus Deus,* published on November 18th in the year 1893, justly and rightly condemned these errors and safeguarded the studies of the Divine Books by most wise precepts and rules.

2. Since then it is fitting that We should commemorate the fiftieth anniversary of the publication of this Encyclical Letter, which is considered the supreme guide in biblical studies, We, moved by that solicitude for sacred studies, which We manifested from the very beginning of Our Pontificate, have considered that this may most opportunely be done by ratifying and inculcating all that was wisely laid down by Our Predecessor and ordained by His Successors for the consolidating and perfecting of the work, and by pointing out what seems necessary in the present day, in order to incite ever more earnestly all those sons of the Church who devote themselves to these studies, to so necessary and so praiseworthy an enterprise.

3. The first and greatest care of Leo XIII was to set forth the teaching on the truth of the Sacred Books and to defend it from attack. Hence with grave words did he proclaim that there is no error whatsoever if the sacred writer, speaking of things of the physical order "went by what sensibly appeared" as the Angelic Doctor says, speaking either "in figurative language, or in terms which were commonly used at the time, and which in many instances are in daily use at this day, even among the most eminent men of science." For "the sacred writers, or to speak more accurately—the words are St. Augustine's—the Holy Spirit, Who spoke by them, did not intend to teach men these things—that is the essential nature of the things of the universe—things in no way profitable to salvation"; which principle "will apply to cognate sciences, and especially to history," that is, by refuting, "in a somewhat similar way the fallacies of the adversaries and defending the historical truth of Sacred Scripture from their attacks." Nor is the sacred writer to be taxed with error, if "copyists have made mistakes in the text of the Bible," or, "if the real meaning of a passage remains

ambiguous." Finally it is absolutely wrong and forbidden "either to narrow inspiration to certain passages of Holy Scripture, or to admit that the sacred writer has erred," since divine inspiration "not only is essentially incompatible with error but excludes and rejects it as absolutely and necessarily as it is impossible that God Himself, the supreme Truth, can utter that which is not true. This is the ancient and constant faith of the Church."

4. This teaching, which Our Predecessor Leo XIII set forth with such solemnity, We also proclaim with Our authority and We urge all to adhere to it religiously. No less earnestly do We inculcate obedience at the present day to the counsels and exhortations which he, in his day, so wisely enjoined. For whereas there arose new and serious difficulties and questions, from the widespread prejudices of rationalism and more especially from the discovery and investigation of the antiquities of the East, this same Predecessor of Ours, moved by zeal of the apostolic office, not only that such an excellent source of Catholic revelation might be more securely and abundantly available to the advantage of the Christian flock, but also that he might not suffer it to be in any way tainted, wished and most earnestly desired "to see an increase in the number of the approved and persevering laborers in the cause of Holy Scripture; and more especially that those whom Divine Grace has called to Holy Orders, should day-by-day, as their state demands, display greater diligence and industry in reading, meditating and explaining it."

5. Wherefore the same Pontiff, as he had already praised and approved the school for biblical studies, founded at St. Stephen's, Jerusalem, by the Master General of the Sacred Order of Preachers—from which, to use his own words, "biblical science itself had received no small advantage, while giving promise of more"—so in the last year of his life he provided yet another way, by which these same studies, so warmly commended in the Encyclical Letter *Providentissimus Deus,* might daily make greater progress and be pursued with the greatest possible security. By the Apostolic Letter *Vigilantiae,* published on October 30 in the year 1902, he founded a Council or Commission, as it is called, of eminent men, "whose duty it would

be to procure by every means that the sacred texts may receive everywhere among us that more thorough exposition which the times demand, and be kept safe not only from every breath of error, but also from all inconsiderate opinions." Following the example of Our Predecessors, We also have effectively confirmed and amplified this Council using its good offices, as often before, to remind commentators of the Sacred Books of those safe rules of Catholic exegesis, which have been handed down by the Holy Fathers and Doctors of the Church, as well as by the Sovereign Pontiffs themselves.

6. It may not be out of place here to recall gratefully the principal and more useful contributions made successively by Our Predecessors toward this same end, which contributions may be considered as the complement or fruit of the movement so happily initiated by Leo XIII. And first of all Pius X, wishing "to provide a sure way for the preparation of a copious supply of teachers, who, commended by the seriousness and the integrity of their doctrine, might explain the Sacred Books in Catholic schools . . ." instituted "the academic degrees of licentiate and doctorate in Sacred Scripture . . . ; to be conferred by the Biblical Commission"; he later enacted a law "concerning the method of Scripture studies to be followed in Clerical Seminaries" with this end in view, viz.: that students of the sacred sciences "not only should themselves fully understand the power, purpose and teaching of the Bible, but should also be equipped to engage in the ministry of the Divine Word with elegance and ability and repel attacks against the divinely inspired books"; finally "in order that a center of higher biblical studies might be established in Rome, which in the best way possible might promote the study of the Bible and all cognate sciences in accordance with the mind of the Catholic Church" he founded the Pontifical Biblical Institute, entrusted to the care of the illustrious Society of Jesus, which he wished endowed "with a superior professorial staff and every facility for biblical research"; he prescribed its laws and rules, professing to follow in this the "salutary and fruitful project" of Leo XIII.

7. All this in fine Our immediate Predecessor of happy memory, Pius XI, brought to perfection, laying down among

other things "that no one should be appointed professor of Sacred Scripture in any Seminary, unless, having completed a special course of biblical studies, he had in due form obtained the academic degrees before the Biblical Commission or the Biblical Institute." He wished that these degrees should have the same rights and the same effects as the degrees duly conferred in Sacred Theology or Canon Law; likewise he decreed that no one should receive "a benefice having attached the canonical obligation of expounding the Sacred Scripture to the people, unless, among other things, he had obtained the licentiate or doctorate in biblical science." And having at the same time urged the Superiors General of the Regular Orders and of the religious Congregations, as well as the Bishops of the Catholic world, to send the more suitable of their students to frequent the schools of the Biblical Institute and obtain there the academical degrees, he confirmed these exhortations by his own example, appointing out of his bounty an annual sum for this very purpose.

8. Seeing that, in the year 1907, with the benign approval of Pius X, of happy memory, "to the Benedictine monks had been committed the task of preparing the investigations and studies on which might be based a new edition of the Latin version of the Scriptures, commonly called the Vulgate," the same Pontiff, Pius XI, wishing to consolidate more firmly and securely this "laborious and arduous enterprise," which demands considerable time and great expense, founded in Rome and lavishly endowed with a library and other means of research, the monastery of St. Jerome, to be devoted exclusively to this work.

9. Nor should We fail to mention here how earnestly these same Predecessors of Ours, when the opportunity occurred, recommended the study of preaching or in fine the pious reading and meditation of the Sacred Scriptures. Pius X most heartily commended the Society of St. Jerome, which strives to promote among the faithful—and to facilitate with all its power—the truly praiseworthy custom of reading and meditating on the holy Gospels; he exhorted them to persevere in the enterprise they had begun, proclaiming it "a most useful undertaking, as well as most suited to the times," seeing that it

helps in no small way "to dissipate the idea that the Church is opposed to or in any way impedes the reading of the Scriptures in the vernacular." And Benedict XV, on the occasion of the fifteenth centenary of the death of St. Jerome, the greatest Doctor of the Sacred Scriptures, after having most solemnly inculcated the precepts and examples of the same Doctor, as well as the principles and rules laid down by Leo XIII and by himself, and having recommended other things highly opportune and never to be forgotten in this connection, exhorted "all the children of the Church, especially clerics, to reverence the Holy Scripture, to read it piously and meditate on it constantly"; he reminded them "that in these pages is to be sought that food, by which the spiritual life is nourished unto perfection," and "that the chief use of Scripture pertains to the holy and fruitful exercise of the ministry of preaching"; he likewise once again expressed his warm approval of the work of the society called after St. Jerome himself, by means of which the Gospels and Acts of Apostles are being so widely diffused, "that there is no Christian family any more without them and that all are accustomed to read and meditate on them daily."

10. But it is right and pleasing to confess openly that it is not only by reason of these initiatives, precepts and exhortations of Our Predecessors that the knowledge and use of the Sacred Scriptures have made great progress among Catholics; for this is also due to the works and labors of all those who diligently cooperated with them, both by meditating, investigating and writing, as well as by teaching and preaching and by translating and propagating the Sacred Books. For from the schools in which are fostered higher studies in theological and biblical science, and especially from Our Pontifical Biblical Institute, there have already come forth, and daily continue to come forth, many students of Holy Scripture who, inspired with an intense love for the Sacred Books, imbue the younger clergy with this same ardent zeal and assiduously impart to them the doctrine they themselves have acquired. Many of them also, by the written word, have promoted and do still promote, far and wide, the study of the Bible; as when they edit the sacred text corrected in accordance with the rules of textual criticism or expound, explain, and translate it into the vernacu-

lar; or when they propose it to the faithful for their pious reading and meditation; or finally when they cultivate and seek the aid of profane sciences which are useful for the interpretation of the Scriptures. From these therefore and from other initiatives which daily become more widespread and vigorous, as, for example, biblical societies, congresses, libraries, associations for meditation on the Gospels, We firmly hope that in the future reverence for, as well as the use and knowledge of, the Sacred Scriptures will everywhere more and more increase for the good of souls, provided the method of biblical studies laid down by Leo XIII, explained more clearly and perfectly by his Successors, and by Us confirmed and amplified—which indeed is the only safe way and proved by experience—be more firmly, eagerly and faithfully accepted by all, regardless of the difficulties which, as in all human affairs, so in this most excellent work will never be wanting.

11. There is no one who cannot easily perceive that the conditions of biblical studies and their subsidiary sciences have greatly changed within the last fifty years. For, apart from anything else, when Our Predecessor published the Encyclical Letter *Providentissimus Deus,* hardly a single place in Palestine had begun to be explored by means of relevant excavations. Now, however, this kind of investigation is much more frequent and, since more precise methods and technical skill have been developed in the course of actual experience, it gives us information at once more abundant and more accurate. How much light has been derived from these explorations for the more correct and fuller understanding of the Sacred Books all experts know, as well as all those who devote themselves to these studies. The value of these excavations is enhanced by the discovery from time to time of written documents, which help much towards the knowledge of the languages, letters, events, customs, and forms of worship of most ancient times. And of no less importance are papyri which have contributed so much to the knowledge of the discovery and investigation, so frequent in our times, of letters and institutions, both public and private, especially of the time of Our Savior.

12. Moreover ancient codices of the Sacred Books have been found and edited with discerning thoroughness; the

exegesis of the Fathers of the Church has been more widely and thoroughly examined; in fine the manner of speaking, reading and writing in use among the ancients is made clear by innumerable examples. All these advantages which, not without a special design of Divine Providence, our age has acquired, are as it were an invitation and inducement to interpreters of the Sacred Literature to make diligent use of this light, so abundantly given, to penetrate more deeply, explain more clearly and expound more lucidly the Divine Oracles. If, with the greatest satisfaction of mind, We perceive that these same interpreters have resolutely answered and still continue to answer this call, this is certainly not the last or least of the fruits of the Encyclical Letter *Providentissimus Deus,* by which Our Predecessor Leo XIII, foreseeing as it were this new development of biblical studies, summoned Catholic exegetes to labor and wisely defined the direction and the method to be followed in that labor.

13. We also, by this Encyclical Letter, desire to insure that the work may not only proceed without interruption, but may also daily become more perfect and fruitful; and to that end We are specially intent on pointing out to all what yet remains to be done, with what spirit the Catholic exegete should undertake, at the present day, so great and noble a work, and to give new incentive and fresh courage to the laborers who toil so strenuously in the vineyard of the Lord.

14. The Fathers of the Church in their time, especially Augustine, warmly recommended to the Catholic scholar, who undertook the investigation and explanation of the Sacred Scriptures, the study of the ancient languages and recourse to the original texts. However, such was the state of letters in those times, that not many—and these few but imperfectly—knew the Hebrew language. In the middle ages, when Scholastic Theology was at the height of its vigor, the knowledge of even the Greek language had long since become so rare in the West, that even the greatest Doctors of that time, in their exposition of the Sacred Text, had recourse only to the Latin version, known as the Vulgate.

15. On the contrary in this our time, not only the Greek language, which since the humanistic renaissance has been, as

it were, restored to new life, is familiar to almost all students of antiquity and letters, but the knowledge of Hebrew also and of other Oriental languages has spread far and wide among literary men. Moreover there are now such abundant aids to the study of these languages that the biblical scholar, who by neglecting them would deprive himself of access to the original texts, could in no wise escape the stigma of levity and sloth. For it is the duty of the exegete to lay hold, so to speak, with the greatest care and reverence of the very least expressions which, under the inspiration of the Divine Spirit, have flowed from the pen of the sacred writer, so as to arrive at a deeper and fuller knowledge of his meaning.

16. Wherefore let him diligently apply himself so as to acquire daily a greater facility in biblical as well as in other Oriental languages and to support his interpretation by the aids which all branches of philology supply. This indeed St. Jerome strove earnestly to achieve, as far as the science of his time permitted; to this also aspired with untiring zeal and no small fruit not a few of the great exegetes of the sixteenth and seventeenth centuries, although the knowledge of languages then was much less than at the present day. In like manner therefore ought we to explain the original text which, having been written by the inspired author himself, has more authority and greater weight than any, even the very best, translation, whether ancient or modern; this can be done all the more easily and fruitfully, if to the knowledge of languages be joined a real skill in literary criticism of the same text.

17. The great importance which should be attached to this kind of criticism was aptly pointed out by Augustine, when, among the precepts to be recommended to the student of the Sacred Books, he put in the first place the care to possess a corrected text. "The correction of the codices"—so says this most distinguished Doctor of the Church—"should first of all engage the attention of those who wish to know the Divine Scripture so that the uncorrected may give place to the corrected." In the present day indeed this art, which is called textual criticism and which is used with great and praiseworthy results in the editions of profane writings, is also quite rightly employed in the case of the Sacred Books, because of that very

reverence which is due to the Divine Oracles. For its very purpose is to insure that the sacred text be restored, as perfectly as possible, be purified from the corruptions due to the carelessness of the copyists and be freed, as far as may be done, from glosses and omissions, from the interchange and repetition of words and from all other kinds of mistakes, which are wont to make their way gradually into writings handed down through many centuries.

18. It is scarcely necessary to observe that this criticism, which some fifty years ago not a few made use of quite arbitrarily and often in such wise that one would say they did so to introduce into the sacred text their own preconceived ideas, today has rules so firmly established and secure, that it has become a most valuable aid to the purer and more accurate editing of the sacred text and that any abuse can easily be discovered. Nor is it necessary here to call to mind—since it is doubtless familiar and evident to all students of Sacred Scripture—to what extent namely the Church has held in honor these studies in textual criticism from the earliest centuries down even to the present day.

19. Today therefore, since this branch of science has attained to such high perfection, it is the honorable, though not always easy, task of students of the Bible to procure by every means that as soon as possible may be duly published by Catholics editions of the Sacred Books and of ancient versions, brought out in accordance with these standards, which, that is to say, unite the greatest reverence for the sacred text with an exact observance of all the rules of criticism. And let all know that this prolonged labor is not only necessary for the right understanding of the divinely-given writings, but also is urgently demanded by that piety by which it behooves us to be grateful to the God of all providence, Who from the throne of His majesty has sent these books as so many paternal letters to his own children.

20. Nor should anyone think that this use of the original texts, in accordance with the methods of criticism, in any way derogates from those decrees so wisely enacted by the Council of Trent concerning the Latin Vulgate. It is historically certain that the Presidents of the Council received a commission,

which they duly carried out, to beg, that is, the Sovereign Pontiff in the name of the Council that he should have corrected, as far as possible, first a Latin, and then a Greek, and Hebrew edition, which eventually would be published for the benefit of the Holy Church of God. If this desire could not then be fully realized owing to the difficulties of the times and other obstacles, at present it can, We earnestly hope, be more perfectly and entirely fulfilled by the united efforts of Catholic scholars.

21. And if the Tridentine Synod wished "that all should use as authentic" the Vulgate Latin version, this, as all know, applies only to the Latin Church and to the public use of the same Scriptures; nor does it, doubtless, in any way diminish the authority and value of the original texts. For there was no question then of these texts, but of the Latin versions, which were in circulation at that time, and of these the same Council rightly declared to be preferable that which "had been approved by its long-continued use for so many centuries in the Church." Hence this special authority or as they say, authenticity of the Vulgate was not affirmed by the Council particularly for critical reasons, but rather because of its legitimate use in the Churches throughout so many centuries; by which use indeed the same is shown, in the sense in which the Church has understood and understands it, to be free from any error whatsoever in matters of faith and morals; so that, as the Church herself testifies and affirms, it may be quoted safely and without fear of error in disputations, in lectures and in preaching; and so its authenticity is not specified primarily as critical, but rather as juridical.

22. Wherefore this authority of the Vulgate in matters of doctrine by no means prevents—nay rather today it almost demands—either the corroboration and confirmation of this same doctrine by the original texts or the having recourse on any and every occasion to the aid of these same texts, by which the correct meaning of the Sacred Letters is everywhere daily made more clear and evident. Nor is it forbidden by the decree of the Council of Trent to make translations into the vulgar tongue, even directly from the original texts themselves, for the use and benefit of the faithful and for the better understanding

of the divine word, as We know to have been already done in a laudable manner in many countries with the approval of the Ecclesiastical authority.

23. Being thoroughly prepared by the knowledge of the ancient languages and by the aids afforded by the art of criticism, let the Catholic exegete undertake the task, of all those imposed on him the greatest, that, namely of discovering and expounding the genuine meaning of the Sacred Books. In the performance of this task let the interpreters bear in mind that their foremost and greatest endeavor should be to discern and define clearly that sense of the biblical words which is called literal. Aided by the context and by comparison with similar passages, let them therefore by means of their knowledge of languages search out with all diligence the literal meaning of the words; all these helps indeed are wont to be pressed into service in the explanation also of profane writers, so that the mind of the author may be made abundantly clear.

24. The commentators of the Sacred Letters, mindful of the fact that here there is question of a divinely inspired text, the care and interpretation of which have been confided to the Church by God Himself, should no less diligently take into account the explanations and declarations of the teaching authority of the Church, as likewise the interpretation given by the Holy Fathers, and even "the analogy of faith" as Leo XIII most wisely observed in the Encyclical Letter *Providentissimus Deus*. With special zeal should they apply themselves, not only to expounding exclusively these matters which belong to the historical, archaeological, philological and other auxiliary sciences—as, to Our regret, is done in certain commentaries—but, having duly referred to these, insofar as they may aid the exegesis, they should set forth in particular the theological doctrine in faith and morals of the individual books or texts so that their exposition may not only aid the professors of theology in their explanations and proofs of the dogmas of faith, but may also be of assistance to priests in their presentation of Christian doctrine to the people, and in fine, may help all the faithful to lead a life that is holy and worthy of a Christian.

25. By making such an exposition, which is above all, as We have said, theological, they will efficaciously reduce to si-

lence those who, affirming that they scarcely ever find anything in biblical commentaries to raise their hearts to God, to nourish their souls or promote their interior life, repeatedly urge that we should have recourse to a certain spiritual and, as they say, mystical interpretation. With what little reason they thus speak is shown by the experience of many, who, assiduously considering and meditating the word of God, advanced in perfection and were moved to an intense love for God; and this same truth is clearly proved by the constant tradition of the Church and the precepts of the greatest Doctors. Doubtless all spiritual sense is not excluded from the Sacred Scripture.

26. For what was said and done in the Old Testament was ordained and disposed by God with such consummate wisdom, that things past prefigured in a spiritual way those that were to come under the new dispensation of grace. Wherefore the exegete, just as he must search out and expound the literal meaning of the words, intended and expressed by the sacred writer, so also must he do likewise for the spiritual sense, provided it is clearly intended by God. For God alone could have known this spiritual meaning and have revealed it to us. Now Our Divine Savior Himself points out to us and teaches us this same sense in the Holy Gospel; the Apostles also, following the example of the Master, profess it in their spoken and written words; the unchanging tradition of the Church approves it; and finally the most ancient usage of the liturgy proclaims it, wherever may be rightly applied the well-known principle: "The rule of prayer is the rule of faith."

27. Let Catholic exegetes then disclose and expound this spiritual significance, intended and ordained by God, with that care which the dignity of the divine word demands; but let them scrupulously refrain from proposing as the genuine meaning of Sacred Scripture other figurative senses. It may indeed be useful, especially in preaching, to illustrate, and present the matters of faith and morals by a broader use of the Sacred Text in the figurative sense, provided this be done with moderation and restraint; it should, however, never be forgotten that this use of the Sacred Scripture is, as it were, extrinsic to it and accidental, and that, especially in these days, it is not free from danger, since the faithful, in particular those who are well-

informed in the sacred and profane sciences, wish to know what God has told us in the Sacred Letters rather than what an ingenious orator or writer may suggest by a clever use of the words of Scripture. Nor does "the word of God, living and effectual and more piercing than any two-edged sword and reaching unto the division of the soul and the spirit, of the joints also and the marrow, and a discerner of the thoughts and intents of the heart" need artificial devices and human adaptation to move and impress souls; for the Sacred Pages, written under the inspiration of the Spirit of God, are of themselves rich in original meaning; endowed with a divine power, they have their own value; adorned with heavenly beauty, they radiate of themselves light and splendor, provided they are so fully and accurately explained by the interpreter, that all the treasures of wisdom and prudence, therein contained are brought to light.

28. In the accomplishment of this task the Catholic exegete will find invaluable help in an assiduous study of those works, in which the Holy Fathers, the Doctors of the Church and the renowned interpreters of past ages have explained the Sacred Books. For, although sometimes less instructed in profane learning and in the knowledge of languages than the scripture scholars of our time, nevertheless by reason of the office assigned to them by God in the Church, they are distinguished by a certain subtle insight into heavenly things and by a marvellous keenness of intellect, which enables them to penetrate to the very innermost meaning of the divine word and bring to light all that can help to elucidate the teaching of Christ and promote holiness of life.

29. It is indeed regrettable that such precious treasures of Christian antiquity are almost unknown to many writers of the present day, and that students of the history of exegesis have not yet accomplished all that seems necessary for the due investigation and appreciation of so momentous a subject. Would that many, by seeking out the authors of the Catholic interpretation of Scripture and diligently studying their works and drawing thence the almost inexhaustible riches therein stored up, might contribute largely to this end, so that it might be daily more apparent to what extent those authors understood and made known the divine teaching of the Sacred Books, and

that the interpreters of today might thence take example and seek suitable arguments.

30. For thus at long last will be brought about the happy and fruitful union between the doctrine and spiritual sweetness of expression of the ancient authors and the greater erudition and maturer knowledge of the modern, having as its result new progress in the never fully explored and inexhaustible field of the Divine Letters.

31. Moreover we may rightly and deservedly hope that our time also can contribute something towards the deeper and more accurate interpretation of Sacred Scripture. For not a few things, especially in matters pertaining to history, were scarcely at all or not fully explained by the commentators of past ages, since they lacked almost all the information which was needed for their clearer exposition. How difficult for the Fathers themselves, and indeed well nigh unintelligible, were certain passages, is shown, among other things, by the oft-repeated efforts of many of them to explain the first chapters of Genesis; likewise by the reiterated attempts of St. Jerome so to translate the Psalms that the literal sense, that, namely, which is expressed by the words themselves, might be clearly revealed.

32. There are, in fine, other books or texts, which contain difficulties brought to light only in quite recent times, since a more profound knowledge of antiquity has given rise to new questions, on the basis of which the point at issue may be more appropriately examined. Quite wrongly therefore do some pretend, not rightly understanding the conditions of biblical study, that nothing remains to be added by the Catholic exegete of our time to what Christian antiquity has produced; since, on the contrary, these our times have brought to light so many things, which call for a fresh investigation, and which stimulate not a little the practical zest of the present-day interpreter.

33. As in our age, indeed new questions and new difficulties are multiplied, so, by God's favor, new means and aids to exegesis are also provided. Among these it is worthy of special mention that Catholic theologians, following the teaching of the Holy Fathers and especially of the Angelic and Common Doctor, have examined and explained the nature and effects of

biblical inspiration more exactly and more fully than was wont to be done in previous ages. For having begun by expounding minutely the principle that the inspired writer, in composing the sacred book, is the living and reasonable instrument of the Holy Spirit, they rightly observe that, impelled by the divine motion, he so uses his faculties and powers, that from the book composed by him all may easily infer "the special character of each one and, as it were, his personal traits." Let the interpreter then, with all care and without neglecting any light derived from recent research, endeavor to determine the peculiar character and circumstances of the sacred writer, the age in which he lived, the sources written or oral to which he had recourse and the forms of expression he employed.

34. Thus can be the better understanding who was the inspired author, and what he wishes to express by his writings. There is no one indeed but knows that the supreme rule of interpretation is to discover and define what the writer intended to express, as St. Athanasius excellently observes: "Here, as indeed is expedient in all other passages of Sacred Scripture, it should be noted, on what occasion the Apostle spoke; we should carefully and faithfully observe to whom and why he wrote, lest, being ignorant of these points, or confounding one with another, we miss the real meaning of the author."

35. What is the literal sense of a passage is not always as obvious in the speeches and writings of the ancient authors of the East, as it is in the works of our own time. For what they wished to express is not to be determined by the rules of grammar and philology alone, nor solely by the context; the interpreter must, as it were, go back wholly in spirit to those remote centuries of the East and with the aid of history, archaeology, ethnology, and other sciences, accurately determine what modes of writing, so to speak, the authors of that ancient period would be likely to use, and in fact did use.

36. For the ancient peoples of the East, in order to express their ideas, did not always employ those forms or kinds of speech which we use today; but rather those used by the men of their time and countries. What those exactly were the commentator cannot determine as it were in advance, but only after a careful examination of the ancient literature of the East. The

investigation, carried out, on this point, during the past forty
or fifty years with greater care and diligence than ever before,
has more clearly shown what forms of expression were used in
those far-off times, whether in poetic description or in the
formulation of laws and rules of life or in recording the facts
and events of history. The same inquiry has also clearly shown
the special preeminence of the people of Israel among all the
other ancient nations of the East in their mode of compiling
history, both by reason of its antiquity and by reason of the
faithful record of the events; qualities which may well be attributed to the gift of divine inspiration and to the peculiar
religious purpose of biblical history.

37. Nevertheless no one, who has a correct idea of biblical inspiration, will be surprised to find, even in the Sacred
Writers, as in other ancient authors, certain fixed ways of expounding and narrating, certain definite idioms, especially of a
kind peculiar to the Semitic tongues, so-called approximations,
and certain hyperbolical modes of expression, nay, at times,
even paradoxical, which even help to impress the ideas more
deeply on the mind. For the modes of expression which, among
ancient peoples, and especially those of the East, human language used to express its thought, none is excluded from the
Sacred Books, provided the way of speaking adopted in no wise
contradicts the holiness and truth of God, as, with his customary wisdom, the Angelic Doctor already observed in these
words: "In Scripture divine things are presented to us in the
manner which is in common use amongst men." For as the substantial Word of God became like to men in all things, "except
sin," so the words of God, expressed in human language, are
made like to human speech in every respect, except error. In
this consists that "condescension" of the God of providence,
which St. John Chrysostom extolled with the highest praise
and repeatedly declared to be found in the Sacred Books.

38. Hence the Catholic commentator, in order to comply
with the present needs of biblical studies, in explaining the
Sacred Scripture and in demonstrating and proving its immunity
from all error, should also make a prudent use of this means,
determine, that is, to what extent the manner of expression or
the literary mode adopted by the sacred writer may lead to a

correct and genuine interpretation; and let him be convinced that this part of his office cannot be neglected without serious detriment to Catholic exegesis. Not infrequently—to mention only one instance—when some persons reproachfully charge the Sacred Writers with some historical error or inaccuracy in the recording of facts, on closer examination it turns out to be nothing else than those customary modes of expression and narration peculiar to the ancients, which used to be employed in the mutual dealings of social life and which in fact were sanctioned by common usage.

39. When then such modes of expression are met with in the sacred text, which, being meant for men, is couched in human language, justice demands that they be no more taxed with error than when they occur in the ordinary intercourse of daily life. By this knowledge and exact appreciation of the modes of speaking and writing in use among the ancients can be solved many difficulties, which are raised against the veracity and historical value of the Divine Scriptures, and no less efficaciously does this study contribute to a fuller and more luminous understanding of the mind of the Sacred Writer.

40. Let those who cultivate biblical studies turn their attention with all due diligence towards this point and let them neglect none of those discoveries, whether in the domain of archaeology or in ancient history or literature, which serve to make better known the mentality of the ancient writers, as well as their manner and art of reasoning, narrating and writing. In this connection Catholic laymen should consider that they will not only further profane science, but moreover will render a conspicuous service to the Christian cause if they devote themselves with all due diligence and application to the exploration and investigation of the monuments of antiquity and contribute, according to their abilities, to the solution of questions hitherto obscure.

41. For all human knowledge, even the non-sacred, has indeed its own proper dignity and excellence, being a finite participation of the infinite knowledge of God, but it acquires a new and higher dignity and, as it were, a consecration, when it is employed to cast a brighter light upon the things of God.

42. The progressive exploration of the antiquities of the East, mentioned above, the more accurate examination of the original text itself, the more extensive and exact knowledge of languages both biblical and oriental, have with the help of God, happily provided the solution of not a few of those questions, which in the time of Our Predecessor Leo XIII of immortal memory, were raised by critics outside or hostile to the Church against the authenticity, antiquity, integrity and historical value of the Sacred Books. For Catholic exegetes, by a right use of those same scientific arms, not infrequently abused by the adversaries, proposed such interpretations, which are in harmony with Catholic doctrine and the genuine current of tradition, and at the same time are seen to have proved equal to the difficulties, either raised by new explorations and discoveries, or bequeathed by antiquity for solution in our time.

43. Thus has it come about that confidence in the authority and historical value of the Bible, somewhat shaken in the case of some by so many attacks, today among Catholics is completely restored; moreover there are not wanting even non-Catholic writers, who by serious and calm inquiry have been led to abandon modern opinion and to return, at least in some points, to the more ancient ideas. This change is due in great part to the untiring labor by which Catholic commentators of the Sacred Letters, in no way deterred by difficulties and obstacles of all kinds, strove with all their strength to make suitable use of what learned men of the present day, by their investigations in the domain of archaeology or history or philology, have made available for the solution of new questions.

44. Nevertheless no one will be surprised, if all difficulties are not yet solved and overcome, but that even today serious problems greatly exercise the minds of Catholic exegetes. We should not lose courage on this account; nor should we forget that in the human sciences the same happens as in the natural world; that is to say, new beginnings grow little by little and fruits are gathered only after many labors. Thus it has happened that certain disputed points, which in the past remained unsolved and in suspense, in our days, with the progress of studies,

have found a satisfactory solution. Hence there are grounds for hope that those also will by constant effort be at last made clear, which now seem most complicated and difficult.

45. And if the wished-for solution be slow in coming or does not satisfy us, since perhaps a successful conclusion may be reserved to posterity, let us not wax impatient thereat, seeing that in us also is rightly verified what the Fathers, and especially Augustine, observed in their time, viz. God wished difficulties to be scattered through the Sacred Books inspired by Him, in order that we might be urged to read and scrutinize them more intently, and, experiencing in a salutary manner our own limitations, we might be exercised in due submission of mind. No wonder if to one or the other question no solution wholly satisfactory will ever be found, since sometimes we have to do with matters obscure in themselves and too remote from our times and our experience; and since exegesis also, like all other most important sciences, has its secrets, which, impenetrable to our minds, by no efforts whatsoever can be unravelled.

46. But this state of things is no reason why the Catholic commentator, inspired by an active and ardent love of his subject and sincerely devoted to Holy Mother Church, should in any way be deterred from grappling again and again with these difficult problems, hitherto unsolved, not only that he may refute the objections of the adversaries, but also may attempt to find a satisfactory solution, which will be in full accord with the doctrine of the Church, in particular with the traditional teaching regarding the inerrancy of Sacred Scripture, and which will at the same time satisfy the indubitable conclusion of profane sciences.

47. Let all the other sons of the Church bear in mind that the efforts of these resolute laborers in the vineyard of the Lord should be judged not only with equity and justice, but also with the greatest charity; all moreover should abhor that intemperate zeal which imagines that whatever is new should for that very reason be opposed or suspected. Let them bear in mind above all that in the rules and laws promulgated by the Church there is immense matter contained in the Sacred Books— legislative, historical, sapiential and prophetical—there are but few texts whose sense has been defined by the authority of the

Church, nor are those more numerous about which the teaching of the Holy Fathers is unanimous. There remain therefore many things, and of the greatest importance, in the discussion and exposition of which the skill and genius of Catholic commentators may and ought to be freely exercised, so that each may contribute his part to the advantage of all, to the continued progress of the sacred doctrine and to the defense and honor of the Church.

48. This true liberty of the children of God, which adheres faithfully to the teaching of the Church and accepts and uses gratefully the contributions of profane science, this liberty, upheld and sustained in every way by the confidence of all, is the condition and source of all lasting fruit and of all solid progress in Catholic doctrine, as Our Predecessor of happy memory Leo XIII rightly observes, when he says: "Unless harmony of mind be maintained and principles safeguarded, no progress can be expected in this matter from the varied studies of many."

49. Whosoever considers the immense labors undertaken by Catholic exegetes during well nigh two thousand years, so that the word of God, imparted to men through the Sacred Letters, might daily be more deeply and fully understood and more intensely loved, will easily be convinced that it is the serious duty of the faithful, and especially of priests, to make free and holy use of this treasure, accumulated throughout so many centuries by the greatest intellects. For the Sacred Books were not given by God to men to satisfy their curiosity or to provide them with material for study and research, but, as the Apostle observes, in order that these Divine Oracles might "instruct us to salvation, by the faith which is in Christ Jesus" and "that the man of God may be perfect, furnished to every good work."

50. Let priests therefore, who are bound by their office to procure the eternal salvation of the faithful, after they have themselves by diligent study perused the sacred pages and made them their own by prayer and meditations, assiduously distribute the heavenly treasures of the divine word by sermons, homilies and exhortations; let them confirm the Christian doctrine by sentences from the Sacred Books and illustrate it by outstanding examples from sacred history and in particular

321

from the Gospel of Christ Our Lord; and—avoiding with the greatest care those purely arbitrary and far-fetched adaptations, which are not a use, but rather an abuse of the divine word—let them set forth all this with such eloquence, lucidity and clearness that the faithful may not only be moved and inflamed to reform their lives, but may also conceive in their hearts the greatest veneration for the Sacred Scripture.

51. The same veneration the Bishops should endeavor daily to increase and perfect among the faithful committed to their care, encouraging all those initiatives by which men, filled with apostolic zeal, laudably strive to excite and foster among Catholics a greater knowledge of love for the Sacred Books. Let them favor therefore and lend help to those pious associations whose aim it is to spread copies of the Sacred Letters, especially of the Gospels, among the faithful, and to procure by every means that in Christian families the same be read daily with piety and devotion; let them efficaciously recommend by word and example, whenever the liturgical laws permit, the Sacred Scriptures translated, with the approval of the Ecclesiastical authority, into modern languages; let them themselves give public conferences or dissertations on biblical subjects, or see that they are given by other public orators well-versed in the matter.

52. Let the ministers of the Sanctuary support in every way possible and diffuse in fitting manner among all classes of the faithful the periodicals which so laudably and with such heartening results are published from time to time in various parts of the world, whether to treat and expose in a scientific manner biblical questions, or to adapt the fruits of these investigations to the sacred ministry, or to benefit the faithful. Let the ministers of the Sanctuary be convinced that all this, and whatsoever else in apostolic zeal and a sincere love of the divine word may find suitable to this high purpose, will be an efficacious help to the cure of souls.

53. But it is plain to everyone that priests cannot duly fulfill all this, unless in their Seminary days they have imbibed a practical and enduring love for the Sacred Scriptures. Wherefore let the Bishops, on whom devolves the paternal care of their Seminaries, with all diligence see to it that nothing be

omitted in this matter which may help towards the desired end. Let the professors of Sacred Scripture in the Seminaries give the whole course of biblical studies in such a way, that they may instruct the young aspirants to the Priesthood and to the ministry of the divine word with that knowledge of the Sacred Letters and imbue them with that love for the same, without which it is vain to hope for copious fruits of the apostolate.

54. Hence their exegetical explanation should aim especially at the theological doctrine, avoiding useless disputations and omitting all that is calculated rather to gratify curiosity than to promote true learning and solid piety. The literal sense and especially the theological let them propose with such definiteness, explain with such skill and inculcate with such ardor that in their students may be in a sense verified what happened to the disciples on the way to Emmaus, when, having heard the words of the Master, they exclaimed: "Was not our heart burning within us, whilst he opened to us the Scriptures?"

55. Thus the Divine Letters will become for the future priests of the Church a pure and never-failing source for their own spiritual life, as well as food and strength for the sacred office of preaching which they are about to undertake. If the professors of this most important matter in the Seminaries accomplish all this, then let them rest joyfully assured that they have most efficaciously contributed to the salvation of souls, to the progress of the Catholic faith, to the honor and glory of God, and that they have performed a work most closely connected with the apostolic office.

56. If these things which We have said, Venerable Brethren and beloved sons, are necessary in every age, much more urgently are they needed in our sorrowful times, when almost all peoples and nations are plunged in a sea of calamities, when a cruel war heaps ruins upon ruins and slaughter upon slaughter, when, owing to the most bitter hatred stirred up among the nations, We perceive with greatest sorrow that in not a few has been extinguished the sense not only of Christian moderation and charity, but also of humanity itself. Who can heal these mortal wounds of the human family if not He, to Whom the Prince of the Apostles, full of confidence and love, addresses

these words: "Lord, to whom shall we go? Thou hast the words of eternal life."

57. To this Our most merciful Redeemer we must therefore bring all back by every means in our power; for He is the divine consoler of the afflicted: He it is Who teaches all, whether they be invested with public authority or are bound in duty to obey and submit, true honesty, absolute justice and generous charity; it is He in fine, and He alone, Who can be the firm foundation and support of peace and tranquility: "For other foundations no man can lay, but that which is laid: which is Christ Jesus." This the author of salvation, Christ, will men more fully know, more ardently love and more faithfully imitate in proportion as they are more assiduously urged to know and meditate the Sacred Letters, especially the New Testament, for, as St. Jerome the Doctor of Stridon says: "To ignore the Scripture is to ignore Christ"; and again: "If there is anything in this life which sustains a wise man and induces him to maintain his serenity amidst the tribulations and adversities of the world, it is in the first place, I consider, the meditation and knowledge of the Scriptures."

58. There those who are wearied and oppressed by adversities and afflictions will find true consolation and divine strength to suffer and bear with patience; there—that is in the Holy Gospels—Christ, the highest and greatest example of justice, charity and mercy, is present to all; and to the lacerated and trembling human race are laid open the fountains of that divine grace without which both peoples and their rulers can never arrive at, never establish, peace in the state and unity of heart; there in fine will all learn Christ, "Who is the head of all principality and power" and "Who of God is made unto us wisdom and justice and sanctification and redemption."

59. Having expounded and recommended those things which are required for the adaptation of Scripture studies to the necessities of the day, it remains, Venerable Brethren and beloved sons, that to biblical scholars who are devoted sons of the Church and follow faithfully her teaching and direction, We address with paternal affection, not only Our congratulations that they have been chosen and called to so sublime an office, but also Our encouragement to continue with ever renewed

vigor and with all zeal and care, the work so happily begun. Sublime office, We say; for what is more sublime than to scrutinize, explain, propose to the faithful and defend from unbelievers the very word of God, communicated to men under the inspiration of the Holy Spirit?

60. With this spiritual food the mind of the interpreter is fed and nourished "to the commemoration of faith, the consolation of hope, the exhortation of charity." "To live amidst these things, to meditate these things, to know nothing else, to seek nothing else, does it not seem to you already here below a foretaste of the heavenly kingdom?" Let also the minds of the faithful be nourished with this same food, that they may draw from thence the knowledge and love of God and the progress in perfection and the happiness of their own individual souls. Let, then, the interpreters of the Divine Oracles devote themselves to this holy practice with all their heart. "Let them pray, that they may understand"; let them labor to penetrate ever more deeply into the secrets of the Sacred Pages; let them teach and preach, in order to open to others also the treasures of the word of God.

61. Let the present-day commentators of the Sacred Scripture emulate, according to their capacity, what those illustrious interpreters of past ages accomplished with such great fruit; so that, as in the past, so also in these days, the Church may have at her disposal learned doctors for the expounding of the Divine Letters; and, through their assiduous labors, the faithful may comprehend all the splendor, stimulating language, and joy contained in the Holy Scriptures. And in this very arduous and important office let them have "for their comfort the Holy Books" and be mindful of the promised reward: since "they that are learned shall shine as the brightness of the firmament, and they that instruct many unto justice, as stars for all eternity."

62. And now, while ardently desiring for all sons of the Church, and especially for the professors in biblical science, for the young clergy and for preachers, that, continually meditating on the divine word, they may taste how good and sweet is the spirit of the Lord; as a presage of heavenly gifts and a token of Our paternal good will, We impart to you one and all,

Venerable Brethren and beloved sons, most lovingly in the Lord, the Apostolic Benediction.

63. Given at Rome, at St. Peter's, on the 30th of September, the feast of St. Jerome, the greatest Doctor in the exposition of the Sacred Scriptures, in the year 1943, the fifth of Our Pontificate.

Ronald Arbuthnott Knox
1888-1957

*Ronald Knox was born in Kibworth, England, the youngest
son of the Anglican bishop of Manchester. He was educated at
Eton and Balliol College, Oxford, took Anglican orders in 1910,
and became chaplain at Trinity College, Oxford. Growing more
and more dissatisfied with his Anglican position, he was received
into the Roman Catholic Church in 1917, and gave an account
of his reasons the next year in* Spiritual Aeneid.

*After theological studies at St. Edmund's, Ware, he was
ordained in 1919 and stayed on to teach until 1926, when he
was appointed chaplain to Catholic students at Oxford. He left
Oxford right before World War II in order to devote himself to
his major life's project, a modern translation of the entire Bible.
The New Testament appeared in 1944, the Old Testament in
1948. It was widely acclaimed as a masterpiece of English style.*

*The Knox Bible was very popular in the 1950s. It was such
an improvement in so many ways over the Douay-Rheims-
Challoner version that English-speaking Catholics accepted it as
a breath of fresh air. One major problem, however, was that it
was begun as a new translation of the Latin Vulgate. The New
Testament was almost complete when Pius XII's encyclical of
1943 called for the return to the original languages. Knox's
knowledge of Greek was far superior to his Hebrew, so his Old
Testament left much to be desired. Nonetheless his knack for*

turning a phrase often resulted in masterful expressions. The Epistles of Paul are usually considered his best renditions.

One of the contributions of Ronald Knox to the Catholics of his day was his irrepressible enthusiasm for the Bible. The earlier Modernist crisis and associated problems had created a situation of fear and uncertainty. Wasn't it safer to leave the Bible alone? If even a man of Père Lagrange's stature got in trouble . . . But times had changed and an era was dawning in which Catholic scholars would plunge completely into the new sphere of Biblical studies as it opened up. Knox accelerated that process, revealing the excitement that could characterize the advance. It was only fitting that his last public appearance was at Oxford in June, 1957, when he delivered a lecture on "Translation."

As the date of the book reveals, he wrote The Trials of a Translator *right after completing the monumental task, while all the tribulations were still fresh in his mind. His wit and good humor are evident throughout, but in the essay which we have selected for inclusion here, "Farewell to Machabees," he reveals some of the principles that he had tried to observe, especially the big three: accuracy, intelligibility, and readability. Even if one man is not likely to try this colossal feat again, in view of the explosion of knowledge in all the sub-divisions of Biblical studies and background, Ronald Knox's observations are still very appropriate, if only because he makes us more aware of some of the problems involved in the thankless task of translating.*

THE TRIALS OF A TRANSLATOR

A s the traveller, lost in some impenetrable jungle, and convinced that he will never make his way out of it alive, sits down to blaze on a tree-trunk the record of his wanderings, for the benefit of some luckier explorer in times to come; so the translator, seeing the end before him of a task which can never be complete, is fain to draw breath, to look round him, and to meditate on the reflex principles which have guided him thus far. Dr. Goodspeed, leaving the Old Testament to be finished by an indifferent team of collaborators, went straight on from the Apocalypse to his *Problems of New Testament Translation*. And shall not I, with Heliodorus' quip still ringing in my ears, be pardoned if I take time off to watch my own proceedings? Not, heaven knows, in the hope of disarming my critics; but with more modest ambition of satisfying the unprejudiced onlooker who asks, in no unkind spirit, what exactly I think I am getting at.

A division of the subject readily presents itself. Your examination of conscience, when you are doing any translating work, is obviously grouped under three heads: Is it accurate? Is it intelligible? Is it readable? When you are dealing with the Old Testament, those three hurdles form a perspective of increasing difficulty.

(i) *To be accurate*, in rendering any passage of the Old Testament, you have to be perpetually exercised over the exact meaning of Hebrew words (and, consequently, of their Latin token-equivalents) which have been rendered inexactly ever since the time of Coverdale. I have already tried to explain how difficult it is to find a satisfactory substitute for 'justice'. But it is not only 'justice' that has no exact equivalent in English; most of the commonest words in the Old Testament, if you give them their traditional values, are nearly always a point or so out of the true. *Nephesh* often means 'appetite'; and elsewhere it nearly always means 'life' rather than 'soul'. *Shalom* is much more like 'health' than 'peace', and much more like 'prosperity' than either—I cannot remember Reuss ever rendering it by *paix*. *Emeth* is what we mean by 'loyalty' or 'honour', not what we mean by 'truth'. *Chesed* is almost any kind of goodness, and the Vulgate's *misericordia* is often misleading; with the adjective, matters are still worse. *Yeshuah* can be 'victory' as well as deliverance. *Am* does duty for 'army'as well as 'people'. And so on. Those of us who were brought up on the Authorized Version have got it firmly in our heads that there were three main types of occasional sacrifice, the meat-offering, the sin-offering, and the peace-offering. But the whole point of the 'meat-offering' was that it consisted entirely of vegetable food; the 'sin-offering' arose, commonly, from a fault of inadvertence; and whatever the 'peace-offering' was exactly, editors seem agreed that it had nothing to do with peace. Always you are conscious of trying to open a door with a key that doesn't quite fit.

Of course, there are occasions where the Latin differs deliberately from our present Hebrew text, as when St. Jerome insists on making the skies rain down a Just Man, instead of justice; in such a passage as 'I know that my Redeemer liveth' you have no course open but to desert the Hebrew. There are occasions, too, where the Latin is almost certainly a mistaken attempt to render the Hebrew we have got, and you must put things right by elaborate footnotes. But worse still is the steady pull of the Latin token-words against the unmistakable meaning of the original. And this creates an especial difficulty, because so many chance phrases of the Old Testament have been encrusted in the Liturgy, and often in a false perspective. *O quam pulchra est casta generatio cum claritate;* the words have got to be used every time we celebrate a virgin's feast. But they have nothing to do with virginity; they are an attempt to console people who die childless. Are you to keep the meaning of the original in its true setting? Or are you to desert the original and preserve the liturgical overtones? The title *Sol justitiae* occurs in the Litany of the Holy Name; is one bound, in loyalty to the *Ecclesia orans,* to give the phrase a personal twist in

Malachy iv. 2? It sounds all right, because the words are familiar, to talk about the Sun of Justice rising with healing in his wings. But the awkward fact is that Malachy says 'in *her* wings'; obviously he wouldn't have made *shemesh* feminine if he had been thinking of a personal theophany. The word 'his' occurs in our versions because it is pre-Jacobean English for 'its'.

You get the same trouble even with New Testament quotations. The word 'faith' expresses two different ideas, as entertained (consciously) by Habacuc and by St. Paul. Did Osee mean 'mercy' when he contrasted *chesed* with sacrifice (vi. 6)? Modern translators give you 'piety'; and it is quite possible that our Lord (Matt. ix. 13) was interpreting his thought. I confess that my New Testament quotations do not always tally verbally with their Old Testament originals. (But how can they? Cf. Eph. iv. 8). In a hundred ways, the vocabulary of Judaism shades off, by imperceptible gradations, into that of Christianity. 'Life' to us means eternal life; to the Old Testament authors it meant, commonly at least, living to be a hundred. *Da mihi animas!* has been the slogan of much apostolic endeavour; yet Challoner did not hesitate to substitute 'Give me the persons' for Douay's 'Give me the souls' in Genesis xiv. 21; was he right? 'The spirit of the Lord'—how often you hesitate about printing, or not printing, a capital S! Douay gives you a capital in Isaias xi. 2, but in Challoner it is lower case. All your pious instincts make you want to emphasize, throughout the Old Testament, its half-conscious foreshadowing of the New. All your scholarly instincts make you want to reproduce the exact *nuance* of the eighth century B. C. To which of those instincts should the translator yield, if he wants to be 'accurate'?

Minor discrepancies between the Vulgate and the Hebrew, or between the Vulgate and modern commentators on the Hebrew, abound certainly, but are not of great significance. If the Vulgate tells me it means a hedge-hog and the commentators tell me it is a bittern, I am inclined to let St. Jerome have his way, as long as my naturalist friends inform me that the hedge-hog does really make a nest. The principle is the same; the loneliness of a ruin is underlined by the presence of shy animal life, whether of bitterns or of hedge-hogs. It would be

331

otherwise if you translated from the Septuagint; in one passage, where the received text gives you 'a holy person' the Septuagint has 'hyena'. It seems the safest principle to follow the Latin—after all, St. Jerome will sometimes have had a better text than the Massoretes—except on the rare occasions when there is no sense to be extracted from the Vulgate at all. You cannot, I think, be tied down to the statement that Saul was one year old when he came to the throne, merely because that is the construction which the Vulgate has put on an obviously defective Hebrew original.

(ii) *To be intelligible* when you are translating a document, it is not enough to produce a series of sentences, each of which, taken by itself, has a meaning. You have got to show the argument running through your piece, or you have not fulfilled your contract; you have not translated.

There are some sentences, even in the Authorized Version, which must be pronounced unintelligible. My favourite one is Amos iv. 2 and 3: 'The Lord God hath sworn by his holiness, that, lo, the days shall come upon you, that he will take you away with hooks, and your posterity with fish-hooks, and ye shall go out at the breaches, every cow at that which is before her, and ye shall cast them into the palace, saith the Lord'. The translator who shows up that kind of thing must not be allowed to get away with it. The sulky schoolboy's defence, 'Well, that's what it says', is no defence at all. He must be sent back to his place and told to do better. There are not many sentences like that in the Authorized Version; sentences, I mean, which make no impact on the mind. In the Douay they are regrettably common; a verse like 'Shall not the land tremble for this and every one mourn that dwelleth therein, and rise up altogether as a river, and be cast out, and run down as the river of Egypt?' is just an ordinary verse in the Douay, not a museum piece. But a non-signficant verse like that, here and there, is no great matter; you can pick up the thread again, if there is a thread to pick up. The trouble is that so often the thread itself is lacking.

Cut the Old Testament in half, at the end of Esther, and you may say that all the first half is intelligible, being either historical narrative, or legal enactments. There are difficult passages, to be sure, like the specifications for building the

Ronald Arbuthnott Knox

Tabernacle, or the Temple. But you know where you are all the time. The second half contains Machabees, which is narrative again; contains the Psalms, Proverbs and Ecclesiasticus, in which you do not expect, from the nature of the case, a continuous argument. All the rest of Part II, except Daniel and Jonas, is unintelligible unless you can translate it, not verse by verse but chapter by chapter (or at least section by section) so that it makes an impression on the reader's mind. Has it, in fact, been so translated? Take the rattling of forks in the refectory for your answer.

The book of Job is a sustained piece of forensic pleading; the subject under debate being, Whether misfortunes are, in every case, a divine punishment for some fault wittingly or unwittingly committed? Nobody would claim that Job and his friends stick to the point with complete relevance; their own rhetoric carries them away. But the argument is going on all the time; and a good translation ought to be such that, running your eye down a few verses, you can see which side is arguing, without having to look up the rubric. Whether such a translation can be done, I don't know; I am very far indeed from feeling that I have done it. But in so far as you fail, the book of Job ceases to be what it was meant to be, a philosophical dialogue, and becomes a collection of purple patches, mainly about natural history.

Ecclesiastes and Wisdom are also philosophical arguments, though not in the form of dialogue. The former is comparatively easy, but you have to watch your step all the time, or you find yourself missing the emphasis and therefore losing the thread. Wisdom is so difficult that I toyed with the idea of writing a thesis to prove it was written by St. Paul, still unconverted. It is largely an appeal to past history, but for some reason the author prefers to write history without using any proper names. Quite certainly, it is the office of the translator to put them in, when their absence make the allusions intolerably obscure.

With the Canticle of Canticles, we are on more debatable ground. Some critics (Reuss, for instance, who was not a fool) have maintained that there is no unity here, it is only a collection of love-ballads. But you are conscious of special pleading. No, if I were allowed to mark a lacuna in the text at one point (the Chariots of Aminadab, where *something,* surely, has gone wrong with the text), I would be prepared to put it on the stage to-morrow. To insert stage directions in a translation would clearly be vulgar; nor would all commentators agree about the division of the lines. But you want to handle it very carefully, and make your footnotes very lucid, if you are to light up the intensely human document that is enshrined in all that reliquary of mystical interpretation.

And then, the prophets! Practically a quarter of the Old Testament, and yet, apart from Daniel and Jonas, hardly a chapter you can read with your feet on the fender. Here, there is no question of a logical sequence of thought, carefully worked out; the Spirit blows where he will, not abiding our question. Yet beware of holding, in defiance of St. Jerome himself, that the prophets spoke in ecstasy; you are *haeresi proximus,* that way lies Montanism. Evidently the prophets— even Zachary—expected their contemporaries to understand what they were talking about. Only, their contemporaries had the advantage of us; they knew where one prophecy ended and another began, knew the occasion on which each was delivered, and the full details of the situation which led up to it. For all this, the modern reader is at the mercy of a set of commentators, who take fantastic liberties with the text. They assume from the first that it has reached us in the form of a broken-up jigsaw, and proceed to reassemble it; they make up their minds from the first what the prophet's message is, and ring off, with dark allusions to the Machabaean period, when he starts talking about anything else. (What they never seem to allow for is a *defective* text; and yet in real life a copyist is far more likely to drop things out than to foist things in.)

You can, I think, trace a continuous structure of thought in Jeremias and Ezechiel, Aggaeus and Malachy; in Joel, too, if you could be quite certain whether the invaders were Assyrians or locusts. Elsewhere, there are such sudden alternations of threat and promise, hope and fear; the dating of events is so uncertain, the grouping of them so confused; there is so little to show whether the punishment of the heathen and the restoration of Israel will happen the day after to-morrow or a few centuries hence—perhaps the best you can do is to treat your text as a

334

series of prophetic fragments, and decide as judiciously as you may where the breaks come. Your lot as a translator will be all the happier, if you remain unconvinced by those modern speculations about 'metre' which have mapped out Hebrew prophecy in a pattern of strophes and antistrophes—but let that pass.

That the prophets, translate them how you will, can ever be easy reading, I neither believe nor pretend. I do claim that you can do something, and are bound to do all you can, towards making them less unintelligible. The transition from one sentence to the next must be made logically clear, even at the cost of introducing words which are not there, but are implicit in the context. Your vocabulary must be chosen, not so much by reference to the use of this or that word elsewhere in the Old Testament, as by reference to the needs of this particular passage—token-words will not do. You must cast your sentences into a form which will preserve not only the meaning but the *rhetoric* of the original, or the flying wrack of imagery will pass you by.

(iii) *To be readable*—reader, have you ever tried to be readable? Ever tried to compile a document which people would read, not because they had to, but because they wanted to? There is not much point in being accurate and intelligible, if nobody is going to read you.

Or rather, I distinguish. You may translate the Bible, as you might translate a French book on atomic physics, for the sake of the *student*. Please God, there will always be earnest people, perhaps one Catholic in a thousand, who will *study* the Scriptures; but the reader and the student (II Mach. ii. 26) are different people. Where are the Catholic *readers* of the Bible? When did you last come across one of your friends with a Bible open in front of him? In old days, non-Catholics used to read the Bible as a devotional exercise, much as we said the rosary. That is all over; nobody of my age who assists at the public solution of a cross-word can understand modern hesitations about the identity of Bildad the Shuhite, or Tiglath-Pileser. We are in an odd situation. Nobody reads the Bible, Popes and Bishops are always telling us we ought to read the Bible, and when you produce a translation of the Bible, the only thing people complain about is your rendering of the diminutive snippets that are read out in Church on Sundays. 'Of course,' they add, 'the book is all right for *private reading*'—in a tone which implies that such a practice is both rare and unimportant.

To be sure, the Old Testament is not everybody's money—parts of it, anyhow. Nothing in the world is going to make Leviticus newsy. But I do not see that the translator has acquitted himself of his task until he has made Paralipomenon as good reading at Berners' Froissart, and Ecclesiasticus as racy as Florio's Montaigne. I am convinced that the thing can be done, however much my own efforts may have fallen short of the target. And I am convinced that the thing is worth doing; what reason have we to suppose that the Scriptures can only be edifying if they are approached by way of the British Museum?

One difficulty confronts you at the very outset; the whole Hebrew way of putting things is diffuse, whereas we, more and more, grow accustomed to terseness. A language which talks about 'the God of Abraham and the God of Isaac and the God of Jacob', so as to make it clear that Isaac and Jacob are in the genitive, encourages you in the habit of leaving nothing to the imagination. Nine times in the fifth chapter of Genesis we are told that such and such a patriarch 'begat sons and daughters'; is it legitimate to convey precisely the same information by adding the postscript, 'All these had other sons and daughters besides'? Even more leisurely is the progress of Numbers vii. Verses 12 to 89 describe the gifts made by the Israelites at the dedication of the Tabernacle; by verse 17 we have finished the inventory of Juda's contribution, a silver dish, a silver bowl, and so on—only to find that Issachar made precisely the same contribution, which is repeated in full, and so on all through the twelve tribes, up to verse 83. The remaining six verses are occupied with adding up the totals. Obviously the translator must not avail himself of the useful word 'ditto'. But is he bound to repeat exactly how much the dish weighed, exactly how much the bowl weighed, exactly how old the lambs were, every time? There is a great deal of 'The word of the Lord came unto me saying, Go and speak unto this people, and thus shalt thou speak unto them, saying, Thus saith the Lord'; you cannot

Ronald Arbuthnott Knox

omit these formulas, but can nothing be done to scale down the effect of them?

But all that is of secondary importance. What matters is that the Bible should speak to Englishmen not only in English words, but in English idiom. Any translation is a good one in proportion as you can forget, while reading it, that it is a translation at all. Do not be deceived when your friends tell you that they *like* Bible-English. Of course they do, reading or quoting a few sentences; there is a slow-moving thoroughness about it which conveys a sense of dignity—you get the same in an Act of Parliament. But if they would try to read a chapter on end, which they never do, it would rapidly become tedious, and the attention would begin to wander; why? Because they are reading a foreign language disguised in English dress. Just so, an indifferently translated French book gets you down; *en effet* is translated 'as a matter of fact' when it ought to be translated 'sure enough', and *d'ailleurs* is translated 'anyhow' when it ought to be translated 'if it comes to that'. Your interpreter is almost imperceptibly failing all the time to hit the nail exactly on the head.

Easy enough to notice, as most of the modern translators do, when there is some positive Hebraism to be avoided; when turns of phrase like 'into the hand of' or 'by the hand of' can easily be exchanged for normal English equivalents. It is a harder part of the translator's job to notice the negative effect produced by the absence of English mannerisms. Here is an interesting question you may put to an unsuspecting friend: 'Which is commoner in the Old Testament; the word *danger* or the word *peril*?' You will find that 'peril' has it; the concordance tells you that it occurs once in the Old Testament (Authorized Version), whereas 'danger' does not occur at all. 'Jeopardy' comes three times. Now, it is nonsense to suppose that the Hebrew mind has no such notion as danger; why is there no word for it? The answer can only be, that in Hebrew you express the same idea by a nearly-allied word which has to do duty, also, for slightly different ideas; a word like 'affliction', 'tribulation' or 'trouble'. That means, that a good translation of the Old Testament will sometimes give you 'danger' or 'peril', where the stock translations give you 'affliction', 'tribulation' or 'trouble'; sometimes, where the stock translations give you 'fear' or 'terror'. The rendering which does not mention danger or peril jars imperceptibly on the mind.

More often, the difference involved is not one of mere vocabulary; it depends on the whole build of a language, the whole strategy of its rhetoric. To take a single example—your modern reader is impatient to know what happened, whereas your ancient author likes to spin out the story, and keep his audience in suspense. If A wants to borrow money from B, the sort of sequel you get in the Old Testament is, 'And B answered him, saying, Yesterday and the day before, when the Lord brought Israel out of Egypt, he commanded us that we should not turn away from our brethren when they were in need ...' and so on and so on, leading up to a refusal five verses later. What the modern reader wants is, 'But B refused; Yesterday and the day before, he said . . .' and so on. The translator may feel bound to give a literal rendering; is it not his duty to preserve the integrity of a literary monument? But his reader has switched on the wireless.

Perhaps the subtlest irritant of all is the Hebrew habit of parallelism. I know I shall get into trouble for saying this. The Hebrews, I shall be told, when they wanted to write poetry, deliberately repeated themselves, in some such formula as *Et intonuit de caelo Dominus. Et Altissimus dedit vocem suam.* You must reproduce that exactly in English, or you will not give the reader any idea what Hebrew poetry was like. My version of the Psalms has been given bad marks for this; Fr. Gruenthaner complains that 'the lines are not printed to bring out the parallelism and remind the reader that he is dealing with lyric poetry in a metrical form'. And Mgr. Barton says, 'There is really no excuse for this attempt to ignore the metrical quality'. Now, if I were prepared to take up that challenge as a mere point of typography, so far from not having any excuse, I have the excuse of a paper-shortage. To print the supposedly 'poet-ical' parts of the Old Testament all broken up into lines, as the moderns do, increases your newsprint length by something like one page in ten. That is all very well, if you are publishing hand-books for students. But if you are doing a translation which is meant to be read, not studied, and hope, consequently, that it will have a wide sale, the waste of space becomes serious. Again, the student in his library is accustomed to deal with bulky volumes. But if you hope that your translation will be handled on 'buses and in bed, you do not want to saddle the reader with extra weight. There is no harm, now and again, in being practical.

But I will come clean; I have tried, in great part, to obliterate the traces of parallelism not merely in the printing of my translation but in the writing of it. I quite understand people like Fr. Gruenthaner and Mgr. Barton, who are concerned with students, wanting to concentrate attention on the technical lay-out of Hebrew poetry. But what the reader wants, I insist, is to get the illusion that he is reading, not a translation but an original work written in his own language. And to our notions of poetic composition, these remorseless repetitions are wholly foreign; when you have read a page or two on end, they begin to cloy. *Ars est celare artem*, and I have been at pains, not seldom, to conceal the art of my original. Thus, Isaias lx. 4 reads (in a modern translation):

> 'Your sons shall come from far,
>   And your daughters shall be borne on the hip'.

Obviously, the sex-discrimination is not intended; the older children, boy or girl, would talk, the little ones, girl or boy, would be carried. You want, therefore, something different; if you were translating from the Hebrew (the Vulgate necessitates a departure from it), you would write: 'Sons of yours, daughters of yours, come from far away; carried at their mothers' sides they come.' It is quite true, that does not show the working of the Hebrew sentence; but why should it? You are not mugging the thing up for an exam; you want to read the kind of thing an Englishman would write, if he were encouraging a modern set of Displaced Persons with the promise of restoration.

'Modern'—I have a confession to make. When I embarked on the Old Testament, I thought I could treat it as I treated the New; aim at a sort of timeless English that would reproduce the idiom of our own day without its neologisms, and perhaps have something of an old-fashioned flavour about it. The further I got into the Old Testament, the more surely it was borne in on me that you could not (as they say) swing it. The New Testament was new, the Old Testament was old. The New Testament was written, mainly, by people who thought in Aramaic and used Greek as a kind of Esperanto; it has not the vigour of a living language. The Old Testament was written, mainly, by people who were using their own tongue, and expressed themselves naturally in it. A different treatment was called for, or the whole thing went desperately flat. What opened my eyes, I think, was a rendering by Reuss of the phrase, *Nigra sum sed formosa.* He went at it in a business-like way, as the French do, and produced *'Je suis brunette, mais je suis jolie'.*

'Je suis brunette, mais je suis jolie'—yes, it is all right, there is no slang there, no neologism, and yet. . . . It is not, somehow, the Canticles. Or take that very painstaking piece of work, the Old Testament companion to Goodspeed. Nahum ii. 9 reads:

> 'Plunder silver, plunder gold;
> For there is no end to the stores,
> An abundance of all sorts of valuable articles'.

Marked out in lines, you see, to give the poetical effect; but *does* it give a poetical effect? Nahum has disappeared, and you are left with the language of a cloak-room notice. You cannot make your rendering into poetry by just chopping it up into lengths.

No, what is needed, if we are ever to have a first-class translation of the Old Testament, is a return to the past; to an earlier and more vigorous tradition of English, such as the old translators had, Florio, and North, and Holland, and Urquhart, and L'Estrange, and Adlington. They really managed to 'English' the classical and foreign authors they dealt with, because their own language was still fluid, and could adapt itself to shades of thought; it was not yet cast into a mould. I say 'if we are ever to have a first-class translation'; that is not mock-modesty about my own efforts. I seriously doubt whether I have had the courage or the skill to go back, sufficiently, to those old models. But I have felt, all along, the impetus. Take the book of Proverbs, for example; why does it all read so flat? Because your

340

Hebrew author always writes at full length, whereas the English tradition is to reduce the aphorism to a minimum of words. 'As the cold of snow in the time of harvest, so is a faithful messenger to them that send him'—that is not English; the Englishman says, 'faithful messenger, harvest snow', and leaves it at that.

May I give a single, short example, to illustrate the kind of problem I have been discussing? In the Authorized Version, slightly more lucid as usual than the Douay, the 65th chapter of Isaias begins as follows:

'I am sought of them that asked not for me; I am found of them that sought me not; I said, Behold me, behold me, unto a nation that was not called by my name. I have spread out my hands all day unto a rebellious people, which walketh in a way that was not good, after their own thoughts.'

At first sight, it would appear that verse 1 refers to the call of the Gentiles, verse 2 to the rejection of Israel; and this allegorical interpretation is put on the passage in Romans x. 20. But modern editors are agreed that the Massoretic text is wrongly pointed; LXX and Vulgate are right in giving 'that did not call upon my name' at the end of the sentence. And they are agreed that verse 1, no less than verse 2, refers to the rejection of Israel. The point throughout is that God made himself available to the Jews; if you may put it in that way without irreverence, he was like a grown-up playing hide-and-seek with his favourite children, peeping out from his hiding-place and making their task of search fool-proof, only to find that they had got tired of the game, and were not looking for him at all. In the context, that is to say, verse 1 means something wholly different from what the older versions tell you; they are inaccurate, because they are over-literal. How to correct the inaccuracy? This was my first attempt, made several years ago, when I was new to the job:

'I let myself be questioned by men who do not begin by asking for me; I let myself be found by men who do not search for me; it is to a nation which never calls on my name that I say, I am here, I am close at hand. All day long I spread out my hands to a rebellious people, that goes astray in following its own devices; a people that is ever openly defying me'.

I claim, here, some merit for ingenuity. You can read verse 1 so as to make it apply, in St. Paul's way, to the Gentiles; you can also read it so that it will apply to the Jews, and lead on naturally to verse 2. The rendering is accurate, and just intelligible. But what a rendering! How is anybody going to read through sixty-six chapters of Isaias, all Englished in so stilted and so pedantic a fashion? I might ask the printer to make good my shortcomings:

'I let myself be questioned
    By men who do not begin by asking for me;
I let myself be found
    By men who do not search for me'—

no doubt I could sell my shoddy goods with a little window-dressing like that; Fr. Gruenthaner would be delighted. But is it worth it?

This is how the passage stands at present:

'So ready I to answer, and ask they will not; so easy to be found, and search for me is none! A people that will not call upon my name; else my own voice should whisper, I am here, I am close at hand! Out-stretched these hands of mine, all the day long, to a nation of rebels, straying this way and that as the mood takes them, openly defying me.'

That is its present form; I do not say, its final form; nearly all this process of revision has been done in railway trains. But I hold to it that you have got to do something *of that kind* if you want to let the reader into the mind of Isaias.

Legentibus, si semper exactus sit sermo, non erit gratus. I wonder where St. Jerome found that thought-provoking sentiment to end Machabees with? It is not in the Greek.

Lucien Cerfaux
1883-1968

Cerfaux was born in Presles, Belgium, and entered the seminary of the diocese of Tournai. He matriculated at the Belgian College in Rome, and then completed doctorates in both philosophy and theology at the Gregorian University, staying for an additional year of study at the Biblical Institute. From 1911 to 1930 he taught Scripture at the seminary in Tournai, then from 1930 until his retirement in 1954 he held the chair of New Testament studies at the University of Louvain. Still active, he went to Lourdes in the summer of 1968, shortly after his 85th birthday, to give a series of conferences on the Bible, and died there.

Up until 1936 Cerfaux concentrated on aspects of New Testament environment: Gnosticism, the mystery-religions, Alexandrian Judaism, and the early Fathers. Thereafter he focused more on the New Testament itself, producing his famous trilogy: The Church in the Theology of St. Paul *(1942);* Christ in the Theology of St. Paul *(1951); and* The Christian in the Theology of St. Paul *(1962).*

It is interesting to keep in mind that Cerfaux was studying in Rome all during the period of the Modernist crisis. His year at the Biblical Institute was only the third year of its existence. This may account in part for his preferring to stay away from the text of the New Testament itself in his early studies. It was a time when it was extremely easy for the best of scholars (e.g., Père Lagrange) to get into trouble with the frightened authorities.

When the atmosphere improved, however, Cerfaux was ready. He had spent his time well in preparing for more intensive Biblical work. While much of the Catholic world was unprepared when Pius XII called for the acceptance of modern scientific methods in viewing the Bible, Cerfaux's leadership put Belgium in a better situation. Louvain soon produced a bevy of faithful, qualified disciples because of him.

The selection that follows consists of the final 35 pages of his Christ in the Theology of St. Paul. *It illustrates his ability to scrutinize the text minutely, then step back and attempt a broad synthesis, using the detailed results of his previous analysis. In this particular case it will also be obvious why such an approach is controversial, since it must engage in conjecture that subsequent studies question and modify. Thus some today would be uneasy with the neatness of his division, finding three levels in the thought of Paul corresponding to three stages in his ministry; others would be nervous at the way he assumes authenticity for all but Hebrews.*

These reservations, however, are minor and secondary in comparison to Cerfaux's achievement. Even those who disagree on particular points will readily acknowledge that he has brought new life and light to the study of Paul, and opened the door to a richness of insight and understanding that simply was unavailable in earlier days.

CHRIST IN THE THEOLOGY
OF ST. PAUL

* * * * *

CHAPTER 6

JESUS AND THE LORD JESUS

Jesus

I t is rare for Paul to say "Jesus" and nothing more. However, he sometimes does it, usually in a passage which recalls the earliest form of faith, either the parousia, or the death and resurrection. Here the apostle is harking back implicitly to the manner of speaking of the Palestine community, of those who were witnesses of the life of Jesus. It is thus that he expresses his faith "in Jesus dead and risen again" (1 Thess. 4:14); he speaks of the "marks of Jesus" (Gal. 6:17); of the putting to death ($\nu\acute{\epsilon}\kappa\rho\omega\sigma\iota\nu$) of Jesus (2 Cor. 4:10). The passage, in which the subject is the death of Christ and faith, explains also Rom. 3:26 ($\pi\acute{\iota}\sigma\tau\iota\varsigma$ ᾽I$\eta\sigma o\tilde{v}$). The name of Jesus is bound up with the resurrection in 1 Thess. 1:10 (with the parousia). Elsewhere the word is found in relation to the apostle's preaching (2 Cor. 4:5; 11:4), to the faith which depends on this preaching (Eph. 4:21), or to the confession of faith (1 Cor. 12:3).

In all there are ten such passages in the epistles. We may bring them together by saying that all these texts lead us back always to the primitive formulas: the name of "Jesus" represents the historical fact and is a reminder of the very beginnings of the rise of Christianity. We get a very clear impression of the concrete and living meaning which this name kept when we read 1 Thess 2:15, which speaks of the Jews "who added the murder of the Lord Jesus to that of the prophets". It was the primitive community which expressed very clearly its resentment against the Jews.

The Lord Jesus; our Lord Jesus

The position of the words is quite regular in these two formulas: κύριος Ἰησοῦς and ὁ κύριος ἡμῶν Ἰησοῦς. The first is an acclamation which becomes a profession of faith, while the second is like a well-known form of etiquette. Both bring us back to the vocabulary of the primitive community. Nearly always they are connected with the essential data of faith: the parousia, the death, the resurrection, the teaching of Jesus handed down by the apostles and the power of the "name".

The *parousia:* 1 Thess. 2:19; 3:13; 2 Thess. 1:7 and 8; 2 Cor. 1:14.

The *resurrection:* 1 Cor. 9:1 (Paul's vision of the risen Jesus raised up in glory: Ἰησοῦν τὸν κύριον ἡμῶν ἑόρακα); 2 Cor. 4:14; Rom. 4:24.

The *death:* 1 Thess. 2:15 (considered essentially as fact).

The *teaching* of Jesus, known because handed down by the apostles: 1 Thess. 4:1 and 2 ("we exhort you in the Lord Jesus", that is, in accordance with his teaching; "the commands which we have given you by the Lord Jesus", by conforming you to his teaching); see 1 Cor. 11:23 ("I have received as handed down from the Lord", with reference to the institution of the Supper). With all these passages we connect Rom. 14:14: "I know and I am sure in the Lord Jesus that nothing is unclean of itself": this refers to the teaching of the gospel in Mark 7:14-23; Matt. 15:10-20.

The *name:* 2 Thess. 1:12; 1 Cor. 5:4, "in the name of the Lord Jesus Christ we are united, both you and my spirit, together with the power of the Lord Jesus". The power of the Lord Jesus is present in the assembly when they are taking counsel; this power takes shape in the "name" which is invoked.

Other formulas are equally ancient, and Paul is either reproducing an expression used by the early Christians or is speaking of the Lord Jesus in the way in which Christians usually spoke of him. Thus: the grace of the Lord Jesus be with you (1 Cor. 16:23; Rom. 16:20; 1 Thess. 3:11; Phil. 2:19).

Lucien Cerfaux

The formula only appears twice in the first letter to the Thessalonians in the form of "in Christ Jesus". It occurs in the passages, "to the churches of God which are in Judaea, in Christ Jesus" (2:14) and "the will of God for us in Christ Jesus" (5:18). It defines the sphere of the religion preached by Paul, the "Christian" religion. The Churches of Judaea are cut off from Judaism by their faith in Christ Jesus. The will of God makes the Thessalonians cleave to the belief in Christ Jesus which is expressed by prayer and unceasing joy.

"Christ Jesus" is found in the openings of both the first and second letters to the Corinthians: "the apostle of Christ Jesus". The object of the apostle's message was the Christ who was manifested in Jesus. The formula ἐν Χριστῷ Ἰησοῦ occurs five times in the first letter to the Corinthians, and defines the sphere of faith or of the deep life of the Christian (1:2; 1:30; 4:15; 4:17—following P, S, C, 33—; 16:24). The phrase "Jesus Christ" is found in 1 Cor. 2:2 (to know Jesus Christ who is the object of the message: Jesus is the Christ); 3:11: the basis of the community is Jesus Christ; 2 Cor. 1:19 (allusion to the message); 13:5 (the same allusion).

The letter to the Galatians has many rich and enlightening examples. The title κύριος is very rare there—it occurs only twice on its own and three times as a composite with "Jesus Christ". On the other hand, "Christos" is found alone more than twenty times, and twelve times as a composite with "Jesus". Moreover, the setting of the epistle calls for the use of the names: we are here at war with the Judaizers, and Paul's thought is dominated by the Law-Christ antithesis (justice through the works of the Law, or by the faith of Christ).

The distinction between Jesus Christ and Christ Jesus is not stable, except that Paul is faithful to the formula "in Christ Jesus". When he wishes to speak of the Christian faith, he writes: the faith of Christ Jesus (2:16), or, in Christ Jesus (5:6), and the faith of Jesus Christ (2:16; 3:22); he also says: to believe in Christ Jesus (εἰς Χρ. Ἰ., 2:16).

Paul is thinking concretely of Jesus (the Christ manifested in Jesus) when he says in 4:14: "You received me as an angel of God, as Christ Jesus." And the same is the case when he reminds them of his preaching: "before your eyes is displayed Jesus (the) Christ crucified", and again when alluding to a revelation received "from Jesus (the) Christ" (1:12). In the opening passage of this epistle, when speaking of his rank as an apostle, he does not write "apostle of Christ Jesus" as he did to the Corinthians, but "Paul, apostle not from men or by the intermediary of men, but by Jesus (the) Christ and God the Father who raised him from the dead".

The phrase "in Christ Jesus" is applied directly to faith (3:26) or justification (by faith): 3:14; 5:6. The meaning grows deeper in 3:28: "there is neither Jew nor Greek, for you are all *one* (the one and only new creature, because identified with the one who is the Christ) in Christ Jesus".

The letter to the Romans deals partly with the same subject as the letter to the Galatians, since it is also concerned with the great Judaeo-Christian controversy. Perhaps it appears more clearly that the expression "Jesus Christ" is the one which comes more readily to Paul's lips, although there is still the exception for the phrase "in Christ Jesus". "Jesus Christ" occurs nine times against the four occurrences of "Christ Jesus". It is usually concerned with the message: 1:1, "servant of Jesus Christ" (speaking of his rank as an apostle); 1:6, "the called of Jesus Christ" (their being called by means of the message); 2:16, "God will judge the secrets of men according to my gospel through Jesus Christ"; 16:25, "the preaching of Jesus Christ (here the genitive is a genitive of object). In 3:22 we meet the expression: the faith of Jesus Christ. Twice the context is the liturgy: 1:8: "I give thanks to my God through Jesus Christ", and this note is even more solemn in Rom. 16:27.

It almost seems as though the "Christ Jesus" form stresses the idea of the confession of Christ: 6:3, "baptized in Christ Jesus" (to connect up with Gal. 3:22: "to believe in Christ Jesus"). For the rest, how are we to find a shade of difference between "the servant of Jesus Christ" in 1:1, and "the minister of Christ Jesus" in 15:16?

"In Christ Jesus" occurs six times. Rom. 3:24: "redemption which is in Christ Jesus"; 6:11; 8:1 and 8:2 (life in Christ). 15:17 is concerned with Christ Jeuss who will reward Paul;

Lucien Cerfaux

in 6:3 "in Christ Jesus" refers to the exercise of the mission which Paul has received.

The usage in the epistles of the captivity is in general less significant. The construction ἐν Χρ. ’Ι. is quite fixed. The regular absence of the article shows that there is a tendency to join up the two names in order to form a sort of composite proper name. However, this combination is less fixed than it is for us, for the elements are interchangeable (while nowadays we only say "Jesus Christ"). But we would not dare to say that "Jesus Christ" is more of a proper name than "Christ Jesus". In both of these expressions "Jesus" or "Christ" can retain its autonomy; the combined elements are not as colourless as they are to-day.

THE LORD JESUS CHRIST AND OUR LORD JESUS CHRIST

The long complete form, the title of Christ, is found three times in the first letter to the Thessalonians: 1:3; 5:9; 5:23, and it always refers to the parousia, which is "the parousia of our Lord Jesus Christ". It is thus "our Lord"—a formal epithet which is very expressive in this context—which gives the special tone. "Jesus" or "Jesus Christ" is the proper name denoting our Lord, our Sovereign (*marana*) whom we await. The same thing is found in 2 Thess. 2:1; 2:14; 2:16; 3:6. This long formula could be very traditional, while the short formula (1 Thess. 1:1; 2 Thess. 1:1 and 1:2) could well be called for by the parallelism with θεὸς πατήρ.

The first letter to the Corinthians preserves the connection between the long formula "our Lord Jesus Christ" and the parousia: 1:7; 1:8; 15:57 (the victory); or its connection with the name (1:2), as does 2 Thess. 3:6; see Acts 15:26. The short formula appears in its usual context: "from God our Father and Lord Jesus Christ" (the Greek has no article in front of κυρίου) (1:3). This is connected with 6:11: "in the name of the Lord (the Greek has the article here because of the article before ὄνομα) Jesus Christ and in the Spirit of our God". In 8:6 we find a theological explanation: κύριος and θεός are as two Powers of God.

349

There are two cases which are irregular at first sight. The first is in 1:9: "God is faithful by whom you have been called into union with his Son Jesus Christ, our Lord." The name "Jesus Christ" is first required by the title "his Son", and then "our Lord" is added by attraction because of the idea of the parousia (see 1:8). The second case is in 15:31: "the glory which I have in Christ Jesus, our Lord". The words "Christ Jesus" are stereotyped, and once again "our Lord" is added because of the parousia; the Christians are Paul's glory for the day of the parousia.

The second letter to the Corinthians provides us with two examples of the long formula: 1:3 and 8:9 (with the new context which shows that it is merely part of Paul's style); the usual short form occurs in 1:2. Note especially 4:5: "We do not preach ourselves, but Jesus Christ, (who is) the *Lord*', while we are his *servants*'." "Lord" is here the attributive complement.

The letter to the Galatians has the long form twice: 6:14 ("the cross") and 6:18 ("grace"); the short form occurs in the usual context of the opening of the epistle.

The letter to the Romans provides the customary examples of the long form: 5:1; 5:11; 15:6. The inversion of the words in 1:4 is explained by the attraction which "Son of God" exercises over "Jesus Christ". We are in familiar country with 6:23: "eternal life in Christ Jesus our Lord", and 8:39: "the charity of God in Christ Jesus our Lord". But here there appears for the first time the form which was to be adopted by the liturgy: "through Jesus Christ our Lord": 5:21 (that grace may reign unto eternal life through Jesus Christ our Lord). The short form occurs in the customary places and in the usual context of the opening of the epistle (1:7).

This enquiry is perhaps not without fruit, for it gives us several conclusions. It was from the primitive community that Paul heard the name of Jesus, which was already so charged with memories of the earthly life of the "Messias" Jesus, and which remained the proper name of Christ *par excellence*. Moreover, he inherited from the primitive community the complete title "our Lord Jesus Christ". We have seen how this was connected, even at the very beginning of Paul's writing of the epistles, with its natural context of the parousia. Our Lord Jesus Christ is Jesus who was the Christ of God and who, through his resurrection, was established in the dignity of heavenly king and sovereign; it is he whom we proclaim as the Lord and invoke under this title, and whom we name our Lord Jesus the Christ in our capacity as servants and subjects. In connection with this we may recall the analogy with the title used in the Aramaic courts: "Our Lord Aretas, King of the Nabataeans."

Paul sees a difference between Jesus Christ and Christ Jesus. When we say "Jesus Christ", our thoughts start with the idea of that man Jesus, whom God raised from the dead and in whom he has caused us to recognize the dignity and the role of "Christ", the messianic saviour. On the other hand, when we say "Christ Jesus", our thoughts start with the idea of the pre-existent Christ, who was manifested in the man Jesus of Nazareth. The constancy of the formula "in Christ Jesus" is largely explained by the use that was made of it: it often replaces our adjective "Christian", and brings to the fore the name "Christ", which tells us of the power of Christ and his role in our salvation.

These names and expressions lost some of their colour in the course of centuries, and we often hesitate when faced with the effort necessary to restore them to some of their first freshness. Such a brilliant stylist and theologian as Paul, realizing what words like Χριστός and κύριος meant, would be sure to use them with deliberation.

CHAPTER 7

SAINT PAUL'S CHRISTOLOGY

Pauline theology as tending towards a definition of the divinity of Christ. The beginnings of speculation on *Theos* and *Kyrios*. Eternal generation. Divine nature. Image of God. Christ is God: validity of the formula, and Saint Paul's use of it. The text of Rom. 9:5. The pastoral epistles—Saint Paul unifies the plan of early christology. His re-use of early material. Development of the Pauline synthesis: the contributions of the Old Testament and (apocalyptic) Judaism. The influence of popular Stoicism. The possibility of an influence exercised by Greek religion. The ideology of gnosis and of the Anthropos myth. The basic intuition of Pauline christology.

THE DIVINITY OF CHRIST

Christ's divinity was a greater stumbling-block for the Jews than his messianity, because it conflicted with their monotheism. It seemed to be a concession, either deliberate or unconscious, to pagan worship. None the less, the faith of the early Christian community was carried along by a deep conviction that Christ was Lord. It was something that belonged to the very core of Christian life. Christ had brought about salvation for mankind, and so he must be the central figure in all worship, just as he is the origin of all holiness. In this respect, Paul thinks exactly as his predecessors did in the community of the apostles, but he thinks as a theologian. His theology, as we have tried to show in these three books, cannot be explained without accepting his underlying certitude that Christ belongs to the sphere of divinity. His originality lies only in his attempts to define exactly the person and the work of this Christ who is God.

Christ's work of salvation was God's work. His death and resurrection fulfil God's plan. Christ is identified with the plan. God delivered up his Son because of his love of men, and it was because of this same love that Christ delivered himself up. Christ will likewise fulfil God's judgment at his second coming, and his glory will be, as it is now, God's glory. The more deeply we ponder upon the mysterious wisdom that presides over the work of our salvation, the more we are faced with the formulas that we have already studied when dealing with the Christian "mystery". The wisdom that gathers a dispersed world back into unity, was manifest from the moment of creation in the action of Christ. Christ achieves the whole work designed by wisdom. The design, as it is gradually fulfilled, reveals Christ. Thus one is inclined to maintain that Christ is the wisdom of God, and that wisdom is at his origin, giving him his purpose.

The gift that Christ brings to the world is the divine gift that is at once wisdom, justice, holiness and life. It is identified with the person of Christ.

The names, titles, and functions of Christ force us to define more closely his transcendental relationships with God, and this is what we shall try to do in this concluding chapter. The various lines of approach that we have suggested in previous chapters will thus be seen to focus on the one principle aim that Paul had in mind.

"Lord"

Saint Paul is not in agreement with rabbinical Judaism (for example, Philo) with its idea that *Theos* and *Kyrios* represent powers of God, while God remains inaccessible beyond all such powers. For Paul, *Theos* means the person of God, or the Father. Both "God" and "the Father" signify one and the same divine person, the one God who is the God of the Old Testament. Then comes the "Lord" who is yet another divine person, a *Kyrios* taking his place by the side, as it were, of *Theos*. It is true that Christianity sees Christ with his glorified humanity, before considering him solely in his divinity, but it is unsatisfactory to suppose that Christ is acclaimed as Lord by the whole cosmos merely in his humanity. Besides, even when he is exalted to heaven, there remains that mysterious phrase of Philippians: "God has given him a name which is above every other name." This supposes that Christ has a dignity even greater than that of Lordship, namely, the state of being at home in the divine subsistence itself. Would a creature be capable of this? Christ takes his humanity into his divine state, only because he himself has never left it. Thus we leave behind the consideration of Christ's earthly existence, and come to the question of his eternal status.

Son of God

Saint Paul gives the only possible answer to the theological problem, working towards the idea of an eternal generation from the starting point of God's son showing the glory and the power of his second coming. He is generated in a sphere inaccessible to creatures, namely, in eternity. He is, as Paul says, "the first born before all creatures".

Paul has to make some adjustments in the perspective provided by sapiential literature. The books of Wisdom would speak of wisdom being created, admittedly with primacy and privilege, yet remaining for all that a creature. "The Lord created me as the beginning of his ways." But Christ who is a personal being, and himself creator, could not be identified with any personification of wisdom. A true creator cannot be created, and so Paul uses the traditional expression, "generation", in regard to the son of God. If Christ belongs to eternity, in a state of equality with the Father, he cannot be created, since creation implies a beginning, an introduction into time. If Christ is in any sense a beginning, an ἀρχή it is because he is orientated towards time on account of his mission. And it is precisely because he belongs to eternity that he can be a creator, an initiator in the temporal sphere. The connection between Χριστός and χρίω in 2 Cor. 1:21 has already suggested such an exegesis.

Ἐν μορφῇ Θεοῦ.

The Fathers give μορφή the sense of "nature" when commenting on the opening passage of Philippians, and no doubt their interpretation is a true one. Christ has his being in God, and so he has the right to those privileges which are God's, in virtue of sharing the same nature as the Father. Christ's title to existence cannot possibly be outside the divine nature, and therefore one has to look for it precisely in the μορφή of which Paul speaks, that is, a mode of being which belongs to God and which is communicated to Christ. Therefore we understand the term μορφή to include all that we mean by the word "nature". It would not be enough to say that μορφή denotes the glory of God which belongs to Christ in his pre-existence. In order to have this glory, Christ must first exist, and in the sphere of eternity, the only way in which he can exist is in the nature of God.

Image of God

This is one of Saint Paul's own expressions. He did not find it in the earlier tradition, and as he used it, it tended to become more or less identical with the notion of *Logos*. His christology had taken a speculative and philosophical turn. The image theme has its place at the climax of two approaches. If we work towards the pre-existing or eternal Christ from the starting-point of his glorification after death, we find that he is God's image first and foremost in virtue of his eternal generation, and only secondarily so because of the glory of his ascension. The expressions "in the form of God", "in the resemblance of God", are more or less synonymous. They both refer to Christ's existence before the incarnation. Paul's other approach starts with creation, and all things are created in Christ who is the image of God before even creation began. "He is the image of the invisible God, the first born before all creatures, because all things were created in him, whether visible or invisible, on earth or in heaven" (Col. 1:15 et seq.). One cannot help thinking that Paul owes something here to a platonic system, hailing perhaps from Alexandrian Judaism, with his connected ideas of image, created world, visible and invisible creation, and invisible God. There is a parallel between the text of Col. 1:15 et seq. and the *Timaeus,* 92 C which is admittedly only verbal since for Plato the visible world (or heaven, or the soul of the world) is the image of an invisible world and of an intelligible god. Philo makes the parallel more exact, with various images of God—the monad, the number seven, heavenly wisdom (ἀρχὴ καὶ εἰκὼν καὶ ὅρασις θεοῦ, *Leg. All.,* i, 43), heavenly νοῦς and *Logos.*

The similarity between this passage from Colossians and Wisdom 7:25 et seq. is more important still. Paul may have been inspired by the sapiential use of such terms as emanation, reflection, mirror, occurring with "image". Any platonic background to his thought can easily be explained by the Alexandrian *milieu.* Wisdom, in Alexandrian Judaism, is an emanation of the glory of God, a reflection of the eternal light, a mirror of God's activity, and an image of his goodness. Speculations bear chiefly on the characteristics that Wisdom would have if it were a true hypostasis. We can say that the fact of being God's image is what constitutes Christ as a real person.

Ὁ ἐπὶ πάντων θεός

Whether or not Christ, the image of God, is actually called "God" implies no change in the direction taken by Paul's christology. The one who is God's image, and whose being comes to him in virtue of the fact that he is the Father's image and reflection, is "God" enough in our manner of speaking. The only reason why Paul does not call Christ God is because "God" means the divine person of the Father for him, as it often does for us.

God (the Father) who gave Paul his Christian vocation, is the God of the Old Testament, *his* God. Paul does not speak of God as if he were conscious of any opposition between the two Testaments. He keeps the traditional confession of faith, and the solemn acclamation εἷς θεός. He keeps to Old Testament phraseology when he takes God as witness, when he speaks of the God of peace, of patience and consolation; when he brings in a doxology to the divine name, or speaks of judgment. Paul knows only one God, who is always the same, whether he is speaking in the context of his old or of his new faith. This one God is henceforward the person of God, the Father.

This is more than a practice with Paul, it is a rule, and something that he has systematized. We have only one God, the Father, and one Lord, Jesus Christ. Christ is not ὁ θεός but he is ὁ υἱὸς τοῦ θεοῦ, the image of God, bearing the name that God (the Father) kept for himself in the Old Testament. Christ is the Son of God. He could not be called ὁ θεός at the time when Paul was writing because the terminology was then so fresh and so concrete in its use that it would have seemed contradictory if Christ had been called God.

The term θεός does, however, mean something other than the person of God, for it connotes God's attributes and his nature, and the divine mode of being. And one can perceive the beginnings of a distinction (both in the Old Testament and the new faith) between the person of God the Father, and his nature or attributes. Saint Paul is familiar with the so-called gods of paganism (1 Cor. 8:1; see 10:20) which are not gods "by nature" (Gal. 4:8). The pagans themselves can contemplate God's power and majesty, the θεῖον, which is made visible by means of creation, and they should be able to use these as stepping stones to a knowledge of the person of God. In Christian revelation, God communicates his glory to us (1 Cor. 2:7). We have access to the knowledge of him, to the depths of his wisdom, and of his riches (Rom. 11:33). We have only to think

Lucien Cerfaux

of the fullness of the divinity in the risen Christ. Thus we can distinguish between the person (the creator, the planner, who sends his son and his spirit) and the mode of this person's being, his nature and his attributes. The man of sin (2 Thess. 2:4) puts himself above all that is called God; he sits in the temple and shows himself as if he were the one and the only God. Cannot Christ receive the same name, in virtue of his inheriting the divine name of *Kyrios*? The man of sin is only an impostor, but the Christ of God only takes what is his by right.

In theory, there is no reason why this should not be the reason why Christ is called God, provided that "God" in the case of Christ denotes divinity only, and not the person of God the Father. We have maintained that Paul follows his own rule strictly, and any evidence that he breaks his own rule must be of the clearest.

Rom. 9:5 is the only text that we can take from Paul's earlier epistles. It does not appear to break the rule, although there are admittedly good reasons and weighty authorities against us. At first sight the passage looks like a doxology: ὁ ὢν ἐπὶ πάντων θεὸς εὐλογητὸς εἰς τοὺς αἰῶνας, ἀμήν. Paul is keeping to the tradition of the synagogue. Rom. 1:18, which speaks of the creator, has something Hebrew about it, and Paul adds: ὅς ἐστιν εὐλογητὸς εἰς τοὺς αἰῶνας, ἀμήν (v. 25). In 2 Cor. 11:31, where he calls on God, the Father of the Lord Jesus, as witness, he slips in the phrase: ὁ ὢν εὐλογητὸς εἰς τοὺς αἰῶνας. The formula is constant. Moreover, when Paul begins to give thanks at the beginning of his letters, he sometimes copies the doxology: εὐλογητὸς ὁ θεὸς καὶ πατὴρ τοῦ κυρίου ἡμῶν Ἰ. Χρ. (2 Cor. 1:3; Eph. 1:3; see 1 Peter 1:3). Other doxologies which replace εὐλογητός by δόξα are rather different from these which we are considering here.

Does the doxology refer to God or to Christ? The Fathers are generally agreed that it refers to Christ, but they refrain from using it in controversy because they admit that their exegesis is not absolutely certain. The moderns are inclined to agree with them.

Much has been written on this text, and there have been attempts at re-fashioning it. This is unwise, however, since the manuscript tradition does not justify the phrase being divided up in various ways, and the punctuation altered.

To keep to more obvious conclusions, we feel that it is important above all to treat it as a doxology. The parallel with 2 Cor. 11:31 is striking, the latter beginning as it does with ὁ ὢν and continuing with εὐλογητός: (God), "the one who is blessed for all time". According to this parallel we should translate Rom. 9:5 as "the one who is God above all, is blessed for all time".

One can back up the traditional exegesis attributing the doxology to Christ by pointing out that the period in which Paul enumerates the Jews' privileges finishes with Χριστὸς κατὰ σάρκα. This formula needs κατὰ πνεῦμα for its antithesis, and we could paraphrase as follows: The one whom the Jews could not know and possess except according to the flesh, we Christians know and possess as the one who, being God, is blessed for all time.

There are still difficulties, even with this interpretation. Why, for instance, should there be a doxology instead of the more normal development by means of an antithesis? It is quite reasonable to transfer a doxological formula to Christ, but at the same time it is being emphasized that he is ἐπὶ πάντων θεός. For what reason, we may ask, does Paul use such an unusual formula, instead of calling Christ "Son of God", or "Lord above all"? It must also be considered that θεός becomes appellative, and is not his proper name in the normal sense. By punctuating the phrase after ἐπὶ πάντων one can of course render the sense much less unusual. Thus "God is above all things. May he be therefore blessed." But in this case the reading would have to be εὐλογητὸς θεός. And it is no help at all to alter the phrase to "He who is above all things, God blessed for all time".

If the doxology is applied to God, Paul's thought would be different again. He has just been enumerating the privileges of the Jews. Let all glory be given to God who has favoured his chosen people, and whose worship, covenant and promises have been the subject of the writer's thought thus far. He is God above all things, and as such is no longer the God of the Jews alone (see Rom. 3:29). As such he is blessed for all time. This was the exegesis of Diodorus of Tarsus. "Christ (according

Lucien Cerfaux

to the flesh) belongs to the Jews, but God does not belong to them, for he is the God who is over all men. This is why the Jews have lost all their privileges."

There is in fact no reason why God should not be the subject of this doxology. If he is, then Saint Paul is faithful to his rule, and God keeps his proper name θεός. Thus we can avoid the great disadvantage of changing Paul's vocabulary.

The christology of the pastoral epistles develops in various respects the basic teaching on Christ that we find in the major epistles and those of the captivity. We shall not be surprised to find in the pastoral letters such a formula as ἐπιφάνειαν τῆς δόξης τοῦ μεγάλου θεοῦ καὶ σωτῆρος ἡμῶν Χριστοῦ Ἰησοῦ. The title μέγας θεός is brought out as an analogy with the formulas of emperor worship, and θεός is an epithet and not a proper name.

* * * * *

GENERAL SYNOPSIS

The principle factors of Paul's christology remain constant throughout the epistles, and thus we cannot speak of a true evolution in his system. The bases of his theology were already determined from the start, together with the essential means of expressing his thought, for Paul inherited the outlook of the first Christian community. He shared their vision of the risen Christ, and like them he was familiar with Old Testament and Judaic formulas.

On the other hand, one gets the impression that it is impossible to make one synthesis of Paul's thought that will be faithful to every stage of his career. Thus we have distinguished three successive levels in his development which are clearly differentiated because at each level his centre of interest is different. The first stage of his thought is found in the epistles to the Thessalonians and the conclusion of 1 Corinthians, before his apostolic labours in the church at Corinth. Here he is at his nearest to the outlook of the Jerusalem community, such as we find it in the synoptics and the book of Acts. This is the archaic level. The second stage in which the major epistles were written is evidently connected with Paul's residence at Corinth. The

359

third comes as the result of his long apostolate in Asia Minor, particularly at Ephesus, and we find everything that characterizes his thought at this period in the captivity epistles.

1. The two letters to the Thessalonians are centred on Christ's parousia and resurrection. 1 Cor. 15 follows the same plan, with particular insistence on the resurrection. This is typical of the earliest form of the creed, in which death and resurrection are not separated. This is the first focal point of the faith, the work of salvation with Christ as the saviour. It is a soteriology which develops the main points of the early creed. Christians await the coming of Christ, whom God has raised from the dead. Christ died for our sins and God has raised him up again. It was the aim of our first book in the present study to show how these early elements are arranged and developed in Paul's first synthesis. Our first chapter was an attempt to set the stage and to study the message of salvation as it was accepted at the very beginning of Christianity.

The parousia is salvation in the future, and the signal of our resurrection. Christ's resurrection is connected with the parousia to the extent of being, one might say, the first act of the second coming. Thus the message becomes centred on the resurrection, and this is the great characteristic of Paul's soteriology in its first period. Christ's resurrection is foremost in his mind. On the one hand it is the prelude to the parousia, and on the other hand it makes the sanctifying power of the future life and its demands present in this world. Salvation then is not something that is awaited; it is already with us. In analysing Paul's formulas dealing with the resurrection, we have stressed the sudden crisis that occurs when Christ's resurrection is introduced into the Christian's life.

Christ's kingdom likewise is conceived not only as a future reality, to be established with the parousia. It is already with us here and now. This is why the theology of Christ's redeeming death, in Paul's development, underlines the present power of that death.

We concluded our first book with a chapter on the incarnation, a point on which Saint Paul's exact position needed to be made clear. His theology does in fact give such importance to the resurrection that Christ's presence in the world before this event seems almost to be in antithesis to his glorified state. Christ's sanctifying power begins with the resurrection, and the whole purpose of the incarnation is to bring "Christ according to the flesh" into this world, so that he may thereby be in a position to die and so accomplish the work of our salvation in his mortal body. It is in this perspective that we find Paul, unlike John or Mark, omitting Christ's teaching and miracles from his synthesis. Just as Saint John found a manifestation of the divine in Christ's words, so did Mark in the miracles.

2. Christ's resurrection and death have power in the lives of Christians. From this beginning, Paul develops the idea of a religious principle at work in the world which constitutes in fact a new religion. This principle is God's power and generosity present in Christ. This is the point at issue in the second level of Paul's christology.

The literary starting point is provided by the opening words of Romans, and of the first letter to the Corinthians. Here we see how Saint Paul presented the Christian message as antithetical to the fundamental ideas of Judaism and paganism. The contrast with Judaism, with which Paul opposes both Jews and Judaizing Christians, is that Christ's work has put an end to the system of the Law. We belong to a new system in which Christ is the originator of our justice, through the faith that we have in him. The second contrast is between Christian faith and Greek philosophy. Some of the Christians at Corinth had been tempted to put Christian religion, with its monotheism and its spiritual experience, on the same footing as those philosophical religions such as Orphism and the mystery cults. For Paul, Christianity is essentially an acceptance of Christ's power. Christian wisdom is the wisdom of God, given to us by the Spirit. The object at which it aims is Christ and the future rewards that we shall receive from him.

Christian salvation deepens into a new life, which comes to us through the power of Christ's resurrection. Paul takes these ideas and develops them simultaneously. Christ henceforward is the "spiritual" Christ, communicating his own life of holiness to us. We have been at pains to define the exact relationships between the spiritual Christ and the Holy Spirit.

Our life is, moreover, a share in Christ's life. Here we have dwelt somewhat on the question of a supposedly "mystic" Christ composed of the totality of Christians. Mysticism does not, however, bring about a mystic Christ. It is far better to keep to Paul's simple formula, and speak of our share in Christ's risen life. The "collective" Christ, the second Adam, and the Church as Christ's body are all themes that Paul touches on, but it would be wrong to suppose that our understanding of historical theology profits by the elaboration of any synthesis that is based on such ideas. Such constructions are more akin to our way of thinking than to Saint Paul's and their chief use has been in claiming Paul's doctrine for oriental syncretism. But Paul's construction is not based on a gnostic plan, nor does it use gnostic materials or the much exaggerated Anthropos myth.

3. The third level of Paul's thought gives us the most complete christological synthesis, still using the materials with which the previous levels have familiarized us. The chief point of interest now is the idea of Christ's "mystery". In other words, the manner in which God has brought about our salvation reveals a secret wisdom centred on Christ, and realized by Christ. Paul draws our attention here less to Christ's presence in the world, or to his person, and more to eschatological and soteriological questions. Thus we have kept for the third book in this study the basic problems of christology, combining the themes which most reveal Christ's person (his divinity, for example) with the development of the mystery.

After a preliminary analysis of the hymns to Christ (a speciality of the churches of Asia Minor apparently) we considered the themes of revelation and of knowledge of the mystery, both in their literary forms and in the special conception of Christianity that is implied by the forms. The apostles, and especially Paul, were given the task of revealing the Christian mystery, the knowledge of which is one of the essential benefits of Christian life. To express the content of the mystery, we have to define Christ's connection with the world. Christ unifies the world of men (both Jews and pagans) and the world of the cosmic forces. He gathers everything into the unity of God. His work of uniting all things to the unity of their origin, allows us

Lucien Cerfaux

to penetrate into the mystery of Christ's person as the image of God.

In the following chapters, we considered the name and attributes of Christ, still focusing our attention on his person. These names and attributes we had already met, but had not thus far concentrated on them at length. Christ's divinity is the principle question. Without faith in that divinity, which underlies eschatology, soteriology and mysticism, the development of Paul's christology would have neither basis, purpose nor system. The whole power of the development becomes obvious when Paul draws our attention to the person of Christ. His titles take on their full meaning—Son of God, and Lord. In our last chapter we dealt explicitly with the theme of Christ's divinity, touching on the problems of the origins of christology.

Thus we conlcuded that Paul's christology was the fruit of revelation. The modern solution that minimizes the idea of an immediate intervention on the part of God, stems from an ideology that is simply not adequate for explaining Paul's christology. Oriental syncretism is a favourite theory at the moment, and it tends to put all else into the background— Christ's incarnation, his revelation of himself in teaching and miracles, his death and resurrection, and the revelations of the apostolic age, including of course Paul's own. Paul did, however, build on the revelation made by Christ. This was implicit in the faith of the first Christian community, and in the doctrine revealed to him personally. These latter he knew to harmonize perfectly with the thought of his fellow Christians. What Paul builds is not the work of a syncretist. The gnostic authors are clearly syncretic, but Paul is an inspired Christian. His system elaborates the traditions he received, and the revelations that shed their light on tradition.

Pierre Maurice Benoit

1906-

Benoit was born in Nancy, France, and was educated there until going to the Dominican college of le Saulchoir. In 1933 he began his lengthy career as Professor of New Testament at the Ecole Biblique in Jerusalem. He was director of the prestigious Revue Biblique *from 1953 to 1968, and director of the Ecole Biblique from 1965 to 1972. He played a major role in the preparation of the* Jerusalem Bible, *being responsible especially for the Gospel of Matthew and Paul's captivity epistles. He was a peritus at the Second Vatican Council and was named a consultor of the Biblical Commission in 1972.*

The two-volume work called Jesus and the Gospel *is the English translation of a collection of his articles, called in French* Exégèse et Théologie. *The most remarkable thing about Benoit is the breadth of his knowledge and interests, and these articles demonstrate that. We have selected for presentation here chapter 5 of volume II, an article that he wrote in 1952 on "The Origins of the Apostles' Creed in the New Testament."*

The article could serve as a model in many ways, for the same kind of thing happens time and again in contemporary Biblical studies. First, there is a long-standing tradition accepted without question by centuries of Christian believers. Then critical studies intervene and call it into question. Then the fashionable position is to debunk, deny, ridicule. Then a further insight alters the scene so that the original tradition turns out to have been closer to the truth than its antagonists.

The consequence of this process is that the original position is reinterpreted, then reappropriated in a much healthier, more intelligent way than the initial credulity allowed. In that process much has been gained in both understanding and appreciation. Here, for instance, one might come to Benoit's article with the naive belief that the Apostles' Creed was written by the Apostles. Upon learning that such a position is untenable historically, one can react negatively and complain that the designation "Apostles' Creed" is false and dishonest. But upon following him carefully through the maze of data and grasping the pattern that emerges, one comes out on the other side of the article with a realization that the Apostles' Creed is the Apostles' Creed in a much more meaningful and important sense than if they had merely composed it.

It has been said that the mantle of Père Lagrange fell upon Père Benoit. He has worn it with dignity and become in the process "probably the best-known Catholic New Testament scholar of our time" (J. S. Kselman in the JBC). Along with Roland de Vaux and M. E. Boismard he has maintained the high tradition of Dominican scholarship that has played so prominent a role in the contemporary renewal.

JESUS AND THE GOSPEL

CHAPTER 5

THE ORIGINS OF THE APOSTLES' CREED
IN THE NEW TESTAMENT

For a long time it was believed that the 'Apostles' Creed' had really been composed by the Twelve Apostles, that the latter, at the moment when they separated to go out and conquer the world, had fixed the formula of the common faith they preached and that this formula, to which each had contributed an article, was no other than our apostolic creed. This belief, which appears at the end of the 4th century and probably goes back to still more remote times, flourished until the 15th century, at which time the critical spirit of the Renaissance became aware of its legendary character.

The reaction that followed was necessary and healthy, but it went too far, so that modern scholars of the 19th and early 20th centuries were able to go to the opposite extreme and deny that the apostolic age had had a datum of faith solidly established and professed by everyone. Deceived by an analytic method which was useful in itself but was practised in a one-sided fashion, they happily emphasised the divergences between St John and St Paul, and even between St Paul and Jesus himself, and concluded that the first century of Christianity had seen only a flowering of disparate and even contradictory doctrines. It would have been only from the beginning of the 2nd century that the Church, now an organised institution, would have undertaken to unify these multifarious data and to canonise the result in a formula of faith; and this unification and canonisation, it is well understood, could not have been carried out without choosing, forcing and in part sacrificing the diverse tendencies of the first epoch.

But this extreme opinion has been corrected in its turn and work carried out in the last few years has given us a more exact picture. It has become apparent that, behind the indisputable divergences of theological development discerned by analysis, a profound unity concerning the essentials of the Christian message reigns throughout the writings of the New Testament. Furthermore, it has been recognised that this nucleus of the message is to be found enunciated more or less by everyone in similar stereotyped terms which, without having the fixity of the formulas to be elaborated in the end, nevertheless foreshadow and prepare us for them. In the light of this it again becomes true to say that the 'Apostles' Creed', in content as well as in form, derives in a direct line from the datum furnished by the writings of the Apostolic age; even if it was not composed by the Apsotles in its present state, it still represents a faithful expression of the message they transmitted to the Church and in terms which even reflect the form in which they transmitted it.

This is what I propose to show in this essay, by studying (1) the content and the form of the apostolic preaching, especially the 'Kerygma' and (2) the content and the form of the first 'Confessions of Faith' which in certain privileged circumstances issued from the life of the nascent Church, since it was from the combination of these two elements that the Creed was born and it is through them that it really is linked to the Apostles.

1. THE APOSTOLIC 'KERYGMA'

What the Kerygma is

The Greek word *Kerygma* is used in the New Testament to denote the first triumphant preaching that the witnesses of Christ addressed to the world to bring to its notice the 'Good News' (the meaning of the word *euangelion*, gospel) of the salvation who God the Father had just achieved in his Son and through his Spirit. It differed from *Catechesis, Didache* and *Didaskalia*, which followed up and taught the converted doctrine they were to hold in a more systematic fashion, and from *Paraenesis*, which inculcated the moral obligations of their new way of life, by having a shock-effect—it was an announcement, a proclamation addressed to men still ignorant of Christ to call them to believe.

In the first contact only the essentials mattered. Like the 'heralds' (in Greek *Kerux*) of a great King, these messengers proclaimed before the world the astounding news that God, in the person of Jesus, had just intervened all-powerfully in the history of mankind: no one could remain indifferent in the fact of this divine initiative, it was necessary to surrender to the evidence of the facts they witnessed to, to believe, to be converted. Peter preaches in Jerusalem in the very first moments of the Church. Paul carries the gospel to the Jews and Gentiles of the Graeco-Roman world. Matthew, Mark, Luke and John write out the one Gospel in more developed forms, setting out this primitive, essential Kerygma in ways that vary according to their aims and their audiences. The author of the epistle to the Hebrews, the Seer of the Revelation, know no basis for their wonderful theological or prophetic elaborations other than the common faith in the dead and risen Christ. Everywhere we find the same doctrine, the same message, the same language, not yet enclosed indefinitive formulas but always sounding the same unique note.

The Kerygma in the Acts of the Apostles

For the study of this primitive Kerygma, discourses contained in the first part of the *Acts of the Apostles* form an especially important source. Admittedly this work, although it tells the story of the first steps of the Church, is not the earliest of the New Testament writings; its author, St Luke, the disciple of St Paul, belongs to the second generation of Christians. But it is equally certain that in the composition of this work he used sources that were earlier, and that these sources, whether spoken or written, go back to the first years of the Church in Jerusalem, shortly after the departure of Jesus.

Proof of this is to be found in the way the Aramaic language in which they were first formulated makes itself clearly heard behind the Greek of Luke's translation; and also in the still very simple way, prior to all theological speculation, that the person of Christ is presented. His divine pre-existence is not denied but it is not yet clearly enunciated. We are at the very first stage, when the dazzling conviction of the triumph of Jesus, raised to the right hand of the Father in heaven after the humiliations of the Passion, occupies the whole field of Christian awareness and does away with the need to reflect on the heavenly existence which might have preceded these humiliations. On this point, a version composed some thirty or forty years after the death of Jesus would have expressed itself much more explicitly. If we cannot be certain that these discourses give us the *ipsissima verba* of the Apostle Peter, we can be certain that in them we hear a direct and authentic echo of the way in which the first community from its very beginnings understood and preached the message of salvation. We can therefore make use confidently of these precious documents to isolate the essential elements of the primitive Kerygma.

There are five of these discourses of Peter. The first (2:14-39) was addressed, on the day of Pentecost, to the crowd which had been attracted by the news of this extraordinary event. The second (3:12-26) was delivered a little later to a crowd which had gathered in a portico of the Temple following on a miraculous healing. When the leaders of the Sanhedrin wanted to control the agitation this miracle had led to and which seemed disquieting to them, Peter had the chance to defend the new faith in front of them in a third (4:9-12) and fourth (5:29-32) discourse. Lastly, later still, having been summoned to Caesarea by the centurion Cornelius who asked to be instructed, the prince of the Apostles gave him an exposition which constitutes the fifth discourse (10:34-43). To these five proclamations of Peter, we can add the discourse given by the Apostle Paul in the synagogue at Antioch in Pisidia (13:16-41), since this discourse differs considerably from the other discourses of Paul reported in the Acts, in being based plainly on the same outline as those of Peter. These discourses of course all differ notably in length and importance, and they show appreciable variations due to their varying occasions. Nevertheless they all resemble one another in the elements which make up the underlying structure and which are precisely the elements that constitute the primitive Kerygma. It is these elements which we are concerned to disengage.

Pierre Maurice Benoit

At the very centre there stand the death and resurrection of Jesus. This is the essential fact that must be brought to the notice of all men, since it contains the whole substance of salvation: Jesus of Nazareth has just been put to death, rejected by the Jews, handed over to Pontius Pilate, executed by the Pagans; but God has raised him on the third day and has exalted him in glory to his right hand with the title of 'Lord' (*Kyrios*) (2:23f, 32-6; 3:13-15; 4:10; 5:30f; 10:39f; 13:27-30).

This cardinal fact, which is presented as a historical event, duly proved, occupies the centre of the Kerygma of which it is the real essence. But it does not stand alone and is surrounded, as by concentric circles, with a halo of other historical facts, antecedent and consequent, which prove it and give it its full value.

A first circle is composed of the facts which immediately preceded and followed this drama. Before the Cross, there was the earthly life of Jesus, the marvellous features of which guarantee his divine mission; he was announced by John the Baptist, and anointed by him with a baptism at which God declared him to be the Messiah (10:37f; 13:23-5), then he went about in public, in Galilee and Judaea, doing good and working miracles (2:22; 10:38f). After his resurrection and exaltation to heaven, there were the signs that proved his triumph: the appearances in which he showed himself alive to his disciples (2:32; 3:15; 5:32; 10:39-42; 13:31) and the outpouring of the Holy Spirit which, in confirmation of his promise, came to confer the first-fruits of the new life on them (2:33; 5:32).

A second circle then surrounds this nucleus of facts and places them in a wider historical perspective, looking backwards to the past as well as forward to the future. In the past, there were the prophecies in the Scriptures which had been announcing these events for a long time and which receive a startling confirmation from them: his Davidic descent (2:30; 13:34), his Messianic sonship (13:33), his mission as 'Prophet', successor to Moses (3:22f), his sufferings (3:18), his role of the stone rejected by the builders (the Jews) which becomes the keystone (4:11), his resurrection (2:25-31; 13:34-7), his exaltation to the right hand of God in heaven (2:34f)—was this not all announced by the Prophets?

To this long preparation in the past corresponds an indefinite repercussion in the future. With the resurrection of Christ and the outpouring of the Spirit, the messianic times have begun (2:17-21), the era of salvation has opened: to it are invited not only the Jews but also the Gentiles (3:25), all those who call on the name of the Lord Jesus (2:39), in whom alone is salvation (4:12). It is a period of waiting during which Christ Jesus remains in heaven; but one day he will return, and then all things will be restored (3:20f). For the moment it is necessary to be sorry for one's sins, to believe in the Lord Jesus and be baptised in his name; in this way one will be granted the forgiveness of sins and the gift of the Holy Spirit (2:38; cf. 3:19-26; 5:31; 10:43; 13:38).

It is, as we can see, *the whole divine plan of salvation* that this schema of the primitive preaching passes in review. This review has a clear historical character, because salvation in the Judaeo-Christian revelation is a history, the history of God's intervention in the progress of human events to bring his creatures dispersed by sin back to him. In this history the kerygmatic schema which we have just analysed isolates three stages: at the beginning, the preparing of salvation in the prophecies of Scripture; then in the centre the work of Christ, his dying and rising; lastly, the fruits of his salvation communicated to men by the forgiveness of sins and life in the Holy Spirit, while they wait for the restoration of the universe at the Parousia. It is easy to relate these three stages of salvation to the Three Persons of the Trinity, the Father who creates, the Son who saves, and the Spirit who sanctifies. We shall have to remember this when we discuss the Trinitarian scheme adopted by the Creed.

The Kerygma in the Epistles

If the discourses in Acts are an especially important source for the study of the Kerygma, because they present it in a complete form and in a logical order, or rather a chronological order, they are not the only witness nor even the earliest. The epistles, especially those of Peter and Paul, also bear witness in their own way, not in the form of a consecutive exposition but of brief allusions.

These writings are addressed to the converted and are answering special questions of doctrine or morals, and in them the Apostles are carrying out catechesis, distributing 'didache', or even 'didaskalia'. They did not have to reproduce the Kerygma, which they had already preached and which they took for granted as known. They do, however, sometimes remind their readers of it quickly, and these brief mentions, which could almost be called quotations, are very precious to us since they allow us to see the substantial identity of the primitive Kerygma, in its foundation and even to a certain degree in its form. These isolated fragments, buried in theological or polemical elaborations, have been compared to the first crystals that form in a substance which is in process of crystallisation: in them we see the first signs of the formulation that will grow more and more stereotyped and will end one day in the Creed.

They are brief assertions, easily recognisable from their style, which is simple, declaratory and often rhythmic. It is not rare either for the context to betray their origin; for example when they are quoted as that which it is necessary to 'believe' and 'confess' (*Rm* 10:9), is that which has been 'received' from tradition and which must be 'handed on' (*1 Co* 11:23; 15:1-3). Paul is glad to remind his readers that assertions like these have their origins in 'his Gospel' (e.g. *Rm* 2:16; *2 Tm* 2:8).

All the elements of the Kerygma that we have encountered above can thus be found again threaded through the epistles. The proclamations of the death, resurrection and exaltation of Christ to heaven, which we saw were the centre of the Kerygma in Acts, are also the most frequent in the rest of the New Testament, and this is an interesting confirmation of their primordial value in the Christian message. Take for example the passage in *1 Co* 15:1ff, whose introduction and style are particularly typical of 'Kerygmatic' quotations; 'Brothers, I want to remind you of the gospel I preached to you, the gospel that you have received . . . I taught you what I had been taught myself, namely that Christ died for our sins, in accordance with the scriptures; that he was buried; and that he was raised to life on the third day, in accordance with the scriptures; that he appeared first to Cephas and secondly to the Twelve, etc. . .' We realise that Paul is here quoting—he tells us so himself—a fundamental proclamation of the faith which is already clothed in a 'traditional' formulation and handed on like that.

This text is particularly clear, but there are many others as well in which we can sense the existence of formulas which are already half-fixed, for example: that 'Christ died (was delivered up) for our sins' or 'for us' (*1 Th* 5:10; *Ga* 1:4; 2:20; *2 Co* 5:14; *Rm* 4:25; 5:6-8; *1 Tm* 2:6; *Tt* 2:14; *1 P* 2:21f; 3:18; cf. *Mt* 20:28; *Mk* 10:45), that he 'died and rose again' (*1 Th* 4:14; *Rm* 4:25; 8:34; 14:9; *1 P* 3:18 etc.), that it was 'God who raised him from the dead' (*1 Th* 1:10; *1 Co* 6:14; 15:15; *2 Co* 4:14; *Ga* 1:1; *Rm* 4:24; 6:4; 10:9; *Col* 2:12; *Ep* 1:20; *1 P* 1: 21), that he is 'seated at the right hand of God' (*Rm* 8:24; *Ep* 1:20; *Heb* 1:3-13; 8:1; 10:12; 12:2; *1 P* 3:22; and cf. *Mt* 22: 44; 26:64; *Mk* 16:19; *Ac* 7:55f) and that he is established there as 'Kyrios', that is, as 'Lord' (cf. *1 Co* 12:3; *Rm* 10:9; and the use of this title throughout the New Testament) of the living and the dead (*Rm* 14:9) and even the heavenly spirits (*Ph* 2: 10f; *Ep* 1:20f; *Heb* 1:4; *1 P* 3:22). All these stages that Christ traversed when he passed through death to regain life are to be restated in almost the same form by the Apostles' Creed. One article alone, the Descent into Hell, is less powerfully attested in the New Testament; even so the kerygmatic passage in *1 P* 3: 18-22, alludes to it without any doubt. Besides, as we know, it is an article of lesser importance, and did not appear in the primitive Roman form of the Apostles' Creed, just as it is still missing from the Nicene.

In the Kerygma in Acts the central fact of the Death and Resurrection were surrounded and as it were prolonged by preparations in the past and consequences in the future. These elements do not fail either to appear in the remainder of the New Testament, ordered here, as they were there, to placing the Cross and Easter in the full sweep of the divine plan. It was in this way that the earthly life of Jesus, his work and his teaching, although it is true that they play a very small part in the epistles whether Paul's (*1 Co* 7:10; *2 Co* 8:9; see also 5:16) or the others (*2 P* 1:16-18), became the object of a broad catechesis which was gathered up in the gospels. It was in this way too that the prophecies and the prefiguration of the work of Christ in the Scriptures were exploited as a theme by all the authors of the New Testament, whether they make it their business to emphasise the fulfilment of prophecy (the Gospels, especially St Matthew), whether they draw material from it for a theological explanation of salvation (St Paul), to the point where this exegesis becomes the principal object of a treatise (the epistle to the Hebrews), or whether they derive inspiration from the oracles of the past to announce the future of the Church (the Revelation of St John). And it is finally in this way that the divine origin of Jesus, which the discourses in Acts still pass over in silence, very quickly becomes one of their most constant affirmations: not only does his descent from David form part of the Kerygma (cf. *Rm* 1:3; *2 Tm* 2:8), but his title 'Son of God' appears in it too (*Rm* 1:3f; *Heb* 4:14), as well as in the confessions of faith (*Ac* 8:37; 9:20; *1 Jn* 4:15; 5:5, etc.), not to mention a large number of texts where it has spread from the Kerygma into the epistles and the gospels. The only thing to notice is that the conception by the Holy Spirit and the virgin birth never appear explicitly outside the infancy gospels of Matthew and Luke (and perhaps in Jn 1:13, according to a form of the text which seems very early). It may be that the Church did not feel the need to assert these truths of faith explicitly until a little later, on the occasion of certain heresies. Even so, this happened very soon: St Ignatius of Antioch always includes the virgin birth in his statement of faith.

As for the future, all the New Testament writings are unanimous in what they affirm of its ultimate perspectives. The expectation of the 'Day of the Lord', of the day when he will 'come', of his 'Parousia', appears so often, from the gospels through the epistles to Revelation, that it is unnecessary to quote texts. It is sufficient to remind ourselves of the liturgical appeal: *Marana tha,* 'Our Lord, come!' (*1 Co* 16:22; *Rv* 22:20). This return of the Lord will be the signal for the general Resurrection and the Judgement, two points of faith which the epistle to the Hebrews (6:2) ranges among the fundamental articles of the elementary teaching. These two points were new to the pagans, to whom they had to be preached and defended (*Ac* 17:18-31f; *1 Co* 15:12), but in fact they originated in traditional Jewish belief (with the exception of the Sadducees, cf. *Mt* 22:23ff; *Ac* 4:1f; 23:6-8).

The new element in the Christian message was to associate these strictly with the person of Christ, and this is precisely what happens in many texts of the New Testament in which we seem to hear an echo of the apostolic Kerygma. The 'resurrection of the dead' is announced by Peter as 'in Jesus' (*Ac* 4:2), which evidently means in relation to the resurrection of Jesus, which is its prelude; and Paul for his part never ceases to base the assurance of our own resurrection on that of Christ (*1 Th* 4:14; *1 Co* 6:14; 15:12-23; *2 Co* 4:14; 13:4; *Rm* 6:4f; 8:11; *Ph* 3:10f; *Col* 2:12f). Similarly, the traditional Jewish doctrine of the eschatological judgement is renewed by the assertion that it is Jesus who 'will judge the living and the dead', a formula which is already fixed in the New Testament (*2 Tm* 4:1; *Ac* 19:42; *1 P* 4:5; *Rm* 14:9f; cf. *1 Co* 3:13; 4:5; *2 Co* 5:10; *Rm* 2:16; *Ac* 17:31; *Mt* 25:31-46) and which will be taken up again by the Creed just as it is.

The Kerygma, whose essential content we have just reviewed, is therefore seen to be the basis of the faith in the first Christian communities. We have shown that its major pronouncements are to be found again in all the New Testament writings, with a strong basic similarity and often even with one of outward form. In it we can perceive a well-defined nucleus of fundamental beliefs which characterise the faith in its primitive state. It is a boon which comes from the Apostles, which we 'receive' from their witness and which must be 'passed on' in its integrity (*2 Th* 2:15; *1 Co* 11:1, etc.). It is a 'rule of doctrine' which we must obey with all our heart (*Rm* 6:17), a 'deposit' which must be kept (*1 Tm* 6:20; *2 Tm* 1:14), a 'sound teaching' (*1 Tm* 1:10; *Tt* 1:9; *2 Tm* 4:3), 'sound words' *1 Tm* 6:3; *2 Tm* 1:13) which must be opposed to 'strange doctrines' and 'subtleties' (*1 Tm* 1:3f) which restless spirits occupy themselves with. It is a 'profession of faith' of which we must never let go (*Heb* 4:14; cf. 3:1; 10:23), a 'faith' which has been 'entrusted' to the 'saints', i.e. the Christians, 'once and for all' and for which they must fight (*Jude* 3).

Behind the inevitable, and fertile, divergences that distinguish the theological elaborations of the different New

Testament writers from one another, there is then a fundamental datum from which they all start, on which they all build, and which they all begin by preaching when they want to conquer the world for the faith of Christ. On their lips and in their writings this datum is clothed in a formulation which is already fairly homogeneous, governed by the simplicity of the message itself and by the frequency with which it was repeated. It is not yet a 'Creed' with a definitively fixed text, but it is its prelude and its authentic source.

II. THE CONFESSIONS OF FAITH

Another kind of literary formation however appeared on the scene to combine with that of the Kerygma and prepare for the establishment of the Creed; that of 'confessions of faith'. These are formulas, often very short, which the Christians uttered on certain special occasions when they had to proclaim their faith. Issuing from the apostolic preaching, from which they drew their entire substance, these formulas are nevertheless distinguished from it, first by the precise occasions which determined their employment, and secondly by their literary form, which is even more lapidary and more stereotyped than that of the Kerygma. They seem to take pleasure in being as concise as a motto, a pass-word or a slogan. And this stripped and trenchant stylisation played its part in the composition of the Creed.

We can get some idea from the New Testament of the principal circumstances in the life of the Church which called out such confessions of faith. The first and most important of course was *Baptism*. In this act of initiation into the Christian life, the neophyte had to profess the faith which justified his admission; being baptised 'in the name' of Christ or of the Trinity (*Ac* 2:38; 8:16; 10:48; 19:5; *1 Co* 1:13-15; *Mt* 28:19); he had to proclaim his faith in that name (*Ac* 22:16). In fact, one passage in the Acts of the Apostles shows us the deacon Philip saying to the Ethiopian eunuch who had asked for baptism: 'If you believe with all your heart, you may', and the latter replying, 'I believe that Jesus is the Son of God' (*Ac* 8:37).

Other texts again could be explained very well as formulas having a baptismal origin: for example, *1 P* 3:18-22, where the elements which have a kerygmatic character (vv. 18, 19, 22) enclose an explicit mention of baptism; or *Ep* 4:4-6 where too baptism is mentioned: 'One Body and one Spirit . . . one Hope; one Lord, one Faith, one Baptism; and one God who is Father of all, over all, through all and within all'. *Rm* 10:9 and *1 Tm* 6:12, which we are going to examine shortly, could also have a baptismal origin.

The *Eucharist,* which was celebrated intimately among the baptised, was not of a nature to call out such confessions of faith. It would rather have been the occasion for kerygmatic catecheses on the institution of the rite by the Lord, such as that which St Paul utters in *1 Co* 11:23-5 and that which served as a basis for the narrative of the Last Supper in the Gospels (*Mk* 14:22-5). In return for this, however, *Exorcisms,* which also introduced the invocation of the Name of the Lord, must have used formulas of faith which would have been imposed to be respected and obeyed by the demons (cf. *Jm* 2:19; *Mk* 1:24; 3:11; 5:7). *Miraculous Cures* can also be assimilated to exorcisms, since sickness was believed to be of demonic origin and was expelled by invoking the Name (*Ac* 3:6; 3:13-16; 4:10). As for the 'profession' which Timothy made 'in front of many witnesses' (*1 Tm* 6:12), some interpreters believe it was made at the moment of his ordination to the priesthood (cf. *1 Tm* 4:14; *2 Tm* 2:2). It is true that others place it at a time of persecution, before a pagan tribunal, because of the allusion in v. 13 to the 'profession' made by Christ before Pilate; and it could again be merely a question of the profession of faith uttered by Timothy at his baptism.

We can be certain too that *persecutions by the pagan authorities* also called out confessions of faith: Christians, pressed to utter blasphemous formulas, opposed them victoriously with the profession of their faith in Christ. The detailed episode in the Martyrdom of St Polycarp (viii, 2), where the old bishop refuses to say 'Caesar is Lord', (*Kyrios Kaisar*) throws a striking light on the formula of faith 'Jesus is Lord' (*Kyrios Iesous*) which St Paul quotes on two occasions: *Rm* 10:9 'If your lips confess that Jesus is Lord and if you believe in your heart that God raised him from the dead, then you will be saved', and *1 Co* 12:3: 'no one can be speaking under the influence of the

Holy Spirit and say "Curse Jesus", and on the other hand, no
one can say, "Jesus is Lord", unless he is under the influence
of the Holy Spirit'. The first of these texts has been taken by
many interpreters to be a profession of baptismal faith, and this
is very probable, but it is very attractive to follow O. Cullmann
and recognise in the second at least an allusion to these declarations that Christians had to utter before the public authorities
and in which they had the confidence to see the inspiration of
the Holy Spirit (*Mt* 13:11).

   Polemic against the enemies of the faith, whether Jew,
pagan or heretic, was another occasion for the creating or
propagating of confessions of faith which condemned their
errors. It was necessary to prove to the Jews that 'Jesus is the
Messiah' (*Ac* 5:42; 18:5-28), and many exegetes have thought
that John has his eye on their refusal to believe when he exclaims: 'The man who denies that Jesus is the Christ—he is the
liar' (*1 Jn* 2:22). However, the particular way in which John
uses the word 'Christ' suggests that he is here visualising rather
the Docetist heresy, which denies the Incarnation. In fact, the
struggle against this heresy inspires him a little further on with
another formula which this time leaves no doubt: 'You can tell
the spirits that come from God by this: every spirit which
acknowledges that Jesus the Christ has come in the flesh is from
God; but any spirit which will not say this of Jesus (or, according to certain witnesses, which dissolves Jesus) is not
from God (4:2f). It is then the Incarnation and the Divinity of
Jesus that John proclaims in the two confessions of faith that
follow, which are practically equivalent: 'Whoever believes that
Jesus is the Christ has been begotten by God' (5:1) and 'If
anyone acknowledges that Jesus is the Son of God, God lives
in him, and he in God' (4:15).—As for the pagans, what has to
be maintained against them above all is monotheism; and this is
clearly the intention that inspires St Paul, in a contest where he
is combating idolatry, to utter this confession of faith: 'for us
there is one God, the Father, from whom all things come and
for whom we exist; and there is one Lord, Jesus Christ, through
whom all things come and through whom we exist' (*1 Co* 8:6).

   Finally, in the heart of the Christian community itself, the
solemn oath which took the divine Name to witness could have

been an occasion for the use of professions of faith: this is how *2 Tm* 4:1 is to be explained; and it throws some light on *1 Tm* 6:13 also.

It is evident that the various occasions we have just been envisaging are not mutually exclusive and the same confession of faith, for example 'Jesus is Lord', *'Kyrios Iesous'*, could be used at Baptism (*Ac* 8:6; 19:5; *Rm* 19:9) as well as in exorcisms (*Ac* 19:13) or before a tribunal (*1 Co* 12:3), and even as a mere liturgical invocation (*Ac* 7:59; *Rv* 22:20). These formulas were important in their own right, independently of the use that could be made of them, and there are some, like that in *1 Tm* 2:5, whose context no longer allows any precise circumstances to be assigned to them.

To these various circumstances in the life of the Church which gave rise to professions of faith, another cause must be added, *Liturgical Worship*. It too necessarily led to the expression of the faith in stylised and stereotyped formulas, but with a rhythm different from that of the confessions of faith, broader, less lapidary and more lyrical. In the New Testament we have traces of liturgical formulas of this kind. Sometimes they are very short invocations like the *Marana tha* of *1 Co* 16:22 (cf. *Rv* 22:20) or like 'The Lord is very near' of *Ph* 4:5. Sometimes they are doxologies as in *1 Tm* 1:17: 'To the eternal King, the undying, invisible and only God, be honour and glory for ever and ever. Amen' (cf. also *Rm* 11:36; 16:27; *Ph* 4:20; *Jude* 25; *Rv* 5:13; 7:12). Sometimes they are benedictions like that in *2 Co* 13:13: 'The grace of the Lord Jesus Christ, the love of God and the fellowship of the Holy Spirit be with you all'. And it has been suggested that the formulary of greetings and thanksgivings with which all the epistles of St Paul begin may take its inspiration from the words he uttered at the liturgical assemblies. Lastly, they are sometimes actual hymns that the Christians sang at their prayer-meetings (*Col* 3:16) and of which it is thought there are traces in *Ph* 2:6-11 and *1 Tm* 3:16, and perhaps also in *1 P* 2:21-4. It will be noticed that the content of these hymns is no other than the Kerygma of the abasement and exaltation of Christ, presented in a rhythmic and poetic mode.

But we must return to 'Confessions of faith' properly so-called, that is to those formulas which proclaim the Name to which the believer declares his allegiance. This name is ordinarily that of Christ, but it happens sometimes that the name of the Father is linked to it, and even that of the Spirit; this structure can develop from a simple to a tri-partite one, and it deserves to hold our attention since it is of interest for the trinitarian scheme of the Creed.

In actual fact, the simple or Christological formulas are the more numerous. Whether they record the word of salvation achieved by Christ, or select his titles of 'Messiah', 'Lord' or 'Son of God' from it, the kerygmatic proclamations and the confessions of faith mention most often only the person of Christ: it is he who is truly at the centre of the message. The 'by-partite' formulas, those which associate the person of the Father with him, are relatively less frequent. Besides *1 Co* 8:6 and *1 Tm* 6:13, which we have quoted above, there are two other texts from the pastoral epistles which are particularly adduced: *1 Tm* 2:5 'There is only one God, and there is only one mediator between God and mankind, himself a man, Christ Jesus, who sacrificed himself as a ransom for all', and *2 Tm* 4:1 'Before God and before Christ Jesus who is to be judge of the living and the dead, I put this duty to you'. As for the tri-partite form, which juxtaposes the three Persons of the Trinity, it is to be found, we are told, only in the order of baptism given in *Mt* 28:19 and in the liturgical blessing in *2 Co* 13:13.

From this state of affairs the conclusion has sometimes been drawn that the trinitarian form of the confession was later and was the result of an evolution which had slightly vitiated the meaning of the primitive faith. Not of course that faith in the Father and the Holy Spirit was not as primitve as that in Christ. But for the very first Christians of all, the former was a function of the latter: they believed in the Father and in the Spirit because of and in relation to the Son, in the Father as the One who raised Christ from the Dead, and in the Spirit as the Gift granted by Christ through Baptism. Christ being at the centre of the faith, to relegate him to the second place in a trinitarian confession would therefore be a distortion of tradition, it would be as it were to displace the centre of gravity in the object of faith.

This complaint, presented in particular by O. Cullmann, does not seem to be justified. It derives from a mistaken perspective which places too much importance on the confessions of faith and too little on the totality of the apostolic preaching contained in the Kerygma. The fact that the confessions of faith put the emphasis on the person or the work of Christ and most frequently do not go beyond that, can be explained easily by the very special circumstances that gave rise to them—the Christians were invoking the name of the Saviour to whom they were attaching themselves through a sacred rite, or affirming their belief in his true dignity as Christ, Lord or Son of God, against the false brethren, the Jews and the pagans who attacked him. But if we turn from the confessions of faith to the Kerygma in all its richness, we find the persons of he Father and the Spirit linked in an indissoluble fashion to the work of Christ from the very earliest epoch. Texts abound in the New Testament which associate either the Father and the Son, or the three Persons of the Trinity; and often they are expressed in formulas which, without being confessions of faith, nevertheless, with their stereotyped form, give us a glimpse of a very primitive tradition common to all.

It will be sufficient to quote as an example the formula 'Blessed be the God and Father of our Lord Jesus Christ' (2 Co 1:3, 11:31; Ep 1:3; cf. Col 1:3) whose origin as a doxology is obvious (cf. also Rm 15:6, where it is a question of being 'united in mind and voice' in the utterance of this formula); or again the formula of greeting adopted by St Paul in all his epistles from 2 Th on: 'Grace and peace to you from God the Father and the Lord Jesus Christ'. It is a remarkable thing that the other epistles, which do not adopt this specifically Pauline expression, nevertheless are careful to associate God and Christ in their prologues: cf. Heb 1:1-2; Jm 1:1; 2 P 1:1-2; Jude 1; 1 Jn 1:3; 2 Jn 3. Alongside these liturgical formulas many others could be adduced which reveal the constant habit of naming the Father and Son together: for example, 1 Th 3:11, 'May God our Father himself, and our Lord Jesus Christ, make it easy for us to come to you'; 2 Th 2:16, 'May our Lord

Jesus Christ himself, and God our Father . . . comfort you . . .';
1 P 4:11, 'So that in everything God may receive the glory,
through Jesus Christ'; *Rv* 1:2, John has 'written down . . . the
word of God guaranteed by Jesus Christ', etc. etc.

The harvest of texts with a manifestly trinitarian intention
would be no less rich. Here are some characteristic examples:
1 Co 6:11, 'You have been . . . justified through the name of
the Lord Jesus Christ and through the Spirit of our God: *1 Co*
12:4-6, 'There is a variety of gifts but always the same Spirit;
there are all sorts of service to be done, but always to the same
Lord; working in all sorts of different ways in different people,
it is the same God who is working in all of them': *Ep* 2:18,
'Through him (Christ), both of us have in the one Spirit our
way to come to the Father': *1 P* 1:2, 'Peter . . . to all . . . who
have been chosen, by the provident purpose of God the Father,
to be made holy by the Spirit, obedient to Jesus Christ and
sprinkled with his blood', etc. etc.

In reality, the whole message of the New Testament is
founded on faith in the concurrence of the Three divine Persons
in the accomplishment of salvation. And if it is true that the
Father and the Spirit are ordinarily considered in relation to the
work of the Son, it would be wrong to conclude from this
that the latter takes place in the faith. It is not possible to
subscribe to O. Cullmann's phrase, 'Because he believes in Christ
Kyrios, the first-century Christian believes in God and in the
Holy Spirit'. It is the contrary which is true: it is because he
believes in the Father who raised him and in the Holy Spirit
whose outpouring manifests his triumph in heaven that the
Christian believes in Jesus *Kyrios.* And if he wishes to express
the totality of his faith in the divine Name in a single formula,
it is logical that he should place the Father before the Son, as
being the one who sent him, delivered him over to death for our
salvation, then raised and exalted him, and that he should place
the Spirit after the Son, as being the one who is sent us from
heaven by the risen Christ to continue his work of salvation in
us. And in fact, this order is not only 'logical', it is 'chronological'; it is the very order of the history of salvation, such as it
emerges from the Holy Books and as we realised its presence
behind the Kerygma in Acts, such too as it is to be found again

in the sublime panorama of the divine plan of salvation at the beginning of the epistle to the Ephesians (1:4-14). This order is no other than that of the interventions of God in our human history. It is the order of our knowledge of the Trinity itself. Our faith in the Three divine Persons did not spring from speculations about their own intimate relations: these came later, in the course of theological elaboration. It is the Scripture itself that reveals the divine Persons through the actions which they have performed for us, creating, saving and sanctifying us. And it is this concrete faith, soaked in history, that is expressed by the trinitarian formula. By taking this as the framework of the Creed, the Church has perfectly preserved the authentic Scriptural orientation of primitive Christianity.

CONCLUSION

The historians of the Apostles' Creed have shown that it sprang from the combination of two formulas with different origins: on the one hand, the trinitarian confession of faith, and on the other a kerygmatic statement of the incarnation and redemption of Christ. These two types of formula, which arose in different circumstances and existed separately to begin with, were naturally brought together and associated in the life of the Church, notably in the liturgy of baptism. The association could be a mere juxtaposition (cf. Irenaeus, *Adversus Haereses,* I, 10:1); but more often it was managed by combining them, the Christological statement being inserted after the mention of the Second Person in the framework of the trinitarian confession. In this way our Creed was constructed. This elaboration took place in the second and third centuries, and we do not have to study it in this article. Our task has been to observe, from the first century, from the very beginning of the Church, the birth of these two types of formula which were to be fused in the Creed and we have been able to show that both equally issued from the teaching of the Apostles: the Christological statement was the result of the fixing of the Apostolic Kerygma the essential elements of which we found in all the New Testament writings; the trinitarian confession of faith derives from the earliest confessions and, if it is from the literary point of view the end-product of a certain evolution, it is no less a completely authen-

Pierre Maurice Benoit

tic expression of the way the first Christians came to know the Three divine Persons through the revelation of the history of salvation.

We have therefore very good reasons for saying that our Creed is truly 'Apostolic'. It is true that it was not composed in its present form by the Apostles: but it descends in a direct line, both in content and in form, from formulas received from the Apostles which expressed the essentials of the Christian message at the beginning of the Church. This is an assurance of the first importance for the firmness of our faith. And another no less fruitful lesson may be drawn from this study. It was in order to convert the world, to gather men to Christ, to conquer devils and fight the enemies of the faith, that our first brethren solemnly proclaimed their belief. Let us, when we utter again with our lips substantially the same formulas which they uttered before us, let us in our turrn make them, not a formal and individualistic declaration, but a proclamation intended to conquer the world, which is sure of its power because it is based on the witness of the Apostles, and through them on Christ.

385

John Lawrence McKenzie
1910-1955

John L. McKenzie was born in Brazil, Indiana, and graduated from Xavier University in 1932. He received a Master's degree from St. Louis University in 1935 and a doctorate in theology from Weston College in 1946. He has taught at West Baden College, Loyola University, and DePaul University. In 1963-1964 he was president of the Catholic Biblical Association.

McKenzie is one of a half-dozen scholars who have formed the real backbone of American Catholic Biblical renewal, and of the half-dozen he may well be the foremost. It is simply impossible today to recreate the scene upon which his Two-Edged Sword burst in 1956. American Catholic fundamentalism was widespread, largely because no alternatives had been offered. The anti-Modernist oath annually restrained seminary professors from straying too far from Lamentabili and Pascendi of a half-century before. The prevailing inclination was to view the Bible through the filter of Denzinger-Bannwart's Enchiridion.

McKenzie opened the field of modern Biblical studies, especially those concerning the Old Testament, to American Catholics at large. With his superb prose style, solid scholarship, and wry humor, he signaled the arrival of a new era. Reviewers greeted the book with enthusiastic acclaim, describing it as "supremely important," "a brilliant synthesis," "stimulating

THE CATHOLIC TRADITION: Sacred Scripture

and fascinating," "the most significant Catholic interpretation of the Old Testament ever written in English."

In 17 chapters the book handles all the major themes of Old Testament theology. The selection that follows consists of two of the best chapters: chapter two, "God Speaks to Man," and chapter 17, "The Old and New." The former deals with a theme that has been more troublesome than any other, especially among English-speaking Christians. The very notion of a "God who speaks" has often led to attitudes toward the Bible as His Word that tended to eliminate any human dimension whatsoever. McKenzie provides insight for side-stepping that fundamentalist trap.

His concluding chapter confronts another area of continuing controversy, how Old and New Testament are related. As long as there is a Bible and a Christian Church this will be a lively, relevant question. The sweeping historical survey which McKenzie provides and the alternatives he presents serve to promote a perspective in which to pursue this question intelligently. Few essays will be encountered which perform so helpful a function so effectively.

In the quarter-century since the Two-Edged Sword *appeared, McKenzie has continued to provide incomparable assistance to all who are interested in the Bible. His New Testament work,* The Power and the Wisdom, *his studies in Biblical theology,* Myths and Realities, *and his* Dictionary of the Bible *have all put American Christians yet further in debt to him. When the factors contributing to the renewal of American Catholicism in the age of Vatican II are tallied, high on the list will certainly be the name of John L. McKenzie.*

THE TWO-EDGED SWORD

The religion of the ancient Hebrews was based upon the belief that God can and does speak to man. Were we to count the number of times when God is said to speak to man in the Old Testament, we should find that they are scarcely less than the number of pages in the book. We can, it is true, draw a line after which the Old Testament books contain very few such allusions; it is the Great Divide of Hebrew history, the period of the Exile, roughly 587-536 B.C. When Ezra returned to Jerusalem from Babylon, he brought with him "the book of the law of the Lord"; but it is not said of him, as it was said of the prophets, "The word of the Lord came to Ezra." His near contemporaries, Haggai and Zechariah, received the word of the Lord; but there is a difference between them and the men of a century or two before. Judas the Maccabee and his companions, faced with the problem of what to do with the stones of the altar which had been polluted, put them away in a suitable place until a prophet should come and tell them what to do; the author, as well as Judas and his men, four hundred years after the Exile, seems sadly aware that the age of prophecy is past.

Can we trace anything like this belief in the religions of the ancient Semitic world? Revelation they knew, and chosen individuals, the vessels of divine revelation, they knew. Two thousand years before Christ, Gudea, the ruler of Lagash in Mesopotamia, learned in a dream the plan of the temple which he should construct. The diviners of Mesopotamia ascertained through the occult arts the intentions of the gods, and thus advised men how to meet the future. A seer of Ashurbanipal of Assyria had a dream in which the goddess Ishtar of Arbela gave him a message for the king. In the eleventh century B.C., an Egyptian ambassador to Byblos in Syria tells how a god seized a young man of the court of the king of Byblos, so that he spoke as one inspired; many scholars think they see a kinship between the young enthusiast and the Hebrew prophets. Monsignor Ronald Knox has recently studied religious enthusiasm and found it to be of wide, almost universal diffusion. The Hebrew belief that God speaks to man appears to be, at first glance, a manifestation of a universally human religious instinct.

Historians of religion, of course, have no difficulty explaining the phenomena of divine communication in ancient religions: it was a fraud or a superstition or an accepted convention. Men have always believed that the will of the gods was not altogether veiled from their sight; in one way or another they have sought it, and they have often believed they have found it: in the babblings of a fanatic, in the movements of the stars, in the liver of a sheep. One thinks that the logic of events would render this superstition entirely incredible, and it does; but the superstition persists. For even in the most debased forms of religion, the will of the gods is the factor of supreme importance in life; if it cannot be ascertained, then unbelief is the only attitude possible to a thinking man. If the will of the gods cannot be ascertained, it is entirely insignificant; if the gods were concerned with what men did, they would make their will known. Many of our contemporaries, aware of this, and aware also that the study of religion shows the human origin of many alleged divine communications, have renounced any belief that the will of God effectively touches human life. If this be true, then the Hebrew religion is based upon a falsehood; and it is a mere accident that the beliefs of the Hebrews have any more value for modern man than the beliefs of the headhunters of the Solomon Islands.

It is not our purpose to demonstrate that the Hebrew belief is sound, but merely to set it forth. It is important, however, to realize that the Hebrew belief that God speaks to man is fundamental. One cannot accept some of the Hebrew beliefs as valid for modern man and abandon the basis upon which they are proposed; for this leaves them precisely baseless, unfounded. One would then accept them because one likes them, or because they are in accord with what one believes already on quite other grounds. One finds the words of the Hebrew Bible appropriate to express one's own thoughts, or the thoughts of one's philosophy or theology, but not the thoughts of the Hebrew Bible. The words of the Bible are often torn from their context to ornament a system of thought or of belief which is a human invention.

If we examine the Hebrew belief in divine communication, we cannot fail to notice some obvious features which do not appear in other religions. The first is the large place which this belief occupies in Hebrew religion. Hebrew history, from the patriarchs to the fall of the kingdom of Judah, exhibits a series of men who claimed attention for no other reason than this, that they spoke in the name of the Lord. They recommended themselves not for their learning, their experience, their wisdom, their power, but for this only, that the word of the Lord had come to them. We find no such history in other religions, especially in those which were nearest to the Hebrews in time and place; this series of men arose in imitation of no one.

A second feature is the content of what these men spoke. If one goes through the divine communications of other religions, one sees that men's curiosity is less about the will of the gods than about the future. Not what the gods want them to do, but what is going to happen is the question which they addressed to their diviners. The Hebrews who spoke in the name of the Lord have no answer to such questions. The law and custom of the Hebrews prohibited the practice of the occult arts, the accepted and ordinary means of ascertaining the divine will throughout the ancient Near East. What these men had to say about the divine will was totally different. They proposed the will of the Lord as determining every activity and every department of human life, regulating it according to a moral standard which rose above anything which the world had yet seen. They spoke of the future, as we shall see; but they spoke of it to threaten evil if the standards of conduct which they set forth were not maintained. The priests and the diviners of the ancient Semitic world generally knew and kept their place, and did not attempt to direct the political and economic life of their people. It did sometimes happen that priestly circles, because of their wealth or superior knowledge, or because the power of superstition is very great, succeeded in acquiring control of secular affairs. But, when it happened, the priests succeeded to a secular power, which they employed for secular ends. Look again at the men of the word among the Hebrews. They remained outside secular ends and means. Power and influence they wished and they possessed, but it was not secular power. If they collided with secular power, it was a collision of two orders, not of two competitors in the same order. They proposed religion, the will of the Lord, as the supreme regulative power of all human activity. There were no others in the world of their time who did so.

A third feature which exhibits itself is the manner in which these men spoke. If we grant that Ezekiel had his trances, and that Elisha called for a minstrel before he spoke the word of the Lord, we can still see, without any need for discussion, that the Hebrew prophets spoke the word of the Lord with none of the external trappings of the seer and diviner of the ancient world. There is no abracadabra, no ranting and raving, no witches' brew from which they educe their mystic knowledge. They speak with passion, but not in a frenzy; they are in full possession of their minds. There is no sign of any adaptation of their message to the desires of their listeners; rather there is a studied effort to run counter to existing practices and prejudices, to overturn accepted conventions. They claim to be the spokesmen of the true and highest traditions of their people; but they are revolutionaries, come, like Jesus, "to cast fire on the earth," and "to bring not peace, but a sword." What seer or diviner of Egypt or Mesopotamia was hated for his message? Do we hear that any of them took and maintained a position in pertinacious hostility to king, nobles, wealthy, commoners at the hazard of his goods and his life? A classification which will include the Hebrew spokesmen of the Lord with the pliant priests and diviners of the ancient world must be broad indeed. Surely, we think, there can be no single explanation of two types of men so different. Surely there must have been factors operating in the Hebrew religious world which were not present in the ancient Semitic world at large.

Shall we find these factors in the "peculiar religious genius" of the Hebrews? We must not underestimate the creative powers of the human genius. The sophists of the Athenian market place did not produce Socrates. What makes the history of the human race differ from the history of the anthropoid ape is the rare but recurring emergence of men who can break out of the framework of their times and initiate a new departure: anonymous heroes like the men who invented the wheel and the alphabet, men better known like Socrates and Isaac Newton. The homely proverb has it that he was a bold man who first ate an oyster. More likely he was a hungry man, but necessity mothers boldness as well as invention; shall we suppose that he too was a bold man, driven by the necessity of some guidance for human conduct, who first arose and announced: "Thus saith the Lord"? Let us admit that the Hebrews had a peculiar religious genius to this extent, at least, that no other people has produced so many men who spoke as these did, and whose words have echoed so far: "their voice goes through all the world, and their words to the end of the earth." The Greeks also had a peculiar genius for philosophy, and abstract thought is their gift to the world. We Americans are accused of a peculiar genius for the machine; certainly no other people has given the world so many gadgets. No, the "peculiar religious genius" of the Hebrews is an attested fact. The question is: to what shall we attribute this genius?

Perhaps the question is idle, as meaningless as if we were to ask to what we should attribute the philosophical genius of the Greeks, or the military genius of the Romans. It is the essence of genius that we cannot account for it. But we must notice that the "peculiar religious genius" of the Hebrews can be found in a few men only. These men habitually accuse their countrymen of a peculiar obtuseness in matters religious; they are "dazed, blind, drunk, reeling, wrapped in deep slumber, with eyes closed and heads muffled," a people that does not hearken to the word of the Lord. It is incomprehensible how one can attribute the words of the prophets to a collective religious consciousness and think of them as the flowering of a folk creation. The prophets, it is true, had never heard of such a collective consciousness; the point is that their words are a denial of any such collective creative genius, and this apart from the fact that the prophets themselves attributed their words to

393

the Lord. We grant that the world has long been afflicted with men who claimed to be divine emissaries; but even the most broad-minded student of the history of religion does not wish to put the Hebrew prophets in the same class with Buddha and Mohammed. Again, the differences are far greater than the similarity. Should it not be within the compass of a peculiar religious genius to distinguish between the divine and the human? But we must not oversimplify. After all, we ought to consider the suggestion that the claim of the Hebrew prophets to speak in the name of the Lord is no more than a manner of speaking, proper to their culture. They were ignorant of psychological analysis, and perhaps what they call "the word of the Lord" can be explained, by careful analysis, as immanent: the product of their own minds, of the mysterious processes of genius, whose nature eludes even its possessors and is, consequently, attributed to some superhuman agent.

To satisfy ourselves about what the Hebrews meant, we shall have to look more closely at the great body of Hebrew letters, in which God speaks so often. We may, for the moment, omit the conversational level on which God deals with man in the first few chapters of Genesis; the Hebrews, like all other peoples, thought that things were quite different in the beginning from what they are now. The significance of this Hebrew belief is important, and it will be considered in its proper place; but it is not relevant to the question which faces us now. Let us rather remove ourselves to the time of the patriarchs: Abraham, Isaac, Jacob. These are historical figures, at least in the sense that they lived in historical times; we know the geography of the places in which they dwelt; we know a great deal about the kings and peoples of their times, and the spade of the archeologist has uncovered the remains of city walls and houses upon which their eyes could have fallen. It was the tradition of the Hebrews that no man knew the Lord when He said to Abram, "Leave your land, your relatives and your clan, and go to the land which I will show you." It was the same tradition that the Lord blessed the patriarchs and promised to bless more abundantly the great people which should spring from their loins. To them God speaks or appears, in what form we cannot say, or is seen and heard in a dream, and, in one startling episode, stops

and dines with Abraham as a guest. In such episodes as
Abraham's hospitality or Jacob's wrestling or Moses at the
burning bush, the story unfolds itself with such convincing
realism that we forget who is involved, and we are suddenly
shocked to recall that it is the Lord God who is an actor in the
story. The gods of Homer also mingled with men; but the gods
of Homer were frankly human, charming rascals. What, we
wonder, was the form and the voice and the manner which
was in the minds of the men who told such things of the Lord?
For the moment, at least, we cannot determine this; but it is
clear that the Hebrew tradition represented the patriarchs as
enjoying an easy familiarity with the Deity such as few men
have ever been believed to enjoy. And this easy familiarity was
at the basis of the Hebrew belief, for the Lord made himself
known to His people through the patriarchs; they felt themselves the heirs of the promises which He made to Abraham,
Isaac, and Jacob.

This easy familiarity was continued with Moses, the true
founder of the Hebrew nation. Of him more often than of any
other is it said that God spoke to him. The traditions of this
familiarity are not entirely of one piece; for, while "the Lord
used to speak to Moses face to face, as one man speaks to
another," "mouth to mouth, plainly and not in riddles," it is
also said that Moses was permitted to see only the back of the
Lord, and not His face. Of Moses are related the striking visions
of the burning bush and of Sinai; not only did the Lord give
Moses the two tablets inscribed with the law, but a whole collection of law which no two tablets could contain is ascribed to
the Lord Himself, to be enunciated through Moses. Throughout the journey from Egypt to the land of Canaan, the Lord
appeared to Moses in every crisis; and when the Lord threatened
to destroy this rebellious people, Moses argued and pleaded on
their behalf until the Lord relented and showed mercy. Again,
we wonder what form and figure lies behind these stories, or
what could be meant by the "face" and the "back" of Him
whom no man can see; but these questions do not alter the fact
that Moses is certainly represented as the spokesman of God,
and that his impact upon the history of Israel, and through
Israel upon the world, is that of a man who brought God to

his fellow men. To understand Moses as anything else is to rewrite the early history of Israel; and this has often been attempted.

We may pass over quickly the turbulent century or two known as the period of the Judges, when every man did what was right in his own eyes; we pass it over with some regret, for we omit the picturesque stories of Gideon and of the parents of Samson. We pass over Joshua even more easily, for tradition described him as a lesser Moses. But with the beginning of the Hebrew monarchy under Saul and David we enter the period of the prophets; and prophecy is a unique Hebrew phenomenon which demands some consideration in detail. We lump together under the one word "prophecy" a great many diverse personalities and incidents which might perhaps be better distinguished; but we are thinking here of the one thing which was proper to prophecy: the word of the Lord. "The word of the Lord" is the consecrated phrase which describes the experience of every man who is called a prophet. The name is given to men as different as Samuel, who would recover lost articles for a small fee, and Isaiah, whose stately dignity did not prevent him, at the word of the Lord, from walking naked and barefoot through the streets of Jerusalem, and Elijah, who dwelt solitary in the wilderness and wore a rough garment of animal skin, and Elisha, who cursed small boys. They are a strange and not entirely attractive group of men, these prophets, and they are not all cast in heroic mold. It is worth notice, and we shall have to recall it again, that the word of the Lord did not ennoble him to whom it came; the Lord can slay a thousand with the jawbone of an ass. It was not by the flash of intelligence or of character that the prophets affected history, but by that two-edged sword, the word of the Lord.

The bare words, "the word of the Lord came to X," do not tell us much about the experience itself. To discover what the words mean, we shall have to find some more circumstantial accounts of what befell the prophets. The material for this, while not abundant, is ample enough to take us a good part of the way. We have the story of the call of Samuel; the Lord called him while he slept, and the boy thought it was the voice of the old priest Eli in the adjoining room. We have the magnificent experience of Elijah on Mount Horeb; the prophet heard a mighty wind, felt an earthquake, saw the flash of lightning, but the Lord was present in the barely perceptible movement of a gentle breeze. We have the story of Micah ben Imla, who saw the Lord with all His heavenly retinue. We have Ezekiel's vision of the marvelous chariot upon which the Lord sat enthroned. But we shall find out most about the mind of a prophet if we consider the experiences of two men, Isaiah and Jeremiah.

Of Isaiah is related what is called his inaugural vision: the experience by which he knew himself commissioned as a prophet, in which he first received the word of the Lord. He was in the temple, and he saw the glory of the Lord: the swish of the skirts of the robe of a gigantic enthroned figure, the sound of heavenly beings chanting, "Holy! Holy! Holy!" and he felt himself doomed, for he, an unclean mortal, knew he was in the presence of Divinity. Yet when a voice asked of no one in particular, "Whom shall we send?" he could not help answering, "Here I am; send me." And there follows a commission to speak the word of the Lord which is itself a brief summary of what the prophet subsequently said. With his lips cleansed by a burning coal in the hands of a seraph, he is fit to speak the word of the Lord.

Now, there are those who would see in this a story entirely imaginary. The invisible Lord is not a robed figure of gigantic proportions. It is a strange seraph which would need tongs to pick up a red-hot coal, and a strange coal which would cleanse the prophet's lips without searing them off. Isaiah was not unskilled in creative imagination; the hot coal symbolizes very well the contrast between the impure lips of man and the pure word of God. And we have no reason to deny that Isaiah clothed his inaugural experience in imaginative vesture. But we should not make the mistake of thinking that he himself created the idea that the Lord had called him to be a prophet. Critics often forget that, if God is going to communicate with man directly, there is almost certainly going to be some psychic disturbance; for the experience can scarcely be called normal. If a severe blow can make one see stars, we hesitate to say what a man would see if God spoke to him. All who have had the experience attest that there was a psychic disturbance. For Isaiah, the psychic disturbance resulted in a lasting sense of the profound gulf between the holiness of God and the unholiness of man, a gulf which only the Lord can bridge. Behind his words one can always discern the sublime and dimly seen figure of the vision, the thrice Holy One; here is the conviction that gives force to his words. He spoke of this as no one else had spoken; and he tells us, very simply, that he so spoke of it because once in his life he had seen the Lord and known, as he could not otherwise have known, what the holiness of God means. If this be delusion, let us have more of it.

Jeremiah, too, had an inaugural vision, but he saw not even the skirts of the robe. He heard the Lord tell him he was predestined to be a prophet; far from volunteering, he pleaded youth and slowness of speech. The answer was: "Go wherever I send you." Then the Lord gave him speech; the Lord touched his mouth, and put His own word in the mouth of Jeremiah. This vision, too, leaves its impress on the career of Jeremiah; for he is not only a man with a message, he is a man under compulsion. Again and again he expresses his own loathing for the hateful message he has for his people, that they are perishing by their own wickedness. Again and again he complains of the hatred and persecution which the word of the Lord brings him, opposition he would gladly end by keeping silence. But he cannot keep silence; for "the word of the Lord is in my heart like a burning fire; I am worn out with holding it, I cannot endure it." And, when his courage nearly fails, he senses of a sudden that the Lord is with him, keeping him, as the Lord promised him in the inaugural vision, "a fortified city, a column of iron, a wall of bronze."

More than this Jeremiah tells us; for he is almost the only one of the prophets to speak of what we now call "false prophets." They too claimed the word of the Lord; and we cannot tell now whether they were the sincere victims of their own delusion or dishonest pretenders. But they called themselves and were thought to be prophets. Jeremiah knew that they felt no compulsion such as that under which he suffered. They ran when they were not sent, they prophesied when the Lord had not spoken to them; they had not stood in the circle of the friends of the Lord and heard His words. They prophesied the delusions of their own mind, lies in the name of the Lord. If the prophet has a dream, let him tell his dream; if he has the word of the Lord, let him speak the word of the Lord.

All these things indicate that Jeremiah was not unaware of the problem of the origin of the word of the Lord, as it has been raised by modern scholars; he was troubled by the possibility that men can believe that their own thoughts are the word of the Lord. Was it possible that he himself was so deluded? Against this possibility he had only that overpowering sense of "otherness" in the word of the Lord; and he knew, as one knows his own mind, that those who gave him the lie had no such sense of compulsion. Yet how could he prove it? To those who challenged his commission he gave a response that seems remarkably feeble: earlier prophets who had threatened evil had usually been right, and those who had said that all is well had usually been wrong; therefore let us wait and see. Not spectacular, this, and scarcely to be compared with the story related of Samuel, who, at a much less critical juncture of Hebrew history, called upon an unseasonal thunderstorm to justify himself; much less impressive than the story of Elijah on Mount Carmel, who challenged the Lord to prove Himself God by lightning on demand. Was the hand of the Lord shortened in the days of Jeremiah, or was Jeremiah of so much less faith? In any case, the answer of Jeremiah is more reassuring than thunder and lightning because it is so genuinely human. It is as certain an attestation as we could wish of the tremendous integrity of his character, the thing that separates him decisively from the false prophets; if anyone ever tried to separate the precious from the vile, the word of the Lord from the word of man, it was Jeremiah, who was flogged and imprisoned because, despite the revolt of his whole being, he could not escape the compulsion that it was the word of the Lord. Let critics join him in his muddy cistern before they quickly judge that he, like the false prophets, could not tell the word of the Lord from his own psychic processes.

We are, of course, faced with the question of analogy. We Catholics believe that Ridley and Latimer were in error; yet Latimer urged Ridley to play the man, and they died bravely for their error. Courage and integrity of character are not found exclusively on the side of truth; men have died bravely for error, as they have surrendered cravenly in defending the truth. Yet there is something about the experience of Jeremiah which puts it into another class. Whether for truth or for error, men must convince themselves that their beliefs are true before they will put forth their all on their behalf; the testimony of Jeremiah is that he did not convince himself, but was convinced by another. His doubts were never resolved, they were simply smothered. He was an unwilling witness. He was strong, but not with his own strength. One cannot think that he, like many others, stuck to his task because he was unwilling to reverse his whole life and admit that he had been wrong all the time. There was nothing he would rather do.

We should not rashly extend what we say of Jeremiah to all those whom we call prophets, even if he himself expresses an awareness of continuity with the prophets of the past. Yet there is a community of idiom among them—"The word of the Lord came," "Thus says the Lord," and a dozen such set phrases which occur in all the books of the prophets. There is a community of visual and auditory allusions to heavenly sights and sounds. Most striking of all, there is a community of content, obvious if one reads the books, which we shall have to discuss at length in later chapters. Thus we have little evidence of such an inner conflict in other prophets as we have in Jeremiah; but we have no reason to think that the prophetic diction in them expresses anything else than the same overpowering sense of otherness. With Jeremiah, we can be sure that the man who lacked this sense was no prophet.

But there were other channels also among the Hebrews in which God was deemed to speak to man; we have to look at these somewhat carefully, for it would be a mistake, it seems, to put them on the same level with prophetic consciousness. What was the mysterious device called "Urim and Thummim," mentioned several times in the stories of Saul and David? One "asked the Lord," and the Lord answered through Urim and Thummim. From the nature of the questions and the answers, it is clear that this device was oracular, quite similar to the oracular devices of the diviners; and we have no reason to think that it was other than a survival of primitive usage,

through which the Lord was thought to unveil the future, probably by the casting of lots. Here we have a combination of popular superstition and a conventional manner of speaking. The
device was no more and no less a revelation of the will of the
Lord than the modern Christian device of seeking the will of
God by opening the pages of the Bible at random. The Urim
and Thummim do not appear after the time of David; in a more
enlightened age there was no room for this primitive device. It
seems evident that it would be a false logic to compare this
device with the prophetic consciousness.

The priests also were channels through which God spoke
to men. They possessed the traditions of the law and custom
through which Hebrew worship and Hebrew life were regulated.
This was "the law of the Lord," for the Lord had given it to
Moses. Yet, with changing social and political conditions, new
problems arose to which the old laws gave no solution. In such
instances, one consulted the priests, and their answer was an
answer of the Lord Himself, for they spoke in His name. If
their answer became an integral part of the law and custom, it
was incorporated into the code, and became a part of the law
of the Lord. Did the priests speak in the name of the Lord as
the prophets did? Hardly; for in the priests we have the basis of
a conventional manner of speech: the priestly authority. They
spoke with the authority of their office, they interpreted the
law of the Lord, or answered questions, or adjudicated disputes
according to the law of the Lord. They expressed the will of
the Lord much as the religious superior expresses the will of
God to his subjects; but they do not exhibit that sense of otherness which we find in the prophets.

But we do meet the question: in what sense is that body of
law which is contained in the four latter books of Moses "the
law of the Lord"? Are we to extend the story of the two tablets,
"written by the finger of the Lord," to cover that vast bulk of
precepts and prohibitions? Open the book of Leviticus at random, and we meet such a sentence as this: "Say to the sons of
Israel: The following are the creatures that you may eat, of all
the animals on the earth: any animal with a cloven hoof that
chews the cud you may eat"; and there follows an enumeration
in which the hare is called unclean because it has not a cloven

hoof, although it chews the cud! The picture of Moses writing this unbiological sentence at the dictation of the Lord is one at which the most devout mind is startled. One thinks of the words of St. Paul: "Is God concerned with oxen?"

But there is more to the question than this. Since the beginning of the twentieth century, many codes of law, some almost complete, have been recovered from the ancient Semitic world of which the Hebrews were a part. When these are read, similarities in detail with Hebrew laws appear which approach very closely to identity. The law which required the man who seduces a virgin to pay the marriage price and marry her is not even a wise law, by modern standards of conduct; it may have been wise in the ancient world, but could not God leave the ancients to settle such problems in their own way, as He leaves us to settle ours? A large number of Hebrew laws are obviously derived from the common law of the ancient Semitic world. In 1902, there was discovered at the site of ancient Susa a massive column of hard stone on which were inscribed the laws of Hammurabi of Babylon, who was a near contemporary of Abraham, four to five hundred years before Moses. In several dozen instances, the resemblance between the code of Hammurabi and the Hebrew codes is very close. Some have thought that the law of Moses not only used the code of Hammurabi as a legal source, but also imitated it in its account of the stone tablets. This impression is not correct; Hammurabi is grateful to the gods for giving him the kingdom and maintaining his power, but he does not attribute the laws to them.

It must be granted that the attribution of the mass of material called the law of Moses to the dictation of God Himself has made it extremely difficult for many to accept any idea of God speaking to man in the Old Testament. And since this attribution was a theological commonplace for many centuries, it was hard to see how it could be abandoned or modified without abandoning what we have called basic in the religion of the Hebrews: the belief that God can and does speak to man. Modern studies of ancient legal collections enable us not only to put the "law of Moses" more clearly in its historical perspective, but to explain it as "the law of the Lord" without fearing that we stultify ourselves. The Hebrew law is a collection of collections, an amassing of laws and customs which arose in various times and places, and which were ultimately gathered in a single corpus under the name of Moses, the Lawgiver. How many of these laws go back to the time of Moses modern criticism has not determined in detail, and it probably never will. But we can see that the picture of Moses receiving all these laws from the hand of the Lord is imaginary, the figured idealization of his position as the emissary of the Lord and founder of the Hebrew commonwealth.

Do we thereby take away from Moses the authority which Hebrew tradition accorded him, and put him in the limbo of legend with Minos of Crete and Arthur of Camelot? Before we do so, let us recall that without Moses there is no such thing as a Hebrew people or a Hebrew religion. Moses in Hebrew tradition is the man through whom the Lord and the people were joined. If Moses did not exist, to borrow a phrase, we should have to invent him. The religion of the Hebrews is a singular episode in the history of man's quest for God, and it demands a singular cause. Hebrew tradition gives us Moses, and we had better take him. In the long line of spokesmen of the Lord who pass through Hebrew history Moses is the first and the greatest. If he was not of the prophets, then there were no prophets, for they all presuppose him. His story raises questions which the story of Jeremiah does not raise just because he was the first. There is no comparison between the story of Jeremiah, partly autobiographical and partly collected from contemporary or very nearly contemporary accounts, and the stories of Moses and the patriarchs. Moses has acquired a halo and a haze of glory in the tradition; his often told story has been overlaid with such touches of grandeur as attach themselves to every great historical figure. It seems unsound to attempt a precise analysis of the Hebrew idea of divine communication on the basis of such stories as that of the burning bush or the Sinai theophany, stories which have been embellished by the vivid imagination of the popular storyteller. On the other hand, the story of Moses, however it be understood, exhibits the same sense of otherness which we find in the prophets; to remove this is to remove Moses from history altogether.

403

There is yet another way through which the Hebrews found that God spoke to men, and this is through the wisdom of the sages. The book of Proverbs tells us that "the Lord gives wisdom; out of His mouth come knowledge and reason." The same idea is expressed in the story of Solomon, the very model of the wise man, who asked the Lord for wisdom rather than riches and honor, and received it; for his prayer was itself the proof of his wisdom. Evidently, however, we are not dealing here with an experience like that of the prophets. What the wise man says is the fruit of the Lord's gift, but it is the word of the wise man; the wise man will deliver his wisdom to his son, and the wisdom of the ages will be accumulated. Without doubt the Hebrews believed that such a blessing as wisdom was a gift of the Lord, and this belief also has its significance; but they do not speak of wisdom as the prophets spoke of the word of the Lord.

This sketch of the Hebrew idea of the communication of God with man has, up to this point, left us with an irreducible core of belief in something which we have designated "an over-powering sense of otherness." It is more than this; but how much more depends on our answer to some further questions. Must we suppose that Jeremiah heard the sound of a voice impinging upon his ear from some invisible source? How could Isaiah see the skirts of the Lord's robe, when he knew as well as we do that the Lord is invisible and has no robe? We spoke earlier of the convincing realism of many of the accounts of the conversation of God with men. Does this realism force us to admit that God did, in the obvious sense of the words, "speak with Moses face to face, as one man speaks to another," or that God took dinner with Abraham, and debated with him the fate of Sodom? No believing Christian can doubt the condescension of God; for if He has condescended to become a man, there is no loss of dignity in speaking with man. But the believing Christian is not less a believer if he wishes to know more exactly how the divine communication became perceptible. Did the prophets, as they spoke the word of the Lord, repeat phrases which they heard ringing like a bell within them?

The last question is the easiest to answer. If the prophets spoke in this way, it is strange that they should speak each in his own language and in his own style. If the Lord spoke to Isaiah in this crassly material manner, then He spoke exactly as Isaiah would speak to himself; and the same is true of each individual prophet. We meet again the obtrusive human element, which forbids us to make men lifeless tools of the divine. God uses them in the manner proper to their nature; that is, He uses them as they are, to the full extent of their distinct personality, their powers of mind, heart, tongue. That the prophets parroted what God dictated is as impossible as the idea that the writers of the sacred books were unthinking stenographers.

We may find a key to the things which the prophets saw and heard if we look to the experiences of Christian mystics. This strange phenomenon of communication with the world of the supernatural has been constant in the history of Christianity. There has been much pseudo-mysticism, perhaps more than we know, and the Church never speaks a final word about the mystical phenomena which are attested. She has no real test of the genuinity of the phenomena except her own faith and the performance of the mystic; if the alleged mystic leads a truly Christian life, if the mystic exhibits heroic Christian virtues, then there is no reason to doubt that the mystic has experienced God in an extraordinary manner. Yet even the true mystic may be occasionally deceived, and no one is more aware of this than the mystic himself. It is remarkable how some pretenders have been able to deceive wise and holy men by false claims to mystical experience, perhaps for many years. There is little in the mystical phenomenon itself, even when it appears in such sober and reasonable people as St. Theresa of Avila or St. Francis de Sales, to prove that it is what the mystic believes it to be, or claims it to be. Many Christians have a fanatic curiosity for novel revelations, and there are always those who for vanity or for gain will satisfy them.

Now it is immediately obvious, if one looks at mystical phenomena, that there is a startling diversity in its character in different people. One cannot imagine St. John of the Cross having the experience of St. Margaret Mary Alacoque, or St. Ignatius Loyola speaking of God in the manner of St. Therese of the Child Jesus. Even in the mystical experience, God is, so to speak, refracted through the personality of the mystic, and apprehended according to the capacities of the one to whom He reveals Himself. We see this diversity in the sensible and external effects of the mystical experience, and so the mystics describe it. They also see things and hear things, their members are affected, they may be rendered unconscious. The mystics tell us that such things are a sign not of holiness, but of the weakness of human nature, and that the highest experience of God is elevating and inspiring, without any external disturbance. They do not confuse the sights and sounds aroused in their sensible perceptions with God Himself; at least, they do their best to avoid this confusion, admitting that it is easily possible and that it often happens. The experience of God, they tell us, is indescribable in human language; the more easily it is described in sensible image, the farther removed it is from the reality. But the experience of God has a tremendous effect upon one's life, giving it new perspective and purpose, new strength and endurance. The Church, as we have seen, judges the genuinity of these experiences by performance. If there is no change in the life of the mystic, the Church is not much interested in the external phenomena, however spectacular they may be. She does not wish Christian holiness to become a sideshow.

If, then, we view the experiences of the prophets in the light of what we can learn from Christian mysticism, we see that that phenomena found in the prophets are of a piece with those found in the mystics. "The word of the Lord" is the shattering experience of the divine reality, with repercussions in the sensible and emotional activity of the prophet. But, just as the mystics do not confuse these sensible and emotional reactions with the experience of God Himself, neither should we, in reading the prophets, identify these peripheral fireworks with the prophetic experience itself. They are not the divine reality. If we look for the transformation of the prophet, the alteration of his life into new dimensions and a new perspective, we see it beyond doubt, especially in Jeremiah. To the prophets we may apply the test of performance, although we should note again, as we remarked above, that the word of the Lord does not of itself ennoble one. There were small and imperfect men among the prophets, as we shall have to point out, just as there have been many whose mystical experiences we can hardly doubt, although the experiences did not raise them to the level of heroism. Even so moving an experience as mysticism does not force men to do that which they really do not want to do; and even "the word of the Lord" did not make a man that which he really did not want to be.

We seem to have reduced "the word of the Lord" to something indescribable, and so to have brought ourselves up against a blank wall. Certainly there is something in the supernatural which ultimately escapes analysis; there is a frontier beyond which experience and analogy cannot pass. But the supernatural does not elude our grasp altogether. This experience of which we are speaking is described by those who know it as a knowledge of the reality of God more profound than is possible by faith or by thinking. It is an awareness of His present and immediate reality in the prophet himself, in the world, in other men, in the course of nature, in the course of human events. It is a marvelously keen perception of the living personality of God; to this thought we shall have to return, for it is one of the most striking features of the Hebrew belief in God that it always sees God with sharply defined personal traits. It is a sense of the divine immediacy which is at once terrible, since it made Isaiah fear for his life, and consoling, since it made Jeremiah secure because the Lord was with him as a dreaded warrior. We cannot call it vision, and we cannot call it hearing or feeling, for God cannot be perceived on the sensible level; God is perceived in what St. Teresa called the interior of the soul. But we cannot, unless we reject all the evidence there is on the question, reduce this experience to any kind of normal sensible or intellectual activity. Without exception, this knowledge of God, wherever it appears, is described as something impressed upon the soul by an over-powering agent outside the soul itself, who thus makes Himself unmistakably known as a human person makes himself unmistakably known.

Such a terribly immediate awareness of the divine alters entirely one's habits of thought. The prophet has a sharper perception of the difference between good and evil, and a finer insight into the unspeakable consequences of human malice. In a way, he comes to share God's attitude toward good and evil. Because he sees the divine reality so clearly, he sees human life as a process tending toward a term, which is God; and he knows that this process must be directed by God, not by man, a direction which man cannot finally avert. He sees the urgency of the divine imperative which governs human life, for he sees this imperative in the will of God as he has felt it. The sense of the divine reality is a glowing light within his mind, casting its beams upon everything which falls within the scope of human knowledge, bringing out each object in sharper focus; in the clarity of this light he sees things somehow as God sees them, and he formulates his words, "the word of the Lord," with all the intensity of feeling and language which he has at his command.

This, indeed, may not be "revelation" in the accepted sense, and we do not intend to speak of revelation in this sense; we make an effort—slow and stumbling, we know, but an effort—to reach into the psychological wellspring of revelation, to enter into a mind where God meets man "face to face." Here one feels that one is an intruder. But our modern sophistication has forced us into many places where our fathers feared to tread; if we do not attempt some analysis of the psychology of prophecy, others will do it for us. There are many modern studies of the subject, few of which are in even substantial harmony with Catholic belief. What we think we have found in the prophet's mind is, we believe, not that which one finds in great creative minds. The processes of genius, as we have noticed, are not easily analyzed; the possessor of genius cannot easily explain the brilliant intuition which is the mark of his gift. We do not mean to call the prophet's insight into God and the world and human nature a "brilliant intuition"; for a brilliant intuition lacks the overpowering sense of otherness which is the mark of the prophet. Socrates said that he was impelled to speak to the Athenians by a "demonic being"; he left it purposely vague and tantalized us beyond patience. Was he merely exercising the famous Socratic wit, and prodding his adversaries, who thought themselves the defenders of piety and orthodoxy, with the hint that he also had an otherworldly guide? Or did the phrase mean any more than "the devil in me"? In any case, it is merely a passing allusion in the life of Socrates; and we really should not make the comparison.

John Lawrence McKenzie

It is worth our attention to notice how this sense of the Lord. More often than not, the prophets deliver the word of the Lord in the first person; usually with an introductory formula, but not always. If the prophet begins to speak in his own person, he will easily lapse into speech in the person of the Lord. This does not, as we have seen, indicate that the prophet was echoing an inner voice; but it does indicate the close communion with the Lord which was the fruit of his mystic insight. We have said that the prophet shared, in a way, in God's views; he knew that his thoughts were clarified by that divine illumination, his emotional response was a human expression of the divine attitude, and he spoke the word of the Lord with a full conviction that he was one with the Lord in whose name he spoke. This exhibits the mystical character of his experience, and at the same time shows the gulf which lies between the word of the Lord and the brilliant intuitions of creative genius. Genius is self-conscious, aware and proud of its power; it does not lose itself in identification with another, even if that other be God. In the prophets we constantly strike against that hard core of "otherness," the sense of something real and objective which is not themselves. Modern writers sometimes speak of the "irrational" in the prophetic consciousness, and the word is apt, if properly understood. The irrational is that which cannot be resolved into its component parts, which is beyond exact calculation; it is something which normal experience and scientific analysis cannot account for, and that something is God.

Shall we call the prophets abnormal? Many modern students of the prophets look for the key of the prophetic experience in abnormal psychology. This approach is not very flattering to the prophets, for abnormal psychology is the study of the malfunctioning of the mind. In this sense, certainly, we do not like to have the prophets called abnormal; and we do not believe that any analysis has shown them to be abnormal, in the technical sense of the word. Mental disorders are classified in certain patterns; the layman will say simply that his neighbor is crazy, but the clinical psychologist will put a name to what he observes. If the prophets are abnormal in the technical sense, then they ought to exhibit certain symptoms and certain patterns; and these the analysts have failed to give us. An isolated instance of abnormal behavior, if it were a sign of mental disorder, would have us all behind bars; for normal mental and emotional stability is far from a perfect equilibrium. The application of such principles to the prophets is ridiculous, and perhaps we should not mention it, except to show how far men will go rather than admit the personal intrusion of God into human life and human affairs.

But the prophets are abnormal in the popular sense of the word, just as genius is abnormal; and if the line between genius and insanity is very thin, as we hear, then perhaps the line between prophecy and insanity is very thin also. Genius does not appear except in persons of extremely delicate sensibilities, and their very sensitivity, which is their strength, is also the weakness which makes it possible for the mind to break down. No doubt the word of the Lord could come to the dull and unimaginative and unfeeling person whom we usually call "normal," but it seems that it rarely did so, if at all; and if it did, its utterance would be comparatively dull, unimaginative, and unfeeling. The fire of Amos burns low in Haggai; and we have all heard the words of the Gospels, which are spirit and life, reduced to intolerable dullness by spiritless preaching. We could infer for ourselves, even if we did not have the introspection of Jeremiah to inform us, that the word of the Lord was a dreadful psychological burden, mentally and emotionally fatiguing; and we should not be surprised if nature occasionally bent under the strain. Prophecy, again like genius, made its possessor a lonely man; the singularity of his psychic processes isolates him from his fellows, for there is no one with whom he can share his thoughts and feelings about the thing to which his life is dedicated. The prophet cannot expect understanding and sympathy from his fellows; he is closer to the Lord than he is to any man.

We have attempted to sketch here something of the way in which God speaks to man: to put the Hebrew belief that he did so into our own language. We believe that God did speak to man, but we have observed that it is not our primary purpose to argue this point; we are more concerned with showing that this belief cannot be analyzed out of the Hebrew faith without essentially altering our own estimate of that faith. We cannot escape, in the Old Testament, the pervading conviction that God intrudes Himself into the minds of men in an extraordinary but thoroughly objective manner, and that men, possessed of this awareness, become His spokesmen. They remain men, and they sometimes remain men who are petty; but Hebrew faith in the Lord God is meaningless apart from this fundamental belief, that they knew Him at all only because He spoke to them.

CHAPTER XVII

THE OLD AND NEW

At the very dawn of Christianity, the relations between the Old Testament and Christianity became an acute question. For Jesus came into the Jewish world as the fulfillment of the Old Testament. The Jews who refused to accept Him as the fulfillment of the Old Testament were forced by the logic of their position to treat their sacred books as terminal, and themselves, ultimately, as the fulfillment of these books. The cleft between Judaism and Christianity took form very early, and it has remained to the present day. We no longer witness the type of controversy between Jews and Christians which was common in the infancy of the Church; many modern Jews and Christians are only vaguely aware of the basis of their separation. But they are divided not only on what they think of Christ, but on what they think of the Old Testament.

In the second century of the Christian era, there appeared in the Church a man named Marcion. Marcion reacted to the Jewish claims of the Old Testament in a startling manner. Let the Jews, he said, have their sacred books, for these books are Jewish; they are not Christian. Marcion asserted that the God of the Old Testament was not the God of the New Testament, that His character and attributes were contradictory to the character and attributes of the Father whom Jesus revealed. God had not revealed Himself to the Jews, their sacred books had no relationship to the New Testament, and had nothing to contribute to the faith of Christians. The Church, of course, could not tolerate such views, and expelled Marcion and his followers, thus affirming the unity and continuity of the two Testaments.

But the relationship between Old and New Testaments did not thereby become a settled issue. We do not intend to take the reader through centuries of discussion and dispute, because such a review would weary even professional theologians. The discussions were not concerned with the unity and continuity of the two Testaments, for this was an accepted doctrine of the Church; they revolved rather about the meaning of this unity, and its application to Christian belief and Christian life.

We have seen that the Bible was the prayer book of the early Church, as it has remained the prayer book of the modern Church. Outside of this, the Old Testament was considered in the early Church as a book which spoke of Christ. We are in danger of stating here the opinions of the Fathers of the Church too simply, and we are sensible of the possibility of rebuke; but we are trying to sum up in a few paragraphs a vast intellectual movement, and it is scarcely possible not to oversimplify. This view of the Old Testament was a reaction, in the first place, to the Jewish denial that Jesus was the Christ; but, in addition, these men thought that the Old Testament, since it is so much more extensive than the New, should tell a great many things about Christ that the New Testament does not tell. The further question, then, was: How does Christ appear in the Old Testament? For it is obvious that the Old Testament is not superficially concerned with Him. Let us pause and try to recapture the thinking of the Fathers of the Church about this problem. They saw no reason why the Old Testament should have been written except that it should speak of Christ. If it did not speak of Him, it would not be a Christian book, and the Jews and Marcion would be right. They saw that the New Testament appeals to the Old, and they believed that, if they could formulate the principles behind the quotations of the Old Testament in the New, these principles could be extended to the entire Old Testament.

There are two ways, the Fathers said, in which Christ can be found in the Old Testament, and these two admit subdivisions: in prediction and in preparation. The predictions may be, or may be thought to be, explicit and formal; if they are, nothing is necessary except to identify them. But even the

Fathers could find relatively few of these within the Old Testament. Therefore most predictions were, they thought, uttered in type or figure; and this requires a little explanation.

This use of the Old Testament, called "typology," has a good foundation in the New Testament. In recent times the basis of New Testament typology has been closely studied, and we can now see more clearly its background in the Jewish interpretation of the Old Testament with which most of the New Testament writers were familiar. There is a fundamental similarity between Old and New Testaments which rests upon a community of ideas, of beliefs, of language. It is the same God whose saving will is revealed in each of the Testaments. Hence one can point out similarities between exhibitions of His saving power, as between the exodus of the Hebrews from Egypt and the exodus of the neophyte from sin through baptism; both were passages through water. Jewish interpretation, which sought the meaning of every single word of the Bible, found such similarities in the words themselves, "catchwords," or in merely external features of the narratives. The method and its purpose are intrinsically sound, for they rest upon a belief of the unity of Old and New Testaments which permits us to illustrate one by the other, and thus to arrive at a deeper understanding of the whole. A searching examination of the use of the Old Testament in the New reveals that typology is much more restrained than it has often been thought to be; unfortunately, these restraints were not always imitated by some of the Fathers who cultivated typology.

We alluded in our first chapter to the modern revival of this kind of interpretation. One takes a text the sense of which, understood by itself, is not concerned with Christ at all—so, for instance, the ark of Noah or the tabernacle which the Hebrews constructed in the desert. But, since the Old Testament, as these Fathers understood it, always and everywhere speaks of Christ, there must be some deeper meaning in these items; and so both the ark and the tabernacle are understood to signify the Church which Jesus founded, either in general or in some particular aspect. For the Old Testament speaks of Christ not only in His life and person, but also in His mission; and it contains in type and figure the whole of the Christian

413

dispensation. Many of the Fathers of the Church thought that God revealed the entire Christian dispensation to such spiritual giants of the Hebrews as Moses and the prophets; but the prophets could not communicate this revelation, because their people would not have understood them. Therefore they veiled the revelation under types and figures which cannot be pierced except by a spiritual understanding; Christians, upon whom the plenitude of the Spirit has come, are endowed with this understanding, at least those Christians who have advanced to a truly "spiritual" life. To the Jews and to more carnal Christians, this spiritual sense remains hidden, and therefore they never perceive the true meaning of the Old Testament; for this spiritual meaning is the true meaning. The Old Testament, properly understood, was thought to contain the fullness of divine revelation, couched in its own figurative style.

The intrinsic weakness of such a system of interpretation is evident; and it was this weakness which led to its abandonment. For it depends almost entirely upon the arbitrary judgment of the interpreter himself, who is by definition a man of spiritual understanding. One cannot argue with a man of spiritual understanding; one listens humbly. The system supposes that the Old Testament was written formally for Christians, not for the Hebrews, that the prophets spoke to men centuries removed, not to the men who stood before them. It supposes also that they deliberately spoke in riddles. Such a consideration of the Old Testament is simply impossible; and it would never have arisen, if these early Fathers had known any other way to think of the Old Testament as a Christian book.

Is it not a Christian book, if it prepares for Christ? This also was proposed by a few of the Fathers of the Church. The two systems were not thought to exclude each other; actually they do, if they are carried to their logical conclusions. For the idea of preparation, properly understood, signifies a progressive revelation of God to man. Man, taken historically, was not apt for the fullness of divine revelation—a proposition which was accepted by the "allegorizing" school also; but if preparation means anything, it means that the fullness of revelation was not granted even to a few privileged souls. There is a growth in the knowledge of God; each new revelation of God makes man more apt to receive the following step, which will take him yet farther. This interpretation of the Old Testament, at once more accurate and more fruitful than the theory of types and figures, was not studied very earnestly during and after the age of the Fathers of the Church; and the "allegorical" school degenerated into fantasy. By and large, those who took the Old Testament seriously throughout most of the Christian era looked at it primarily as a mine of evidence, of texts by which they might prove the divinity of Jesus and the truth of His claims.

In the sixteenth century, Catholics as well as the theologians of the Protestant sects dug into the Old Testament as a mine of theological evidence. Each side, as we saw earlier, accepted the Bible on the same terms as the word of God, and each sought to find in it arguments for its own exposition of revealed truth. This meant, of course, that most of the Old Testament was not seriously studied, because most of it had no relevance to the current controversies; in fact, the idea of the Old Testament as a whole, and even of its parts as distinct literary units, was not very prominent in the theological schools of the seventeenth and eighteenth centuries. Finally, some were discouraged by the extravagant claims made by theologians, and decided that a book which could be pulled in so many directions at once could hardly be the word of God at all.

We hesitate to exhibit hindsight by criticizing the work of these great men of the past, who achieved marvels within their limitations; we should be fortunate if we do as well within our limitations. But each age, as the Sovereign Pontiff has reminded us, can and should contribute something of its own to the understanding of the Bible. The Old Testament has been viewed as a Christian book, one that speaks of Christ; it is that, even if we cannot understand the proposition in the sense in which it was understood by so many of the Fathers of the Church. It has been viewed as a preparation for Christ; it is that also, even if the idea of progressive revelation which we formulate will not be quite the same as that of the Fathers. It has been viewed as evidence of Christianity; it is that also, even if we admit, regretfully, that this involves more than a search for proof texts. But above and beyond these, there are some points of unity and continuity between the two Testaments

415

which are not contained in these formulae of the past, or, at least, are not too openly stated in them.

Let us consider first the proposition that the Old Testament is a Christian book. This we must maintain, even though its authors were not Christians. We maintain it because of the unity of faith and of spirit which governs the two Testaments. One need not abandon the Old Testament in order to accept the New; indeed, one may not. We maintain this despite the unparalleled novelty of the Incarnation, the great revolutionary event which overturns all human ideas and human values—except the knowledge of God. Novel the Incarnation was and is; but it is not out of character with the God of the Hebrews, although it is entirely out of character with any other idea of divinity which has ever entered the human mind. We do not say that the Incarnation was announced with studied obscurity in the Old Testament, that the prophets left clues to identify Christ as if biblical study were a treasure hunt; we say that they knew and spoke of a God who is the same as the God who took human flesh, and that they spoke of a world which was apt for this desperate remedy.

Many modern Catholics are not sure that the Old Testament is a Christian book. We have all heard the preacher's commonplace that the Old Testament is the law of fear, the New Testament the law of love. This fallacy becomes current because it is such a successful parody of the truth. Readers of the Old Testament know that it is false, and we hope that readers of this book have become suspicious of it. They know that the Hebrews would say that a God who is only fearsome is no true God; that a God who neither exhibits nor excites affection is true God. If they turn to their Bible, they will find that the Old Testament expresses the love of God for man and of man for God in unrestrained language. They know, too, that a God who does not arouse fear is no true God; they are aware that the Old Testament contains nothing so fearsome as the New Testament doctrines of hell and judgment. A distinguished modern theologian, Father Jules Lebreton, once quoted with approval a more ancient distinguished theologian, Origen, as saying: "We have searched the Scriptures, and we do not find that God is called father in the Old Testament." It is hard to

understand how two men so learned should have overlooked or
misunderstood at least twenty-six instances in which paternity
or paternal traits are applied to God in the Old Testament; it is
very dangerous to say that something is not contained in this
bulky book.

On the other hand, the Old Testament never knew the love
of God which is revealed in the Incarnate Son of God. It knew
the divine condescension, but it did not know that God could
empty Himself and take the form of a slave, becoming obedient
unto death: love supposes equality or creates it. Neither did it
know the capacity of man to love God, if man be adopted as
a son of God. When Jeremiah and Ezekiel spoke of the transformation of the heart, they did not know the power of God to
transform. In these, as in other things, the New Testament is
novel, revolutionary. But the continuity is not broken. Those
who knew the God of the Hebrews could recognize Him in the
Incarnation; but they would see that they had not known Him
very well. His character does not change, but its depths are newly perceived.

Christians are sometimes startled at the moral level of the
Old Testament. Where Catholics have not escaped the influence
of Puritanism or Jansenism, it is whispered that there are some
parts of the Old Testament which really had better not be read.
Religious communities which read the Bible in their dining
rooms piously omit some lurid episodes. They probably have
not considered that they agree in this with the peddlers of
pornographic literature, who plead in their own defense that
their wares contain nothing which cannot be paralleled in the
Old Testament. Catholics are not quite sure of a book in which
those who appear to be the heroes and heroines tell lies, steal,
murder, practice polygamy—all, they think, with divine approval.
It is easier to forget about such stories, and to believe that the
Hebrews lived in a very special world under a very special
dispensation. This, of course, makes the Hebrews entirely un-
real and entirely meaningless for the modern Christian.

Again, we hope the the reader of this book has learned
that the Hebrews were altogether real people with an altogether
real God. They have heard of the moral will of moral earnestness of the Old Testament is of one piece with the moral

earnestness of Jesus and the New Testament. They may be able to understand that the unenlightened moral insight of the Hebrews has no more effect upon the substance of Hebrew belief than the unenlightened morality of the Crusades or the Spanish Inquisition has upon the substance of Hebrew belief of Catholic belief. They will agree that God could not enter the world unless He had first created an atmosphere of moral seriousness. A merely human morality may be, at a given moment, higher than a morality based upon faith in a God with a moral will. But a merely human morality can never have any more force than there is in the good will of the men who have formed it; and the insight of a merely human morality can never exceed the capacities of the human intelligence from which it proceeds. A morality based upon faith in God grows both in strength and in vision, and it has no limit except the limits of the knowledge of God. And what limits shall we place upon the power of God to reveal Himself to man?

The Old Testament is a Christian book because it is a book of hope. We have referred earlier to the often-voiced despair of the ancient world, a despair which could be silenced only by worldly prosperity, which represented the summit of man's hopes. The Old Testament is the monument of the Hebrew belief in the power and will of God for good, which nothing can defeat. We ought to notice that this is not the simple and untested faith of the child. The hope of the Hebrews was indeed passed through the fire, and that not merely once; but each time it emerges stronger than it was before, with a clearer vision of its object. And thus we may answer the question: Does the Old Testament point to Christ? We cannot accept the idea that the Old Testament is a collection of clues which point to Him; but it points to the ultimate fulfillment of the power and will of God for good. It hopes for something to which Jesus is the answer. The ancient ideal of a society living in submission to the will of God is what Jesus established, the society which is in the world without being of the world, and therefore not subject to the corrupting influence of the world. He is the ultimate term of the divine condescension. He is the man who realizes in His own person all that the Hebrews hoped that man, led by the Lord, might become, and through whom other men reach

418

their destiny. He is the true Israel, and all who know the Lord are members of Him; in Him Israel attains its destiny and dies, to rise again to a new and undying life. Yes, the Old Testament points to Him; for it is a book that always looks forward, and carries us with it in its forward glance until it reaches Him, and then it reposes, as if to say: "Here it is."

We said that the Old Testament is also considered as a preparation for the New. We might ask: Why should there be a preparation? Cannot God act without preparing the conditions for His activity? Is He bound by the conditions of space and time, so that the divine operation must be extended in space and time? And we must confess that we run up against a mystery. Certainly the effects of the divine operation are extended in space and time; but we really do not understand the mystery of the divine patience. We would wish to hurry things; to us, delay implies an imperfection. We know that we must wait until the time is ripe, but we do not see why God must wait. We might understand the mystery of the divine patience better if we had a better grasp of the mystery of human iniquity. We do not see what a tremendous obstacle we place to the operation of God. It is not an insuperable obstacle, but we must let Him overcome it in His own way; and His way is the way of patience. Men do not easily admit God into a world from which they have expelled Him; and we cannot say that they would admit Him more quickly if God forced His way into the world more impatiently. We have already seen that the Old Testament knows the violence of the divine impact upon the world. But it also knows that where God might force us, He prefers to persuade us. So the Old Testament finds Him in the gentle breeze rather than in the earthquake and the lightning. He is the waters of Shiloh that go softly and imperceptibly, the summer sun that invisibly and effortlessly ripens the grain. He is all these things in the Old Testament, because the Hebrews knew something about the mystery of the divine patience. They knew it because they knew something about the hard resistance which man sets up against the advances of God.

But let us accept the mystery, as we must all mysteries, and ask how the Old Testament prepared for the New. To begin with what is obvious and superficial, the Old Testament gave

Jesus and His Apostles a language in which they could speak the Gospel. Only a thorough word-for-word study of the New Testament shows to what an astonishing degree its language reflects the language of the Old Testament. H. B. Swete has said that there is not a single page of the New Testament without an allusion to the Old Testament. Jesus announced the revolutionary novelty of the Gospel in a familiar language which, to some extent, disguised its radical character and made it easier to assimilate. And when we see that the religious vocabulary of the New Testament—which is our own religious vocabulary— is drawn from the Old Testament, we see that ideas as well as words are involved. The key words of the New Testament are charged with a new meaning; but if this new meaning were not a development of the meaning which the words have in the Old Testament, the words would have been unintelligible. If we look for a reason for the divine patience, we shall find it in the necessity of educating at least a portion of mankind to the point of religious understanding where it could listen to the words of Jesus with elementary intelligence.

For this reason, familiarity with the Old Testament has always been a key to the understanding of the New Testament. The full impact of the words of Jesus is not grasped unless we hear His words against the background of the history and the prophecy, the wisdom and the poetry of His own people. Even in apostolic times, this was so obvious that the Apostles took with them the Old Testament in Greek, to give to the Gentiles who knew nothing of the Jewish world. The New Testament had not yet been written; but the Old Testament was "background reading" for the Gentiles, so that they could put this strange Gospel into its proper perspective. For it would have been gibberish to them against the intellectual background of the Greek world, as St. Paul found at Athens. And even if we do not think of the Old Testament as primarily a means by which the Gospel was made more intelligible to the Gentiles, we must admit that it was the means by which the Apostles themselves acquired the concepts and the language in which they could preach the Gospel.

This is preparation on the surface; we can go beneath the surface, however, and find more profound effects of the Old

John Lawrence McKenzie

Testament upon the New. Not least in importance, we think, is that feature of the Old Testament which we have emphasized many times: its affirmation of the futility of human wisdom, human power, human civilization, of the inability of man to save himself from himself. St. Paul put it into a single line when he said that the folly of God is wiser than the wisdom of men, and the weakness of God is stronger than the strength of men. We should not think that the men of the Greco-Roman world who St. Paul attacked were too much different from ourselves. After long wars, they had reached an era of general peace. They could trust public order to maintain itself, and thus they could pursue trade and commerce without fear, and exchange goods and create wealth on a scale which had never been attained in the world's history. They did not live in an age of great creative genius in literature, art, philosophy; but they were in secure possession of the great tradition of Greece, and they produced an abundance of literature, art, and philosophical thought which, if not great, was fairly competent. It was a wealthy, peaceful, literate, cultivated world, based upon the most stable government which man had ever set up. Was this a world to which a few wandering Jews could easily tell its poverty and nakedness, its spiritual destitution? Only a man steeped in the Old Testament, like St. Paul, could have written the burning lines of the first chapter of the Epistle to the Romans. Paul writes like a cultural barbarian; he has no eyes for philosophy, literature, the arts, which are the rich robes wrapped around a harlot. This great civilization was a vast human failure, as he judged it; to him and to other early Christians it was the Scarlet Woman, Babel come to life again. Through St. Paul and the Apostles, as well as directly, the Old Testament uttered its despair of human achievements and human institutions, and forced men to consider where real and lasting security might be found.

We mentioned a third way in which the Old Testament is considered: as evidence for the truth of Christianity. For a long time this has meant the "proof text": the verse or the line in which is enunciated some proposition of the Christian faith. This use of the Old Testament has never meant very much to the laity, nor even to the clergy at large; it is a use which

421

belongs to the theological schools and to professional theological discussions. It is a method which is still in use and still in honor; hence what we have to say about it may arouse some resentment among those who are trained in this method, and who have come to regard it as an essential part of theology. Nevertheless, we think ourselves obliged to say that an approach to literature which looks for single lines rather than larger contexts is not a proper approach to any form of literature; and there appears to be no reason why it should be proper in theology.

Here, again, we must recall what we have said earlier, basing our remarks on the words of Pius XII: it should be possible for our age to contribute something to biblical studies which past ages have not contributed. The past fifty years have been as active for the study of the Old Testament as any comparable period since the beginning of our era. Must we not admit regretfully that there has been scarcely any perceptible development in the theological use of the Old Testament as evidence for the truth of Christianity? If it be not impertinence in a simple exegete, we submit the suggestion that the theologians can well afford to re-examine their approach to the Old Testament and the methods according to which they use the Old Testament, and incorporate into their approach and their methods those discoveries of modern times which they find relevant to their purpose. We can hardly believe that theology will be poorer for such work; and we cannot believe that St. Thomas Aquinas, who wished nothing more than acquaintance with the most modern works of his day, even the works of the infidel Arab philosophers, would be slow to take advantage of the opportunities which modern biblical studies would afford him. We think he would be even more eager to do so if he lived in an age when the Protestant scholars who are grouped as "neo-orthodox" show not only a profound interest in the Old Testament, but also a remarkable creative facility in their treatment of it.

But the apologetic use of the Old Testament will hardly ever be the primary interest of its readers outside of professional circles. The Old Testament is indeed evidence for the claims of Christianity; in the preceding pages, we have tried to suggest some of the ways in which this evidence appears to us. We are aware that it is imperfect apologetics. We do not know that very many have ever been led or will be led to accept Christianity by reading the Old Testament, although we see how it can happen; we know the story of the eunuch of the queen of Ethiopia. But we would rather give those who seek instruction in the faith the New Testament and the Baltimore Catechism. One may to some extent agree with Origen that the spiritual understanding of the Old Testament is for Christian "gnostics," those who are well enough instructed in their faith to read it with profit and without danger; unlike Origen, we would not restrict this understanding to a privileged few. They will read the Old Testament not as evidence for their faith, but with a faith that seeks understanding. They expect to learn from this book a fuller meaning of the things they believe: about God, His impact on the world, and the revolutionary effect of His impact upon the world and upon their own personal life. We think that the New Testament also would be read more widely and more intelligently by the faithful if the Old Testament also were read, for the Old Testament is the first and the indispensable commentary to the New. If some might wonder in surprise whether the commentary here is not more obscure than that upon which it comments, we can only challenge them to make the effort. That the effort is great we cannot deny; those who wish to read the Bible intelligently and spiritually will have to give it the time they now give to other things. We think also that priests would present the Epistles and the Gospels to the faithful with some of the incendiary zeal of St. Paul if, like St. Paul, they were steeped in the Old Testament. Many of the faithful, if not most of them, will know little about the Bible as a whole except what they hear from their priests; can we priests communicate to them the force of this book unless we have sensed it ourselves?

The child's voice which Augustine heard in his garden still speaks to us: "Pick it up and read it." When Augustine, moved by the incredible coincidence of this unseen voice, read the Bible, the spiritual crisis followed which altered the course of his life and the character of his personality. We need not expect anything so sensational in ourselves; but, if we can trust God who wrote the book and the experience of the ages which have used it, our faith will develop an understanding greater than we thought possible.